D0857020

On the Nature of Consciousness

On the Nature of Consciousness

Cognitive,
Phenomenological,
and Transpersonal
Perspectives

HARRY T. HUNT

Yale University Press
New Haven and London

Designed by Nancy Ovedovitz. Set in Times Roman and Gill Sans Condensed type by Keystone Typesetting, Inc., Orwigsburg, Pennsylvania. Printed in the United States of America by BookCrafters Inc., Chelsea, Michigan.

Library of Congress Cataloging-in-Publication Data

Hunt, Harry T., 1943–

On the nature of consciousness : cognitive, phenomenological, and transpersonal perspectives / Harry T. Hunt.

   p.   cm.

   Includes bibliographical references and index.

   ISBN 0-300-06230-3 (alk. paper)

   1. Consciousness.   2. Cognition.   3. Transpersonal psychology. I. Title.

BF311.H79   1995

153—dc20   94-48759

                            CIP

A catalogue record for this book is available from the British Library.

The paper in this book meets the guidelines for permanence and durability of the Committee on Production Guidelines for Book Longevity of the Council on Library Resources.

10   9   8   7   6   5   4   3   2   1

Contents

The cognitive unconscious experienced: The microgenesis of awareness

"Absorption" in immediate state as a dimension of individual difference

Lewin's topological psychology and its limitations / Dynamics of change in the life space and catastrophe theory / The boundary between life space and foreign hull as double torus

Preface

This book is a synthesis of cognitive, phenomenological, and transpersonal approaches to consciousness. The need for synthesis in an era of specializations has been widely remarked. The actual work of creative synthesis, however, is often less happily received, for synthesis transforms its materials in ways that are often unexpected and unorthodox. In addition, synthesis usually means that the fuller context of debate in separate specializations is sacrificed to considerations of space.

The need for synthesis within the contemporary human sciences persists in the face of these drawbacks. After all, the context of competing views can be reflected somewhat in discursive chapter notes. In addition, the resulting mutual modifications of each area also bear on the context of debate within separate disciplines. The very fact that disparate materials do go together in a particular way must strengthen the one perspective among the many possible in each area that allows just that synthesis.

In what follows I begin by reviewing multidisciplinary approaches to the question of consciousness, with progressive levels of synthesis developed as we proceed. Part I reviews the renewed interest in "ordinary" consciousness and its functions within cognitive psychology. This cognitive perspective is then related to the more descriptive study of "altered" and "transpersonal" states of consciousness, considered here as the maximum development of the experiential side of human intelligence. Three themes begin to emerge through this mutually modifying en-

counter: the possibility that states of consciousness provide unique, largely uncon-
sidered evidence for a general cognitive psychology; the centrality of consciousness, especially as manifested in the varieties of mystical experience, for the major
paradigm creators of psychology, sociology, and anthropology; and the necessity of
physical metaphor for any description of consciousness, with its implications of an
inseparability of consciousness and world.

Competing views of consciousness in cognition, neurophysiology, and animal
psychology are the focus of Part II. A view of perceptual awareness as the core of a
consciousness potentially shared across species is derived from the "ecological"
perspective of James J. Gibson. A view of self-referential symbolic consciousness is
then developed from Norman Geschwind's theory of symbolic cognition, as based
on a capacity for cross-modal translation and transformation among multiple perceptual modalities. Synesthesias, so ubiquitous in all altered states of consciousness, appear as the "inner" side of cross-modal processes. The transpersonal experiences of mysticism are considered as maximally abstract synesthesias — a view
later extended and defended in chapters 7 and 10.

Part III is the turning point of the book in its journey through cognition toward
the transpersonal. The separate strands of these "realist" approaches to perception
and thought, the phenomenology of consciousness (ordinary and transpersonal),
and theories of metaphor are first brought together fully in a reconsideration of
William James's "stream of consciousness." We see its dialogic social organization
and potential relations to contemporary nonlinear dynamics (chaos theory).

Part IV offers a more detailed study of a cross-modal translation model of human
consciousness through a review of the cognitive and phenomenological literature
on synesthesias, the abstract imagery of Arnheim, Lakoff, and Johnson, and the
classical Greek theory of the fusion of the senses as *sensus communis*. This forms
the context for the heart of the book, Part V, which presents an original cognitive
theory of the transpersonal experiences in meditative and related states. A consideration of the "process" of such experiences (chapter 10) leads to a broadly naturalistic, but nonreductive, account of their object or intent (chapter 11). Here, following
the lead of Herbert Guenther, I pursue a synthesis of the Mahayana Buddhist view
of meditative realization and the experiential account of Being in the later Heidegger. This is supplemented by a further development of Gibson's analysis of the
primacy of perception, lacking in Heidegger but strongly implied throughout his
work. The understanding of meditative states in terms of the basic organization of
perception allows us to avoid the various "new age" supernaturalisms that too often
blight the transpersonal literature.

The last three chapters are more speculative and return to several lines of inquiry
begun earlier: the inseparability of human self-referential consciousness and temporality; the grounding of the widely discussed parallels between consciousness

and modern physics in common metaphors resting on the structure of perception; and the communal basis of transpersonal states as reflected in both the sociology of mystical experience and a naturalistic reinterpretation of parapsychological research in terms of Durkheim's "collective consciousness."

In the course of writing this book I was struck that over my professional lifetime as an academic psychologist there has been no fundamental revolution within my own discipline to compare with the advent of nonlinear dynamics in the physical sciences or the impact of Heidegger and related deconstructionisms in philosophy. The only real candidate for a revolutionary paradigm is, I realized, Gibson's ecological perspective on perception, and its ultimate reception remains sadly uncertain. Of course, many would point to our widely heralded "cognitive revolution," but this seems less a unifying paradigm than a disparate collection of isolated subdisciplines. It is true that the last thirty years has also seen the development of a systematic study of dreams and transpersonal states, but, again, this promising area has remained fragmented and, with the striking exception of A. H. Almaas, largely uninterested in synthesis with psychodynamic and cognitive perspectives.

I have been led to wonder if, aside from the many institutional pressures toward specialization, a major reason for this relative stasis of psychology is precisely its general neglect of consciousness. How can a discipline that purports to study mind and person pretend to "ecological validity" if its heritage of methodological behaviorism prevents it from seriously considering "experience"?

In what follows, then, I seek to place consciousness at the defining center of cognition, as a capacity for sensitive attunement to a surround traceable down to protozoa. In the much-debated relation of consciousness and mind I reduce the latter to the former. Consciousness is not a "mechanism" to be "explained" cognitively or neurophysiologically, but a categorical "primitive" that defines the level of analysis that is psychology. Its existence may become a fundamental problem for a holistic, field-theoretical biology of the future, but for the human sciences it is the context of our being.

Correspondingly, and in marked contrast to views of consciousness as inherently private and cut off from consensual validation, our experience is understood here as a "consciousness-with" — and this at least three times over. First, all forms of perceptual awareness are, with Gibson, organized in terms of common dimensions resonant to an array potentially shared both within and between species. Second, our human self-referential consciousness is based on a "turning around" on this perceptual template by means of cross-modal syntheses. These have the structure of a dialogue, an internalization of the first kinesthetic and visual cross-translations in the "mirroring relation" between infant and mothering one. Finally, transpersonal states are themselves the maximum experiential articulation of this same cross-modal capacity, and so are not inherently "narcissistic," but are shared and common.

What I have done, I think, is to exemplify a perspective on the discipline of psychology based on the primacy of experience. In this I would hope to point the way toward psychologies of the future that would do a fuller justice to the original promise of the human sciences to address both the problematic nature of our species and the social and spiritual crises that define our times.

Acknowledgments

Since I am someone who works in relative isolation, I find myself at the end of this labor surprised at the number of people to whom I am indebted. Perhaps if I divided them by the number of years these thoughts actually cover, the list would shrink toward the very limits of scholastic autism. More likely, if the proper unit of analysis is the topic of consciousness itself, I have been very richly interconnected.

I would like to thank the following colleagues who, whether recently or over many years, have helped me with suggestions, sources, and discussions: Jack Adams-Webber, Charles Alexander, Lynne Angus, Willard Bradley, Kevin Dann, Jayne Gackenbach, George Gillespie, Gordon Globus, John Mayer, A. Joffre Mercier, Carol Munschaur, Robert Ogilvie, David Orme-Johnson, Peter Rand, and Fred Travis. I thank Gordon Globus for his suggestions for the manuscript. I also thank William Webster, dean of social sciences at Brock University, for his support.

I am especially indebted to Paul Kugler for sharing his deep understanding of Jung and for his invitations to present portions of this present work at the Analytical Psychology Society of Western New York, there also to participate in discussion groups that have included Barbara and Dennis Tedlock, David Miller, Karl Pribram, Peter Kugler, Stanton Marian, and Terry Pulver. The stimulation of these discussions over the past few years is one of the most valuable experiences I have ever had. For invitations to present earlier forms of this material, I also thank Leendert Mos and Paul Swartz of the Center for Advanced Study in Theoretical Psychology, University of Alberta, Edmonton, and Maxim Stamenov, organizer of the 1988 symposium "Models of Meaning" at the Bulgarian Institute of Language, Druzhba, Bulgaria — both being highpoints of my professional life.

I wish to thank Cho Je Lama Namse Rinpoche, the Venerable Khenpo Karthar Rinpoche, and His Eminence the late Jamgon Kontrol Rinpoche for many years of teachings from the Tibetan Mahayana Buddhist tradition, for which I am profoundly grateful. It should be clear that the treatment of Buddhist meditation herein reflects my own understanding only, but hopefully enriched, at whatever level it finds itself, by these teachers of insight and compassion.

I would also thank several scholars whom I consider as my postgraduate teachers and whose example and encouragement have meant more than I can say: Hameed Ali, Roland Fischer, the late Paul Seligman, and Mervyn Sprung. In this context I must also go further back and thank the late Eugenia Hanfmann and Edward A. Tiryakian, my two earlier teachers who most inspired and encouraged me in the breadth of my interests.

At the other end of this continuum I owe thanks to my thesis students, who over the years have been my collaborators in our studies of states of consciousness and metaphor: the late Cara Chefurka, Ernest Atalick, Paula Harder, John Carducci, John Walker, Jan Kraft, Mike Dillon, Mark Galka, Coralee Popham, Roc Villeneuve, Aurelia Spadafora, Arlene Gervais, Sheryl Shearing-Johns, Dyan Pariak, Rich Janzen, Jason Ramsey, Karen Csoli, Marc Poirier, Lori Ayers, and Al Morrison.

I am very much in debt to Terry Swanlund for our many years of friendship and conversation. He persuaded me both of the need to address my work on states of consciousness to a broader critical context and of the importance of Gibson for the full understanding of Heidegger (and vice versa). His impact on this book has been immense.

I thank my children, Amanda and Nathaniel, whose interest in what I am doing made for many helpful discussions and suggestions. I am also very grateful to Frank Rocchio for his helpful reading and response to the first draft of this work. I am especially grateful to my secretary, Linda Pidduck, for the extremely high quality of her work and her perseverance and equanimity in the face of ever-further revisions.

At the risk now of either confirming or denying my readers worst fears or highest hopes concerning the more personal side of my endeavors, I wish to thank Simon Weber-Brown for his generous supply of soundboard-quality concert tapes of the Grateful Dead, to which this book was written. In the same spirit I thank Bruce Jackson for loaning me his collection of all the out-of-print Phillip K. Dick novels I had not yet read, which in some sort of balancing counterbinge helped preserve sanity when away from my desk.

Finally I express my deep gratitude to my wife, Kate Ruzycki-Hunt, for her encouragement, careful editing, and most especially for her presence in my life. This book is dedicated to her. Whether it could have been written without her I happily do not get to know. I do know it was a lot nicer this way.

On the Nature of Consciousness

Part I Consciousness in Context: Psychology, Philosophy, Culture

Mystical utterances reflect a very peculiar and important way of look-ing at things which is as definite and characteristic as any other. . . . This mystical way of looking at things, so far from being the special possession of peculiar people called mystics, rather enters into the ex-perience of most men at many times, just as views of the horizon and the open sky enter into most ordinary views of the world. At the hori-zon things become confused or vastly extended, parallel lines meet and so on; just so, in the mystical sectors of experience, some things behave and appear quite differently from things in the near or middle distances of experience. . . . The so called great mystics are merely people who carry to the point of genius an absolutely normal, ordi-nary, indispensable side of human experience. . . . There are people whose incapacity for mathematics leads them to form an aversion from the whole subject, and there are people whose incapacity for mysticism leads them to form a similar aversion, yet it does not follow that either capacity is not a form of normal human endowment, ex-pressing itself in a peculiar type of utterance and discourse, in fact with such regularity as to merit the title of a "logic."
J. N. Findlay, "The Logic of Mysticism"

There is no chance of progress in [psychology] until there are enough people who respect the human mind, whether they like it or not, whether they think it is the wrong kind of mind or not, or whether they disapprove of the way that particular kind of mind works.
W. R. Bion, *Brazilian Lectures*

1 The Most Fundamental of Empirical Questions or the Most Misguided— What Is Consciousness?

Consciousness and Its Controversies

What is consciousness? It is a "something" that is before each of us at this very moment yet not sought or noticed as such until questioned. Then, like the water in which the fish swims, it is everywhere and nowhere.

Our immediate awareness is as clearly present as it is resistant to definite characterization. Consciousness — and not coincidentally, as we will see — is much as Augustine said of time in his *Confessions*: we seem to understand it quite well until we are asked about it, and precisely then do we find ourselves confused. While our own consciousness has its definite thatness, our very participation in everyday social reality seems to require that we look through it and not at it. So again there is the parallel with time, which, it has been said (Pöppel, 1988), is what we notice when nothing else is happening — implying that there will be circumstances when consciousness as such becomes manifest and *is* noticed.

In psychology, consciousness has again become a focus of interest and controversy. On the one hand, contemporary "cognitive science," as the dominant paradigm within most of the human sciences (Gardner, 1985), is involved in a fierce debate over the nature and function of consciousness. This is a debate that is strikingly reminiscent of the struggle over the status of introspectionism earlier in this century. On the other hand, "transpersonal psychology" has gradually crystallized as the discipline involved in the study of transformations of consciousness, especially those associated with the various meditative traditions, as potential expressions of the maximum synthesis and integration open to consciousness.

Although it has been suggested (Hunt, 1985a; Baars, 1988; Natsoulas, 1991–92) that such transformations of consciousness might shed a unique light both on the ordinary consciousness with which we began our discussion and on its underlying cognitive bases, there has been very little formal dialogue between the transpersonal and cognitive perspectives (Hunt, 1984, 1985a, 1985b; Globus, 1990, 1992; Varela, Thompson, and Rosch, 1991). Within the cognitive-science paradigm itself we find equally stark contrasts. There are some, such as Daniel Schacter (1989), Bernard Baars (1988), Thomas Natsoulas (1984), George Mandler (1975), and the philosopher John Searle (1992), who have sought to reintroduce consciousness as the basis of the synthesizing, directing, and volitional capacities of mind. They make the relation between brain and mind the most fundamental scientific problem of our time. Others, especially those enthralled with artificial intelligence (Dennett, 1991) and "eliminative materialism" (Churchland, 1988), see consciousness as a pseudo-problem. Awareness becomes the noncausal, epiphenomenal expression of a more fundamental computational capacity. A future science of the brain and/or computational simulation is supposed to replace our "folk psychology" of intentions and mental states with a genuinely causal language (Stitch, 1983), and this with no discernible effect on our actual experience of ourselves (Rorty, 1979).

There is, however, serious debate about the relationship between consciousness and its neural substrate. Certainly, clinical neurological studies of adult brain damage show a localization of specific symbolic functions in areas of the neocortex. Neuropsychologists like Schacter (1988, 1989) and Weiskrantz (1988) have even suggested that syndromes like aphasia and agnosia reflect a separation of symbolic functioning from a central "consciousness awareness system" that would be localized at the intersection of the occipital, parietal, and temporal areas of the neocortex. Yet brain damage in young children, prior to the localization and automatization of function in the neocortex, shows an immense plasticity and interchangeability in neural areas. Advances in the postbirth treatment of hydroencephaly have shown that full human capacities will develop with as little as 10 percent of normal cortical mass — here spread in a thin rim across the inside of the skull (Dixon, 1991). More generally, as both psychologists (Natsoulas, 1981) and philosophers (Searle, 1992) have noted, even if we knew the exact neural processes occurring with the experience of pain or color, that would not necessarily show us how these processes *were* those conscious experiences, let alone eliminate the language and categories that describe them.

Is consciousness then a nonreducible capacity emerging at some point in the evolution of central nervous systems? The neurologist Roger Sperry (1991) pictures consciousness as a higher-order emergent from holistic neural properties that will in turn exercise a "downward control" over lower neural functioning. The idea of an evolutionary emergence — if not autonomy — is widely shared. But then does it not follow that there will be a point below which creatures are somehow not conscious? Would that not make them insentient? Certainly an evolutionary emergence model is consistent with the idea that consciousness at its various levels would be neurologically localized. On the other hand, the cognitive psychologist George Miller (1981) has suggested that all motile creatures must be "conscious" in some form because their motility both requires it for safe navigation *and* indicates it behaviorally — perhaps even down to the single-cell protozoa, which have no separate nervous systems at all. If all motile life is by definition sentient, then "unconscious" functioning is based on a progressive automatization of capacities originally requiring awareness. If so, it is "the unconscious" that evolves in evolution as much or more than consciousness.

How far "down" do we carry such an analysis? Plants move too, just at a slower rate, and Gustav Fechner, the father of experimental psychology, argued eloquently for their consciousness (James, 1912). Alfred Binet (1888), another foundational figure for experimental and cognitive psychology, concluded from his microscope studies of protozoan behavior that they were most plausibly regarded as sentient, and that neurons themselves are best regarded as protozoa specialized for sentience in much the way that stomach cells are specialized for digestion (see chap. 5). On this view, the evolution of "neural nets" does not create consciousness but allows the sentience of their constituents to fuse into ever more complex fields of conscious awareness. The brain would not create or "cause" consciousness so much as "gather" and focus it. If so, the physiological characteristics of nervous systems will never tell us as much about consciousness as many cognitive scientists today would like to believe.

The Place of Consciousness in Psychology and Its Fragmented History

Whether one places consciousness at the center of psychology or regards it as purely epiphenomenal seems to depend on one's understanding of social science and its potential program, both in relation to and in contrast with the humanities and physical sciences.

Psychology entails a curious dialectic — perhaps one that is ultimately self-contradictory and paradoxical, perhaps one that will also prove novel and emergent. We find a subject matter — thought, feeling, dreams and visionary states — that has traditionally been expressively rendered in the great works of art and mythology (the humanities) but now is to be formally conceptualized in terms of the experimental methods that have enjoyed such conspicuous outward success in the physical sciences. Accordingly, both conceptually and methodologically, psychology has uneasily tended toward a division between those who would see the discipline primarily in terms of what Dilthey (1914) termed *Geisteswissenschaften*, based on methods of "understanding" or phenomenology, and proponents of a more traditionally scientific psychology considered as natural science. *Naturwissenschaften* are based on a knowing by experimental manipulation and measurement.

The response to this tension, inherent in the very idea of social science, has most often been an attempt at the complete assimilation of one of these views by the other. Accordingly, there are those psychologists — the would-be "hard scientists" — who hold that all matters pertaining to experience will ultimately be assimilated to a future neurophysiology and experimental functionalism. Such reductionism or eliminativism elicits a more faint echo back from an equally extreme spiritualist counterpart that would seek to explain neurophysiology as an epiphenomenon of consciousness. This is a position fully developed within idealist metaphysics (east and west), but scientific psychology cannot completely expunge it from its history owing to "father" Fechner's view that, not just plants, but matter itself is conscious.

In addition, there are those, perhaps best represented by Michel Foucault (1970), who see the multiple juxtaposition of themes and methods that characterize the human sciences as but a temporary historical amalgam, eventually to be resolved back into its constituents — as some psychologists are properly reclaimed by history and philosophy and others by biological science. Still, what is particularly striking about the foundational figures of psychology — Fechner, William James, and Sigmund Freud — is the creative tension in their work that comes precisely from a staged interaction between the languages and methods of subjectivity and objectivity. It may be that this very juxtaposition is the source of a genuine emergent identity in the social sciences, allowing multiple and shifting integrations across the traditional sciences and humanities that will also reflect our conflicted and divided nature.

The root of this division between the subjective and the objective in the human sciences, and the impossibility of either side totally eliminating or assimilating the other, may lie in a curious duality in our experience of ourselves and others. Each of us is given or presented twice over, once from the first-person view of our immediate awareness and then again from the third-person perspective of the other. A second-person tense already attests to the continuous interplay of these two perspectives as part of our very concept and experience of person and mind. "Let me tell you what it was like" and "Just do it" are the immediate reflections of these disparate but overlapping attitudes that give us a psychology of subjectivity, on the one hand, and a laboratory-based experimental psychology, on the other — along with at least the potential of an emergent, if uneasy, dialogue between them.

After all, the immediate consciousness with which we began our discussion, and all of its potential transformations, are certainly facts of nature. If we keep in mind that, historically, subject matters in the sciences have tended to dictate their own methodologies, we have every right to ask for a science of these phenomena as well and to expect that this might require its own techniques. The challenge becomes all the greater, however, when we note that this consciousness is associated or linked in ways to be determined with either nervous systems or motile organismic activity in general — both of which our tradition has historically attempted to explain from a third-person perspective of impersonal causes and principles.

The genuine emergence of any cross-dialogue about our "nature" will require the development of an empirical science of consciousness — with its own methods and traditions — to begin to balance our historical leanings towards a psychology of function, behavior, and process. Such a "science" of consciousness will entail its own dialogue back and forth across the dividing lines between phenomenology and cognition, states of consciousness and neurophysiology. It will also have to think across the surprising isolation between the diverse subtraditions in psychology and philosophy that have attempted to address consciousness in all its multiple forms. Much has been made of the experimental cognitive research on visual imagery that began in the 1960s as a "return of the ostracized" (Holt, 1962). Yet the more descriptive work on altered states of consciousness (sensory deprivation, hypnosis, psychedelic experience) and transpersonal states (meditation and high-dosage psychedelic experience) that emerged at the same time has had essentially no cross-influence on its experimental counterparts (Walsh, 1992).

There is an astonishing fragmentation within this less predominant phenomenological perspective in the history of psychology. For instance, there has been almost no cross-dialogue among the classical introspectionism of Wilhelm Wundt and E. B. Titchener (1912), the later microgenetic introspectionism of Felix Krueger (1928), Paul Schilder (1942), and Heinz Werner (1961), the early applied phenomenologies of immediate consciousness in William James (1890) and Henri Bergson (1889), the formal phenomenologies of Edmund Husserl (1907) and Alfred Schutz (1962), the existential phenomenologies of Martin Heidegger (1927), Jean-Paul Sartre (1939), and Maurice Merleau-Ponty (1964), or the applied phenomenologies arising out of gestalt psychology and culminating in Kurt Lewin's (1936) topology of the life-space. Similarly, none of the above has commonly been related to the psychologies of narcissism in Sigmund Freud (1914), Carl Jung (1921), and Heinz Kohut (1977), or James Hillman's (1978) psychology of imagistic and metaphoric self-reference, or the observations of clinical neurology (Luria, 1973), or the descriptive phenomenologies of schizophrenic onset (Chapman, 1966; Bowers, 1974), let alone to the development of research and phenomenological investigation of altered states of consciousness (Tart, 1965) and the transpersonal psychologies of meditation (Goleman, 1972). Yet all these subtraditions do seem to describe overlapping phenomena and processes, as we shall see. An empirical psychology of consciousness, fully developed enough to dialogue with its more dominant and functionalist "cognitive science" counterpart, will only be possible as these strands within the subjectivist tradition of psychology are interwoven to the same degree now found in the more continuous history of the cognitive tradition (Gardner, 1985).

Lines of Further Inquiry

Transformations of Consciousness as Primary Data for Cognitive Theory

I have mentioned the reintroduction of consciousness into contemporary cognitive science as a causal cognitive system involving synthesis, direction, and volition by, among others, Baars, Marcel, and Schacter. We will see, however, that the consciousness thereby posited as central to actual functioning remains as curiously empty of content as the "impalpable awarenesses" of Külpe's introspectors at the University of Würzburg. That very lack of specifiable pattern led to the loss of interest in consciousness by experimental psychologists in the 1920s. What is still missing is, paradoxically, just that dialectic between cognition and phenomenology, third- and first-person criteria, that would define a genuine psychological science of consciousness.

It is here that we can turn to the spontaneous transformations of consciousness that constitute "nature's experiments" on mind, initially at least in its first-person aspect, and that have been variously termed "altered states of consciousness," "transpersonal states," or, as below, "presentational states." These phenomena appear to offer just the empirical clues both to the nature of consciousness in general and to its cognitive-symbolic processes that are lost in the transparency of ordinary awareness. Indeed, these subjective states, both in their positive form as an enhanced experiential synthesis and in their more disintegrated and psychotic aspect, constitute the uniquely privileged "microscope" for an emergent psychology of consciousness — and perhaps even of symbolic cognition itself in its broadest aspects.

For instance, consider the ubiquity of synesthesias in spontaneous altered states (Hunt, 1985ab, 1989b), where one sensory modality is subjectively experienced in terms of another — as in the experience of color and geometric form while listening to music and sensed as inseparable from it. Synesthesias fit very well with the neurologist Norman Geschwind's (1965) theory of all symbolic cognition as based on a capacity for cross-modal translation between the different perceptual modalities. They may even provide a unique "window" for the inner processes of such cross transformations (see chapters 4, 7, and 10). Similarly, reports of complex and aesthetically intricate geometric designs from the hypnagogic period sleep onset, psychedelic drugs, and meditation may offer both a confirmation and a unique extension of the heterodox cognitive theories suggesting that abstract geometric imagery is basic not only to nonverbal symbolic thought but even to verbal thought and syntax (Arnheim, 1969; Lakoff, 1987; Johnson, 1987; McNeill, 1992; see chapters 8 and 10).

Finally, consider accounts of so called "out-of-body experience," sometimes reported at sleep onset or as a common element in "near-death" experience. From a naturalistic perspective, we can regard this state as an especially powerful and vivid imaginal experience of seeing oneself as if from outside, although it can appear to be vividly perceptual. The imaginal status of out-of-body experience, however, seems to follow from the fact that so many of these accounts contain features that do not correspond in full detail with one's actual physical surroundings and thus are an imaged approximation to perception (Green, 1968; Irwin, 1985). Although subjectively astounding, these experiences actually fit quite well with certain general models of human cognition. George Herbert Mead (1934) suggested that the dividing line between lower animals and the human symbolic capacity comes with our ability to "take the role of the other" — simultaneously to send a communicative message while monitoring, changing, and reformulating it in terms of its perceived adequacy. This capacity for the ongoing self-reference of our symbolic communication and our symbolically structured awareness is of course most obvious in speech and verbal thought. In the out-of-body experience we would seem to have a manifestation of this same self-referential capacity, but expressed as such in a visual-spatial mode that is no longer subordinated to the pragmatics of everyday verbal cognition.

In later chapters I will pursue the full variety of transformations of consciousness with respect to their implications for a theory of mind. One of the things that is especially interesting about these states is that they appear to be spontaneous expressions of a self-referential, abstract, symbolic capacity that has traditionally been explained as a consequence of language but here is manifested in a nonverbal form. Accordingly, these experiences may provide a unique kind of evidence for Howard Gardner's (1983) view of the symbolic mind as consisting in a loosely bound set of multiple, semi-autonomous "frames" — including mathematics, interpersonal relations, music, and the visual arts, along with language. The latter may be the frame of the most practical importance but not the source or explanation for all the others. We will see how spontaneous transformations of consciousness may help to reveal the processes underlying all symbolic frames.

"Higher States of Consciousness" and Social Science:
A Renewal of Discourse between Science and Religion

Our preceding account of social science as an emergent, open-ended integration of the modes of thought in the sciences and the humanities raises the issue of how a genuine "cognitive science" would understand spiritual and religious experiences

— the fullest experiential realizations of the mode of awareness within the humanities. What are these experiences psychologically and what might they show us about the human mind in general?

It was Friedrich Nietzsche, who often called himself a "psychologist" (*The Will to Power*), who began this interrogation. God, and all other conceptual and valuative "absolutes," are seen as unwitting projections of the human mind. The "overman," the new human being to come, would be able to reown this level of mind, which provides us our sense of ground and purpose, but without succumbing to its illusory aspects. Nietzsche was perhaps the first to call for a "natural physiology" of ecstasy — a program that perhaps reached its purest expression, for good or ill, in the psychedelic drug research of the 1960s. For William James (1902) and Carl Jung (1953), as inheritors of Nietzsche's project, the direct experience of what Rudolf Otto (1923) has termed the "numinous," the cross-culturally common felt core of religious experience, is to be understood as an empirical fact of mind. As such, it can be "scientifically" studied. For both James and Jung, and down into the current transpersonal psychologies, while the existence of spontaneous religious experiences can never establish their "objective" truth, such experiences can be empirically studied in terms of both their cognitive processes and their impact on the lives of people and societies. Accordingly, our characteristically western debate between science and religion can be engaged on a new level of discourse, where spirituality becomes a series of empirical experiential states and social science attempts to understand their implications for a theory of the human mind.

The nature of religious and transpersonal experience was hardly a topic of peripheral or incidental interest to the foundational figures of social science, but has rather been at the heart of the very idea of "human sciences." Fechner (1901) postulated a spiritual panpsychism and addressed the psychological reality of life after death in terms of the survival of the deceased in the minds of the survivors. James (1890) wrote his two-volume *Principles of Psychology,* masterfully integrating the psychology of his day, specifically in order to address the issue of free will within the worldview of science. In *The Varieties of Religious Experience* he tackled the empirical diversity of religious experiences, suggesting that their function is to offer a needed ground and confidence for our open-ended intelligence. Freud and Jung, of course, split over the issue of whether religious experience is a defensive illusion or a positive expression of an innate archetypal imagination. The nature of religion and religious experience was also central to the sociologies of Emile Durkheim (1912) and Max Weber (1922), as well as to much of early anthropology (Tylor, 1871; Frazier, 1922).

Here is the question these "ancestors" left for us: do "numinous" or "transpersonal" experiences reflect the specifically human development of an aspect of our symbolic self-referential capacity, or even its core, as Jung would have it? Or does our ostensibly cross-cultural propensity for such experience show, instead, with Freud, a "primitive" mode of thought, perhaps even the residue of an infantile "oceanic" feeling that is the core of primitive narcissism? Do these states show us something about the fullest capacity for synthesis of the symbolic mind or do they instead betoken a built-in tendency to disintegration and primitivization, perhaps stemming from our very cognitive complexity and the pressures it places upon us as a species?

Heidegger, in *Being and Time* (1927), states that our potential for an experience of a sense of transcendence rests on our uniquely human form of temporality — that dimension of human life that leads out ahead of itself and into that which is open and unknown. Our ability to directly sense this openness as such is the immediate occasion for the direct awareness of Being. The experience of Being is the sense of openness that lies at the basis of all religious experience and which religious mythologies attempt to circumscribe conceptually. This capacity for wonder and fascination that oneself and the world are at all is not possible in the "closed" worlds of lower animals. On the other hand, Wilhelm Reich (1949), an early follower of Freud who broke away in pursuit of a "science" of life energy, understood the sensations of "streaming" and dynamic flow in bodily experience during transpersonal states as the direct sensing of the vitally embodied "aliveness" we share with all organisms. Here, religious experience would be a direct awareness of the structures of a perceptual world common to all motile, sentient creatures (see chapters 10 and 11).

The very idea of social science demands that these questions about the nature of religious experience and traditional spirituality be addressed on this new level of discourse, where experiences are "facts" in their own right, to be understood as expressions of mind and society. The difficulty is to locate a line of inquiry that will avoid the false reductionism of merely explaining away aspects of ourselves that do not fit easily with our modern self-images of rationality and control, so central to contemporary cognitive science. Yet it must also avoid that advocacy and "over-belief" (James, 1902) wherein much current humanistic and transpersonal psychology slips past social science and into a new mysticism of its own.

Consciousness and Physical Metaphor

A diverse range of thinkers, beginning with Giambattista Vico (1744), have called attention to the seeming necessity that all references to consciousness — whether as "higher states" or as immediate ordinary awareness — must remain indirect, resting on the use of physical metaphor. Such metaphor appears not just in the descriptive utilization of words like "flow" and "horizon," but also is reflected in the etymologies of all languages for words related to "consciousness" and subjective experience in general (Asch, 1961; see chapters 6 and 9).

William James (1912), years after his seminal chapter in the *Principles* on consciousness as stream, concluded that there was ultimately no way to separate consciousness as such from the world in which it is embedded and which it is about. "All . . . painfully accumulated points of difference run gradually into their opposites and are full of exceptions" (p. 18). In effect, he seems to be saying that the system (the mind) that generates and responds to all possible physical metaphors could not conceivably be fully described by just one such metaphor — even one of the obvious power and appropriateness of flowing water. The meditative traditions have their own version of this nonrepresentability of consciousness as something in its own right apart from the world. "Consciousness has no independent nature of its own," says one of the founders of the Soto tradition of Zen Buddhism (Cleary, 1980, p. 19). Consciousness, so definitely before the reader at the beginning of this chapter, seems now rather like an elastic, infinitely accommodating and transparent medium that molds itself instantly and without ostensible remainder to any fist that would "grasp" it. The more we try to fix consciousness conceptually, the more clearly we will register each wrinkle on each knuckle, missing yet again the all-encompassing nature of the medium itself. As self-referential beings, we have no place to stand outside this process, for anything *we* discover about the world must also be a potential metaphor for the medium through which it is presented.

Consciousness and world are inseparable. Is consciousness as a topic for empirical research thereby rendered outside any would-be system or science, however emergent, if the metaphors needed for such self-depiction are arbitrary and endlessly open? So it is for contemporary deconstructionism. If consciousness is always constructed out of an open, unformalizable set of metaphors, it can then have no nature of its own. Consciousness per se then becomes a kind of projective illusion, and our self-awareness must slip away into a strangely absolute relativism. Yet, are not some metaphors — such as flowing from an unknown source, luminosity or glow, and horizonal openness — somehow privileged? Indeed, these are the very metaphors that seem to engender and form self-awareness in the higher stages of meditation. These metaphors utilize patterns of nature that are dynamic and emergent enough to reflect something of our own sense of an openness of consciousness and self. Their similarity to certain aspects of nonlinear dynamics (chaos theory) raises the possibility that the basic principles of perception — shared across motile sentient creatures and reused as the abstract structures of symbolic cognition — are mirrored "inward" from the nonlinear fluidities of air and water that constitute the most immediate constant surround for living systems (chapters 6 and 13). If so, then certain aspects of world will be privileged for the self-depiction of a consciousness whose infinite malleability becomes more a matter of function and less one of actual structure. Water, too, flows ubiquitously over and through all forms but does not thereby lack for its own identity.

A Circumambulation of Consciousness, Courtesy of the *Oxford English Dictionary*

For Ludwig Wittgenstein (1953), ordinary language is the maximally complex expression of the human mind, with all logical and scientific systems being simplified formalizations abstracted out of its multiple, overlapping strands. Accordingly, psychologists could do worse at early stages of inquiry than to look up their topic in the dictionary. Thomas Natsoulas (1981, 1983, 1992) has done just that in a series of articles surveying the basic meanings of "consciousness" (seven in all) found in the *Oxford English Dictionary* and exploring their implications for cognitive theory. I will follow the logic of that investigation, reordering the definitions somewhat and using them to introduce some additional lines of inquiry for what follows. Much of the debate in current cognitive-science approaches to consciousness comes from a failure to distinguish among these meanings.

The first and second definitions of consciousness in the *OED* are closely related and seem to reflect the social symbolic bases of perhaps all human awareness. Consciousness$_1$, Natsoulas's "interpersonal meaning," is defined as a mutual knowledge — "knowing or sharing the knowledge of something together with another" or "privy to something with another." Here, indeed, we have the Latin root of the term *consciousness* as literally a "knowing" (*scientia*) "with" (*con*). As Natsoulas (1983) points out, for A to be conscious of something with B implies a symbolic role relationship between them — A is aware that B is aware that A is aware of some state of affairs, and vice versa.

This recursive cycle reminds us of the existence of limits to our symbolic capacity and our periodic awareness of them. I can know that you know that I know that you know something, but our everyday social and political realities are often determined by the fact that we cannot go much beyond three or four such levels. As the psychoanalyst W. R. Bion (1962) says, "The capacity to think is rudimentary in all of us" (p. 14). The self-referential structure of our interpersonal awareness allows us to sense these limitations as such at those points where our "calculations" break down into indeterminacy. Certainly, it is hard to imagine an eagle sensing that its capacity for flight lacked something. The nested complexity and fragility of this capacity for knowing-with is well captured by R. D. Laing in *Knots*:

Jack can't tell Jill what he
wants Jill to tell him.
Jill can't tell him either
because although Jill knows X
Jill does not know
that Jack does not know X.
Jack can see
that Jill knows

he realizes that she
does not know she knows X.
Jill can only discover she knows it
by realizing what Jack does not.
But Jill
cannot see what
Jack does not know.
If she did she would be glad to tell him.
(Laing, 1970, p. 74)

Even the most ordinary relationship can carry us close to that "negative capability" which is the capacity of the highly creative to sense and still remain open to what they do not know rather than what they do.

The first manifestation of this reflexivity is probably found in the early facial mirroring games between neonate and mothering one, which the psychoanalyst D. W. Winnicott (1971) and the cognitive psychologists Heinz Werner and Bernard Kaplan (1963) saw as the developmental origination of the symbolic capacity. The infant sees its own face in the face of the mothering one and can also see — with delight — that she responds with her own face to its expressions. Recent research shows that this capacity is already present for certain specific behaviors immediately after birth in nontraumatized neonates (Meltzoff and Moore, 1989). Not surprisingly, perhaps, we are specifically human from birth, there being no preliminary "animal" phase as in the theoretical fantasies of Freud and so many others. On this view of the developmental roots of reflexive consciousness, we see again that the core of human cognition lies outside linguistic forms and verbal expression. It is only later that these become integrated into the visual-kinesthetic sequences of mirroring.

Consciousness$_2$, Natsoulas's "personal meaning," is defined in the *OED* as "internal knowledge," as in the carrying forward of consciousness$_1$ to the level of the individual — being witness to one's own deeds, knowing one's own innocence or guilt. Here, in G. H. Mead's (1934) terms, I "take the role of the other" toward myself and so come into view as a self. For Mead, as well as in the cognitive psychology of Vygotsky (1962), an awareness of self emerges from imaginatively "internalizing" the expressions of others toward us. Freud (1933) similarly understood the core of the superego (*Über Ich*), prior to its more obvious function of self-evaluation in a moral sense, as the capacity for immediate self-awareness. Later, Winnicott (1971) and Kohut (1977) pictured the sense of self as resulting from the "internalization" of the empathic "mirroring" relationship with the mother, so that the child gradually comes to "mirror" and "hold" itself.

The major implication of these first two usages is that consciousness in a symbolizing being can never be intrinsically private — despite our best attempts, in our

culture of autonomous "individuals," to fear or pretend otherwise. Our consciousness comes to us structured through and through like an interior conversation. We
can withdraw from any of the contents of sociality, but not from its form. Rather
than being an "inner container" into which others cannot see, consciousness is
dialogic — although the dialogue need not be linguistic, but can be based in visual-
kinesthetic imagery. Accordingly, our consciousness of ourselves is certainly not
"infallible" — that fruitless and misleading debate still current in cognitive-science
circles (Dennett, 1991). Rather, our self-awareness can be both immediately and
directly present, with its characteristic clarity and transparency, *and* nonetheless
constructed cognitively as the view back from "the other," real or imaginary. This
awareness of my consciousness is inevitably, if slightly, delayed by the fact that it is
"about" what "I" have just seen, done, or felt. These are the numerous "me's" that
in Mead's account constitute self-referential attempts to see an ultimately unspecifiable "I."

Mead's account of consciousness as self-referential also provides a descriptive,
potentially empirical way to understand Freud's concept of "unconscious mind." In
descriptive interpersonal terms, the form of Freud's unconscious is based on the
inevitable, if normally slight, imbalance between what I am aware of at a given
moment (first-person criteria) and what I show to others (third-person criteria).
Placing to one side his misleading metaphor of mind-as-container, Freud is describing the maximally extreme delay between what I have just said or shown and what I
can consciously know of my own message — my fluctuating inability to "take the
role of the other" fully with respect to my own expressions. Neurosis represents the
exaggeration of what on Mead's account must apply to all of us, namely, that we can
never fully catch up with and know what we have just done in the manner to which
that is available to someone who knows us intimately. Thus, psychotherapy for the
classical neuroses is a mirroring back to the client of what he or she shows. Con-
sciousness$_2$ becomes more fully correlated with consciousness$_1$, and their inevitable
temporal asymmetry gradually returns to its normal range. Jung's very different
form of therapy, based on the cultivation of an autonomous "active imagination,"
reflects the development of the opposite asymmetry. Here, in the cultivation of
spontaneous imaginal states and dialogues, consciousness$_1$ has been temporarily
suspended in order that consciousness$_2$ may become more fully manifest. The
eventual reintegration of what has been thereby learned "inside" with what can be
lived out with others marks that "integration" so central to Jung's concerns and so
different from Freud's valuation of "control."

With the next two *OED* definitions we shift from the specifically human to
meanings that could in principle be shared with nonsymbolic, sentient creatures.
Consciousness$_6$, Natsoulas's "general state" meaning, is defined as being awake,
alert, or aroused. In effect, this form of consciousness varies in intensity or degree in

a way that seems related to the organismic response to novelty, also termed the "orientation response." It is not at all clear whether this meaning could ever be fully separated (other than as its third-person behavioral criterion) from immediate sentient perception, since to be awake and alert will also entail being sentiently present within a life-world or surround. This brings us to consciousness$_3$, Natsoulas's "awareness meaning," as the immediate consciousness of something, sentience, or the moment-by-moment contents of consciousness. Natsoulas argues that this awareness meaning is fundamental to all the other definitions and ultimately is presupposed by them. Potentially, and perhaps most parsimoniously, it is shared by all sentient organisms. Each species would be sentiently present within its own specific "bubble" of perception and motoric effectance (Von Uexküll, 1934).

With Natsoulas (1981) we can say that this immediate awareness has two aspects. The debate, central to cognitive science and artificial intelligence, comes over whether they are inextricably joined or potentially separable (chapter 3). First, there is the intentionality or "aboutness" side, as reflected in the early Brentano (1874), James (1890), and Husserl (1907). There is something each moment of awareness is about. Consciousness points, and necessarily, with James, at something other than its immediate self. Gilbert Ryle (1949) similarly speaks of the index finger that can point at anything except itself. "Aboutness" means that our access to our immediate subjective state always glides just beyond itself. Our awareness of this very moment is always slightly post hoc. This delay, however slight, again follows from the self-referential basis of human consciousness. The second side, then, is precisely that unmistakable, immediately felt side of aboutness — the "raw feel" aspect often referred to as "sensation" or "qualia." Following Wittgenstein (1953), ongoing subjectivity is differently accessed than intentional cognitive capacities. Subjective states are "suffered" or "undergone," with a potentially specifiable "duration," in a way that is not true for propositional knowledge. We can tell how long a pain lasts and even time the persistence of the felt meaning of a word in semantic satiation research. The question is whether, with artificial-intelligence theorists like Daniel Dennett (1991), this "state" aspect is merely an epiphenomenal by-product of the more primary aboutness functions of perception and cognition. On the other hand, for the philosopher Thomas Nagel (1974), there is something it is *like* to be a sentient organism — whether a bat (Nagel's example) or perhaps even a protozoan (chapter 5). Perhaps this "is like" is indispensable not only to our being alive but also to our very capacity for cognitive functioning.

Of course we can only infer this aspect of immediate sentience in other species as an extrapolation from our own self-referential capacity. In effect, it is our consciousness$_2$ that locates the subjective-state side of cognition as a specific result of introspection. The ephemeral qualities of immediate awareness are normally not noticed as such and so are lost within the cognitive acts they are about or for. While plausibly inferrable in nonsymbolic animals, they may well be doubly lost there-in — because those creatures do not show any of the outward signs of a self-referential awareness that would allow them to be aware of a sentience separate from the world it is about. From this perspective, bats just are. They manifest their bat-ness, which is "been" or "felt" but not self-referentially experienced. It might be tempting to liken the immediate sentience of nonsymbolic creatures to so-called "blind-sight" neurological syndromes, in which the primary receptor areas of the visual cortex have been damaged, as observed in human subjects or experimentally ablated monkeys (see chapter 2). Both human and monkey subjects seem initially unable to see at all in the affected regions but may gradually learn that they have some residual, if nonconscious, powers of discrimination. It cannot, however, be the case that ordinary awareness in nonsymbolic animals is like blindsight, because immediately after their experimental operations, the monkeys indeed act differently and as if they were blind, hesitantly exploring their environment by means of touch and sound alone. This must attest to their loss of visual sentience as something suddenly noticeable by its absence. The absence of self-reference in nonsymbolic creatures cannot mean that they operate as "automata" without any immediate qualities of ongoing awareness. Rather they can only bring such awareness into view by means of their functional attunements to their surroundings.

Consciousness$_4$, the "reflexive awareness" definition, is precisely the capacity for this direct awareness and recognition of one's own ongoing subjective experience. It makes explicit that there is a further emergent capacity necessary in order to have direct access to the qualitative side of consciousness$_3$. In this genuinely introspective aspect, one's immediate subjective state, or the "is like" of experience, becomes the focus of a self-consciousness. It is here that people cannot have the same access to another's experience in the moment as they do to their own. My hypnagogic imagery is not accessible to you, although it may be that an inner dialogic process both creates it and allows it to be shared, after the fact. Reflexive awareness of immediate subjective state is a special consequence of our capacity to "take the role of the other" toward ourselves as personal awareness (consciousness$_2$). The reflexive awareness of self, however, is predominantly evaluative and judgmental (that is, socially engaged), while our immediate sentience can only be brought into view by cultivating a radically detached and observational attitude. This is the potentiality that is the gateway for the unfolding of those more radical transformations of consciousness often termed "altered states."

In a tantalizing way, the "is like" of immediate momentary consciousness does not exist in the context of the pragmatic engagement of everyday life. It is almost entirely lost within our perpetually renewed and self-referentially evaluated concern with ourselves, others, and our projects. Only when we step back from such pragmatic involvements and either cultivate or involuntarily withdraw into a more detached attitude does anything like an immediate consciousness, of an empirically specifiable sort, come into view. Held in view, it begins to undergo certain characteristic transformations. This is, after all, what is involved in so called "insight" or "mindfulness" meditation, where functional verbal thought is deliberately inhibited in order to witness unfolding "mind moments" that gradually begin to approach the properties of classical mystical experience (Goleman, 1972; Deikman, 1982). It is less well known that the classical introspectionist techniques developed by E. B. Titchener (1912) and the early Raymond Cattell (1930), based on the attempted inhibition of the "stimulus" or "naming" error and the cultivation of a bare observational attitude, elicited transformations of consciousness very much like those observed with low levels of psychedelic drugs or early stages of meditation (Hunt, 1984, 1985ab, 1986). The verbatim protocols from these early introspectionist studies show, at least to the contemporary eye, copious instances of spontaneous experiences of derealization, depersonalization, physiognomic transformations of perception, synesthesias, changes in sensed time and spatial localization, and trancelike absorptive states (see chapters 2 and 6).

Along similar lines, Milton Erickson's model of hypnosis, as interpreted by Erickson and Rossi (1981) and Plotkin (1979), suggests that the hypnotist induces in the subject a reflexive turning around on his or her ongoing states of consciousness. This is similar to classical introspection and meditation — except that the explicit role relationship with the hypnotist allows the dialogic basis of this self-awareness to appear more obviously and be more directly utilized. By commenting directly on features of the subject's immediate state that normally have only a first-person access, and a partial one at that — "you are getting sleepy," "your left arm is feeling tingly and light" — the hypnotist invites the subject to take an unusually detached, observing perspective on his or her ongoing sentience. At the same time, by calling attention to such awareness and then anticipating and finally directing it, the hypnotist makes the unusual move of taking the role of the other's first-person sentience and thereby speaking to the subject's ongoing experience as if from "within." Common to hypnosis, meditation, classical introspection, and spontaneous alterations of consciousness is precisely this attitude of receptive witnessing. This gives the resultant sense that one's experience is no longer in an ordinary sense "mine" but rather appears as if imposed from "outside."

As we will see (chapter 6), this sudden noticing of awareness as something impersonal and imposed would appear to be a consequence of our dialogic account of human consciousness. The more primarily observing and detached one becomes in an actual ongoing conversation, the more the other is forced to show and reveal themselves. Something like this seems to happen internally in hypnosis and meditation. It is as if one took up an observing role relationship to immediate awareness as such. Here indeed is a microscope for normally unconscious cognitive processes, as well as a path of experiential development in its own right.

To go on to complete this survey of the *OED*, however, consciousness₅ — Natsoulas's "unitive meaning" — and consciousness₇ — the "dissociative meaning" — would seem to be two sides of the same human potentiality. Both progressive degrees of integration and of disintegration and splitting are necessary consequences of Mead's description of the intrinsic incompleteness of our capacity to take the role of the other at any given moment. Consciousness₅ is defined as the "totality of impressions, thoughts, and feelings making up a person's conscious being." It sounds like a kind of integration of all the other definitions and yet one that must also vary in degree. In other words, this aspect of integrated awareness will differ greatly across and within individuals. It is coupled with its opposite, consciousness₇, which is defined as the "double consciousness" of multiple personality — the existence of two separate trains of thought or feeling in the same person. Obviously we are also very close in this account to the seemingly infinite nuances of self-contradiction and self-deception that seem intrinsic to any form of self-referential symbolic cognition.

The necessary, yet fluctuating asymmetry between interpersonal and personal/reflexive consciousness, understandable as a consequence of Mead's taking the role of the other, suggests that our experience of ourselves will continuously vary along a dimension of integration versus division and splitting.[1] Reflexivity, for Mead, is never fully completed. We cannot fully turn around on and encompass ourselves because we are continuously under way and there is nowhere to stand outside the recursive spiral of cognitive symbolism. Mead stresses the inevitable failure of the various partial "me's" that we automatically construct as personifications of ourselves to ever exhaust the spontaneously expressive "I" that does our feeling, acting, and personifying. The "I" cannot be characterized other than as the stream of consciousness itself:

> Where in conduct does the "I" come in as over against the "me"? . . . We may have a better self and a worse self but that again is not the "I" . . . , because they are both selves. We approve of one and disapprove of the other, but when we bring up one or the other they are there for such approval as "me's." The "I" does not get into the limelight; we talk to ourselves but do not see ourselves. . . . The "I" of this moment is present in the "me" of the next moment. There again I cannot turn around quick enough to catch myself. I become a "me" in so far as I remember what I said. The "I" can be given, however, this functional relationship. It is because of the "I" that we can say that we are never fully aware of what we are, that we surprise ourselves by our own action. (Mead, 1936, pp. 173–74)

Mead is presenting the lived version of Kurt Gödel's famous mathematical theorem (Hofstadter, 1979). Any system that refers to itself, including basic mathematics as well as human personality, can never finally be shown to be either complete or consistent with itself. Such a system will self-referentially modify itself in ways that cannot be predicted from its present state. These resulting self-generated reorganizations also fit well with Ulric Neisser (1976) and Frederic Bartlett (1932) on the human symbolic capacity as based on a turning around on and reorganization of the perceptual schemata. Such a turning around on perception must lead to its spontaneous rearrangement, introducing that "novelty" which many have made intrinsic to human intelligence.

Indeed, it is our overall sense of significance or context in a situation that seems most especially vulnerable to spontaneous reinterpretation. Context suffers a per-petually renewed occlusion as we attempt to grasp it. As Mead stresses, the basis of symbolic cognition in a "taking the role of the other" means that we gain any perspective on our experience and actions only retrospectively. We know how that perceived context can seem so painfully obvious that we are incredulous that we could have missed something so clear. We can then wonder what we might be missing now.

We arrive here at the cognitive basis for the psychoanalyst Jacques Lacan's (1973) notion of a "deletion of the subject" intrinsic to human experience, and for Jung's (1951) notion of the unknowability of a Self that can never be fully encom-passed but only circumambulated. Yet the difference between Jung and Lacan is immense. Lacan's deletion is absolute. The "I" cannot be "filled," and it is only language and its "reality principle" that can guide us past this narcissistic lure and into the world. All "inward," imaginative, or metaphoric techniques that seek to reflect the "I" must produce illusion — as if one point on a flywheel were to think that it might somehow catch up with another point on its circumference. Jung (1944, 1951), on the other hand, in a fashion similar to the Tibetan Buddhist tradition and its imageries of light and open space (Tarthang Tulku, 1977), posits a metaphori-cally based circumambulation of the "I" using images that do have a definite structure and are related to the physical world. These metaphoric structures "hold" and "contain" our sensed openness in much the way that Winnicott sees the infant's experience as held by the empathic mothering figure. This allows our spontaneous nature to come forth, be held, and be reflected back in order to be known. Is consciousness a lure to be rejected or a metaphorically based process of genuine self-awareness?

Some Philosophical Reservations about the Concept of Consciousness: Wittgenstein and Heidegger

Martin Heidegger and Ludwig Wittgenstein are doubtless the most influential phi-losophers of this century. Though quite disparate in their methods of thought, both were fundamentally preoccupied with the nature of experience and its relation to language. They were also scathingly critical of the concept of consciousness in western thought. Consciousness is either inextricably tied into the misleading notion of the "privacy" of experience (Wittgenstein) or inseparable from the sterile, ultimately alienating dichotomy between subject and object, mind and world, that has bedeviled our tradition (Heidegger). Our traditional concept of consciousness becomes emblematic of a deep historical confusion or even cultural pathology. We cannot proceed much further in our present discourse without considering their mutual repudiation of any special "realm" of consciousness as something separate from the world it is in, shares, and knows. This rejection will prove well supported over the course of our inquiry.

Wittgenstein (1953, 1980, 1992) was equally critical of the use in psychology of any general concept of consciousness, as in Husserl's systematic phenomenology, and of the more "molecular" concept of an immediately introspected sentience (primary consciousness$_3$ as revealed by reflexive consciousness$_4$). Neither usage will be of help in understanding the processes of thought and language for Wittgenstein. The first usage is too broad, the second too narrow. The general concept of consciousness for Wittgenstein amounts to little more than the redundancy of putting "consciousness of" in front of all references to cognitive capacity and mental activity. At the other extreme, and with critics of classical introspectionism like George Humphrey (1951), the "raw feel" aspect of our experience does not tell us anything about pragmatic cognitive and linguistic activity in the social world — any more than we would, normally at least, accept telephone doodles in lieu of the conversation that engendered them. Thus, his widely quoted statement: "Even if someone had a particular capacity only when, and only so long as, he had a particular feeling, the feeling would not be the capacity. . . . An inner process stands in need of outward criteria" (Wittgenstein, 1953, p. 181).

That said, Wittgenstein was not missing the fact that we do have a first-person access to mind. Indeed, it is not even clear that Wittgenstein would want to deny that subjective states might provide unique evidence of normally invisible cognitive processes that underlie, but are not the equivalent of, the practical expressions of intelligence and language. Rather, it follows from the social and self-referential bases of our symbolic capacity that the mind will be accessed from both a first- and a third-person perspective, in a dynamic and shifting exchange in which neither can be considered primary or causative. "Consciousness is as clear in his face and behavior, as in myself" (Wittgenstein, 1980, p. 164). What is invalidated for Wittgenstein is any notion of consciousness as intrinsically "private" and "interior." As with Mead, our experience as symbolic beings is inherently dialogic and self-referential. First- and third-person criteria are formally inseparable, functional phases of symbolic activity. Their conjoined asymmetries constitute the continuum along which we can order various "forms of life" that are part of our symbolic capacity.

Wittgenstein (1992) traces an overlapping family of phenomena in a continuous series that includes lying, pretending, knowing, and even the social implications of the claim that one's experience is, after all, private — "I know what I am thinking but you cannot."[2] I have already added Freud's unconscious, as accessed whenever third-person criteria give important information about others that is ostensibly not available to them, and I have also mentioned Jung's very different first-person-centered "imaginal" unconscious. There seems no reason not to include as well in this series of phenomena certain transformations of consciousness consequent upon a self-referential symbolic capacity. These can involve an enhancement of the unitive aspect of experience — as in the sense of being, presence, or "I am" experience described within the meditative traditions and in accounts of "peak experience" (Maslow, 1971). Although first-person access may predominate initially in these spontaneous transformations of awareness, there is clearly, as James (1902) insisted, a third-person impact of such experiences on the social surroundings of the individual. Max Weber (1922) termed this "charisma" — the third-person face of the numinous — and made it central to his theory of the social impact of religious experience. Indeed, on a more descriptive level, so nonprivate are such experiences that the person involved appears to others as entranced or absorbed and may behave toward them afterwards with unusual expressions of compassion and personal power.

From Wittgenstein's perspective, the traditional doctrines of mind-body relationship, so widely debated historically and equally avoided in what follows, appear in the first instance as misleading formalizations of the actual dynamic interplay of the first- and third-person criteria in everyday experience. As John Searle states, "Dualists asked, 'how many kinds of things and properties are there?' and counted up to two. Monists, confronting the same question, only got as far as one. But the real mistake was to start counting at all" (Searle, 1992, p. 26). The various "doctrines" of mind and brain may attempt to make one form of access the source of the other. Idealism makes first-person criteria causative. Materialism elevates third-person behavioral criteria to the status of explanation. Other views insist on an equally artificial division. I am suggesting that in all these views, "brain" is unwittingly assimilated to "the other" and either elevated accordingly or banished from the scene. Dualisms of mind and brain that entail either a parallelism or interactionism, although at least more eclectically comprehensive, also assume an intrinsic division utterly denied by our actual experience of ourselves. Again, for Wittgenstein, we have in such views simplifications of ordinary language, not advances beyond it. "Double aspect" theories might sound more like it, but that is less a theoretical doctrine open to empirical investigation than a formalized and abstract statement of the conjoint access we already have to ourselves and others, with mind substituted for self and brain substituted for other.

Of course, there is still a fundamental scientific issue, perhaps the most fundamental of our time, concerning the relation of experience to neurons and their networks. A big part of its fascination as "problem," however, may come from its historical confusion with our daily dialectic and struggle across the categories of self and other. To what degree our current mind-brain theories reflect metaphysical elaborations that seek to elevate a megalomaniac's self over society or a mighty and impersonal society over the individual will remain, for now, an open question.

On a very different level of analysis, Heidegger, in *Being and Time* (1927) and its companion work, *The Basic Problems of Phenomenology* (1982), sought to demonstrate that any would-be phenomenology of consciousness — with its claims of a constitutive, world-creating intentionality — simply cannot be separated from a more primary being-in-the-world, of which it is but one, falsely formalized aspect. Heidegger seeks to undercut the traditional subject-object dichotomy in terms of which we have all been trained to think. "World," in modern thought, has become something increasingly physical, objective, and measurable. Accordingly, part of the virtue of Husserl's earlier phenomenology of consciousness was to call attention to the primacy of our living presence in a world given to us to experience. Yet such consciousness still had the misleading connotation of something "interior" and "subjective." It risked leaving our being-in-the-world as something ephemeral and unreal. If both subjectivity and objectivity are equally given to us through our symbolic mode of "being there" (*Dasein*), then: "Intentionality is neither objective nor subjective. . . . Dasein . . . is already immediately dwelling among things. For the Dasein there is no outside, for which reason it is also absurd to talk about an inside" (Heidegger, 1982, p. 65, 66).

"Consciousness" has equally misleading connotations of world-creating subjectivity or epiphenomenal residue. It only emerges, for Heidegger, with the birth of our sciences of objectivity, based on the assumption of the primacy of a "matter" held to have an existence somehow outside the qualitative patterning of our experience. In our objectivity everything that "matters," including people, becomes some sort of "commodity." That objectivity has brought about a world that is to be known by a subject who somehow stands outside it (Heidegger, 1977). Subjectivity is, paradoxically, created by the notion of an external objectivity, much as, with Rudolf Arnheim (1974), the illusion of perspective in naturalistic painting creates a "unique" viewing point occupied by the distanced observer. Our concept of consciousness as subjective and interior emerges with a social order that values an increasingly autonomous, isolated, and interchangeable individual as its ideal. The problem herein is the simultaneous tendency to see the mind of that individual as similarly autonomous from its social context and to construct a theory of consciousness falsely separated from body, other, and world. Whether such a consciousness then becomes foundational or irrelevant, it has been falsely conceptualized as primarily alone. Whether we like it or not, this is how we, as a people, now think.

Heidegger begins his analysis in *Being and Time* from what he sees as western humanity's loss of any vital, immediate sense of what "isness" or "being" means — a loss of the sense of being alive and fully present with others in our world. This diagnosis of modern culture is very reminiscent of Winnicott's (1971) characterization of many contemporary clients in psychotherapy as suffering primarily from a sense of not feeling real or vitally embodied and alive. For Winnicott, and later for Kohut (1977), this felt loss of reality is the core of the narcissism of modern life (Lasch, 1978). More and more of us fall into either personal grandiosity or emotional withdrawal as the ever-present alternatives that lie on either side of felt presence. Social scientists perhaps should not ignore the fact that Descartes — the progenitor of the subject-object dichotomy in its modern form — actually managed to doubt whether he *existed* and had to construct logical proofs in order to convince himself *intellectually* that he did. Proofs for the existence of God may or may not be charmingly quixotic, but needing a proof of one's own being or isness is, more simply, sad, if not overtly schizoid. The danger is that our contemporary psychological and philosophical concepts of consciousness are not merely conceptually confused, as Wittgenstein would have it, but actually clinically disturbed. We unwittingly enshrine an endemic narcissism and personal isolation at the core of our thought about our own nature and potentialities.

Heidegger's analysis of the subject-object dichotomy and loss of Being is quite congruent with the more sociological language of Robert Bellah and his co-authors in *Habits of the Heart* (1985). For Bellah, it is the extreme development of our western ideal of the private, autonomous individual that has led to values based on self-actualization and a culture of psychotherapy. Are these, in their social impact, essentially narcissistic? In our worship of the individual and his or her consciousness and personal development we lose any sense of genuine community with others. Yet it should also be noted (chapter 14) that in traditional hunter-gatherer societies it was primarily consciousness and states of consciousness that could be the most profoundly shared, as in socially defined ecstatic states and forms of archetypal dreaming. In nonliterate native societies these "states," which we now tend to regard as narcissistic, seem to have been the immediate source for a binding sense of community and shared experience. Any attempt to conceptualize consciousness and its potential transformations must address how something that could seem so obvious to traditional peoples now appears to us as paradoxical and merely magical.

In what follows we will want to be on guard against understanding consciousness in a way that merely echoes valuative and conceptual systems that are coming into increasing question in terms of their impact on the ability of contemporary people to feel real and vitally present with others in a shared world. We walk a treacherous and shifting ground when we seek a formal account of "consciousness." Consciousness is surely a foundational concept in the western tradition, but too many attempts to approach it both theoretically and empirically may have rather served primarily to perpetuate an ideology that actually splits us from our world and leaves us, at least conceptually, in a falsely isolated and private stance. Otherwise what is intended as an investigation of the foundations of our human mind risks becoming, instead, just another expression of a dilemma about which our major thinkers have been alerting us throughout this century.

2 Cognition and Consciousness

The Renewed Debate over Consciousness:
Secondary By-Product or Fundamental Capacity?

Cognitive psychologists and neuropsychologists like Marcel (1983ab), Humphrey (1983), Baars (1988), Weiskrantz (1988), and Schacter (1989) now understand consciousness as a formal system or capacity involving the direction, choice, and synthesis of nonconscious processes. This movement, however, has also been answered with renewed versions of the traditional functionalist and behaviorist rejections of the study of consciousness as anything other than an incidental by-product of computational capacity (Dennett, 1991). Consciousness is seen as private and hence outside scientific scrutiny, confabulated and deluded in its pretended access to cognitive process, and ultimately nonfunctional. Such a rejection is in fact central to the artificial-intelligence movement. If sentient awareness should prove necessary for the understanding of symbolic cognition, especially in its recombinatory and novel aspects, then computer simulations of cognition must finally be confined to those part functions that can become completely automatized within the more open context of life experience.

Our most basic understanding of ourselves and other life forms rides on this debate. Indeed, a significant portion of contemporary cognitive science may have unwittingly backed into a view of consciousness as having much the same features that we attribute to the chronic schizophrenic. Namely, it is private and withdrawn, completely deluded about itself, and without any adaptive function. I have already questioned both the theoretical and sociocultural consequences when subjectivity becomes something progressively useless and futile. How much of our concept of consciousness is open to potential empirical investigation and how much rests on the implicit metaphysics of modern mass societies and their valuation of utility over all else?

The view that consciousness is something intrinsically private, even ineffable, and so unresearchable in any genuinely empirical sense, seems doubtful on both theoretical and empirical grounds. If, with Mead and Wittgenstein, our self-referential awareness is dialogically structured through and through, it should be, by definition, potentially communicable. On the idea of there being multiple symbolic frames, such communication need not be linguistic to be both abstract and intelligible. On the level of empirical accessibility, research on altered states of consciousness (recently reviewed by Farthing, 1992) has consistently shown that subjective reports from hypnosis (Hilgard, 1968), sensory deprivation (Zubek, 1969), LSD and related psychedelic drugs (Barr et al., 1972) and meditation (Hunt and Chefurka, 1976; Shapiro, 1983) can be assessed by questionnaire and content analysis in ways that are reliable and even formally scalable. Several questionnaires have also been developed based on general features of spontaneous alterations of consciousness, independent of specific causal setting, in order to assess what seems to be the rather high "base rate" of spontaneous transformations of consciousness in the ordinary population (Pekala, 1991). There are even scales and questionnaires for the changes of consciousness in that most private of subjective horrors, psychotic onset (Chapman and Chapman, 1980).

Consider next the claim that access to our own consciousness is necessarily indirect and inferred, being based on the same ad hoc assumptions and even confabulations upon which we base our inferences about the state of mind of others in everyday social relationships. Widely cited in this context is the research of Nisbett and Wilson (1977) showing, in a way that Freud could only have applauded, that subjects who have no knowledge of reliable findings concerning position preferences for either end in the free selection of objects placed in a line will confabulate highly idiosyncratic explanations for their own choices. Their stated criteria, such as color and design, are clearly refuted by their actual behavior. In effect, they are simply not conscious of the actual bases of their own judgments.

While "taking the role of the other" toward ourselves is clearly a cognitive-symbolic construction, and so is necessarily partial and incomplete, that does not necessarily render it without function. Indeed, self-consciousness is thereby no more limited than the similarly intrinsically incomplete and partial mathematical languages of the sciences (Bronowski, 1971). The correct rejection of any supposed infallibility for first-person access to experience does not then prove its irrelevance — in practice or in theory. Although all experience comes to us within a cultural tradition (Katz 1978), the cross-cultural commonalities in hallucinatory geometric designs (Jung's mandala images), synesthesias, out-of-body imaginal states and lucid dreams, and the "white light" experiences of shamans and meditators (Reichel-Dolmatoff, 1975; Siegel and Jarvick, 1975; Hunt, 1989b) seem to indicate that such nonverbal states have a common underlying structure. These states can plausibly be interpreted as exemplifications of the "deep structure" of a kind of intelligence that directly reuses and reorganizes the structures of perception. Such an imaginal intelligence would be analogous to Bickerton's (1984) cross-cultural template for syntax but is difficult to explain in purely linguistic terms.[1] The limits of a verbal self awareness may not be those of an imagistic one.

The most fundamental argument against any functional role for consciousness, however, has always been that subjective states are really secondary by-products of actual cognitive competencies, to which they provide little or no access. Karl Lashley, in a manner reminiscent of Wittgenstein (1953), put this most forcefully: "No activity of mind is *ever* conscious . . . . When we think, the connections are just there. We have no *perception* of how a thought or a sentence is structured. Experience gives us no clue as to the means by which it is organized" (Lashley, 1960, p. 532). An ostensibly telling illustration of Lashley's point comes from N. F. Maier's (1931) famous "two cords" problem. Subjects were required to secure two widely separated hanging cords together, with the experimenter eventually providing a surreptitious clue to the only possible solution by brushing against one of the cords and so setting it in motion. The subjects, however, *never* mentioned the clue in their later reports, even though their sudden "insights" that the cords could only be joined by such swinging had immediately followed it. Maier concluded that the insight, or "ah ha" experience, with its sudden impact, felt novelty, and reorganization of previous awareness, is without any content of its own, other than the impalpable knowledge of the solution. It may actually "obliterate" or "mask" the cognitive processes that would lead up to it.

Can we be quite so sure that the "ah-ha" experience has no function — that it plays no necessary causal role in symbolic cognition? In turn, might not its phenomenology offer empirical clues, if not to the separate cognitive processes it synthesizes, then to the cognitive processes involved in the act of synthesis itself? This is perhaps the point at which to begin to consider more specifically views of consciousness as a cognitive system in its own right, first along phenomenological lines and then in terms of experimental and clinical neurological research. Later, we will return to the possibility that spontaneous transformations of consciousness could provide the specific microscope for such a system.

Humphrey (1951), in his analysis of the famous Würzburg controversy that led to the rejection of systematic introspection, agreed that consciousness during symbolic cognition consisted in an impalpable "sense" of significance that could not be further specified or described. Although it is commonly held that this conclusion led to the demise of introspectionism and the advent of behavioral functionalism, it is important to stress that early introspectors like Ach (1905) and Woodworth (1906) believed that although the moment of insight might be largely unspecifiable, it did real work in the course of thinking — that it mattered. Their initial phenomenology of this insight state and its potential function has been extended by the clinical psychologist and phenomenologist Eugene Gendlin (1962). In his account, "felt meaning" is the immediate state aspect of the sense of understanding that must accompany all moments of transition and novelty in symbolic cognition, to the extent that we can be said to follow what is happening.

As with the Würzburg introspectors and their allies, felt meanings are a definite "something" for Gendlin, yet not open to description other than as what they are about. They are preliminary enough to admit of multiple possible lines of further articulation, but specific enough to suffice without any more specific articulation in most situations. They are, indeed, precise enough so that we directly sense when a given articulation or even line of thought departs from our original experience in any way. Felt meaning is by no means "primitive," since it must immediately follow the most complex symbolic communications, including mathematical expressions, if we are to understand them. Felt meanings are causal in that they demonstrably guide communicative thought. Their sudden loss or absence is immediately and sometimes painfully felt and often socially disguised, and their quality of involuntary capture means that a given "sense" of understanding will temporarily block other potential and competing insights. In the more specific form of word meaning, the loss of felt sense of meaning in semantic satiation, following from prolonged repetition or staring at the written word, can literally be timed by stopwatch. It may even be delayed by an accompanying gesture or imagery (Werner and Kaplan, 1963).

William James (1902) suggested that classical mystical experience can be regarded as an especially enhanced and intensified felt meaning (to use the more current terminology). With nothing specific that it is about, it is sensed as about everything. We can also see the power of a generalized sense of felt meaning through its absence in the syndromes of derealization and depersonalization that can accompany psychotic onset (Chapman, 1966). Here we seem to find an intensified form of ordinary semantic satiation. Perhaps even entire cultures and civilizations can similarly lose their *sense* of direction and meaning, and in spontaneous "radical salvation movements" begin to regain it. Indeed, the fact that felt meanings *feel* like the overall context or sense of totality in one's situation means that it is precisely that context, the total organization of a situation rather than its specifics, that is most open to shifting and unexpected reorganizations. Accordingly, much of "everyday"

(Schutz, 1962) and "high" (Kuhn, 1966) culture can be seen as a socially endorsed, communal attempt to contain and control this potential for unexpected openness and novelty. Since creativity must involve a destruction of the previous status quo, it will often appear as frightening as it does liberating.

Rather than conclude that the state of felt meaning can offer no clue to its underlying cognitive processes, I would suggest that it is precisely its involuntary imposition, experienced "as if" from outside and so described in various creative endeavors, that demonstrates the social, dialogic structure of human consciousness. We will see later (chapter 6) how in a phenomenological sense felt meanings are given to us by a phenomenal other, as a demonstrable phase of our own awareness in dialogue with the waiting, thinking "me."

In an influential series of experiments, the cognitive psychologist Anthony Marcel (1983a, 1983b, 1988) has outlined a cognitive-science version of Gendlin's felt meaning. Consciousness, for Marcel, is a cognitive system in its own right that synthesizes, organizes, and directs largely unconscious parallel processes through successive moments of "figurative unity." Subjects were presented with words flashed by a tachistoscope too rapidly for any conscious recognition. They were asked to make forced-choice guesses among list words that were similar either in meaning or in letter composition to the words actually flashed. As the exposure times were progressively decreased, the subjects still remained able to pick words semantically related to the ones actually shown after they had lost the ability to guess words containing similar letters. Thus, at the lower range of exposure time, if the word *acquaintance* had been exposed, they could successfully guess a word like *friend* over *acquiescence,* even though the latter had greater graphic similarity to the original word. Marcel concluded that the most immediate and rapidly constructed moments of consciousness must make available the highest and most developed levels of semantic synthesis first, before any available awareness of the constituent parts of what had been synthesized. Even though the letters out of which the words had been composed must have been processed unconsciously in order to allow accurate semantic matches, it required significantly longer exposure times for awareness of these constituents of symbolic meaning. In effect, the whole preceded the simpler parts in terms of availability to awareness — presumably showing part of the basic function of consciousness.

A similar phenomenon emerges from Heinz Werner's (1956) earlier introspectionist study of the experience of word meaning with subliminal tachistoscopic exposure. His subjects were asked to describe whatever they felt, however vague and undefined, about what the unseen word might mean. He found that in response to, say, successive exposures of "cloud," subjects could "feel" that it was something "high" and "soft" and "light," before they could accurately intuit the word itself. As illustrated in this research, felt meaning comes to us with a definite sense of "feel" or "physiognomy" — perhaps even with synesthetic, cross-modal features. This constitutes an abstract and sensed synthesis which will in turn normally be masked by its more specific and articulated completion. As tachistoscopic and introspectionist research have revealed, immediate symbolic consciousness first provides us with the maximally intuitive synthesis and sensed meaning of our situation at its most abstract level. The analytic constituents of such meanings require longer to unfold, leading generations of cognitive psychologists to conclude that consciousness can tell us nothing of its part processes, when in fact it directly exemplifies its own capacity for immediate felt synthesis.

Jack Yates (1985) similarly called attention to the way that our ostensibly amodal consciousness offers no clues to the underlying perceptual modalities of the information being synthesized, in that subjects find it harder to recall whether they have seen or heard sentences than to recall their actual meanings. As with Werner's example, this may show, rather, that the impalpable aspect of felt meaning entails and actually illustrates ongoing processes of positive synesthetic fusion (see chapters 4 and 7). Again, the phenomenology of a conscious awareness system may not offer clues to the nonconscious operations it synthesizes, but may show instead the rather different cognitive processes involved in the synthesizing activities of consciousness itself.

The Conscious Awareness System and Its Multiple Manifestations

The major recent attempts to develop a cognitive psychology of consciousness as a capacity in its own right have been made by the cognitive psychologist Bernard Baars, the neuropsychologists L. Weiskrantz and Daniel Schacter, and, from a more clinical neurological perspective, Norman Geschwind and M. Mesulam.

In *A Cognitive Theory of Consciousness* Bernard Baars defines consciousness as the capacity for selection, serial integration, and volitional direction necessary within a complex nervous system that must integrate multiple and parallel automatized unconscious processes. Consciousness is responsible for the selectivity of experience, attunement to novelty, and "system-wide" activation or publicity. It is the "global workspace" for ongoing synthesis. In terms of localization of cortical function, Baars suggests that it is the reticular-thalamic projective system, functionally manifested in the "orientation response" based in the brain stem, that receives the maximum input from all other neural areas (see chapter 4). It alone is broad enough in its synthesizing potential to be the neural locus of consciousness. Cortical activity per se is not conscious. Rather, consciousness is indicated by the 300 millisecond wave of activation that constitutes the cortical evoked response (CER), and requires the engagement of the thalamic projection system in order to arouse and orient the cortex. The orientation response is associated with a CER that is spread across the entire cortex, subcortex, and autonomic nervous system. But with habituation and presumed automatization it becomes localized within more and more specific cortical areas and so becomes more and more marginally conscious. For Baars, then, the orientation response is the physiological side of the qualitative, perceptually based dimensions that are the experiential core of all awareness. Perhaps consistent with his emphasis on the orientation response and CER as the primary expressions of a conscious awareness system, Baars does not make a major distinction between an immediate, perceptually based consciousness, potentially inferrable in lower organisms, and a more specifically human self-referential, symbolic consciousness.[2] It is the latter capacity that becomes the primary focus for Schacter, Weiskrantz, and Geschwind.

Schacter (1988, 1989) and Weiskrantz (1974, 1988) both review a series of neocortical and subcortical damage syndromes that seem to be most parsimoniously interpreted as involving the disconnection of various perceptual and symbolic capacities from a self-referential awareness system localized predominantly in the right hemisphere of the neocortex. It may be useful here to distinguish between "vertical" disconnection syndromes, based on some sort of dissociation between subcortical and cortical functions, such as blindsight and the form of amnesia related to bilateral hippocampal damage, and more specifically neocortical or "horizontal" disconnection syndromes, like aphasia or prosopagnosia (inability to recognize faces). In all these syndromes the subject is acutely self-aware of the deficit or loss in capacity, although some degree of nonconscious preservation of implicit functioning, outside the person's control and awareness, is often demonstrable behaviorally and physiologically.

For instance, in blindsight, where the primary striate visual cortex is damaged in humans or experimentally ablated in rhesus monkeys, subjects indeed act as though they were blind. In the case of humans, they complain of a total inability to see in the affected areas of the visual field. Nonetheless, they show eye movement fixations of moving objects in the "blind" area. If forced to guess basic dimensions of perceptual stimuli, such as horizontal versus vertical stripes, they show correct responses that improve over time — all the while claiming that they cannot see anything. The monkeys even gradually recover some capacity to navigate through the surrounding array, although our insistently self-referential awareness of the lack of qualitative perception may prevent that sort of "faith" for human subjects.

Bilateral hippocampal damage in humans is associated with a subjectively devastating loss of episodic or personal memory, so that the subject will not remember a test taken five minutes before or the psychologist who gave it (Tulving, 1983). Yet here again an implicit function can still be demonstrated. Subjects who report no conscious memory of previous testing will nonetheless show actual improvement with repeated practice. Similarly, subjects suffering from receptive aphasia and prosopagnosia, with an acute awareness of their inability to understand language or recognize faces, will show appropriate galvanic skin responses (GSR) to test stimuli — demonstrating an implicit, nonconscious discrimination.

Schacter (1989) suggests that it is simply not very parsimonious to divide every cognitive function into its conscious and nonconscious forms. It makes more sense to see all these syndromes of deficit as involving a disconnection between multiple specific functions and their access to a single, central awareness system. Such disconnections in fact show, with Baars, the functional importance of such a central awareness system for the synthesis of perceptual and cognitive capacities.

There does exist a neurological syndrome that specifically and directly affects this capacity for self-awareness. In anosognosia patients demonstrate a total lack of self-awareness of the more particular linguistic, perceptual, sensory, and motor deficits we have been discussing. Patients with this additional loss of awareness show specific damage to the parietal regions of the right hemisphere. Schacter cites Geschwind's (1965) reference to this area as the "association area of association areas" — the zone of convergence for both the higher-level symbolic neocortical areas as well as subcortical projections. Thereby it would be the equivalent, on the level of symbolic cognition, of Baars's more perceptual "global workspace." Not only do we have evidence of syndromes based on a disconnection from self-referential awareness, but in anosognosia we see direct damage to such a neocortical awareness system. As John Kihlstrom has suggested, this would be the locus for our awareness of self (Kihlstrom and Tobias, 1990).

Geschwind and Mesulam (Geschwind, 1982; Mesulam and Geschwind, 1978; Mesulam, 1985) complete this neurological location of self-consciousness as a separate functional system. They point out that the most common clinical neurological syndrome, and the only one that all normal subjects will have experienced at certain times, is delirium or confusional state. Delirium most commonly follows from diffuse trauma to the right parietal and right frontal regions — the former manifested in more immediate hallucinatory and confusional conditions and the latter in difficulties of selective attention. In other words, such syndromes have as their primary symptom the impairment of consciousness. Geschwind (1982) suggests that while the left hemisphere is dominant for language, the right hemisphere is dominant for attention and response to novelty — in short, consciousness. The pervasiveness of delirium syndromes and their appearance within ordinary drowsiness and intoxication supports the notion of a conscious awareness system as the point of maximal synthesis of cognitive activity and accordingly as the function that is most easily impaired.

The defining "negative" or deficit symptoms of confusional states include disorientation for time and place, loss of interest, lack of awareness of any deficit, and, often, retrospective amnesia for the episode. The more "positive" or disinhibitive symptoms (Hughlings-Jackson, 1958) include witty or playful verbal associations and intrusive hallucinatory imagery (Lipowski, 1967, 1990). These are also the basic features of ordinary REM (rapid eye movement) dreaming — confusion, memory deficits, lack of awareness that one is in fact asleep and dreaming, and intrusive perceptions and thoughts that are out of place in the immediate dream setting (Hunt, 1982, 1989a). Itil (1970) has called attention to the similarities between the electroencephalogram (EEG) of clinical delirium and the human REM state. They share a superimposed mixture of beta, theta, and delta rhythms that on average reflect a slight lowering of activation compared to normal alert wakefulness.

If delirium is best conceived as a pure and primary disturbance of consciousness, then its polar opposite may not be so much the incomplete self-referential awareness of everyday life, itself so often confused and clouded, but the enhanced clarity and sense of presence associated with long-term meditative practice and spontaneous peak experience. Meditation, indeed, is usually understood as a means for the higher development of consciousness. Interestingly, lucid dreaming — knowing that you are dreaming while the dream continues — has been regarded on phenomenological and physiological grounds as a spontaneous meditative state (Hunt, 1982, 1989a; Gackenbach and Bosveld, 1989). Such dreams seem to be associated with a specific activation of the parietal areas — particularly in the right hemisphere (Holtzinger, 1990). The unusually coherent alpha and theta rhythms from across the entire cortex that are associated with deep meditation (Alexander et al., 1990) also seem to imply a maximum synthesis of functioning across the cortex. An enhanced balance between left and right hemispheres would allow the normally subordinated right hemisphere — associated with felt meaning and self-awareness — a greater influence on the more verbal intelligence of the left hemisphere (Hunt, 1989a).

Meditation is based on a deliberate suspension of our more practically oriented cognitive activity, especially verbally organized thought. This inhibition of capacities associated with left-hemisphere predominance would allow the potential synthesizing capacity of self-awareness more time to complete itself to the greatest degree possible. The result seems to be just those feelings of presence, clarity, and "isness" that were central to Heidegger (chapter 11). After all, if we are willing to entertain the idea that conscious awareness in itself is a "system," and that that system can be selectively impaired, we ought to be prepared to consider the possibility that it can be selectively enhanced and developed as well.

Note, however, that apart from Geschwind and our related extrapolations of his clinical phenomenology of clouded consciousness into dreaming, lucid dreams, and meditation, what is lacking in recent attempts in cognitive science to formulate a causal conscious awareness system is precisely phenomenology. In most such approaches, consciousness is "responsible" for volition and active synthesis, so that we are led back again to the conclusions of Maier, Lashley, and Humphrey — which left nothing of consciousness to research other than its outward behavioral and functional expressions. Consciousness is once again a causal "something," but it is still impalpable and unspecifiable. It is just here that we will find the contribution of research and phenomenologies based on spontaneous transformations of consciousness. These will provide perhaps the only available microscope for the processes that would constitute our ordinary, and so invisible, conscious awareness system. They indicate the lines along which such a system would undergo both its own pathologies and its own development.

The Cognitive Unconscious: Separate System or Proto-Consciousness?

The findings of Schacter and Marcel show that perception, semantic recognition, and verbal thought can all remain "implicit" or "unconscious" and are capable of expression independent of any conscious awareness system. The rediscovery of such a "cognitive unconscious" is also part of a second revolution in current cognitive science that is in potential competition with the renewed fascination with consciousness. Any first-person psychology will again seem truly residual if it cannot be characterized apart from functions that can also be unconscious. A "cognitive unconscious," as the staging area for cognitive-symbolic processes, might seem to leave only the still "impalpable" act of direction and choice for a conscious awareness system (Bowers, 1987; Kihlstrom, 1987). If we conclude that our most complex capacities are intrinsically unconscious, we will not have traveled very far from the functionalist-behaviorist tradition of experimental North American psychology. Its inheritor, artificial intelligence, would then have every confidence of finally "simulating" all functionally important aspects of mind.

The philosopher John Searle (1990, 1992) has argued, on the other hand, that all cognitive processes that can be considered intentional (that is, psychological rather than purely physiochemical) must in principle be capable of consciousness. In this view, only the physiochemical properties of neuronal nets themselves are intrinsically and truly unconscious. Strictly applied, this suggests a litmus test for the line between phenomenology and neuron: what cannot be reflected in awareness in some fashion or other can accordingly be regarded as nonpsychological. From this perspective, any unconscious that is genuinely cognitive must be understood not as some sort of separate realm or system but as processes that are on their way *toward* consciousness and, under certain conditions, capable of some form of reflection within ongoing awareness. Cognitive processes that are unconscious, so similar in conception to Freud's preconscious system, are best regarded as part of an inherent tendency toward "becoming conscious." They would be aspects of a proto-consciousness unfolding into explicit awareness. We will see how some of the most striking experimental evidence for a cognitive unconscious is actually most consistent with a primacy of consciousness as the organizing principle of mind. "The unconscious" then becomes a consequence, one of immense functional importance, of the automatization of processes that were originally reflected in awareness.

Consider the sort of research so carefully reviewed by Norman F. Dixon (1981), on so-called subliminal or implicit perception. Marcel (1983b) exposed words tachistoscopically and immediately masked them with a following competing stimulus to prevent any conscious recognition. He found that the cognitive processes underlying semantic recognition that were stopped short of focal consciousness seemed to be differently organized than if a completed awareness had been allowed. Ordinarily, if a word like *tree* is flashed to subjects at above-threshold levels and is followed by the polysemous word *palm,* then, owing to the semantic set thereby created, recognition of a word like *wrist* presented shortly afterward will be slower than normal. Whereas *wrist* will be facilitated if the first word is *hand* rather than *tree.* However, when Marcel masked *palm* in the earlier sequence, so that it was left well below the threshold of recognition, the recognition of *wrist* was equally facilitated regardless of whether *hand* or *tree* came first. In other words, unconsciously processed semantic associations fan out into all related categories simultaneously, whereas focal awareness is sequentially controlled by set and context. In what may be a physiological reflection of this widely diffused semantic activation, subthreshold words of high emotional content, as opposed to nonemotional ones, show a marked electrodermal response that is absent if the emotional words are exposed long enough for focal awareness (Masling et al., 1991).

Dixon interprets such research neurophysiologically in terms of two cortical projection systems — an ultrarapid one based on afferent pathways direct to the cortex, reflected in the normally unconscious, first 100 millisecond phase of the cortical evoked response, and a slower reticular-thalamic projection system. The latter is associated with the second 200 millisecond wave of the CER, which in turn is the phase of the CER that disappears during the state of unconsciousness induced by anesthesia. These phases, however, seem to be inextricably linked as stages of a single dimension of "becoming conscious." Haber and Hershenson (1965) found that tachistoscopic repetitions of words and letters, each well short of the threshold of awareness and even with considerable time delays, eventually produced a complete and clear awareness of the stimulus. The simple repetition of unconscious processing finally appears as focal awareness. Indeed, the broad synthesis and semantic activation of subliminal symbolic recognition, as located by Marcel and Masling, implies that the cognitive unconscious is characterized by exactly the same synthesis and "systemwide broadcasting" attributed by Baars to consciousness. The two then differ only in the relative breadth of the material synthesized. A "cognitive unconscious" seems unintelligible other than as a system that inherently moves toward becoming conscious unless it is directly impeded. Rather than assuming that a cognitive unconscious is inherently polysemic, in contrast to the selective serial order of a conscious awareness system, we should remind ourselves that poetry, for instance, is based on the same cross-category resonance studied by Marcel at subthreshold levels. In poetry, however, polysemy appears as something to be directly sensed and aesthetically appreciated as a form of consciousness.

A similar conclusion emerges from experimental and anecdotal research on implicit awareness during surgical anesthesia. Several experimental studies have demonstrated some postoperative recognition for words read to the patient during anesthesia (as compared to control lists), as well as higher test scores for obscure facts presented to the unconscious patient, greater postoperative free-association responses for primed words, postoperative performance of suggestions for unusual hand movements, and significantly quicker recovery for those given positive suggestions during the operation (Kihlstrom and Schacter, 1990; Kihlstrom et al., 1990). Such demonstrations of "implicit" perception during surgery probably belong together with the occasional appearance of spontaneous self-referential awareness under anesthesia, usually without any outward behavioral manifestations. Sometimes this can take the form of dreamlike, delirious imagery and unbearable pain; sometimes it includes awareness of upsetting remarks made by the surgeons (Utting, 1990). Retrospective recall of states of consciousness during anesthetic coma is correlated with greater anxiety and nightmares during recovery (Bonke, 1990). Factors leading to these states include lighter levels of anesthesia (36 percent of cases in a study by Coglio et al., 1990), higher levels of preoperative anxiety (44 percent), and, perhaps, special training in self-observation — as reflected in the fascinating case of Edmund Jacobson (1911), a major introspectionist colleague of Titchener. Jacobson, in the midst of a dawning subjective awareness of his surgical situation and the pain involved, had a sudden insight and said, as later confirmed by the doctors, "I've made a discovery. The secondary consciousness . . . ," which was finished in his thoughts as, "is the primary consciousness." By this he meant that consciousness actually continues during the periods for which we are later amnesic and is not split off as a secondary realm or system.

The implication seems to be that ostensible physical unconsciousness, without any behavioral reactivity, can at times be accompanied by both implicit and explicit awareness — consistent with the idea of a single continuum of becoming conscious. Given the accounts of Jacobson and many others, it seems most likely that the phenomenon is mediated by the self-awareness capacity of the right parietal zones of convergence of Geschwind (1982) and Schacter (1989). It may be impossible to distinguish in any fixed or absolute way between implicit or unconscious perception and a more or less continuous "stream" of background proto-consciousness. The latter would perhaps be akin to delirium syndromes with retroactive amnesia, but also capable of achieving a more complete self-referential form. This fits well with the assertions of some subjects in "subliminal" tachistoscopic research that they were immediately aware of a specific content flashed on the screen which was as quickly forgotten, leaving at best the beginnings of a felt meaning that resists any further specification — somewhat like knowing that one has dreamt but having no idea of what.

The final demonstration of an inseparability between unconscious cognitive activity and a process of becoming conscious comes from a reinterpretation of Benjamin Libet's (1985) widely cited claims concerning the unconscious bases of volitional behavior. Libet had located a "readiness potential" in the EEG that preceded voluntary finger movements by about 550 milliseconds. However, when subjects were asked to indicate the subjective timing of their decision to deliberately crook their finger, by marking a revolving line on a clock face, they located their conscious decisions to move only 200 milliseconds before the actual movement. This suggested to Libet that an unconscious process preceded volitional behavior by up to 400 milliseconds! The function of focal consciousness, on Libet's model, would be confined only to a final veto power exercised over the last milliseconds of a decision process whose volitional initiation would be unconscious. An even more striking illustration of this same phenomenon comes from an earlier study by the neurologist Grey Walter (see Dennett, 1991) in which subjects were instructed to advance a slide projector on their own decision, while the 500 millisecond readiness potential had been directly programmed into the projector and actually caused its advance. Subjects were startled when the projector seemed to anticipate their decisions, moving just before they had consciously chosen to press the advance button.

What Libet overlooked in attempting to make even volition — as utterly impalpable as its awareness may be — into an unconscious process is the similarity of his procedure to the widely researched differences between motor and sensory sets in early studies of response time (Woodworth and Schlosberg, 1954). Setting oneself for the movement one will make allows significantly faster responses than setting oneself for the signal that will trigger that same movement. This results in the common observation, with the "motor set," that the movement itself feels totally automatic and without any awareness of the decision to move. A practical illustration of this principle comes from sprint starts in track, where runners are instructed to forget the gun and instead to try vividly to imagine the movements they are about to make. When successfully achieved, the result can be that the runner suddenly "comes to" with the race under way and with no memory of anything at all at the start. Note, however, and contra Libet, that the initiation of this sequence is quintessentially conscious, in that the runners (and the subjects in Libet's experiments) form an anticipatory conscious image of the movement to be made. Grey Walters's demonstration can be similarly interpreted, with the readiness potential arising out of the movement *image* which precedes the decision itself. Otherwise his subjects could not have been aware of any connection at all between their incipient intentions and the slide advance. They would have been merely annoyed, rather than mystified by an ostensible psychokinesis. Whatever else is involved in the motor set, it rests on imagery and so on consciousness.[3]

Consciousness and the cognitive unconscious appear as the two sides of a common dimension of becoming conscious. They are stages in a process of expression. There may be no unconscious cognitive capacity that is not on its way toward consciousness, and no consciousness that does not emerge out of previous stages that are not *ordinarily* accessible to full self-referential awareness.[4]

The Cognitive Unconscious Experienced: The Microgenesis of Awareness

It would appear that the proper metaphor for becoming conscious is that of growth rather than of opening a door between separate areas — one of which is intrinsically outside awareness. Becoming conscious is a relatively rapid unfolding of successive phases of synthesis and selection. Cognitive processes that are subordinated and held unconscious within one symbolic frame may constitute the actual form of consciousness in other frames, as we shall see. This seems to be the best way to understand classical introspectionism and the microgenesis of experience — as showing how something closely related to an aesthetic attitude allows normally unconscious processes to assume the form of focal awareness.

Contemporary histories of the introspectionist psychology of the early 1900s rightly dismiss Titchener and Wundt's theory that systematic laboratory introspection could reveal the "building blocks" or compositional units of experience. The method of introspection itself, however, is also similarly dismissed. It is seen not as an observational technique in its own right but as an unwitting intellectual exercise in which perception and thought are artificially decomposed into separate sensory-imaginal dimensions (Humphrey, 1951). Such accounts miss the clear evidence from published introspective protocols that what Raymond Cattell (1930) called successful "subjectification" was more like a spontaneous state into which the experimental observer fell by cultivating a passive receptive attitude. Titchener's definition of introspection as "avoiding the stimulus error" turns out, as we will see, to be much like meditation. Traditional histories also ignore the rather different microgenetic model of consciousness, referring to the ultrarapid, moment-by-moment growth of experience posited by the European introspectionists (Krueger, 1928; Sander, 1930; and Heinz Werner, 1961) and their British counterparts (Spearman, 1923; Cattell, 1930).

Felix Krueger was particularly interested in the way that introspective observers, trained to adopt a passive receptive attitude and presented with visual forms that were tachistoscopically truncated to prevent complete recognition, were able to tune into earlier and earlier, normally unconscious stages of experience formation — thereby allowing aspects of its ultrarapid microgenesis to appear directly within awareness. At the most rapid levels of exposure of emotionally significant objects or scenes, observers were able to describe only a diffuse burst of light. With successive exposures this was replaced initially by various geometric patterns, reorganizing from exposure to exposure into different forms, then by isolated parts of the object actually shown, and ending with the fully recognizable stimulus. The latter could still undergo "hallucinatory" transformations, with repeated exposures, until the entire picture was stabilized at around 200 milliseconds. Krueger was struck by the aesthetic qualities of these subjective transformations, while Schilder (1942) called attention to their similarity to the geometric and kinematic imagery of psychedelic drugs and the hypnagogic period of sleep onset. The better introspective observers — and not everyone could be so trained (Titchener, 1912) — could achieve very similar effects without the tachistoscope (see Hunt, 1984, 1985ab, 1986).

Avoiding the "stimulus" or "naming" error in introspection involved adopting a receptive attitude, open to ongoing experience without seeking to control or identify it in any way. This entailed a deliberate suppression of all labeling and semantic recognition. The immediate "is" of experience was to be undergone as a momentary subjective state, in place of the ordinary, pragmatic "is for" of everyday life. Considerable novelty and variety in experimental stimuli were generally needed to help even highly practiced introspectors replace this more natural tendency to name with a more aesthetic, detached attitude. In response to these various stimuli, successful introspectors ended up describing ultrabrief subjective states closely related to derealization, depersonalization, loss of localization in space and time, trancelike absorption, synesthesia, and physiognomic imagery. These are also the effects that are common, in more protracted forms, in altered-state experience. Some evidence that these observers were "exteriorizing" normally subliminal cognitive processes comes from Cattell's (1930) finding of a delayed GSR during these induced subjective transformations. In other words, the holding off of a functional semantic response seemed to offer a brief, almost meditatively detached plateau during which these subjective transformations could unfold.

On the basis of Marcel's more functionalist studies of tachistoscopic word recognition, we could say that avoiding the stimulus error actually allows more time for the broader synthesis typical of subliminal processes to come forward as direct awareness. As with Marcel's finding of the greater exposure times needed to identify the constituent letters of words, compared to their semantic significance, it takes longer to fully experience the more expressive, less functional aspects of awareness. Yet it seems implausible to believe, as Werner and Schilder apparently did, that the subliminal phases of ordinary experience somehow "contain" the full panorama of altered-state phenomena. Surely, our experience would not pass through every form of alteration of consciousness on its way to focal awareness. Rather, processes that are normally nonconscious and in the background are turned into a *form* of consciousness different from our ordinary, language-based awareness — and resulting from an attitude closely akin to both meditative and aesthetic contemplation.

It was William James (1890) who originally put forward the related view that sensation is not a "building block" or "stage" of perception, but that the two are alternative organizations of the same material. Depending on one's attitude, one notices either perception, with all its associations with functional meaning, or "states" full of the sort of portent and expressive physiognomy cultivated by artists. One of James's own accounts shows that this shift to subjectification can also occur spontaneously. We see how closely it is related to the state of experience common to aesthetic perception and altered states:

> Sitting reading late one night, I suddenly heard a most formidable noise proceeding from the upper part of the house which it seemed to fill. It ceased and in a moment renewed itself. I went into the hall to listen, but it came no more. Resuming my seat in the room, however, there it was again, low, mighty, alarming, like a rising flood. . . . It came from all space. Quite startled, I again went into the hall, but it had already ceased once more. On returning a second time to the room, I discovered that it was nothing but the breathing of a little scotch terrier which lay asleep on the floor. The noteworthy thing is that as soon as I recognized what it was, I was compelled to think it a different sound, and could not then *hear* it as I had heard it a moment before. (James, 1890, p. 100)

What is striking here is the way that such awareness is filled with felt meaning and a sense of symbolic significance — not verbal-semantic but expressive, physiognomic, and polysemic. The sound is "mighty," "alarming," "coming from all space." This is right out of the aesthetic sensibility of an H. P. Lovecraft, but here undergone as a spontaneous state. James Gibson (1950, 1966, 1979) later also suggested that "sensation," which for a time he termed the "visual field" in contrast to the "visual world," is the product of a special self-referential attitude closely related to aesthetics and nonverbal metaphor. Painters and poets must be sensitive to just these expressive properties of the immediate array. Rather than reflecting building blocks or microgenetic stages, contemplation of experience for its own sake induces a *transformation* of consciousness, in another sense, its *completion*.

It will be helpful here to introduce a distinction between representational and presentational symbolism, as two fundamental forms of symbolic cognition — a distinction developed by the philosopher Susanne Langer (1942), the psychoanalyst Marshall Edelson (1975), and the cognitive psychologist Robert Haskell (1984). Each mode of symbolism clearly involves a self-referential capacity. Neither can be said to be more primitive or more advanced than the other, yet immediate awareness plays a very different role in each. In representational symbolism, as typified by ordinary language and perhaps most fully developed in mathematics, specific intentional reference is paramount and the medium of expression is a relatively automatized, and so largely unconscious, code. Here, indeed, with Lacan, Saussure, and postmodernism, the relation between signifier and referent *is* arbitrary—one of "difference." Signs are ultimately defined only in relation to other signs. To become totally absorbed in the expressive sound properties of another's words is to lose the referential thread of ordinary discourse. Consciousness enters representational thought primarily as the impalpable felt meanings of the Würzburgers, in order to choose and direct our thought and not as its substance. In the presentational symbolisms, on the other hand, meaning emerges as a result of an experiential immersion in the expressive patterns of the symbolic medium. It appears as spontaneous, preemptory imagery and is fully developed in the expressive media of the arts. Here, felt meaning emerges from the medium in the form of potential semblances that are "sensed," polysemic and open-ended, and so unpredictable and novel. It is the receptive, observing attitude common to aesthetics, meditation, and classical introspection that allows such meaning to emerge.

These forms of symbolism are necessarily intertwined. Referential language use is filled with intonation, gesture, and emphasis as its presentational aspect, while presentational states, although ineffable in ordinary discursive terms, nonetheless have their definite *sense* of intentional meaning in the form of an incipient portent. In effect, each of these symbolic modes has the other as its relatively subordinated "unconscious" or background. I have already discussed Gendlin's felt meaning as the animating source of referential discourse, most clearly manifested in its underlying gesture and tone and all too easy to miss as a necessary component of discursive speech. In the arts, referential intentionality and shared codes in the form of styles are also absolutely central, but meaning emerges more intuitively and spontaneously from an ongoing absorption in the expressive medium itself as the "surface" of conscious awareness.

The delay or inhibition in pragmatic semantic meaning common to meditation, classical introspectionism, and tachistoscopic exposures has more to do with allowing the time needed for the maximum felt synthesis of presentational symbolism than with exposing any supposed "building blocks" or "stages" of ordinary perception. James Gibson (1979) is correct that the tachistoscope, along with a related introspective absorption in the psychological moment, has nothing to do with functional perception or recognition. Instead, these special self-referential techniques delay a normally predominant semantic categorization long enough to allow the emergence into awareness of the expressive perceptual dimensions that are basic to the presentational symbolisms. Since the presentational side of our symbolic capacity conveys more about context or setting than about referential focus, the repetition of successive "mind moments" allows a melding of our experience into the "state" we are "in" — with a resulting self-awareness that is not primarily post hoc but continuous. We all vary in the degree to which we delay "function" in order to bring forward this presentational-state side of our experience. It ranges from ordinary moods, to aesthetics, to the "be-here-now" sense of presence in peak experiences and meditative states.

A related conclusion has been reached within the recent revival of the microgenetic tradition (Froehlich, Smith, Draguns, and Hentschel, 1984; Hentschel, Smith, and Draguns, 1986a; Hanlon, 1991; Smith and Carlsson, 1990; and Brown, 1988, 1991). The consensus now is that the earlier work of Ulf Kragh (1955; Kragh and Smith, 1970) on what he termed percept genesis — the gradual development of "perception" as isolated by tachistoscopic glimpses — can have little to do with functional perception in the sense of either navigation within or recognition of the ordinary environment. Kragh's earlier studies were predominantly focused on different clinical groups. He found that schizophrenic and hysterical patients had more symbolic or fantastic elements in response to the truncated tachistoscopic exposures of various scenes, more different meanings, and higher thresholds for accurate recognition than did depressive or obsessional patients. This work was interpreted in an exclusively diagnostic fashion, missing the possibility that these patient groups actually varied on a more general dimension related to creativity and imaginative absorption.

In my own research (Poirier and Hunt, 1992) some subjects reported elaborate reorganizations of tachistoscopically exposed pictures on repeated flashes that continued well after a first accurate recognition and at clearly post-threshold time intervals — making this entire technique more like a Rorschach task than anything to do with ordinary recognition. The multiplicity of forms that subjects see both before and after accurate recognition would appear to parallel, in a presentational symbolic mode, the breadth of verbal associations with subliminal word exposures found by Marcel (1983b) and others (Dixon, 1981). In point of fact, it has proven very difficult to elicit microgenetically primitive stages from exposures of perceptual forms that do not have emotional significance, such as abstract geometric shapes (Hentschel, Smith, and Draguns, 1986b; Smith, 1991). The connection between creativity and the tendency of certain subjects to elaborate "bizarre" reports with tachistoscopic exposures was advanced by Smith and Carlsson (1990), who found that creative normal subjects and artists generated the most such reorganizations. This would suggest that the similar responses in schizophrenic and hysterical patients were based on their relatively higher capacity for imaginative absorption. Poirier and Hunt (1992) similarly found significant correlations of questionnaire measures of imaginative absorption and prior history of spontaneous mystical experience with reports of more diverse and fantastic patterns in tachistoscopically presented pictures.

We are left with a renewed cognitive science that views consciousness as one of its fundamental principles and a "cognitive unconscious" as its automatized derivation. Consciousness, however, is not one thing — nor is its subordinated unconscious. Representational symbolism rests on highly automatized communicative codes, whose sequential selection and direction forces awareness of its expressive medium into a subordinate role. In presentational symbolisms this relation between conscious and unconscious is inverted. The medium becomes focal and its intentionality, here polysemic and layered, must have time to well forth out of its "unconscious." It would appear that one theorist's "system unconscious" is another's "conscious awareness system." This view is already implied by both Freud's (1914) idea that narcissism allows conscious access to what would be dynamically unconscious within a more averagely neurotic orientation and Jung's (1921) generalization of that into the typological reciprocities of "introversion" and "extraversion." More recently, there is the contrast between Geschwind (1982), who, on the basis of his clinical phenomenology of delirium, located immediate self-awareness in the right hemisphere, and Galin (1974), who suggested a similar localization for Freud's "dynamic unconscious."[5]

Certainly, it has been a huge error to assume, on the basis of mainstream cognitive psychology's bias toward the linguistic and the representational, that consciousness is necessarily a transparent medium empty of all content and limited to the functions of selection and choice. Consciousness per se is much more directly manifested in the arts and spontaneous altered states, where it is richly grained, polysemic, and felt as imposed as if from without. Such "presentational states" will provide far more evidence about consciousness as such and about aspects of symbolic cognition that are normally subordinated to language than will the impalpable awarenesses of a more propositional and representational thought.

"Absorption" in Immediate State as a Dimension of Individual Difference

The suggestion that there are two forms of self-referential awareness, one subordinated to instrumental "set" and the other manifested in spontaneous presentational states, does also imply that the predominant form of consciousness will vary along a dimension of individual difference. Certainly, some people are much more responsive to the various consciousness-altering techniques than others (Zubek, 1969; Hilgard, 1968; Bowers, 1976, Fischer, 1975). Several general questionnaires have been developed to assess individual differences in proclivity to spontaneous transformations of consciousness and their relation to what can be termed a more experiential attitude. The tendency to notice the medium of consciousness and its transformations has been variously termed imaginative involvement (Hilgard, 1974), absorption (Tellegen and Atkinson, 1974), and openness to experience (McCrae and Costa, 1983). Questionnaire and rating-scale measurements of these dimensions have been found to correlate in multiple studies with aesthetic and metaphoric sensitivities (McCrae and Costa, 1983; Hunt and Popham, 1987), the occurrence of spontaneous alterations of consciousness in everyday life (Hilgard, 1968; Hunt and Popham, 1987), hypnotizability (Tellegen and Atkinson, 1974), and more developed transformations of consciousness such as lucid dreaming (Spadafora and Hunt, 1990; Gackenbach and Bosveld, 1989), out-of-body experience (Irwin, 1985), and mystical experience (Spanos and Moretti, 1988; Hunt, Gervais, Shearing-Johns, Travis, 1992).

Roche and McConkey (1990) suggest that imaginative absorption is one of the most basic dimensions of individual difference in personality and cognitive style. McCrae and Costa conclude that the closely related openness to experience is one of the fundamental dimensions of individual variability, including extraversion and neuroticism. Gordon Claridge (1972), extending Hans Eysenck's earlier tri-dimensional model of personality, suggested that imaginativeness and aesthetic sensitivity should be considered as the positive, adaptive side of a general dimension whose negative expression is proneness to schizophrenia. A related developmental model of "absorption" has been proposed by Wilson and Barber (1981) and Lynn and Rhue (1988) based on early childhood proclivities to fantasy involvements and spontaneous alterations of consciousness. In children whose familial surroundings are generally benign and supportive this dimension will manifest itself as a positive imaginative and creative sensitivity. Whereas in children exposed to more traumatic or deficient circumstances it will appear as a potential for dissociation, culminating in psychotic, borderline, and multiple-personality syndromes.

Along these lines, Andras Angyal (1965), in his holistic cognitive reformulation of psychoanalysis, posited a "universal ambiguity" in all human capacities and traits. All our experience comes in two forms — an adaptive, integrative aspect in the context of hope and optimism or, with the very same function, a negative, defensive side of despair and dread. Although Angyal did not extend his formulation to the relation of mystical or related integrative states to psychotic or other dissociative states, it seems likely that a capacity as general as imaginative absorption would also show this dual structure. Thus, we note the contrast between presentational states reflecting a maximal experiential synthesis and those reflecting experiential disintegration. There is, in fact, considerable overlap in the specific subjective transformations of attention, perception, feeling, and thinking that occur in the high-stress inductions of psychotic onset and the exaggerated relaxation and detachment of meditation. Yet the overall gestalt of these experiences is unmistakably different in terms of their impact on cognitive organization, sense of self, and relationships with others.

This becomes a good point, then, to consider empirical evidence that would support the idea of transformations of consciousness as a general tendency related to imagination and creativity that could manifest itself in both adaptive and non-adaptive forms. There are, on the one hand, the widely cited studies showing hospitalized schizophrenics scoring unusually high on some measures of imaginative creativity (Dykes and McGhie, 1976) and, on the other, Frank Barron's (1969) repeated demonstrations that highly successful artists and scientists, who are the very opposite of withdrawn or deluded given their cultural contributions, have profiles on the Minnesota Multiphasic Personality Inventory (MMPI) like those of the hospitalized patients. By implication we could say that the patients succumb to sensitivities that the more creative manage to access in an integrative fashion. More recently, Spanos and Moretti (1988) found that subjects who scored high on a questionnaire measure of mystical experience also showed high levels on a scale of imaginative absorption but not on a questionnaire measure of neuroticism, while those who described "demonic" experiences of possession and felt malevolence showed high levels on both absorption *and* neuroticism.

With respect to the cognitive-symbolic and developmental bases of this bivalent dimension, my own research found a relation between high levels of spatial analytic ability and balance and more positive forms of dream state, such as lucid dreaming and archetypal-mythological dreaming, and the opposite relation for high levels of nightmares (Spadafora and Hunt, 1990). In a later study (Hunt et al., 1992) we found that adults who retrospectively recalled high levels of "positive" transpersonal experiences before the age of ten, such as out-of-body imagery and "white light" mystical states, showed superior spatial-symbolic abilities in adulthood (block designs test), while those with high levels of recalled childhood nightmares and night terrors showed comparative decrements. Correspondingly, Swartz and Seginer (1981) found that subjects reporting high levels of spontaneous mystical experience did better on tests of spatial orientation and balance, a finding confirmed by Jayne Gackenbach for lucid dreaming (Gackenbach and Bosveld, 1989).

Meanwhile, on the negative side, there has long been a small literature showing spatial and vestibular decrement in catatonic schizophrenia (Angyal and Blackman, 1940) and childhood autism (Ornitz and Ritvo, 1968). This would make sense if presentational states, as expressions of nonverbal symbolism, reused basic spatial and perceptual structures that could be disrupted by serious psychological trauma early in childhood. High levels of spatial ability might also operate as a sort of inoculation against disintegrative subjective states. Either way, spatial abilities would be the framework needed for the full development of presentational states that are based on their reuse and rearrangement (Hunt, 1989a).

It is interesting to note that essentially all of the hunter-gatherer groups studied by cultural anthropologists have sanctioned methods for inducing transformations of consciousness, which they regard as psychosomatically healing and socially integrative. These methods range from meditation, ritual dance, incubation for "sacred" dreams, fasting, and isolation to the use of psychedelic substances (Bourguignon, 1973). These same "dream-centered" societies also recognize negative or malevolent forms of consciousness transformation, often in terms of a "soul loss" corresponding to schizoid withdrawal or more agitated possession experiences reminiscent of acute paranoid states. The shaman, as the expert in the induction of positive transformations of consciousness, is also the agent of cure for these negative forms — strongly implying that these peoples, too, distinguish positive and negative expressions of a more basic human capacity.

Spontaneous transformations of consciousness and closely related aesthetic sensibilities are founded on the symbolic rearrangement of nonverbal perceptual structures and are the maximum *experiential* expressions of a conscious awareness system. In its more adaptive, positive manifestations this dimension shows the potential synthesizing function of consciousness at its furthest development. Its disintegrative, psychotic counterpart illustrates the failure or disorder of that same capacity.

Finally, it is worth reemphasizing that the cognitivists seeking the reintroduction of a consciousness awareness system, the transpersonal psychologists interested in the phenomenology and cognitive bases of meditation and related states, and the personality researchers centered on imaginative absorption and its relation to presentational metaphor have shown almost no tendency to refer to each other in their work. Truly, the different traditions within the study of consciousness in contemporary psychology are like the fragments of a dismembered Osiris, spread along the course of the history of psychology in this century and confronted with a dominant Seth-like functionalism as its opposing "mainstream." Any genuine "cognitive science" must reassemble the former in order to balance it against the latter and so locate a consciousness that could do justice to the full range and variability of the human mind.

Part II Consciousness, Brain, and Organism:
How Much Can Neurophysiology Tell Us about Consciousness?

Thinking in terms of physiological processes is extremely dangerous in connection with the clarification of conceptual problems in psychology. . . . [It] deludes us sometimes with false difficulties, sometimes with false solutions. The best prophylactic against this is the thought that I don't know at all whether the humans I am acquainted with actually have a nervous system.
Ludwig Wittgenstein, *Remarks on the Philosophy of Psychology*

Perception *and that which depends on it* are inexplicable by mechanical causes. . . . *Supposing that there were a machine so constructed as to think, feel, and have perception, we could conceive of it as enlarged and yet preserving the same portions, so that we might enter it as into a mill. And this granted, we should only find on visiting it, pieces which push one against another, but never anything by which to explain a perception. This must be sought for, therefore, in the simple substance and not in the composite or in the machine.*
G. W. Leibnitz, *The Monadology*

A higher animal is nothing more than a colony of protozoans. Every one of the cells composing such an animal, has retained its primitive

properties, giving them a higher degree of perfection by division of labor and by selection. The epithelial cells that secrete the nails and the hair are organisms perfected with reference to the secretion of protective parts. Similarly, the cells of the brain are organisms that have been perfected with reference to psychical attributes.
Alfred Binet, *The Psychic Life of Micro-Organisms*

3 Consciousness as Emergent: The Irrelevance of Specific Neurophysiology

There is a widespread agreement among those psychologists who see consciousness as a causal system in its own right that its qualitative features are somehow "emergent" from underlying neural processes. That said, however, all major questions remain. Is consciousness, in the sense of a primary or immediate sentience, only emergent at a particular level of central nervous system complexity, as most investigators certainly would agree for self-referential symbolic processes? If so, is primary awareness regionally localized? Or, with the artificial-intelligence (AI) community, would any computational system of sufficient "cross-reference" also perform the basic functions attributable to consciousness? On both views, an unconscious, automatized organization of mind would obtain up to some level of complexity, evolutionary or otherwise. At that point, consciousness would be emergent.

A broadly phenomenological tradition would have it, however, that awareness is primary and irreducible, perhaps characteristic of all motile organisms. On this view, it is the unconscious that is the evolutionary emergent, perhaps culminating in the emancipation of an automatized unconscious system as the underlying principle of artificial intelligence. By implication, the psychologist of perception James Gibson (1979) exemplifies such a primacy of awareness with his approach to a "direct perception" as intrinsic to motile organisms that must be able to resonate sensitively to their shifting surroundings. The properties of neural systems would then not explain the basis of such sensitive attunements but rather serve to focus and specify them on more and more differentiated levels.

Sperry's Emergent Holism

The neurologist Roger Sperry (1987, 1991) was one of the first[1] to formalize the idea that the qualia of consciousness are emergent from "higher-order organizational processes" of the brain, in much the same way that molecules, with their own chemical laws, are emergent from, but not directly reducible to, subatomic reality. Consciousness has its own holistic properties and functions which not only are not reducible to any specific neural substructure but indeed causally control their own lower-order neural constituents. This downward control is characteristic of all emergent levels in nature, as when the macrodynamics of liquid flow determine the movement of a particular molecule of water in a stream and not its own specific chemistry. Sperry is not positing some sort of dualist interaction of separate "substances." Consciousness is nothing other than a dynamic property of certain higher-order patterns of neural organization. These properties just *are* consciousness and in turn exert the same kind of influence on more specific neural function, as does a wave on its molecules.

Although there is nothing magical or mysterious in this widely shared model of emergence, there is, in addition to the obvious questions of just how these higher-level properties are conscious and how far "down" they go in terms of evolutionary simplicity, the related issue of just what *sort* of emergence might be involved. For Sperry, the emergence of consciousness out of neural processes is something that crosses categorical levels, as from quantum fields to molecules. It could also be, however, that the emergence of consciousness occurs entirely within a single level, already characterized by a preliminary capacity for sentience as something that is always present in motile organisms and cannot be reduced to anything nonconscious. This alternative conception can be illustrated in the relation of large social institutions, like the Pentagon, to small groups. Large social organizations have holistic properties that can be said to be emergent from a small group level (originally the hunter-gatherer band). The latter is in turn subordinated to the new whole as downwardly controlled, lower-order departments. There is genuine emergence here, but it takes place entirely within the category of social group.

Complex forms of consciousness may only emerge out of neural networks because a simpler form of sentience is already present as the subjective side of all organismic locomotion. Does such sentience already exist in single-cell organisms, without any neurons at all? If that should turn out to be the most parsimonious view, many cognitive psychologists have been looking for emergence in the wrong place and in the wrong way. Theories of consciousness as based on higher-order properties of neural organization can easily be recast along these lines — in terms of neural nets gathering, focusing, and organizing sentience but not creating it. The models of emergence put forward within artificial intelligence, however, would be in for more difficulty. If the first level of analysis is not already sentient, then it may be that no account of further complexity and recursive feedback will be able to "bootstrap" into the actual functions of consciousness.

Here, I will outline those perspectives that refuse to localize consciousness in specific brain areas and neural properties but picture it instead as something more general and fundamental.

Doctrines of Synthesis and Self-Organization as Emergent Neural Properties

Holonomy (The Law of the Whole)

The hologram, with its laser technology, has been adopted by Karl Pribram (1985, 1991), in particular, as a model for how neural networks could integrate simultaneous, widely diffused neural regions into an experiential whole. In the optical hologram a laser is passed through a half-silvered mirror, so that part of its light goes directly onto a photographic plate while the rest is reflected from a complex object and then onto the same plate. This superimposition creates interference patterns, much like ripples from several stones thrown simultaneously into water spreading across its surface and intersecting. The subsequent exposure of any part of the plate allows the reconstruction of the entire original pattern as a virtual object that appears as if photographed from multiple angles simultaneously. The physicist David Bohm (1983) generalized this phenomenon into an inclusive model of both physical reality and the central nervous system. In both, particular events are simultaneously "enfolded" within a total "implicate order," any part of which can be "unfolded" in terms of the organizing principles of the whole.

Pribram (1985) used such holonomic principles to show how neural networks might enfold multiple forms of information that are superimposed simultaneously in various cortical regions and in turn can be unfolded as consciousness. He suggests that the translation of sensory signals into two-dimensional component sine waves (spatial frequency) is accomplished by Fourier transformation. This enfolding process will radiate across the cortex, just like the wave fronts from stones tossed into water, producing multiple and widely spread nodes of reinforcement and interference. Inverse transformation unfolds these patterns from any portion of the cortex — making neural networks something like the harmonic resonators of musical instruments. Pribram sees support for such a holonomic organization in the way that long-term memory loss appears to be a function of the overall amount of cortical damage rather than of injury to specific areas. Bohm (1983) stressed the way that each moment of awareness fuses into an experienced whole, within which it is impossible to separate the various modules of perceptual modality, feeling, and thought. Gordon Globus (1992a) has extended this approach to the structure of perception itself, suggesting that for each species all possibilities of perceptual configuration in their environment are latent in their nervous systems—and, we might add, equally latent within the structure of each situation they encounter. Holonomics fits well with Gendlin's account of "felt meaning," where a given "sense" of understanding has no discernible parts or components and yet can be specifically unfolded or articulated in very different ways.

Evidence that the central nervous system actually operates in a holonomic manner was initially confined to the way that columns of neurons in the visual cortex operate together as "feature detectors" (Pribram, 1985). Recent research by Gray, Konig, Engel, and Singer (1989), however, reports synchronous electrocortical frequencies lasting a few hundred milliseconds from widely separate neural columns, leading Pribram (1991) and others (Barinaga, 1990) to speculate that these are the unifying waves of immediate awareness or focal attention. If similarly synchronous frequencies were found across the different association areas involved in perception, we might have a neural reflection of the redundancy of sight, sound, touch, and smell that Gibson (1966) made central to the perception of concrete reality. Such evidence, or indications of similar synchronies on the higher cortical levels involved in the cross-modality translations that Geschwind (1965) makes central to symbolic cognition, would illustrate the synthesizing activity of holonomic systems.

Although holonomy may well show an interesting congruence between a physical system (the brain) and the capacity for widespread synthesis in moment-by-moment consciousness, note also the existence of a major problem—one that will also hold for the connectionist models to be considered below. It is still not at all clear how such a physical process would generate the qualitative nature of immediate perceptual awareness in the first place, unless, as seems most likely, its existence has already been smuggled in surreptitiously from the start. Once again, we find ourselves with a causal "process" that gathers, organizes, and reorganizes a "something" that still remains outside any quantitative conceptual net. Of course, any demonstration of isomorphism of brain, world, and consciousness is tremendously important in helping us past the various subject-object dichotomies that have so misled us, but they do not thereby "explain" what experience is. For help there, we will need to look, with Gibson, much more closely at perception and what it does.

Connectionism

The depictions of the nonspecific organizational and synthesizing properties of neural networks that seem to offer the closest reflection of the functions of a conscious awareness system have been variously termed connectionism (Smolensky, 1988), parallel distributed processing (Rumelhart, Smolensky, McClelland and Hinton, 1986), and self-organizing (autopoietic) systems (Maturana and Varela, 1987; Varela, Thompson, and Rosch, 1991). The massive anatomical connectivity of the human cerebral cortex links fifty-five billion neurons, each with tens of thousands of dendritic connections to other neurons, and each neuron firing an average of forty times a second (Baars, 1988). This, taken with the simultaneous activation of widely separate areas of the cortex and subcortex, had already lead Donald Hebb (1949) to his "cell assembly" model of diffuse parallel processing and continuously reorganizing neural connections in perception and learning. What has been added by connectionism is the mathematics to represent this interconnectivity, based on the probabilistic calculus needed to represent the fluidic processes of thermodynamics in terms of multiple attractors, repellors, limits, and saddle points (Abraham and Shaw, 1985).

In contrast to the serial computations of traditional artificial intelligence (see below), computations in parallel systems are based on waves of excitation and inhibition moving across neuronlike units that compete and cooperate, enhancing and suppressing particular patterns of connectivity (Globus, 1992b). Such a network, based on the statistical properties of fluid dynamics, will "settle" into momentary states of maximum "harmony" in terms of the tasks "constraining" or directing it. Following Globus, these networks are n-dimensional, their possible "states" consisting in the total patterns of interconnection that they could "self-organize." Different states, however, come to have very different probabilities as a function of the loadings, or "weights," at key nodes of interconnection, which "tune" and constrain the system, as reflected in psychological terms by motivating drives and previous learning. Each node is in potential competition with all other nodes. Network states with high computational energy push the surrounding system into unstable peaks, whereas states with low or equalized energy constitute basins that function as attractors. Discrete input into such a system creates "perturbations" that "settle out" into the most harmonious organization available — this settling out corresponding to the various psychological states of perception, memory, and feeling. Apart from continually shifting constraints, such a system is spontaneously self-organizing rather than rule-following. The serially structured rules and executive routines so central to mainstream cognitivist and AI accounts emerge as special cases of regularity in a system that always operates as a unified whole. Its successive syntheses radiate across the entire network, which is always available in its entirety in every situation.

The connectionist paradigm has sparked considerable analysis and criticism within contemporary cognition. Both proponents (Smolensky, 1988) and critics (Fodor and Pylyshyn, 1988) point out that as conceptual and empirical units, "harmonies," "peaks," and "basins" lie somewhere between neurophysiology and functional cognition, with linkages in both directions open to question. These concepts are postneurological yet "sub-symbolic" (Smolensky, 1988). Gordon Globus (1992b) offers a solution to this debate over whether connectionism is closer to neurology or to cognition by suggesting instead that its fields of connectivity may be most congruent with the emergent properties of consciousness itself. "Harmonies" seem to fit especially well with gestalt principles of form perception such as simplicity, balance, and *Pragnanz.* Also, "settling" between "peaks" and "basins" is strikingly reminiscent of William James's use of the metaphors of streaming and waves for the basic form of consciousness. Indeed, there is a distinctive aesthetic quality in all this talk of harmonies, waves of excitation, and perturbations.

Gardner (1985) suggested that the parallel networks of connectionism could be considered as the core of a cognitive unconscious, with consciousness as its selective, serial expression. We have already seen, however, that immediate consciousness — especially in its presentational symbolic aspect — is itself a simultaneous synthesis and that the relation between conscious and unconscious organizations is entirely relative to symbolic frame. It would be ironic, indeed, if this most rigorous of cognitivist paradigms, which has proven so hard to link to either neurology or cognitive function, were actually best suited to reflect a conscious awareness system that has proven similarly difficult to place within contemporary cognitive theory.

Globus (1989, 1990) develops this insight by showing how various features of dreaming, as also for John Antrobus (1991), can be understood in terms of connectionist networks under minimal constraint. The tendency toward condensation and superimposition of imagery in dreams would reflect unsettled states of high computational energy during REM sleep, while Freud's other major process of dream formation, displacement, would reflect a sudden shift from higher- to lower-energy computational networks. Meditation would be based on the gradual suspension of the constraints of linguistic internal dialogue, allowing the maximum expression of spontaneous self-organization. This is exemplified, for Globus, in the common occurrence of abstract geometric or *mandala* designs in such states, which would provide a self-reflective picture of the structural tendencies within the neural network at that particular moment.

Certainly, the diversity of substances eliciting psychedelic and/or delirious transformations of consciousness have close chemical similarities to various endogenous neurotransmitters and modulators that excite or inhibit connections across the synapses, in particular serotonin, norepinephrine, dopamine, and acetylcholine (Dowling, 1992; Kolb, 1990). Accordingly, it makes sense that all consciousness transformations, however ostensibly caused, could be mediated at some point by shifts in these endogenous substances. These shifts do seem to operate on the overall connectivity of neural networks and to bring about both lower constraints and a maximized, spontaneous self-organization.

Setting to one side for now the issue of whether neural networks "cause" or "gather" consciousness, it does seem to be the case that Globus's exposition of connectionism is deeply resonant with phenomenologies of consciousness and its transformations. Contrary to the way it has been interpreted by its major cognitivist exponents, connectionism offers an interesting reflection of the capacities for immediate synthesis and integration basic to recent cognitive psychologies of consciousness. This, in turn, might help to explain the problems encountered in establishing linkages between connectionist principles and more specific cognitive and neural functions. For Globus, connectionism brings us closer to those higher organizational principles of neural networks, from which, on Sperry's account, consciousness would be emergent.

Nonlinear Dynamics and Chaos Theory

Globus (1992b) and Walter Freeman (1991; Skarda and Freeman, 1987) have pursued a potential link between the continuous reorganization of perceptual and symbolic awareness and connectionist principles, by interpreting the latter in terms of nonlinear dynamics — the so-called chaos models emerging simultaneously from several disciplines. In mathematics (Hofstadter, 1981), the physics of thermodynamics (Abraham and Shaw, 1983) and fluctuating systems like the weather (Gleik, 1987), the biology of embryonic morphogenesis (Thom, 1975), and EEG research (Aihara and Matsumoto, 1986; Skarda and Freeman, 1987), scientists have begun to focus on the way in which certain form constants found on all levels of the natural world, from galaxies to fluid eddies to seashells (Stevens, 1974), self-organize out of ostensibly chaotic or turbulent backgrounds. Traditionally, such turbulence, based on the intersection of multiple-flow dynamics that set up complex interference patterns, was regarded as random — in the traditional or literal sense, "chaotic." Now, however, turbulent systems can be represented mathematically by means of relatively simple equations based on repeated iteration and feedback.

Although capable of settling into the more basic spiral and branching patterns found throughout nature, turbulent systems have their own organization based on ostensibly random but actually deterministic patterns called "strange attractors." Chaos is representable by equations that depict a sensitive dependence on initial conditions, continuous feedback, and relationships of mutual inhibition and constraint. Equations based on sensitivity to initial conditions have been developed for the computer simulation of weather patterns, where small local changes can have impacts on a much larger scale. Equations based on mutual inhibition and constraint have been used to predict regular but sudden oscillations in predator/prey ratios in animal populations.[2] Examples of strange attractors that define turbulent systems include the Lorenz attractor for the solenoid or torus bases of air currents (Gleik, 1987) and Mandelbrot's (1982) fractal patterns, in which two flow patterns streaming against each other produce the repeating scale-invariant geometries characteristic of coastlines, mountain topographies, clouds, frost patterns on windows, and branching patterns in trees and perhaps dendrites (Globus, 1992b). If continuous repetitions of very simple processes can self-organize into such elaborate patterns, which do seem to be found on all levels of physical reality, then nonlinear dynamics has considerable implication for understanding the potential connectivities of neural nets. These are indeed based on the myriad crossings of neuronal fibers and their electrochemical activations. Chaos models may similarly apply to the sudden reorganizations and discontinuities in complex social systems (Gregerson and Sailer, 1993).

Chaos theory also offers the beginning of a science of the isomorphisms in structure across the physical universe, the environments of living organisms, the organization of the brain, and the flows and eddies of consciousness, since all these levels of reality would exemplify the same self-organizing principles (see chapters 6 and 13). For the present, however, there are a number of more specific implications that emerge when we attempt to relate nonlinear dynamics to neural nets, cognition, and consciousness. Strange attractors have already been located in human neocortical EEG rhythms (Friedrich, Fuchs, and Haken, 1991), electrical activity from the olfactory lobes of rabbits (Freeman, 1991), and the spontaneous firing of the squid axon (Aihara and Matsumoto, 1986). The ostensible turbulence of the EEG has its own dynamic pattern, or "phase space," after all. Given their common holonomic organization, it would make much sense if such nonlinear dynamics could be found in the repeating and gradually changing patterns of perceptual flow within a given modality, the redundancy of multiple modalities of perception within a single situation, and the cross-modal resonances that may be basic to symbolic cognition.

Although Globus (1992b) has suggested a nonlinear dynamic basis for connectionist cognitive models, it still is not clear how we go from these "strange" geometries, including representations of the fractal properties in the branching of neuronal dendrites, to the dynamic flow of qualitative awareness. Certainly, if the same iterative organizations emerge on all levels of nature, we do have a complexly mirroring relation or isomorphism across seemingly disparate categories. But it is difficult to see how one of these becomes the privileged level of explanation for the others — even though most cognitivists today would seek to ground consciousness in the brain. Instead, what we have is the descriptive generalization that multiple levels of reality self-organize along broadly similar lines, including perception and consciousness.

It could just as well be the dynamic flow properties of perception itself, based in the movement of creatures within their shifting surroundings, that lead and form the nonlinear organization of neural conductivity. Neural networks would then instantiate and localize properties that are the sentient side of living forms. Do neural nets explain perception, or is it the other way around? The latter view seems less doubtfully "idealist," if we keep in mind that in evolution and ontogenetic development functions do tend to appear before the fixed structures that further specify them and allow their more complex development. If we extrapolate from this principle that in evolution function is present before the structure that localizes it, then it follows that neural networks are involved in the gathering and differentiation of consciousness but not necessarily in its creation. Neurophysiology may not so much explain consciousness, or perception, or thought, as show how they are instantiated and progressively developed. On this view, neuroscience does not explain the capacities that it claims to. Rather, they explain it.

Varela, Thompson, and Rosch (1991) similarly insist that self-organizing connectionist networks must be embodied and enacted through perceptually guided actions that lack "explanation" on a physiological level of analysis. Experience and action would be irreducible categories of motile organisms. After all, streams and weather systems, while strongly inviting anthropomorphism, are not themselves sentient. We may need to know much more about perception on its own terms before we will know what to do with these isomorphisms.

What is leading what when we approach consciousness by means of the nonlinear dynamics of interconnectivity and strange attractors? Has the dynamic, open flow of consciousness been explained in quantitative, physical terms? Or has there perhaps been an intriguing sea-change in much of contemporary science, such that, after several hundred years of specific concentration on the linear and inanimate, we now begin to seek out those physical properties of nature that actually mirror the form of our own existence?

Artificial Intelligence: The Functions of Consciousness as Emergent from Recursive Computation

Mainstream artificial intelligence, based on the digital, serial modeling of cognitive functions, has always been divided in regard to the nature and function of consciousness. For most AI researchers, consciousness is purely epiphenomenal, and certainly irrelevant to the algorithmic computations on which artificial intelligence simulates various "expert systems." For a minority, however, consciousness refers to functions that could be regarded as emergent at sufficiently complex levels of computation — and so need not be considered as specific to neural systems at all. On this view, the executive capacities associated with consciousness are emergent properties of any computational system with sufficient levels of recursive self-modification. A very few (Hofstadter, 1979) do not rule out the possibility that a complex-enough computational system would somehow become qualitatively conscious, or at the least that it would be indeterminant whether it might have done so. The fact that all such self-referential systems have hitherto been based within sentient beings is here regarded as an evolutionary and historical accident. The irony is that the notions of holism and emergence, traditionally associated with vitalist, gestalt, and systems-theory approaches, are utilized within this maverick AI subculture to support a "mechanistic" account of the functions of a qualitative consciousness.

A basic tenet of the AI perspective is the notion that the mind can be compared to a computer software program, instantiated in a hardware that can be either digital or neural — the brain being seen as a kind of digital system based on the on/off structure of neural firings. Philip Johnson-Laird (1983, 1988) pictures the functional capacities of consciousness for direction and self-reference as entailed by any higher-order computational system with an executive processor that has access to models of itself and the ability to embed such models inside each other recursively. Although any model that a system would have of itself must, on logical grounds, remain partial and incomplete, for Johnson-Laird there would be no danger of infinite regress, as in some narcissistic cul-de-sac of mirrors held up to mirrors, since any computational executive function would have a limited processing capacity. This is also a point that struck R. D. Laing (1970) in his elaborately recursive phenomenology of interpersonal awareness.

Most AI approaches couple a strong version of behavioral functionalism with the irrelevance of neurophysiology for a theory of mind and consciousness. The exception, of course, is contemporary connectionism, which attempts to model a system like the brain with respect to its interconnectivity and parallel processing. For the mainstream tradition, however, stemming from Newell and Simon (see Gardner, 1985), the brain is just one of potentially very differently organized systems complex enough to have "minds" from the point of view of functional capacity. This has led to a great deal of rhetorical fascination with the infamous Turing Test (Turing, 1950). If a computer can convince a skeptical observer that it is humanly conscious on the basis of its functional output alone, then, from the perspective of the radical behaviorism implicit in this tradition, it is. For the so-called "strong" AI perspective, so effectively critiqued by Searle (1980) and others that it now has few adherents as such, something like self-referential consciousness would actually emerge with complex-enough recursion. For the "weak" view, in which anything, in principle, can be simulated computationally, that would certainly include consciousness *if* its actual performative functions could be sufficiently specified. The problem, of course, is that much of what consciousness "does" is open-ended, unpredictable, and not rule-specifiable.

Douglas Hofstadter (1979) has attempted the incorporation of just these features of consciousness into his account of computational recursive systems, in terms of their potential for complete reorganization and the sort of novelty traditionally regarded as the province of self-referential symbolic cognition. On his account, complex-enough cycles of feedback would finally become subject to Gödel's theorem, already encountered in more qualitative terms in Mead's "taking the role of the other." In Gödel's theorem, any system that refers to itself will also potentially modify itself to the point of unpredictability with respect to its completion and consistency. This notion of the limitation of self-referring systems has generally been used to refute the idea that self-awareness could ever be given a fixed, formal, computational structure (Lucas, 1961; Kugler, 1987). Hofstadter is logically correct, however, when he states that if, presumably to the fury of those programmers attempting to utilize it, a computational system were to become complex enough to spontaneously "Gödelize," its open-ended self-reorganizations would become functional versions, at least, of our recombinatory awareness. It is important to remind ourselves, however, that the lived source of this phenomenon, and the place from which it was abstracted into Gödel's mathematical computations, is the recursive dialogue of "I" and "me," self and other. We have located the roots of this capacity in the nonverbal, nonsystematic visual-kinesthetic mirrorings of infant and mother. In other words, it is grounded in self-referentially generated patterns of embodied sentience.

Daniel Dennett (1991) would similarly replace what he calls the "Cartesian Theatre" model of consciousness, and its private homuncular observer, with what he terms a multiple-draft version of consciousness. This would allow a moment-by-moment synthesis of awareness but would require no executive internal observer. Again, however, he may miss the possibility that the actual multiplicity of moments of consciousness rests on the lived, embodied shift within self-referential awareness from one role to another. These functions are only open to computational simulation at all because they are already directly lived as sentient.

Hofstadter faces this issue of the origination of consciousness functions more directly than any other expositor of the AI tradition. If mind, on the analogy of software, is independent of the hard wiring of the system from which it is emergent, then it is in his terms "skimmable" — meaning that it might also be instantiated within a nonneural system. For Hofstadter, this would be the case if our self-referential capacity were directly emergent from what he takes to be the binary, on/off structure of neuronal firing. This is a surprisingly hallowed tenet of the AI tradition, descending from McCulloch and Pitts and their conception of a neuronal logical calculus (see Gardner, 1985). Hofstadter concedes that if symbolic cognition actually rests on the hard wiring of sentient perception, rather than neuronal switching, it may not be so readily skimmable. He concedes that his own computer-generated random sentences, while occasionally mimicking the whimsical side of creativity, precisely lacked "imagery." This might suggest a grounding of thought in the qualitative patterns of perception that would prohibit Hofstadter's enterprise. If the "turning around" of symbolic cognition is not "on" neural switching, but instead "on" *perceptual* schemata that are ultimately *sensed,* this implies a qualitative core to all symbolism. Mind could not emerge spontaneously from a nonsentient system — whatever its recursive complexity.

A recent attempt to address this issue of the relation between thought and perception in AI terms comes from Ray Jackendoff (1987). Extrapolating from the Würzburg introspectors on thinking as an impalpable, imageless "knowing that," he suggests that the central computational level at which such processes would emerge must be specifically independent of perceptual modality; otherwise, it would not be experienced as impalpable. Accordingly, in neurophysiological terms, he locates thought at the "tertiary" convergence zones joining the modality-specific association areas. Symbolic cognition will accordingly be "neutral" or "common" in terms of subjective qualities, in contrast to the highly specific perceptual modules for vision, touch-movement, and hearing. Thinking would be potentially computational precisely as it is independent from qualitative perception. Jackendoff's model works only for representational symbolism, however, not for the presentational symbolisms of aesthetics. These require, as we have seen, an experiential immersion in their qualitative media. In addition, Jackendoff misses the possibility, to be pursued throughout much of what follows, that the experiences emergent from the tertiary zones of convergence in the neocortex are not neutral or common, but rather are specifically synesthetic and cross-modal — giving symbolic felt meaning its indisputable and indescribable "feel."

There are a number of difficulties with computational approaches to consciousness as an emergent synthesizing capacity. With Searle (1980, 1992), we might say that computers have rules and syntax but no semantics — the exact opposite of higher apes in sign-language training (see chapter 5). Programs offer rules for manipulating signs, but even when such manipulations pass the Turing Test — that is, trick us — it is only the programmer, and not the program, that can attach any meaning to the signs produced. This point can be made even better by contrasting representational symbolism, as explicitly rule-following and using highly automatized codes, with the qualitatively felt polysemies of presentational symbolism. Artificial-intelligence simulations of syntax and rule-governed cognition work very well, since these utilize highly routinized codes. But when we consider the presentational side of symbolic cognition, we see that an experiential immersion in expressive media hardly lends itself to algorithmic formulation. Those who see artificial intelligence as modeling the emergent properties of consciousness have it exactly wrong. Computer simulations may reflect the further evolution of a fully separated cognitive unconscious rather than have anything to do with the actual functions of consciousness. In other words, the success of artificial intelligence comes with its instantiation of highly automatized, rule-based processes, indeed with their further development to levels of complexity beyond anything that sentient beings could automatize. The key step in this development would be the separation of rule-following systems from the sentient capacities to which they have otherwise been subordinated and out of which they were developed in the context of organismic evolution.

Hubert Dreyfus (1982) calls attention to a related difficulty in the AI project for a complete computational science of mind. With Wittgenstein (1953) and Heidegger (1927), we can understand formal closed systems — capable of algorithmic formulation — as abstractions from ordinary language and our everyday experience of the world. There is then the problem that these latter are not computable or enclosable within a formal system. Dreyfus echoes Wittgenstein on ordinary language,[3] Heidegger on *Dasein,* Baars on the implicative "context" for ongoing awareness, Searle's (1992) related idea of "background," and Schutz (1962) on a necessarily implicit, unquestioned "common sense" that will reorganize itself continuously in terms of the demands of one's current situation. We cannot explicitly formulate such a background, and if we try, we get something like Heidegger's *Dasein* — whose "rule" is existential openness to the world. A tacit common sense cannot be fully specified, in that the approximation to such a formal computability must immediately create a new tacit background of understanding in a self-referential symbolizing being. It is not at all clear how such continual reorganization could be handled, either, by recent proposals for an interactive, non-representational artificial intelligence (Preston, 1993). As Dreyfus and Searle emphasize, it is hard to picture such a continual reconstitution of context as part of any computational system, without losing thereby the very strength of formal or expert systems in their capacity for astonishingly complex, rule-based algorithms.

Consciousness, as something it is like to "be," is "of" and "in" a "world." Consciousness must be as open as its primary perceptual awareness of that world and, in us, as the dialogic self-reference that reorganizes such immediate sentience. We look the wrong way if, with Lashley (1960), we look for evidence in any phenomenology for the unconscious functions synthesized in moment-by-moment awareness. Rather, perception and the surround it is "of" may offer the best clues to a self-referential consciousness turned around upon and reorganizing that perception.

James Gibson and the Ecological Array: A Primacy of Perception

Gibson's Ambient Optic Array

Traditional psychological and philosophical approaches to cognition posit internal processes or representations that somehow "construct" our consciousness of the world. Information from an external world is understood as deconstructed by binary neural firings and then reassembled within the central nervous system. Our thought about perception seems always drawn toward the view of a solipsistic subject who weaves reality out of a mosaic of quantitative bits of information by subjecting them to the rationalist categories of space, time, and causality.

Accordingly, there has been both excitement and controversy in response to James Gibson's (1966, 1979) account of perception as a noninferred, noncon-structed, direct "readoff" of information from the immediate patterning of an am-bient ecological array. Contrary to our entire epistemological tradition, Gibson was struck by the complexity of the patterning offered directly to the peripheral senses, constituting a dynamic flow of gradients and textures around the organism — most especially when it is in motion. Gibson is critical of traditional "static" approaches to perception as passively imposed on a stationary observer. The artificial removal of locomotion from functional perception leaves laboratory studies of perception with highly simplified appearances "now from here" that require complex and artificial strategies of inference in order for them to give back to us the ambient world with which motion always presents us. Much of the interest of gestalt psy-chology in form perception reflects, for Gibson, just such a simplified analytic or pictorial attitude that is closely related to an aesthetic fascination with "optic struc-ture" as such. This is not the functional perception that allows us actively to navi-gate an environment. For Gibson, nothing needs to be reassembled deep "inside" anything, because there was no disassembling to begin with. Instead, the surround-ing array affords us complexly structured information as soon as the organism is in motion.

Perception is first and foremost a matter of navigation. It is inseparable from the movement of sentient creatures through their ambient or surrounding array. The resulting flow of gradients past the organism allows it to extract "invariants" out of the specific dynamics of shifting surface textures, the looming or diminishing of surfaces, and the continuously shifting occlusion of background by surfaces that delete and add information. Certain patternings persist through these complex flow gradients — some now might prefer to say "self-organize." These invariants can give the organism direct, noninferred information about what the particular array "affords" or allows as possibilities for movement for a creature of that particular size, shape, and speed. Although the specifics of this "envelope of flow" that surrounds every motile creature will vary for each species, its principles are univer-sal, since they are based on the laminations, loomings, and occlusions created by locomotion.

For Gibson, all perception of an ambient array is simultaneously and intrin-sically a proprioception or self-perception of the specific position of the organism in that array. In other words, a particular flow of lamination, looming, and occlusion is only possible from an equally specific position and path. The array, in effect, always gives back the unique position and bodily stance from which just that flow could be experienced. Accordingly, Gibson's ambient ecological array undercuts any subject-object dichotomy. He insists that there is no information about a "there" that does not simultaneously give its specific "here," as two phases of a unique coalition. Perception, action, and proprioception are not different functions or alternatives:

> The optical information to specify the self, including the head, body, arms, and hands, *accompanies* the optical information to specify the environment. The two sources of information coexist. The one could not exist without the other. . . . The dualism of observer and environment is unnecessary. The information for the perception of "here" is of the same kind as the information for the perception of "there," and a continuous layout of surfaces extends from one to the other." (Gibson, 1979, p. 116)

Gibson's refusal to separate subject from object, perception from action, affordance from "effectancy" (Shaw and Turvey, 1981), places his ambient ecological array with Heidegger's similarly conceived being-in-the-world — as irreducibles not subject to analytic decomposition. Organism and environment are a uniquely attuned coalition:

> The mutuality of animal and environment is not implied by physics and the physical sciences. The basic concepts of space, time, matter, and energy do not lead naturally to the organism-environment concept or to the concept of the species and its habitat. Instead they seem to lead to the idea of an animal as an extremely complex object of the physical world. . . . This way of thinking neglects the fact that the animal-object is surrounded in a special way, that an environment is ambient for the living object in a different way from the way that a set of objects is ambient for a physical object. (Gibson, 1979, p. 8)

The similarity to Heidegger's attempt to characterize the "being there" of life forms in-the-world is striking.[4]

More specifically, for Gibson, each position/path of a moving creature creates a specific "visual cone" that wells forth out of the indefinite horizon ahead and becomes uniquely differentiated in texture as it converges on the organism — whose shape becomes the occluding edge of the array (fig. 1). Gibson describes this as a "streaming perspective," "envelope of flow," or "melon-shaped family of curves." It expands in the direction one is going and contracts in the direction from which one has come, showing the organism both where it is and where it is going (fig. 2). This envelope of flow has the shape of a continuously reorganized funnel or vortex open at both ends. Note that both an horizontal openness ahead and an occlusion of flow behind the moving creature must always obtain in principle, even for an animal burrowing under the ground, since the earth just ahead of its digging is similarly

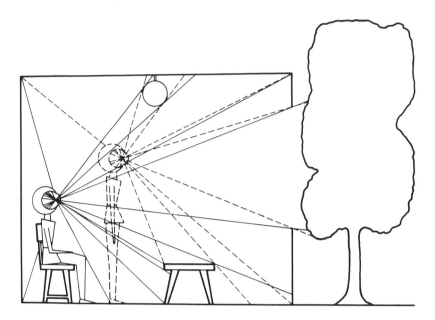

Figure 1. Gibson's visual cone. From The Ecological Approach to Visual Perception ©
1979 by James J. Gibson. Courtesy E. J. Gibson.

indefinite and open to the more immediate specifications that also cease in the area
immediately behind. Gibson is identifying a whence-whither gradient as intrinsic to
the experience of all motile organisms. Each pattern of flow will have its specific
whence-whither structure.

This is very similar to Heidegger's description of our existence as always "ahead
of itself." Where Heidegger, however, made such a "temporality" specific to human *Dasein* and our being toward the more abstract unknown of the future, for
Gibson, a whence-whither gradient, flowing out of horizonal openness, is intrinsic
to the ambient array of all sentient creatures. Temporality is built into any ambient
array: "There are attempts to talk about a 'conscious' present, or a 'specious'
present or a 'span' of present perception, or a span of 'immediate memory,' but they
all founder on the simple fact that there is no dividing line between the present and
the past, between perceiving and remembering. . . . A perception, in fact, does not
have an end. Perceiving goes on" (Gibson, 1979, p. 253). I will explore later the
implications of finding this key aspect of Heidegger's *Dasein* in the ambient array
of all sentient beings (see chapter 11). Certainly, it will have a considerable impact
on where we might best look in evolutionary terms for Sperry's "emergence."

Gibson's ambient ecological array, with its inseparability of "there" and "here,"
also provides the original perceptual template for that self-reference that is often

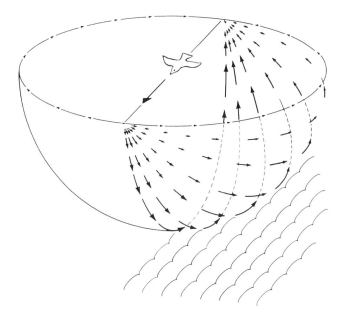

Figure 2. The envelope of flow in Gibson's optic array. From The Ecological Approach to Visual Perception © *1979 by James J. Gibson. Courtesy E. J. Gibson.*

regarded as specific to human symbolic cognition and consciousness. If the experience of one's immediate physical position and the streaming of the array are necessarily co-given and co-determined, then, to modify Mead's terminology slightly, all motile perceiving organisms "take the position mirrored back by the environing other." The mirroring games of mother and infant, in which we located the first manifestation of Mead's "taking the role of the other," also exemplify Gibson's exclusively perceptual coalition of "here" and "there," since it is its own face that the infant locates in the reflecting face of the mother. We can certainly say that symbolic cognition reuses and rearranges the structures of perception, but the template for its self-referential organization seems to be located within Gibson's array.

We even seem to find in Gibson's array and its horizonal openness the template for Mead's unknowable "I," Jung's "circumambulation of the self," and Lacan's "deletion of the subject" — all rightly understood on the human level as necessary consequences of symbolic self-reference. Yet, to the extent that a sentient motile creature is always oriented, among other things, toward a horizonal openness as the source for the gradient of flow and the potential origin for any looming forth of the unexpected, its "stance" must on some level also mirror that very openness. There must be a perceptual readiness in any creature for the sudden reorganizations of the world that are always pending. Just as the more detailed textures and surfaces of the array "give" the organism its specific location in terms of that specific envelope of flow, the horizonal openness ahead, in all its indefiniteness, gives back a corresponding openness and readiness. This readiness in the face of the indefinite horizon is at the least analogous to Heidegger's notion of a specifically human "care" called forth by the openness of time ahead. Again, horizonal openness must be the originating template whose reuse on the level of symbolic cognition creates our orientation toward a more abstract unknown. All sentient beings are oriented toward the unexpected, ready for the next, and that seems to be afforded by the horizon always opening ahead.

Two Systems of Perception: Gibson's "Direct Perception" and "Recognition"

Much controversy has come from Gibson's insistence that perception is always "direct," immediately given by the array, and so without any preliminary microgenetic phases of organization or separate subprocesses devoted to dimensions like size, shape, and motion (Ullman, 1980). The idea of perception as having components that undergo a definite process of construction has been central to traditional doctrines of perception. It does seem, however, that by *perception* Gibson often means something quite different than do the gestalt tradition, Irwin Rock's (1983) "unconscious inference" model, microgenetic theories, and most neural network approaches. Ulric Neisser (1989, 1991) and others (Leibowitz and Post, 1982) have helped clarify this issue by suggesting that we distinguish between two systems within perception: Gibson's "direct perception" that specifies "where" we are in relation to the navigational affordances of the array, and a "recognition" capacity for identifying the various "what"s of potential significance within that array. Lesion studies in monkeys (Mishkin, Ungerleider, and Macko, 1983) suggest that each system may use different cortical pathways—the thalamic projection system for recognition, the superior colliculus for direct perception.

Direct perception operates by means of asymmetry, in that for navigation to continue and collisions to be avoided, symmetrically looming surfaces have to be transformed back into asymmetrical flow. Recognition, on the other hand—at least that aspect requiring basic capacities for memory and anticipation that are common to minimally complex organisms—requires the "static" and symmetrical. It is based on the abstraction of fixed "releasor" patterns out of a flowing array, such as the two-dimensional hawk shape responded to so strongly by rabbits and chickens. As Neisser (1989) states, to identify something, we have to hold it still. Recognition is stymied by rotation, as when gradual adaption to distorting prisms allows subjects to drive cars (direct perception) but not to read license plates. Approach behaviors elicited by need-based recognition lead to the symmetrical magnification of such abstracted forms, while avoidance requires an equally symmetrical minification if final escape is to be effected.

Finally, and consistent with Gibson's rejection of the tachistoscope as a device for the study of direct perception, the recognition system must be able to orient itself to information presented in brief flashes — as in ultrabrief views of distant objects when we are moving through a thick forest. Under those circumstances the tachistoscope could hardly be alien to the way in which recognition operates in the natural world, in contrast to its irrelevance to navigational flow. It seems impossible to see one of these systems as evolutionarily primary and the other as its derivative. It is as difficult to imagine a creature oriented in an array in which it does not "recognize" selected patterns as especially relevant as it is to imagine a recognitive creature moving in a surround to which it was otherwise insentient. Motile creatures must both navigate and identify patterns of significance.

It does appear that much of what is considered as "form perception" by Rock (1983) should be included within Neisser's "recognition" and not confused with the core of direct perception, which would remain, as Gibson suggested, as the navigation of one's surroundings. Most of what Gibson discusses as direct perception goes on in the periphery of vision (Marr, 1982), in what the gestaltists had termed "ground." It is direct perception that allows us to navigate through a cluttered living room while reading a book (Leibowitz and Post, 1982). The phenomena that Rock examines as evidence for cognitive inference in perception, such as reversible and ambiguous figures, illusory contours, and the gestalt principles of form perception, all involve what Gibson terms a "pictorial" attitude to the abstracted properties of an optical structure, which Gibson carefully separates from the navigational requirements of direct perception.

Rock's model of the intelligencelike operations embedded in form completions, apparent motion, and size constancy judgments, along with his concession that "noncognitive" processes might be more involved in the perception of simpler organisms, misses the more plausible evolutionary view that it is intelligence that emerges from the reuse and rearrangement of the processes involved in both direct perception and recognition, rather than the other way around. As we have seen (chapter 2), the separate manifestation of processes related to size (expanding and contracting motions), shape (geometricizations), and motion (expressive dynamics) in both tachistoscopic phenomena (Schilder, 1942) and psychedelic drugs (Klüver, 1966) suggests that these effects have more to do with the perceptual rearrangements entailed in symbolic cognition than with either system of primary perception.

Consciousness and World in Gibson, Heidegger, and Leibnitz

Gibson's concept of direct perception as a sensitive and proprio-locating resonance to the flow of the array seems unintelligible without the immediate, nonreflexive consciousness that Natsoulas (1983) terms primary awareness — with its own inseparability of intentionality and "is like." Such a primary awareness will come in two forms: a more selective and serial recognitive awareness and a more peripheral "streaming," whose relation to a background consciousness becomes immediately clear when we try to navigate unfamiliar surroundings with our eyes closed. We do not need to add sentience or primary awareness to Gibson, because it is already intrinsic and presupposed.[5]

Since the read-off of information from the array during functional navigation is "direct," perception is primary and irreducible. It cannot be explained by the computations of neural nets, since any creature that moves within an ambient surround will be sentient to that array and will illustrate Gibson's basic principles, whether or not it has a neural net (see chapter 5 on protozoan behavior). Certainly, the evolutionary differentiation and organization of neural networks would allow the organism to become progressively more *attuned* to more complex and distant gradients of flow, surface, and texture. It would also allow a progressive differentiation between the dimensions of the multiple perceptual modalities. Karl Pribram (1991) is perhaps the only major neurophysiologist to take up Gibson's challenge here. He shows how holonomic neural networks might be understood as transducing Gibson's flow gradients into distributed Fourier components via a recently discovered dendro-dendritic connectivity that would create receptive neural fields operating independently of specific axonal firing. These repeated transductions and distributions of the flow perspective would allow an instantiation of the resonance process described by Gibson. Correspondingly, a more localized "top-down" extraction of particular object features such as edge, color, and motion properties would be part of a primary recognitive system and its operation in successive, rapid "pulses." Pribram's receptive fields of neuronal networks would not so much explain direct perception as allow for its progressive differentiation, organization, and automatization.

Gibson's ambient array emerges as the potential source for the specifically human structure of Heidegger's being-in-the-world, a conclusion that will require some modification of Heidegger's basic assumptions (see chapter 11). In both thinkers there is the same codetermination of surround and sentient being, the same whence-whither structure welling forth out of horizonal openness, and, by implication, the same "deletion" of the basic stance of the organism in terms of its readiness and openness to the "unconcealed" ahead. If self-reflective symbolic cognition is, as Neisser (1976) and Bartlett (1932) have insisted, based on the reorganization and recombination of perceptual processes, then we might expect Gibson's flow dynamics to reemerge as part of the organizing template for higher mental processes. This perceptual basis for symbolic cognition, would, of course, be best illustrated in presentational states, and we will later locate key aspects of Gibson's array within meditative realizations of the openness of all experience (chapters 10 and 11).

Contrary to traditional assumptions that consciousness is private, it is important to note that Gibson's "streaming" is in principle *shared,* not just across symbolizing persons, but also across species, since the basic characterization of lamination, looming, and occlusion must apply to all motile organisms. Global physical invariants are available to guide the navigation of moving creatures — including, in addition to the horizon, the direction of gravity, the textural gradient of the ground plane, and changing patterns of shadow resulting from the course of the sun (Shaw and McIntyre, 1974). These have been present throughout the course of evolution. Of course, there are profound differences in the resulting envelopes of flow, depending on creature size and maneuverability and whether its primary medium is on the ground, under the ground, in the air, or in the water, not to mention the differently organized need systems that will attune organisms to different aspects of their array. All this, with Nagel (1974), makes it impossible to *know* what it is *like* to be a bat. But the bat's sonar resonates to the same properties of flow, occlusion, and looming that characterize the optic array. Primary awareness is certainly *shared* in terms of its organizing principles as the most basic level of its "is-like." Nonreflexive, perceptual consciousness is a "consciousness with" in a way most western psychology and philosophy has insisted on missing.

The implications of Gibson's analysis of the ambient ecological array go against the Kantian assumptions of most contemporary psychology, in which mind constructs world on the basis of representational categories. Gibson's view is, instead, thoroughly Leibnitzian (see also Weimer, 1982). For Leibnitz, mind and universe were organized in terms of common forces or dynamics that constitute a pre-attuned harmony more medieval than modern. The operative principle with Gibson (Shaw, Turvey, and Mace, 1982) is similarly one of coalitions, in which "here" mirrors "there" and each species-specific array mirrors common principles of a dynamic flow in the physical environment.[6] In this sense, contemporary interest in form constants and nonlinear dynamics as appearing on all levels of physical reality, including perception and neural nets, is deeply congruent with Leibnitz.

Monads, for Leibnitz (1898, 1951) are the fundamental units of reality, in the sense of something not further reducible or fractionable, in contrast to physical atoms. Monads are characterized by "perception" and "appetite" or drive. They are best illustrated by the awareness of animals (Gibson's direct perception), which he terms living mirrors of the universe. The infinitely many universes constituted by the perceptions of each living species exist in a preestablished harmony based on common organizing forms. Human beings are "self-conscious" monads, whereas "bare" monads are sometimes characterized as natural forces that are "analogous" to desire and appetite, and which he illustrates with reference to the dynamics of fire and air currents.[7] It was such physical processes that Leibnitz's "infinitesimal calculus" opened to eventual quantitative representation in thermodynamics and now nonlinear dynamics. From a contemporary point of view, it makes a great deal of sense to make one's fundamental unit of analysis "perception" or "sentient life-world." Making perception both a fundamental epistemological and ontological category highlights the view that all "reality" must first and foremost be known by living creatures — as for Heidegger, who saw *Dasein* as a further development of Monad (Heidegger, 1928). Indeed, if one becomes primarily interested in self-organizing dynamic systems in nature, these may well be best represented by living forms.

Apart from Heidegger's *Dasein* and Gibson's ambient ecological array, Leibnitz's Monads are the other major point in the history of western thought — for Heidegger, since the pre-Socratics — where consciousness is intrinsically attuned to the dynamics that surround it, as well as to all manifestations of itself in multiple species. Subject-object, mind-body, and consciousness-brain dichotomies are purely derivative in this thinking. They are secondary, even perverse, consequences of sociocultural crisis and personal alienation.

4 Consciousness as Localized: Neural Zones of Convergence and Consciousness Awareness System(s)

Localization of Function: Explanation or Instantiation?

Even if we conclude that consciousness is an emergent property of neural connectivity, it soon becomes clear that certain areas of complex nervous systems show especially dense interconnections. These "zones of convergence" become the obvious candidates for any more specific neural localization of consciousness, especially in relation to its capacity for immediate synthesis. Before pursuing the various candidates for such zones, it is important to consider what such attempts can and cannot explain. I have stressed that both in the evolution of the nervous system and in ontogenetic neural development, functions seem to be nascently present before the appearance of the specialized neural and sensory regions that would localize these functions. For instance, although the ear of dolphins is anatomically structured so as to aid in the triangulation of sound sources under water, human divers gradually develop a cruder form of this sensibility without the corresponding anatomy (McNulty, 1976). The location in vertebrate neural systems of specific zones of convergence whose special interconnectivity seems to "embody" the synthesizing functions of consciousness does not lead automatically to the conclusion that sentience is not present in still simpler organisms. The very simplicity of their organization and behavior may not require any such specializations.

Many theorists have attempted to infer an evolutionary emergence of consciousness from the presence of sufficiently complex neural structures. Such purported localizations may, however, reflect more an instantiation of functions already present than the explanation of a capacity as basic as the sensitive navigation of one's array. It could also be, of course, that there is much to learn about the functions thus instantiated from the physiochemical "tracks" left by their progressive differentiation, as localized through more and more complex neural networks. If structure does not always explain function, then it surely reflects it. It is not that the current excitement over genuine breakthroughs in neuroscience is unwarranted, but the question must remain whether these physiological processes explain or are explained by what organisms do in their active attunements to their surrounds. I will address more directly what organismic behaviors may be able to show us about sentience and its multiple levels in the next chapter.

Among those seeking a neural localization, if not necessarily explanation, for consciousness, there has been considerable debate in recent years over whether a neurally instantiated consciousness would be one or many. Of the multiple zones of convergence or even holonomic superimposition that have been put forward as localizations for consciousness, should one be regarded as predominant? Or do they operate together as a single, multiply-distributed synthesizing system? On the one hand, there are those who posit a unitary system of consciousness, with, however, some debate as to the predominating zone of convergence. For instance, Schacter (1989) and Dimond (1976) place such a system in the parietal lobe of the right hemisphere, while Baars (1988) and Penfield (1975) focus on the reticular-thalamic system of the brain stem. Then there are those, such as Kinsbourne (1988), Goldman-Rakic (1988), and Damasio (1989), who, supported by just such disagreements, would see the reticular-thalamic system, the limbic area (with its temporal and frontal connections), the frontal lobes, and the parietal areas of both the left and the right hemispheres as each constituting separate sentience systems. Those would be reciprocally interconnected in a shifting, multiply-determined field of awareness. Damasio suggests that there is no need to pick among these, since they would operate as a single system based on a synchronous electrochemical rhythmicity.

We will consider three zones of convergence in particular, all involving polymodal integration but on very different organizational and potentially evolutionary levels. First, there is the confluence of direct connections from the peripheral senses within the reticular formation of the upper brain stem, common to all vertebrates. This area also includes the orientation response to novelty and more specific thalamic projections to the association areas of the cortex (Moruzzi and Magoun, 1949; Penfield, 1975). Gibson's notion of the "redundancy" of information from different perceptual modalities, probably mediated by the superior colliculus of the midbrain (Stein and Meredith, 1993), is also related to this general system of sensory superimposition. Second, there is the more specifically mammalian hippocampal and amygdala areas of the limbic system involved in the capacity for mnemic imagery and in the coordination of different modalities in association learning under the influence of reinforcement. In humans, at the least, these capacities are organized in terms of an episodic or autobiographical memory that is lost with damage to these forebrain areas (Tulving, 1983). Third, we will consider the "tertiary" neocortical areas, especially in the right hemisphere, that are involved in the cross-integration and reorganization of the perceptual modalities. Geschwind (1965), Luria (1973), and Schacter (1989) make those areas basic to symbolic cognition and self-awareness. In addition we will need to examine the attendant debate with those who would locate the human self-referential capacity exclusively in the left hemisphere and as an aspect of language (Gazzaniga, 1988).

Debates about which of these areas might be predominant in a consciousness awareness system also seem to depend on whether one sees perception, memory and learning, or thought as the more fundamental and inclusive capacity. I have suggested already that perception, in both its direct and recognitive aspects, is the organismic capacity that most clearly requires a primary awareness. Memory involves the abstraction of significant cues and associations from recognitive perception, thence to be progressively extended as the capacity to remember and anticipate. Thought would reflect a more radical reorganization and recombination of perceptual processes. We could say that consciousness is first present in immediate perception, as both a general and modality-specific sensitization to the immediate surround. It becomes considerably extended in its purview by the imagery of anticipation and recall, and is then radically transformed with the appearance of symbolic self-reference and "schematic rearrangement."

That said, it also seems clear that the self-referential, symbolic capacity will also transform memory into something more constructively autobiographical and entail that the novelty response, based in the brain stem, will be increasingly engaged by matters imaginative and linguistic. In other words, although more basic forms of awareness can be traced within higher, more complex forms, these more integrative levels will in turn reorganize and transform lower levels of the same function. It will be difficult, indeed, to separate false projections of the symbolic capacity into our understandings of a more basic memory and perception from the equally misleading reduction of an emergent self-referential consciousness to its simpler roots. We are about to find ample illustrations of these dilemmas.

Penfield and the Reticular-Thalamic System

Wilder Penfield (1975), echoed by Baars (1988), argues that the upper brain stem constitutes the highest level of central nervous system integration, since it has the most inclusive interconnectivity with other neural regions. The lower and upper areas of the reticular projection system send ascending excitatory and inhibitory fibers to all areas of the association cortex and subcortical limbic areas, receive modulating feedback from all these areas in turn, and integrate collateral input directly from the peripheral sensory neurons prior to their connections in the association cortex. In addition, the descending reticular pathways are the final conduit for excitatory and inhibitory motoric activation.

Penfield recast the more traditional view of the reticular activating system as the most primitive level of vertebrate brain organization. Because the reticular system is highly similar in structure and function across all vertebrates, many have found it very tempting to see its level of integration as essentially "reptilian" — as in Paul MacLean's (1973) model of a "triune brain." The limbic lobes, necessary for complex associational learning, are then broadly mammalian, with the tertiary layers of the neocortex reflecting a specifically higher primate and human development. Penfield, however, was struck by the large areas of the cortex that could be damaged without impairing consciousness, while damage to the reticular formation can produce coma. Rather than seeing the reticular formation as a mindless engine for diffuse activation, Penfield concluded that its maximum inclusiveness should locate it as the primary source of a synthesizing consciousness. It would be this consciousness system that plays on the more automatized capacities of the cortex, like a selectively activating spotlight that assimilates their functions into its ongoing awareness. That direct stimulation of the temporal lobes, pioneered by Penfield's research (Penfield and Perot, 1963), sometimes elicits mnemic and dreamlike states can be understood in terms of its elicitation of "orientation" from within the brain stem. Penfield is suggesting that a reticular system that is continuously exposed to feedback from both cortical and limbic areas becomes, in an interesting sense, "sensitized" or "educated" in a specifically human way. *Our* reticular system cannot be regarded as reptilian, but must be seen as the maximally inclusive locus of a thoroughly human awareness.

On the other hand, the occasional reports of a continuing self-awareness with anesthetics that act most directly on the reticular system (Kihlstrom and Schacter, 1990), along with the occurrence of both delirious and stuporous syndromes with right-hemisphere damage (Geschwind, 1982), help to confirm the view that "centers" for awareness are distributed across multiple layers of complex nervous systems. In addition, there have been suggestions (Vanderwolf and Robinson, 1981) that the lower reticular system is more a collection of relatively differentiated subsystems than the single system implied by Penfield's grand synthesis. Sleep and wakefulness subsystems, for instance, should be distinguished from reticular-thalamic projections. These in turn should be divided into two subsystems — one, amine-based and associated with molar movement (the head-turning aspect of the orientation response), and the other, cholinergic-based and involved in the "still-reaction" aspect of orientation and various "consummatory" behaviors. There seems to be an orientation response that is directed more toward navigating the array and an orientation response involving the recognition of organismically significant forms. What one generation of researchers integrates (Moruzzi and Magoun, 1949), the next will differentiate and distribute, and, of course, vice versa.

There is, however, an important relation between the reticular-based orientation response, including its more emergency-centered "tonic-immobility" aspect, and the behavioral side of imaginative absorption, as reflected in both meditative states and catatonia. Tonic immobility is essentially a defensive response, typical in prey but inducible in predators as well under extraordinary circumstances. It is an exaggeration of the "still" component of the orientation response to novelty, but intensified to the point of involuntary paralysis and "waxy flexibility." The latter refers to an involuntary motoric rigidity, such that any imposed position of the limbs will be maintained for up to several minutes. Tonic immobility is an organismic defense, since it can ensure survival in encounters with predators, but it verges on shock, and a certain portion of creatures who go into tonic immobility die. It also involves a general parasympathetic overactivation and intense salivation (Gallup, 1974).

Both waxy flexibility and intense salivation are common not only to the stress-induced state of human catatonia (DeJong, 1945) but also to spontaneous ecstasy in deep meditation (Bernard, 1950). The presence of behavioral aspects of the most intense human absorption states in such a basic, brain stem–based, organismic response might seem to support the view that transformations of consciousness are inherently "regressive" or "primitive." But there also is ample evidence of widespread cortical activation and integration, as well as right parietal predominance, in such states (Alexander et al., 1990; Fischer, 1975). This fits well with Penfield's approach to the orientation response as necessarily inclusive of all levels of neural interconnectivity. I will pursue, in chapter 5, a line of evidence suggesting that human imaginative absorption is based on a symbolically mediated reuse of the still reaction and tonic immobility.

Edelman and Tulving: The "Remembered Present" and Its Limbic Localization

Gerald Edelman (1989, 1992) has developed an approach to what he terms "primary consciousness," which he understands as the capacity for imagery that underlies memory and anticipation. This extension of the perceptual present is the root of consciousness for Edelman. It requires the evolutionary complexity associated with the development of the limbic and hippocampal areas in mammals and perhaps birds. This latest version of the North American tendency to make learning and memory the template for all cognition, and so for consciousness, may unwittingly combine features of a primary perception, in Gibson's sense, with a more symbolic self-reference.

Edelman calls his model of neurological specialization and maturation "neural Darwinism," as an extension of his earlier biological research on the molecular basis of cell specialization in the embryo. In that work, he showed how the release of "cell adhesion molecules" begins to group initially identical cells into regions that gain more specialized features, as in the early formation of neuronal cells. After birth, a related process of "natural selection" determines which neural connections will be strengthened, but now based on repeated association rather than the earlier molecular demarcation process. Edelman suggests that the selective strengthening of neural connections creates different regional "maps," which then interact by means of a parallel and reciprocal "re-entrant signaling." This model of the selective strengthening of neural connections relies on processes also postulated within connectionism. It helps to account for the plasticity of neural functioning in the face of early developmental damage, and posits a greater specification of connections in those regions that are most exercised in repeated tasks.

Edelman extends this model of neural differentiation into a theory of the emergence of consciousness in sufficiently complex neural networks. He focuses, in particular, on processes of re-entrant mapping between maps based on patterning from the outer senses and maps based on inner bodily homeostasis. This means that the core of consciousness is, from the beginning, a kind of self-reference — although Edelman insists that it is far short of the autobiographical awareness of self on the human level. He suggests that primary consciousness is the capacity to image an immediate past and anticipate an immediate future. It emerges as the result of a subsequent re-entrant mapping that registers overlap and disagreement between maps of current, "value-free" sensory experience and maps of previous re-entrant influence between past sensory experiences and "valuative" homeostatic processes. He locates the connectivity needed for this re-entrant mapping between the senses and organismic value in the septum, amygdala, and hippocampus of the limbic area, with a lower, nonconscious perceptual capacity being mapped within the thalamus and homeostatic functions being mapped within the hypothalamus. Primary consciousness appears with the mutual influence of current perception and these mappings of valued past perceptions, in the prefrontal cortex adjacent to the limbic area.

Edelman does not provide any explanation for how the perception of lower organisms could appear to be so immediately and sensitively attuned to their surroundings but nonetheless lack any primary awareness of the sort posited by Natsoulas and presupposed by Gibson. It is hard to see how perception could begin as a value-free structuration principle, given Gibson's analysis of the coalition between bodily actions and array affordances. Of course, the capacity for imagery, in Neisser's (1976) terms the capacity for a detachment of significant patterns from perceptual schemata, does reflect the extension of the "life-space" beyond that possible for immediate perception and recognition. Yet it seems arbitrary in the extreme to deny perception a more primary here-and-now form of consciousness, as in Gibson's whence-whither envelope of flow. Instead, Edelman initiates another version of the endless homuncular regression created by positing nonconscious neural processes (maps) that will do "inwardly" what simple organisms already show in their outward behavior. Again, it comes down to a question of theoretical parsimony in locating the first functional expressions of a primary awareness. Edelman locates consciousness at the stage of memory image as the "remembered present." This seems to be because he falsely promotes to that level processes of re-entrant propriosensitivity already found in Gibson's account of perception. In part, this may follow from his wish to explain functions in terms of underlying structures rather than the other way around.

A related problem, but one that moves in the opposite direction, comes with the approach of Endel Tulving (1983, 1984, 1985) to "episodic" memory, which he posits as the source of self-referential cognition rather than as one of its manifestations. It was Tulving's great contribution to distinguish an episodic or "source" memory from the "semantic" memory of knowing something without specific recall of the situation in which one learned the information. The more episodic or specifically autobiographical form of recall, which Tulving suggested was specific to human beings, does not develop in childhood until between the ages of two and four. Its slow development may reflect the cognitive side of that childhood amnesia of which Freud made so much. In support of the separation of these two forms of memory, Tulving cites research on the radical amnesia that results from bilateral damage to the hippocampus. Although these subjects actually do process new information in the form of semantic memory, they have no episodic memory whatsoever — no source recall beyond a minute or so for any life experiences subsequent to the damage. These subjects also lack the ability to anticipate highly probable future events (Tulving, 1985).

Further support for the role of the hippocampus in this episodic sense of past and anticipated future comes from the original work of Penfield (Penfield and Perot, 1963) and others (Horowitz, 1970) on the episodic form of remembering and more dreamlike sequences that are triggered by direct electrical stimulation to the endorhinal areas of the temporal lobe adjacent to the hippocampus. Indeed, the REM dreaming phase of sleep is associated with both a prolonged activation of the still reaction and the brain stem–based release of norepinephrine and acetylcholine into the hippocampal and forebrain areas. There is now considerable behavioral evidence (see Hunt, 1989a) that REM sleep in mammals is associated with the consolidation of recent novel learning. On the experiential side, it is also striking that dreams are full of what in another context Tulving (1983) termed "free radicals" — specific quasi-mnemic images no longer identifiable by the subject with respect to their original episodes and potentially on their way toward a more general semantic status. Indeed, this is exactly what Freud's "day residues" seem to involve. These are the holdovers from the previous day's experience that are so influential in dream formation but are almost never identified as such by the subject in the dream or even on immediate awakening.

The controversy comes with Tulving's claim that episodic memory is a specifically human capacity, and the point of origin for our "autonoetic" or self-referential awareness. Indeed, our memory is, as Bartlett (1932) also insisted, inseparable from the imaginative reconstruction of what plausibly would have occurred and from even more fanciful revisualizations. Our memories are permeated with an autobiographical organization that does reflect something like Mead's capacity to take the role of the other toward our own past. They are already "thoughts" in the sense of being more like metaphors that mirror our current concerns than any depiction of previous situations as actually lived. Nigro and Neisser's (1983) "observer memories," in which we recall past events from an out-of-body perspective on ourselves within the original situation, similarly show the restructuring of a more primary memory by self-referential consciousness.

The view, however, that this autonoetic consciousness could originate in structures and functions shared by all mammals, including the REM state itself, seems very doubtful. Olton (1979, 1984) has shown that episodic memory is not specifically human and self-referential, but has a perhaps more "eidetic" precursor in lower animals. He calls attention to a form of memory in rats that is crucial in foraging, by which they appear to recognize paths previously taken on other occasions so that they do not need to be re-entered. Like human episodic memory, this capability takes a comparatively long time to develop in rat ontogenesis and is similarly sensitive to hippocampal damage in a way that their longer-term memory is not. There is no reason to regard this ostensible evolutionary core of episodic recall as self-referential or autobiographical, nor as recombinatory. Rather, it would mark that point in evolutionary complexity where a primacy of perception begins to extend ahead and behind in the form of life-spaces that are broader than and potentially different from the concrete perceptual situation. Our episodic memory becomes self-referential, but its more eidetic roots served primarily to extend the range of perception.

Tulving (1985) and Marcia Johnson (Johnson and Hirst, 1992) share a view that different forms of consciousness will be based on different aspects and levels of memory. They reflect a tendency, strong in Anglo-American traditions, to treat learning or memory as the fundamental psychological capacity from which all others must emanate. I have commented elsewhere (Hunt, 1989a) on the conceptual dangers of such a Pax Memoria, which runs the risk of forcing perception, recombinatory imagination, and self-reference into a single reductive template. From this perspective, perception itself becomes nothing but a form of recognition and recall, while thought can be accounted for by sufficiently complex and recursive cycles of associative memory. It may fit well with our utilitarian preference that everything in the mind be malleable and learned, but one wonders how we came up with words like *perception, imagination,* and *thought* if *memory* would do as well. The word *attention* has come in for a similar universalization by those who would deal with consciousness in purely functional, "outward" terms. As Wittgenstein (1953) suggests, if a concept explains everything, then it explains nothing. Of course, memory can be involved *in* thought and perception, without eliminating them as distinct levels of cognition in their own right.

Self-Referential Consciousness

Gazzaniga: The Traditional Primacy of Language
versus Right-Hemisphere Consciousness

Recent debates emerging from research on the lateralization of function in the cerebral hemispheres, now itself hotly debated (Efron, 1990), raise the fundamental and ancient issue of the relation between language and self-referential consciousness. The traditional view, going back to Plato and Aristotle, is that language or linguistically based thought defines our species. Other symbolic forms, as found in the arts, and self-awareness itself would be consequences of language. A more recent view, as articulated by Susanne Langer (1942) and Howard Gardner (1983), is that the mind is a multiplicity of symbolic forms, with language expressing, but not originating, a capacity for reflexive awareness intrinsic to all symbolic frames.

Initial research on neocortical damage syndromes in clinical neurology favored the multiplicity view. So did the first studies of split-brain or commisurotomy patients, where the corpus callosum connecting the hemispheres is cut as a way of controlling severe epilepsy — leaving the hemispheres without any neocortical connection. In commisurotomy research, the hemispheres can be tested separately if perception is confined to the right or left visual field or the right or left hand (although this division does not hold for audition or somatic stimulation). The usual view from both the clinical and commisurotomy studies was that while the left hemisphere is specialized for language use, the right hemisphere is predominant in emotional response, facial recognition, spatial analytic skills (including block designs, embedded figures), and the visual arts. It is also central to the awareness of novelty in general, particularly as reflected in the "gist" or felt-meaning phase of language (Sperry, 1979, 1984; Gardner, 1975).

These conclusions are well illustrated in Oliver Sacks's (1987) curious account of the discomfiture and puzzlement of a number of left- and right-hemisphere stroke victims watching a televised speech by Ronald Reagan. Having lost the ability to understand speech in a literal discursive sense, left-hemisphere patients develop an exaggerated sensitivity to tonal and gestural expressions of felt meaning, making them acutely aware of deception and insincerity. Correspondingly, right-hemisphere damage leaves discursive speech intact but affects the ability to follow the gist or point of speech, as well as metaphors, jokes, and irony. I have already discussed Geschwind's observations that diffuse right-hemisphere damage is associated with delirium, and Schacter's emphasis on the loss of bodily and symbolic self-awareness with right-parietal damage. With Reagan's speech, both groups of patients were confused and disturbed. The left-hemisphere patients knew that the tone and gestures were incorrect, while the more literal-minded right-hemisphere patients could make no sense of his actual message. Non-brain-damaged listeners were apparently able to synthesize the two halves of the speech such that each compensated for the other and so were able to overlook what the patients could not.

One of the early researchers on split-brain patients, Michael Gazzaniga (1983, 1988), has called into question this multiplicity model of symbolic cognition. He concludes that apparent symbolic abilities in the isolated right hemisphere were a function of an atypical localization of some linguistic capacity in the right hemisphere of these patients — likely as a by-product of earlier undetected damage to the left hemisphere in childhood. Right hemispheres with no such localization of language showed little or no ability in the visual identification of objects, causal reasoning, or block design performance. He suggests that the price of our normally exclusive left-hemisphere specialization for language, as the core of all symbolic cognition, is a right hemisphere with a cognitive capacity "vastly inferior to the cognitive skills of a chimpanzee" (Gazzaniga, 1983, p. 536). Since some hemispheric connections will inevitably be preserved in ordinary brain damage syndromes, only commisurotomy studies would be able to detect this radical imbalance. For Gazzaniga, then, all symbolic cognition and self-awareness rests on a left-hemisphere linguistic "interpreter." This will be necessary for all narrative, sequential order and for identifying the separate steps in all computations — whether ostensibly linguistic or spatial.

There is an alternative to Gazzaniga's traditional linguacentric account of mind. If the right hemisphere were in fact central, as almost all clinical neurologists have concluded, for a novel, self-aware felt meaning that feeds the more specific linguistic processes of the left hemisphere, then a surgical separation of the hemispheres will have a more radically isolating effect on the right than on the left. The more routinized aspects of representational language use can continue without our usual sensitivity to context and gist, but a global self-awareness is utterly helpless if it has no more specific phases of articulation to guide it or to which it can respond.

The question becomes, as Natsoulas (1991) rightly states, whether the isolated left hemisphere shows a functional loss as well — precisely, a decrement in a much more difficult-to-research sense of context and felt meaning. Indeed, Gazzaniga (1988) provides numerous examples of left-hemisphere attempts to interpret the reactions of the right hemisphere that seem strikingly confabulated and affectively flat, rather like the explanations that amnesic hypnotic subjects give for posthyp- notically suggested behaviors. It does not seem that there has been any attempt to administer Rorschach or Thematic Apperception Tests to the isolated left hemi- sphere in order to test for just such a superficiality of symbolic feeling and self- awareness. Certainly, the few attempts to study left-hemisphere dream reports in such patients (Greenwood, Wilson and Gazzaniga, 1977; Hoppe, 1977) found dreams to be strikingly short and imaginatively limited. By itself, the left hemi- sphere would appear to suffer from a more extreme form of the lack of access to ongoing experience found in normal subjects in the experiments of Nisbett and Wilson (1977) and Maier (1931). I have already discussed (chapter 2) how the phenomena of aesthetics, altered states of consciousness, and clinical neurology attest to a right-hemisphere-predominant self-awareness, one that assumes a more directly presentational form than our ostensibly impalpable representational sym- bolism.[1]

Geschwind: Cross-Modal Transformation, Self-Awareness,
and the Multiplicity of Symbolic Forms

Often it is difficult to think simply enough to locate the fundamentals of one's subject matter. This was the basis of Gibson's impact, a gradual stripping away of the assumptions of the traditional experimental psychology of perception so that its phenomenological basis in a flow that simultaneously confers "here" and "there" could finally stand forth. Something similar can be said of the insights of the neurologist Norman Geschwind (1965). Symbolic cognition, as a higher rearrange- ment of perception, rests on a capacity for the cross-modal translation between the patterns of the separate perceptual modalities. We can add that this translation will also entail their "transformation" or creative rearrangement. The tertiary zones of the neocortex, which are the areas of localization for the specifically human sym- bolic forms, are found at the junctures between the secondary association areas of the occipital, parietal, and temporal areas devoted to the analysis of sight, touch, and hearing. This very anatomical structure already implies that symbolism may be based on a cross-modal mediation and mutual translation among patterns specific to each of the perceptual modalities. This is what Geschwind put forward as a formal theory, also consistent with A. R. Luria (1973) and more recently taken up again by Schacter (1989).

A cross-modal synthesis theory of human consciousness is also implied by Heinz Werner's "orthogenetic" principle of development. For Werner (1961), any- thing that undergoes genuine development can be said to move from an initially undifferentiated or global organization to a differentiation of multiply coordinated parts, and finally toward a hierarchic integration of these previously differentiated levels. First comes the progressive differentiation of perceptual attunement in multiple modalities on the vertebrate and especially mammalian levels, where recognitive need systems are largely governed by modality-specific releasing cues. That will bring about the developmental possibility of a subsequent reciprocal translation of these modalities — which would be us.[2] Cross-modal translation would be developmentally distinct from both the associational linkage of differentiated modalities in learned reinforcement and the more undifferentiated polymodal redundancy that is part of navigating an array.

Geschwind based his theory on the multiplicity of connections in the human neocortex that converge on the inferior parietal area (angular gyrus) from the secondary association areas for vision, touch, and audition. These bypass the more primary mammalian linkages between the secondary association areas specific to each perceptual modality and the pleasure-pain and mnemic processes of the limbic region. Damage to these neocortical zones of convergence affects various forms of symbolic cognition and, especially in the right hemisphere, self-referential awareness. These areas, with the frontal lobes, also mature more slowly than the rest of the cortex (Luria, 1973), strongly implying their more advanced and integrative nature. Geschwind is suggesting the emergence in us, and partially in the higher primates, of a capacity for cross-translating and so reorganizing the differentiated patterns of the perceptual modalities. It would operate in terms of its own spontaneous potential for emergent structure and relatively independent of the reward and punishment centers of the limbic region.

Geschwind called attention to the existence in the higher apes (chimpanzees, gorillas, and orangutans) of cortical cross-modal connections between vision and touch, but excluding audition-vocalization — which remains primarily linked to the limbic area. The importance of direct cortical integrations between vision and touch-movement in higher apes seems reflected in the emergence of capacities for self-awareness (behavior with mirrors), recombinatory insight (Köhler's crate-stacking chimpanzees), and a widely debated protolinguistic capacity — the latter available for study only when experimenters bypassed vocalization and concentrated on visual-motor signing (see chapter 5). Vocalizations in the higher apes have generally been regarded as tied into more automatic cues for basic social behavior, which is certainly consistent with their primary linkage to the limbic region. Human symbolic intelligence, on Geschwind's model, emerges with the addition of vocalization-audition to this emergent capacity for visual-tactile translation, creating the potentiality for three-way transformations among the perceptual modalities.

Three-way cross-modal syntheses would allow the more open-ended translations and retranslations across perceptual patterns that would eventuate in the symbolic frames of human intelligence. Indeed, described most simply, language entails the transformation of patterns seen into patterns kinesthetically articulated, in turn producing vocal sounds whose enunciation induces in others visualizations that are akin to the initiating visual forms. We see something and transform it into movements that make a sound. The existence of sign languages as naturally emerging alternatives to spoken languages in congenital deafness further illustrates this cross-modal basis of language. Although bypassing audition entirely, signing is localized in the same left temporal areas found in ordinary language, with, in addition, evidence for more parietal (spatial) involvements (Sacks, 1989).

Geschwind's prediction that the higher apes would show an ability for cross-modal matching that would form the basis for their nascent recombinatory and self-referential abilities, but which would be absent in lower primates, has produced a controversial research literature. At times this has obscured rather than clarified the real fundamentals of his theory and its potential impact. Davenport (1970, 1976), in a series of studies, first demonstrated successful transfer in both directions between tactile and visual patterns in chimpanzees, but not in rhesus monkeys. Consistent with Geschwind's model, cross-modal matching was not found with visual-auditory pairings. In the latter, the auditory stimuli were choices between one or more tones, to be matched with corresponding visual dots. However, Covey and Weiskrantz (1975), Elliott (1977), and Norris and Ettlinger (1978) were able to find tactile-visual cross-modal matching in rhesus monkeys, using food shapes presented in the dark, to be chosen later on the basis of visual appearance alone. Meanwhile, Jarvis and Ettlinger (1977) found no differences between rhesus monkeys and chimpanzees in their success rates of visual-tactile matching. They used two stimuli, one of which is reinforced when presented either visually or in the dark, to be matched with its corresponding appearance in the other modality.

Although the latter findings led to skepticism concerning Geschwind's original theory (see Ettlinger and Wilson, 1990), it does appear, nonetheless, that different processes (and neural levels) may underlie cross-modal choice discriminations in monkeys as opposed to higher primates and humans. Jarvis and Ettlinger observed that the monkeys went about these tasks very differently from the chimpanzees. The monkeys responded on the basis of rapid, cursory touches, with initial choices based on position preferences; whereas from the beginning the chimpanzees, touching the tactile shapes in the dark after initial visual exposure, carefully explored back and forth before making their choices. It is not surprising that some degree of multi-modal coordination would be present in any lower mammal with hands. The question is whether such a more primary ability would require neocortical mediation. Such connections could easily be based on areas of the thalamus that respond to multiple modalities as well as the amygdala of the limbic lobe, which is involved in learned associations based on reward and punishment and contains adjacent areas specifically sensitive to each perceptual modality. Indeed, Murray and Mishkin (1985) found a complete loss of cross-modal matching ability in rhesus monkeys subjected to bilateral amygdalectomy, which certainly suggests the subcortical basis for matching in these creatures. However, both Lee et al. (1988) and Nahm et al. (1993) found no such loss in human subjects with corresponding neural damage.

I conclude that there are two levels of cross-modal integration in primates, higher primates, and humans, one limbic and the other neocortical—the latter as postulated by Geschwind.[3] Savage-Rumbaugh, Sevcik, and Hopkins (1988) found perfect first-trial performances on cross-modal matching tasks using chimpanzees who had previously been taught proto-linguistic signing. Savage-Rumbaugh concludes that since signing behaviors are themselves cross-modal, such training would account for the considerably enhanced performance that these apes showed on the direct cross-modal matching tasks. Later evidence, to be reviewed below, finds cross-modal matching in preverbal human infants, also predicted by Geschwind as the first manifestation of symbolic cognition. This helps to prove that it is neocortical cross-modal translations that lead to language, and not the other way around.

In summary, Geschwind's insight that a neocortical cross-modal translation is the basis for self-referential symbolic cognition and consciousness has been broadly supported—however much we have also now learned about an earlier, limbically mediated, associational capacity. The conceptual power of this theory of mind is astonishing, both in its own right and in its capacity to link together ostensibly diverse aspects of cognition.

I. CREATIVITY AND NOVELTY A theory of mind as based on a capacity for cross-modal translation/transformation helps to explain why the human symbolic capacity entails that recombinatory novelty and creativity which most accounts of the human mind have made one of our most fundamental features. Vision, audition-vocalization, and touch-movement are disparately structured sources of information, each with its own rate and ratio of simultaneity to sequentiality. There is no one way that a moment of vision will flow into and transform the very differently patterned moments of audition and touch. Cross-modal fusions will necessarily be multiple and creative. To cross-translate among the patterns of multiple modalities will be to set up cycles of reciprocal transformation that will reorganize the patterns of perception in an open-ended and emergent fashion.

These spatial-temporal reorganizations of reciprocally translated sights, sounds, and movements would entail an openness in the human life-world strikingly absent in the relatively "closed" worlds of nonsymbolic creatures. Certainly, the behavior of simpler creatures is based on a separation of perceptual modalities that must seem surprising *to us*. The "ritualized" unfolding of behaviors associated with basic need systems depends on the appearance of modality-specific releasing cues (Lehrman, 1964). Along these lines, there is the famous demonstration by Von Uexküll (1934) in which mother hens showed no discomfort at the mere sight of their endangered chicks and remained uninterested as long as they did not hear their agitated peeping, which alone released maternal protective behaviors. We will also see (chapter 5) how cross-modal fusions of patterns specific to different need systems could, in addition to producing an endemic novelty in our experience, create the "instinctual" conflicts and "perversions" so central to Freud's account of our peculiarly human "drivenness." A capacity for cross-modal fusion may entail an endemic, open-ended conflict between need systems that are separated in lower mammals. Such a collision of modality-specific patterns and associated need systems fits well with the "catastrophe" models of Thom (1975) and Zeeman (1976), where conflicting systems alternate dominance in sudden, specifically unpredictable reorganizations (see also chapter 13). Creativity and conflict may be two expressions of the same recombinatory potential of cross-modal translations.

2. SELF-REFERENTIAL AWARENESS AS DIALOGIC MIRRORING A cross-flow between sentient modalities into and against each other will also entail an awareness that is self-referential — literally, a sentience of sentience. Such a capacity simultaneously accounts for the intrinsically social organization of all symbolic forms. The cross-translation of modality-specific forms is a necessary feature of the very first manifestations of "taking the role of the other" in infant-mother mirroring games. Such imitative facial behavior is present from birth, albeit initially narrowed to the specifics of tongue protrusion and mouth opening (Meltzoff and Moore, 1977, 1989, 1992; Reissland, 1988). Later, any visually presented facial expression of the mother will be mirrored back by the infant's facial expression. Note that the neonate has not yet seen or recognized its own face in mirrors. So it is hard to see how else such mirroring behaviors are to be explained other than as cross-modal translations between the seen face of the mother and the kinesthetically felt face of the infant. I have already suggested that these mirroring exchanges are the first manifestation of genuinely symbolic communication. Certainly they show an inseparability between the ability to take the role (face) of the other and the capacity for cross-modal translation between perceptual modalities.

It is likely that the cross-modal matching among dynamic patterns of sight, sound, and touch, demonstrable in young infants between eight and twelve months of age (Wagner et al., 1981; Bryant et al., 1972), is a further extension of this earlier cross-modal translation. Kaye and Bower (1994) have also found oral-visual matching in neonates at twelve hours after birth, which they likewise interpret as an abstract, protolinguistic, cross-modal coding capacity. Legerstee (1990) has even demonstrated that infants at three and four months of age are significantly more likely to imitate sounds that match, rather than mismatch, the mouth positions of adults. This suggests that the early visual-kinesthetic mirroring capacity extends into early proto-linguistic vocalizations and their mirroring as well. Supporting the relation between early neonatal mirroring and subsequent interpersonal development, a study by Heiman (1989) found a significant relationship between the amount of early neonatal mirrorings (assessed at two days of age) and later expressions of social intimacy. Specifically, the infants who did the most early mirroring showed the fewest "gaze aversions" in response to the mother's face at three months — which is the age at which most developmentalists date the beginning of communicative intent and the more elaborate facial mirroring behaviors. Accordingly, the earliest neonatal mirrorings, as narrowed and specific as they are, show a clear relationship to the more elaborate cross-modal mirrorings that emerge at three months.

Social mirroring — as incipient "taking the role of the other" — and cross-modal translations — as the core of the symbolic capacity — are coemergent and inseparable. Human cognition is, from the beginning, structured in the form of a dialogue. We find here strong support for the conclusions of both Wittgenstein and Mead that our experience can never be intrinsically private. Rather, human experience is dialogic through and through and from its most nonverbal beginnings. The mother-infant mirroring relation is the template for the first manifestations of cross-modal transformations. It is, accordingly, the meeting point for cognitive psychology and psychoanalytic object-relations theory. The subsequent development of cross-modal translations would rest on the sort of internalization of the mother-infant mirroring relationship posited by Kohut (1977) and Winnicott (1971) as basic to the growth of mind and person. The depth and breadth of these reciprocal exchanges of identity and difference in early mirroring, and the emotional context in which they occur, become the "container" that "holds" both intellectual development and presentational expressions of felt meaning. Deficiencies at these early stages, if not made up by later internalizations of an empathic mirroring capacity (Kohut, 1984), could well be associated with "thought disorder" (Bion, 1962) and proneness to dissociation. Here, the potential "fantasy proneness" or "imaginative absorption" of the young child has proven unable to contain and self-referentially mirror its own spontaneous states, with an impact as disintegrative as, in a more positive context, it might have been integrative and imaginatively creative.

3. MULTIPLE SYMBOLIC FORMS AND THE RELATION BETWEEN THOUGHT AND WORLD A cross-modal concept of mind has the virtue of reconciling the tension between the multiple-frame models of symbolic cognition and more traditional perspectives that posit a single "deep structure" for human intelligence — generally linguistic or propositional. On the one hand, all symbolic frames share a capacity

based on the synthesis of patterns taken from the different "angles" of vision, touch-movement, and audition. These superimpositions would be based on a continuing cycle of translation and retranslation of creative structural possibilities and without any fixed stopping point, until a pattern of practical consequence emerges. In turn, the separate frames (verbal, mathematical, visual arts, etc.) would result when one modality, or two in combination, function as the determinant template or deep structure to be cross-translated into the other(s) as its outward medium of expression. Michel Dufrenne (1973) developed a related typology of the various arts in terms of the type and order of cross-modality fusions that they entail. There can be no center or essence to this multiplicity of symbolic forms other than this very cycle of self-transforming, cross-modal flow itself.[4]

The approach to consciousness as cross-modal synthesis also has the virtue of avoiding that separation of thought and world endemic to most cognitive, neural, and AI modeling. That left a higher symbolic cognition to be constructed "in" the head at a categorical remove from an "outside" world, and left the actual worldly efficacy of thought a source of wonderment. The present approach does not require this contemporary estrangement of subject and object. If the patternings of the senses are afforded by the ecological array as its resonance, then the novel fusions and harmonies emerging from the cross-modal flow of these same patterns are already equally attuned to the possibilities and necessities of the world. Such processes are best conceived not as "in" the brain but rather, in Heidegger's sense, in-the-world.

4. TRANSPERSONAL EXPERIENCE AS INTRINSIC TO SYMBOLIC COGNITION   The addition of vocalization into cross-modal syntheses separates the mind of human beings from the nascent symbolic cognition present in the higher apes. It adds a necessarily extended and open sequentiality into hierarchic visual-tactile integrations. The abstraction of a pure sequentiality from audition and its concomitant cross-translation into visual-spatial simultaneity would create a "realm" of temporality without any sensed limitation or containment. This appears in Heidegger's account of *Dasein* as a being-ahead-of-itself toward an unknown future ending in death. The direct experience of that openness as a presentational state would constitute classical mystical awareness, resting on visual-spatial metaphors of "glow" and "luminosity" that are as open and unfinished as temporality itself. A three-way synesthesia will have an immensely adaptive potential, as its resulting reorganizations are applied to the pragmatics of physical and social reality. It also gives birth to the need to contain spatially an inherently open sequential dimension. The only complete match for the latter would be the entire sequence of visual microgenesis itself — opening out from a diffuse empty luminosity that corresponds to and recasts the horizonal openness of Gibson's visual optic array. Much of my later discussion will pursue a more detailed

account of this "white-light" experience and the related synesthesias so prominent in meditative and spontaneous presentational states (chapters 7, 10, 11).

5. THE RECOMBINANT FUSION OF GIBSON'S DIRECT PERCEPTION AND NEISSER'S RECOGNITION Open-ended cross-modal translations will also have the consequence of combining the principles of Gibson's flowing array with more static, modality-specific recognitive forms, transforming both in terms of the other. The cross-modally based reuse and reorganization of these two systems, functionally distinct in lower mammals, will blur the lines between them. A static recognitive imagery becomes a kinematic imagination based on the dynamic tension between modality-specific patterns and their cross-flow, while the properties of the array itself become available for aesthetic contemplation. Indeed, one of the effects of a cross-modal referencing will be the isolation of each of the "senses" as such, creating abstract patterns ready for further extrapolation. This paves the way for the very psychological models of the separate senses that Gibson rightly rejects as based on a secondary intellectual analysis.

Although language is in one sense clearly a recognitive system, in that we use it to identify and "name" events of significance to us, it also entails a reuse of key features of the flowing array. Syntax is a sequential flow across parts of speech that are fixed in a strict sequential order, much like the limb movements in running creatures (Vowles, 1970). At the same time, the logical grammatical relations of "if-then," "but," and "and" that James made so central to his notion of the stream of consciousness would seem to have their roots in the implicative, whence-whither flow of Gibson's array. The gradients of continuous texture convey the sense of a continuing "and," while surfaces that loom forth interrupt the asymmetrical flow with their "but," and the accretions and deletions of occluded surfaces are full of "if-then" implications. Within the presentational symbolisms, the continuous flow of dance is full of successive "flashes" of expressive portent and significance, while ostensibly static paintings, with their "recognitive" portent, unleash an imaginative sense of abstract dynamics and flow that is essential to their full appreciation (Arnheim, 1974).

6. IMPLICATIONS FOR THEORIES OF HUMAN EVOLUTION A cross-modal translation basis for the symbolic capacity fits very well with approaches to human evolution that posit a process of progressive fetalization or neoteny. This entails a slowing of the rate of maturation and affords a longer period of post-birth growth at a pace normally associated with fetal development, but here unfolding while the young child is exposed to the vicissitudes of the environment. Neoteny (Montagu, 1962; Gould, 1977) is the retention of fetal forms of organization into later developmental stages. The shift from mammals, adapted to highly specialized niches, to primates, and thence to hominid forms seems to reflect a process of progressive fetalization in

the outer forms of mature adults. Different mammalian species are difficult to tell apart at their early embryological stages. The more specialized mammals develop their snouts and hooves late in gestation, while humans retain this more basic mammalian form beyond birth as our final body shape. Major neotenous features in human beings include a retention of the parallel line of head and trunk that is lost in the late embryological stages of more specialized mammals, as well as absence of brow ridges, thinness of the skull bones, flatness of face, large volume of brain and head compared to the rest of the body, globular form of the skull, thin nails, and hairlessness of the body. These are all neotenous features in adult human beings that are also found in early juvenile but not adult forms of the higher primates, as well as being characteristic of the earliest embryological stages of all mammals.

The usual version of the theory of human evolution as based on neoteny is that there is a prolongation of the rate of growth and extreme plasticity characteristic of embryological maturation, which allows our characteristically lengthy childhood. To put it crudely, we are pictured as a kind of walking mammalian fetus. This gives us the long and vulnerable childhood that is also associated with our continued mal-leability and capacity for learning. Although this may be true, we need to consider the implications of Stephen Jay Gould's (1977) suggestion that a structuration or forma-tion principle should be added to specific Darwinian adaptation as a factor of biological evolution. From this perspective, we can see that the prolongation of growth allowed by neoteny would also allow the completion of the structural-developmental potentiality for a hierarchic synthesis of perceptual modalities. These have already undergone an extreme differentiation within the more complex mam-mals. In other words, a more prolonged period made available for central nervous system maturation would allow the increasing cross-translation of the separate association areas for the perceptual modalities. This appears first in the higher primates, with their relatively neotenous tendencies, and is more fully realized in human beings. Cross-modal integration is the developmental principle latent within the differentiation of the perceptual association areas of the mammalian cortex.[5] A lengthened period of maturation would allow its completion, with a concomitant loss of the more specialized adaptations that drove the differentiation of perception in terms of specialized environmental niches.

We have already noticed the manifestation of a related principle in meditation, where the holding off of more specific functional responses, here including prag-matic verbal thought, allows the development of experiential patterns that would have been forestalled by more specific adaptive involvements.

If a principle of structuration based on the hierarchic integration of the senses predominated in our evolution, then whereas in most of evolution, and in our own ontogenesis, function will indeed precede instantiation in structure, human evolu-tion itself might reverse that relationship. In us, the structural potentialities of cross-modal synthesis would have preceded their functional realization in culturally mediated symbolic frames. This fits well with the view that modern human beings are no different in neocortical symbolic capacity than our ancestors, at whatever point our level of cross-modal synthesis was achieved (somewhere between fifty thousand and two hundred thousand years ago, on most accounts). What has developed in us are the increasingly elaborate, culturally mediated forms of symbolization and their progressively differentiated uses. All our modern applications of human intelligence, from science and technology to the arts, are expressions of the same structural potentialities for cross-modal translation that were already present in our late-Pleistocene ancestors.

If our structural potential has remained unchanged and human development is all a matter of progressive application, then, as with many mythological and spiritual traditions, we are indeed "unfinished" as a species. This would be true first in the possibility that a greater degree of cross-modal integration might, in principle, have developed in an adjacent hominid species, whose more vulnerable and complex evolution would have been forestalled by our very success. It would also be more palpably reflected in our ability, as self-referential beings, to sense our own incompleteness — both on a collective and on a personal level. Our self-awareness, wherever it is permitted to unfold outside of the specific practical projects that normally entrain it, keeps showing us the truth of W. R. Bion's insight that "the capacity to think" — and, we might add, feel — "is rudimentary in all of us."

5 Animal Consciousness: The Emergence of Primary Sentience in Protozoa and Self-Referential Consciousness in the Higher Primates

If consciousness is always enacted behaviorally in a world and neuronal connectivity instantiates consciousness but does not necessarily explain it, there is every reason to hope that we might come to understand both self-referential consciousness and the primary sentience it reorganizes by studying their likely points of evolutionary emergence. Any attempt, however, to infer forms and levels of consciousness in the activities and sensitive attunements of organisms simpler than ourselves runs immediately into one of the most fundamental debates of modern science. The issue of animal consciousness clearly pits the basic criteria of theoretical parsimony and availability of methodological verification against each other, perhaps in a unique way. For many traditional psychologists this issue has come to reflect one of the dividing lines between science and romanticism.

Of course, the predominant point of view in modern psychology has been both "mechanistic" and "operational," placing issues of methodology over the requirements of consistent theory. The animal-learning tradition of Pavlov, Watson, and Thorndike, which displaced introspectionism in North American psychology, was based on the assumptions of a nineteenth-century physiology (Boring, 1950; Radner and Radner, 1989). The earlier attempts of Jacob Loeb and others to reduce the behavior of even complex organisms to the rudiments of reflex and tropism reflected a still earlier Cartesian ideal of reducing the complex to the simple. No need for notions of emergence and holism here. For this tradition, association learning and conditioning became the fulcrum of all psychological explanation. Symbolic cognition is to be understood in terms of its simpler stimulus-response and mediational constituents. If allowed at all, the tendency to ascribe any awareness to animals was limited, as with Gerald Edelman today, to mammals and birds — where behavior is most readily modified by conditioning and reinforcement.

From Charles Darwin himself (1872), however, has come a very different tradition, precisely the one occluded by the behavioristic era in psychology and its extension into mainstream "cognitive science." If consciousness exists in us, then it must serve some set of adaptive functions. These functions must have a continuous evolutionary history, like everything else. Such a history should be traceable through the systematic observation of organismic behaviors and sensitivities. The major early practitioner of this tradition was Darwin's student George Romanes (1883), who used an anecdotal, observational method to infer the development of consciousness across diverse species. He concluded that amoebae show enough variability and reactivity in outward behavior to ascribe to them a primary sentience. Lloyd Morgan's (1894) canon of parsimony, which advocated always choosing the simplest kind of mentality possible to explain a given behavioral capacity, was later used by the behaviorist tradition to justify the rejection of consciousness for all but the most complex organisms. Its original intent, however, was to introduce a consistent rule of inference into the Darwinian enterprise of inferring gradiated levels of consciousness, in order to correct for some of Romanes's more anthropomorphic leanings (Radner and Radner, 1989; Costall, 1993).

Morgan's rule of inference was adopted by Margaret Washburn (1917) in her systematic "introspectionist," but certainly scientific, approach in *The Animal Mind:* "One does not have to be a vitalist to believe that animals have minds: one may hold that every action of an animal will someday be explained as the result of physico-chemical processes and yet maintain that the actions of animals are conscious. The consciousness would be an accompaniment, an inner aspect, of the physico-chemical processes" (Washburn, 1917, p. 22). Washburn suggests that to infer a primary awareness, there should be sufficient variability of behavior in problem situations, and that these variations have to show some influence from previously encountered situations. In addition, such reactivities have to be relatively immediate, in contrast to the gradual changes in the growth of plants or in the increasing size of a blacksmith's muscles. Following these rules, as we will see, Washburn was able to ascribe an immediate sentience, nonreflective and without memory, to the behavior of protozoans. This was consistent with the earlier observation based conclusions of Romanes (1883) and Alfred Binet (1888).

More recently, Donald Griffin (1976, 1978, 1984), on the basis of his review of observational and experimental studies of animal behavior, concludes that considerations of theoretical parsimony demand of us the ascription of consciousness to a wide range of organisms:

> The possibility that animals have mental experiences is often dismissed as anthropo-morphic because it is held to imply that other species have the same mental experi-ences a man might have under comparable circumstances. But this widespread view itself contains the questionable assumption that human mental experiences are the only kind that can conceivably exist. This belief that mental experiences are a unique attribute of a single species is not only unparsimonious; it is conceited. It seems more likely than not that mental experiences, like many other characteristics, are wide-spread, . . . but differ greatly in nature and complexity. (Griffin, 1978, p. 528)

The identity of neuronal structure and activity across species must lead us to the postulation of a related continuity in subjective experience. In this regard, Griffin cites the shared commonality of the secondary component of the cortical evoked response, which betokens conscious awareness in us and the orientation response in other organisms. It is much more parsimonious to posit a "something" that it might be "like" to be a particular species, based on its behavioral responsivity, even if we have no methodology to "prove" it, than it is to construct an overly elaborated theory in order to explain why a creature that looks sentient really cannot be so. It is not clear that we should allow the very real methodological limitations involved to force us into a falsely complex and counterintuitive theory about what may be the most fundamental feature of motile living organisms.

Two very different paradigms of thought meet precisely at this issue of animal consciousness. On the one hand, we have the various spiritual traditions, for whom all physical reality is in some sense "animated" or at least potentially conscious. On the other hand, there is the mechanistic version of physical science, in search of experimental and mathematical specifications of whatever is to be its subject mat-ter. These traditions must meet and collide at "animal consciousness." Is conscious-ness indexed in other species by the same behavioral manifestations that seem, to most of us, to betoken it in human beings? Is there a logical and empirically defensible level of organization beyond which motile organisms will be different enough from us to be deemed nonconscious? If consciousness serves no function, such a debate does not matter. We have seen, however, that all recent discussions of consciousness within cognitive psychology have placed it at the center of a capacity for synthesis and integration that is eminently causal. The risk on the one side is, of course, a false anthropomorphism, but the risk on the other is the actual denial of the most fundamental characteristic not only of ourselves but of other sentient beings as well. Here we have a different sort of "best-judgment" Turing Test, with its own consequences for the ethics of how we treat our fellow planetary inhabitants, since in this matter ethical consequences surely flow from theory.

If all sentient beings but ourselves are to be considered primarily as "commodity," can we ourselves and our own presumed uniqueness be far behind? Is this not exactly the concern about twentieth-century culture and science that has been expressed by so many philosophers and thinkers? Our quest for a plausible account of human consciousness and its transformations may also require the courage to ask about its comparative development elsewhere, albeit emulating the care and caution of Washburn and Griffin. If consciousness in its various forms is emergent, and its evolution at least semicontinuous, we must avoid a theory that, by default, makes all its forms a consequence of being human. Or have we, on grounds of methodological purity, ceded away our right as scientists to make our own best judgments concerning matters of such consequence?

Primary Awareness in Motile Organisms

There will be considerable difficulty for us, as self-aware symbolizing beings, in comprehending an immediate awareness that might be lacking in both reflexivity and any imaged extension of the present. Yet, from an evolutionary perspective, such must be the first form of primary awareness — which we need both to imagine as such and to locate in terms of its likely behavioral and physiological expressions.

Jakob von Uexküll (1934) made perhaps the most serious early effort at the imaginative construction of the life-worlds of simple organisms. For von Uexküll, the *Umwelt* or surround of non-self-referential beings cannot be understood in terms of *our* experience of an environment full of "things." For human beings, "things" are always open to be taken in multiple ways, probably based on our capacity for an open-ended cross-modal translation. The world of lower organisms would instead consist of sets of "functional tones" or "effector cues" — similar to Gibson's "affordances." These release the specific actions that constitute the creature's response repertoire. Action, in the absence of self-referential awareness, serves to replace or delete the sentience that has initiated it and by which it will be guided until the organismic situation has been transformed and a specific need has been realized.

The animal's experience of its world, then, is in terms of what it does in response to particular cues for need and movement, and not in terms of "sensory qualities" per se. "Sensations," too often seen as the supposed "simples" of experience, would not be part of the sentient world of lower animals:

> We may say that the number of objects which an animal can distinguish in its own world equals the number of functions it can carry out. If, along with few functions, it possesses few functional images, its world, too, will consist of few objects. As a result its world is indeed poorer, but all the more secure, for orientation is much easier among

few objects than among many. If the *Paramecium* had a functional image of its performance, its entire world would consist of homogenous objects, all of them bearing the same obstacle tone. To be sure, such an *Umwelt* would leave nothing to be desired as far as certitude is concerned. (von Uexküll, 1934, p. 49)

Although von Uexküll's specific imaginative reconstructions of the multiple space-times of the wood tick and sea urchin are based on behavioral research that is often out of date, something very like these distinct organizations seems inevitable. Each species exists in its own highly characteristic "bubble" of perception, as illustrated in von Uexküll's famous example of the utterly different "tone" or affordance of "tree" in the worlds of the wood tick, bird, squirrel, and fox. Such a radical relativity of space-times and "surfaces" might seem to contradict the realism of Gibson and the physical basis of the array, but only if we forget that its ecological affordances must be defined entirely in terms of the size, shape, sensitivities, and speed of movement of the responding organism. The widely differing environmental niches of living organisms, and the functional tones thereby afforded, imply the existence of utterly disparate worlds. Yet their principles of organization in terms of Gibson's "envelope of flow" and its instantiating neurology should be the same.

As to the point of emergence of a primary sentience in lower organisms, it is interesting that both the vitalist philosopher Henri Bergson (1907) and the contemporary cognitive psychologist George Miller (1981) seem to agree that the most parsimonious approach is to posit consciousness on what we might refer to as a "need-to-know" basis. If a creature is actively mobile within an array that accordingly flows past it in a whence-whither gradient and contains surfaces that will release various specific behaviors, then such a creature *requires* some sort of sentient capacity in order to safely navigate that world. In other words, a motile organism moving through its array must be able to locate itself proprioceptively in terms of those surroundings — thereby requiring the here-there, whence-whither dimensions of Gibson's navigational model of perception.

Accordingly, we would need to posit some form of diffuse sentience, prior to any differentiation into separate perceptual modalities, in all protozoa that actively navigate through their surround. It is true that Gustav Fechner (see James, 1912; Lowrie, ed., 1946) suggested that the much slower movements of plants also warranted the hypothesis of a kind of sentience. However, the comparative slowness of these changes, measurable over hours and days, shows the wisdom of Washburn's criterion of a radical-enough change to require some immediate proprioceptive feedback. Contra Fechner, we could speculate that immediate sentience would rest on some ratio (to be established) between the rapidity of shifts in functional tones in the surround and the latency and speed of the organism's response. A gradual enough movement in response to a slowly exerted pressure would not require the proprioception for position so basic to Gibson's account of perception. Considerations of parsimony would not then require the attribution of consciousness. This is not to say that plant growth is thereby necessarily unconsciousness, only that it falls beyond the rules of inference set out by Lloyd Morgan and applied by Washburn and so many others.

What we are saying is that there is no perception outside of the movement capabilities of organisms. They must locate themselves within the whence-whither and here-there dimensions of their array and respond to surfaces valued in terms of approach and avoidance. To move in some such ratio as above is to be "sentient," and vice versa. As Bergson stated, "The humblest organism is conscious in proportion to its power to move *freely*. Is consciousness, here, in relation to movement, the effect or the cause? In one sense, it is the cause, since it has to direct locomotion. But in another sense it is the effect, for it is the motor activity that maintains it, and, once this activity disappears, consciousness dies away or rather falls asleep" (Bergson, 1907, p. 123). This is not necessarily or merely a philosophical vitalism in the present context. Rather, it is what certain beings *do* in terms of a surround specific to their capabilities that warrants the term *consciousness*.

Reflections of Primary Sentience in Protozoa

Numerous early psychologists were interested in the natural observation of the microscopic protozoa, including Romanes (1883), Binet (1988), Jennings (1906), and Washburn (1917). They concluded that the variability and complexity of their behavior warrants some attribution of an ongoing sentience — in probable contrast to the relative automaticity of bacterial movement (Ordal, 1977). Of course, these single-cell creatures do not have neurons, let alone neural nets. Yet the complexity of their approach and avoidance behaviors, and observations in some species of predation, group aggregations, and sexual behavior (Binet, 1988), along with clear, if inevitably anecdotal, demonstrations of the modification of current behavior in terms of prior experience (Washburn, 1917), led most observers to the conclusion that here was the evolutionary beginning of sentience. We will see below how strongly this assumption is supported by more recent discoveries of the identity of the electrochemical activity during protozoan movement and neuronal action potentials in creatures complex enough to have brains.

On the level of behavioral observation, several protozoan species show the proprioceptive sensitivity central to Gibson's description of perception. Washburn (1917) concluded that the reactive responsivity of various motile protozoa just before physical contact with objects in their path was based on turbulence reflected back to them from these looming surfaces and caused by their own movement — a kind of self-generated liquid sonar. Amoebae, separated from the tensile surfaces which they need for movement, go into what we might term an explicitly pro-prioceptive mode and put out pseudopods in all directions until one of these locates a surface, to which the creature then moves (Washburn, 1917). If there is no immediate reafferant feedback from a surface, the amoeba seeks it. These sorts of re-afferant behaviors are at the core of Gibson's notion of a here-there dimension created by resonance to a flowing array.

Anecdotally, there have been many reports of the ostensible modification of behavior in particular protozoa on the basis of prior experience — if not showing genuine learning, then certainly demonstrating sensitization and habituation as its most rudimentary processes. Jennings (1906), for instance, describes a sequence he observed in which a large amoeba had ingested a smaller one. It left, however, a small gap in its enclosing protoplasm through which the latter quickly escaped. The larger one pursued, reingested and now totally enclosed the smaller one, which then lay dormant until the protoplasm of the larger became thinner in one direction, at which point the smaller one broke out and escaped — something Jennings had never before seen. This sequence recurred several times, until the larger amoeba desisted in its pursuit and the smaller one finally escaped. This account shows aspects of behavioral modification in both creatures — in the smaller one, a progressive sensitization to the requirements of escape, and in the larger one, the final habituation to that escape. Romanes (1883), while he did not observe any prior experience that might have been involved, described a single amoeba that crept up the stem of a spiny acineta — which it would normally avoid. It waited at the aperture until the birth of a young unarmored acineta. This it immediately ingested and then removed itself.

Although these and other such accounts show a variability in behavior that might well attest to "learning from experience," the presence of the more complex processes of associational learning and conditioning in protozoa have been a matter of considerable debate. Research showing a growing avoidance of electric currents by large groups of protozoa, as well as the increase of white blood cells in response to disease, is difficult to evaluate in terms of learning because of the possibility of selective adaptation based on their rapid reproductive rates. Philip Applewhite (1979), after reviewing decades of related research attempting to demonstrate approach-avoidance learning, maze behaviors, and classical conditioning in protozoa, describes some positive results, but with largely failed subsequent replications. He concludes that although learning in protozoa is possible in principle, it has not been conclusively demonstrated.[1] We will see how the difficulty of establishing anything beyond immediate sensitization and habituation in protozoa (whereas more complex learning and conditioning are easily demonstrated in the simplest metazoans) may have an anatomical basis.

Washburn (1917) hazards a version of what the life-world of the amoeba could be "like." Its pulsating physical expansion would be associated with an elementary pleasure, while its more defensive and avoidant contractions would have a corresponding negative tone. Its awareness would obviously be highly diffuse, without the differentiations associated with sensory modality. She further suggests that there would be no figure-ground structure in such awareness, since that would require the more specific distance senses, and no sense of self as a separate entity or of any memory or anticipatory "imagery." Its temporal orientation would be based on the immediate "now" — its consciousness coming in a series of "flashes" with only a minimal continuity between them. An analogue to the world of the amoeba, she suggests, would be trying to imagine ourselves navigating through a strange room in total darkness, with no visual memories or anticipatory images whatsoever. If we then add a tendency to ingest all surfaces that felt soft and small and to withdraw from all that seemed harder and larger, we gain a notion of a world as utterly simple as it is exquisitely sensitive.

Whatever the ultimate worth of such constructions, it is interesting that all of the theoretical "structuralisms" proposed for more complex organismic behaviors also apply to the motile protozoa, and indeed in some cases have been generated from protozoan behavior and generalized to all psychological functioning. Structuralism in psychology comprises various descriptive approaches that seek to contextualize specific behaviors and functions. Their most general organismic context is described on levels of analysis so abstract that they operate in lieu of the laws or explanations that may in fact elude us in the social sciences. The structures thus abstracted are considered to be sui generis and not reducible to more basic constituents. The paramount example of such a structuralism is Jean Piaget's (1952) "descriptions" of complex intellectual development in young children in terms of equilibrating cycles of assimilation and accommodation. Assimilation and accommodation cannot be further subdivided, and, indeed, Piaget illustrates them in his most basic definitions with respect to the way in which amoebae physically assimilate whatever they can encompass, and accommodate to all more unyielding surfaces. Konrad Lorenz (in Erikson, 1963) pointed out similarly that Erik Erikson's modes of basic organismic responsivity, with which he sought to contextualize Freud's psychosexual stages in the more general terms of incorporation, retention, expulsion, and intrusion, also describe the behavior patterns of protozoa. Freud (1919) himself likened the transition from narcissistic to object libido to the putting forward of a pseudopod by an amoeba. Wilhelm Reich (1942) similarly modeled his categories of human body sensation — flow and expansion versus tensed contraction — on his observations of protozoan approach and avoidance behaviors. Finally, if we consider Gibson's basic characterization of the ecological array as a potential cross-species structuralism, we have already seen how well its flow gradients and propriosensitivity apply to protozoa.

Considered most parsimoniously, sentient life-worlds are emergent at the level of the protozoa. Certainly, the most general categories describing the patterning of their behavior also describe ours.

The Action Potential of the Neuron as Protozoan Movement

In 1888, in the preface to his *Psychic Life of Micro-Organisms,* Alfred Binet, one of the founders of the discipline of psychology, suggested that neurons could be considered as protozoa that have become specialized for sentience in the same way that stomach cells are specialized for the function of digestive assimilation. Gathered into neuronal networks in metazoans, the capacity of protozoans for sensitive motility becomes the direct discharge of the neuronal action potentials to other neurons and ultimately to the muscles. Following the preceding analysis of protozoa as sentient, this approach is consistent with the theory of neural networks, not as "causing" sentience, but as gathering and differentiating it—creating more and more complex fields of sentience that can become attuned to more specific properties of the array. Ultimately such attunements would approximate the more distant attributes of vision and audition.

Binet's tantalizing, almost offhand suggestion finally gained experimental support through a series of studies demonstrating that protozoa move through their surround by means of the very same electrochemical processes that are involved in neuronal firing (Naitoh and Eckert, 1969ab; Wood, 1972; Anderson, 1988). The resting polarization in most protozoa is remarkably close to the 70 microvolt negative charge on the inner membrane of neurons. External stimulation to paramecia held by tiny glass pipettes results in sudden depolarization of the protozoan membrane. Like neuronal action potentials, these depolarizations are based on the influx of positive ions (here calcium) moving along the membrane. This leads to a sudden action potential, in paramecia associated with their movement, and with the same 50 microvolt positive charge found with neuronal spiking. In at least several protozoan species, the same efflux of positive potassium ions (K^+) that also occurs in neurons restores the resting membrane balance, sometimes with a transient hyperpolarization. In several species of protozoans, graded receptor potentials, based on transient depolarizations and hyperpolarizations in response to external stimulation, have been recorded before the all-or-none action potentials.

Again, the comparison with neuronal functioning in metazoans is startling. Both protozoan movement and metazoan neuronal activity utilize the same processes of membrane conductance based on sudden shifts in ion currents. These potentials also show the same patterns of sensitization and habituation to external stimulation: "It is evident that the surface membrane of a unicellular organism can perform the functions of sensory reception, simple integration of receptor signals, and control of the motor response—and that a rather simple modification of membrane function can give rise to an elementary form of memory. . . . The similarity between the electrical properties of nerve cells and those of protozoa suggests that these properties, primarily related to the functioning of ion-selective membrane channels, are both ubiquitous and very ancient" (Eckert, Randall, and Augustine, 1988, p. 254).

A number of researchers (Eckert et al., 1988; Van Houton, 1981; Wood, 1975; Hamilton, 1975; Chen, 1975) hoped that further research on protozoan motility and sensitivity would provide the key to understanding the specifics of neuronal activity. Certainly, this is plausible in the sense that protozoan processes of motility constitute the most general organismic template for neuronal activity and its probable relation to a primary sentience. In short, the neuronal current and spike is, at its core, identical to the processes of sentient motility in protozoa — both thereby illustrating a transduction of a flowing array into discrete electrochemical processes. In what follows, however, we will also see that methodological limitations, the wide variety of sentience and motor organization across different protozoan species, and the important differences between freely motile protozoa and bound neural interconnectivities have so far held this research to the level of more general implication.

In order to see how protozoan and neural activities will contextualize each other in ways not yet widely appreciated, it will also be necessary to look at the limitations of this comparison. First, on methodological grounds, there has been the sheer difficulty of studying electrical potentials in protozoa without intruding profoundly on their natural activities and sensitivities, making it problematic to use such studies as the primary template for neuronal action. This has meant that fundamental research on the activity of neurons is likely to remain, for now, with the widely studied axon of the giant squid, which is, of course, relatively large — several feet long — and can be maintained as a separate experimental preparation for days (Dowling, 1992). Second, neurons are highly specialized forms of protozoa, routinely firing forty times a second and more. Protozoa are crude and sluggish by comparison. Third, depolarization in protozoa and neurons utilizes a related but differing ionic chemistry. Whereas the neuron depolarizes via an influx of mainly sodium (Na^+) through the ion channels in its axon, most protozoa utilize calcium (Ca^+) instead. Correspondingly, whereas hyperpolarizing neurons undergo an influx of negative chloride ions (Cl^-), most protozoa approximate the same phenomenon only by means of the efflux of potassium (K^+).

Eckert et al. (1988) conclude that the predominant use of calcium for depolarization in protozoa, also characteristic of crustaceans and of vertebrate neurons in embryo, means that the switch to sodium resulted from an evolutionary specialization in impulse conduction, so that protozoa illustrate the original template for motile sentience. A further indication of the subsequent specialization of function in neurons would be the use of calcium at metazoan synapses, instead. Where it is the major catalyst for neurotransmitter and neuromodulator emission and uptake. Since calcium is also concentrated in vertebrate muscles, it would appear that the development of sodium conductants in the axon went along with a shift of the original calcium flux toward the effector end of neuronal activity.

Whereas motile protozoa are functionally autonomous entities, no neuron is ever found alone in nature. The neuron is, by definition, always part of a conjoined neural network. Accordingly, it should be clear that nothing in the present discussion implies that each neuron is separately sentient in the way most parsimonious to ascribe to motile protozoa. Compound protozoa, specialized for sentience-motility, would presumably pool and gather their sentience into emergent "awareness fields." What must be absent in protozoa, making them at best a limited model for the neuron, are synaptic connections and the mediating neurochemicals that facilitate excitatory or inhibitory connections between neurons.[2]

It is at this point that we might also begin to get some purchase on the experimental difficulties in establishing association learning and avoidance conditioning in motile protozoa — while they as clearly show the same sensitization and habituation demonstrable in isolated neurons. Kandel and Schwartz (1982), in research on the avoidance conditioning of the tail of the mollusk, concluded that conditioning is based on the same habituation and sensitization effects found in the single neuron, but mediated by the "inter-neurons" in multineuron networks that would connect together separate reflex arc sequences. If Kandel is correct, then protozoa would lack the minimal structure required for the reliable demonstration of association learning, without, of course, negating the possibility that a less reliable but difficult-to-repeat functional capability would occasionally be demonstrable. Protozoa, then, provide the template not for learning but for the most immediate flow of sentience-motility.

There is a further ambiguity in the nature of neuronal hyperpolarization and its variable presence in protozoa which partly limits and partly illuminates our comparison. Although hyperpolarization in neurons reduces the likelihood and frequency of depolarizing action potentials, and is commonly termed "inhibitory," it is also true that the graded sensory receptor potentials in vertebrates (but not invertebrates) are based on hyperpolarization (Eckert et al., 1988). The first- and second-order neurons of vertebrate visual systems respond to light stimulation with hyperpolarizing currents, depolarizations and action potentials appearing only at the geniculate level. Dowling (1992) suggests that these hyperpolarizing gradiations may provide a more sensitive discriminative capacity — which would be consistent with the idea (James, 1890) that holding off motoric response allows more complex perceptual differentiations.

There seems to be a considerable diversity in the presence and function of membrane hyperpolarization as a distinct phase of protozoan behavior. Several protozoa may have no separate hyperpolarization phase at all (the stalked heliazoans and the stentor [Febvre-Chevalier et al., 1986; Wood, 1975]). On the other hand, Mogami and Machemer (1991) found a distinct hyperpolarization in a stalked ciliate during the emptying of its eliminative vacuole. At least one free-swimming carnivorous ciliate shows hyperpolarization on immediate contact with prey (Hara and Asai, 1980). The paramecium (Naitoh and Eckert, 1973; van Houton, 1979, 1981) shows hyperpolarizing currents, which with noxious stimulation from behind cause it to swim faster but will also cause it to spin around in the vicinity of food. Finally, amoebae show alternate depolarization and hyperpolarization during the shift from gelatinous to liquid phases of pseudopod formation, whether the stimulating contact occasions approach or avoidance (Eckert et al., 1988).

Perhaps it is neuronal functioning that will best contextualize this variability in protozoan hyperpolarization — in turn pointing us toward a basic structuralism for motile organisms. If neurons do what protozoa do — sentience-motility — then perhaps the more elaborate neural nets in vertebrates allow a specialization in function only latent in earlier forms. In this case, we would conclude that protozoan hyperpolarization is part of an immediate sensitization to the surround — the root of a recognitive perception prior to immediate motility. It may even be that since some degree of compensatory hyperpolarization is necessarily involved after all depolarization, we have here an indication of an immediate reafferant feedback after movement, demarking and placing the protozoan within its new surround. Sentience appears to emerge with the "opponent-process" play of both depolarizations and hyperpolarizations, separate phases of which will ultimately be utilized somewhat differently in various protozoa. Certainly, the increased disparity between electrical charges inside and outside the membrane in hyperpolarization might connote an overall increase in "tension," whereas the sudden collapse of this difference and its temporary shift in depolarization would reflect "tension release." It would be a mistake, however, to equate this fundamental polarity with approach-avoidance behaviors. Even Freud (1924), by the end of his career, saw that decrease in tension could also be unpleasant (as in a panic attack), while increase in tension could be pleasurable (as in exploratory behavior).

There is, indeed, much variability in the way that protozoa organize graded depolarizations, all-or-none action potentials, and hyperpolarizations as identifiable aspects of their life-worlds. In some species, the action potential is only avoidant (Febvre-Chevalier et al., 1986; Wood, 1972; Moreton and Amos, 1979), while in others the action potential is associated with both flight and predation behavior (Hara and Asai, 1980). In the paramecium, which is always in motion due to an internally regulated ciliate activity, gradiated surface depolarizations and hyperpolarizations are associated with both approach and avoidance behaviors, depending on their strength and their location on the outer membrane (Van Houton, 1979, 1981). The ubiquity of these basic processes,[3] combined with the variability of their interface with functional behavior, leads to the conclusion that protozoa actually present a variety of ways to organize sentience-motility in terms of the shifting currents of polarization. Metazoan neurons, with their fundamental identity across evolution, would represent a particular specialization among these possibilities. It may even be that our particular "path taken" is not found as such on the single-cell level, precisely because it became the basis for all further metazoan evolution.

What we can say, however, about the relation between protozoa and neurons turns out to be far more important than what we cannot. The reciprocal comparison of the two casts a unique light on each. Neurons are protozoa specialized with respect to their motile sensitivity to a surround, as Binet first said. The action potential of the neuron is a protozoan movement, but one transferred between now stationary neurons to generate pooled fields of sentience and reactivity. Graded depolarizations in protozoa would constitute a readiness for movement, which, in the full context of protozoan behaviors, can be a part either of approach or of avoidance patterns. Hyperpolarizations are part of a "still" phase, showing perhaps the beginnings of a separable capacity for sentience, and one that is again potentially bivalent. Receptor and compensatory hyperpolarization potentials of protozoa would then be transducing gradients of "outer" flow into an "inner" perceptual resonance and proprioception.

The widespread assumption of much of cognitive science and artificial intelligence that neurons manifest an on-off binary pattern, as a sort of logical calculus within the nervous system, stands forth now as a deep error. Neurons are not organized as on-off computations. In living protozoa, "off" would have to be death, while "on" has multiple values, being the relatively distinct aspects of an organism-environment coalition. If we go in search of a neuronal logical calculus based on the full range of protozoan behavior, we do not come up with anything binary. Instead, we could perhaps posit a five-value "organismic calculus" of sensitive motility based on recognitive and navigational aspects in both approach and avoidance contexts as well as a category for spontaneous motility. The quality of being-in-a-world emerges as a sui generis form. It is not to be reduced to more preliminary electrochemical processes, but rather utilizes these membrane polarizations, at times quite variously, in its instantiations.[4]

This does not mean that the strictly computational, non organismic modeling in artificial intelligence of advanced forms of memory, syntax, and logic, in digital or parallel, must be rejected simply because it is based on binary switches. It does mean that living organisms, including metazoan neurons and protozoa, do not "work" in this fashion. We already know how greatly the cognitive processes involved in human and computer chess differ (Gardner, 1985). The point here is that this difference goes all the way down to their respective "hard wiring" — a point many cognitive scientists will not want to accept. If these latter insist on starting with on-off connections, their systems may constitute interesting analogs to symbolic cognition and consciousness — and in so doing be quite instructive. However, if the aspiration is to more than an analogy in final output, then their starting point is *dead* wrong.

There is no mind-brain problem at all — no point in a continuum of neuronal complexity at which consciousness is suddenly emergent. There *is* a question of how it is that sentience would be an intrinsic aspect of certain electrochemical processes associated with cell motility — making this an issue more fundamental to biology than to neurology. The key to any notion of "emergence" in science is to locate the level of reality that is involved. The neurotransmitters of such contemporary fascination may well pertain to how consciousness is pooled and segregated within complex neural nets, but they will not tell us how consciousness is created. What we can say is that the behaviors indicating sentience to a surrounding flow co-emerge with electrochemical transductions of that same flow. The interface between protozoan behavior, protozoan electrochemical reactivity, and neuronal polarization locates the most parsimonious and plausible point for an emergence of sentience. Central nervous systems do not create sentience but gather and focus it so as to resonate to more and more differentiated versions of the ecological array.

The Emergence of Self-Referential Cognition in Higher Apes

At the other end of an evolutionary continuum of awareness we can locate the first clear signs of a self-referential consciousness, at least within our own direct evolutionary line, in the multiple capacities emerging in the higher apes (chimpanzees, orangutans, and gorillas).

First, there is the evidence, reviewed by Gordon Gallup (1977), of a fascination with mirrors in the higher apes, which is widely taken as indicating a capacity for self-recognition that seems to be absent in baboons and monkeys. An especially striking demonstration of this nascent sense of self-awareness is found in the ability of the gorilla to recognize as its own a red dot painted on its forehead when first seen in the mirror, as indicated by immediate exploratory touches to the head. Consistent with Mead's analysis of self-awareness as a taking the role of the other toward oneself, such mirror recognition is absent in chimpanzees reared apart from other chimpanzees. Further indication that the recognition of self requires some sort of internalization of social relationship comes from the persistence shown by home-reared chimpanzees, not having been exposed to other chimpanzees, in grouping photographs of themselves with human photographs rather than with those of other chimpanzees.

Along with these indications of a consciousness of self we find other emergent features of human cognition — including the capacity to recombine and rearrange in novel ways the components of physical and social situations. The most famous example here is Wolfgang Köhler's (1926) early demonstration of the spontaneous ability of his captive chimpanzees to stack crates one on top of the other in order to reach food placed beyond normal access. There are also Jane Goodall's (1971) fascinating observations of this same recombinatory capacity applied to social situations in the wild. One of the most striking of several such accounts was the ability of one nondominant chimpanzee to lead the others away from a feeding area — normally the province of an alpha male — in order to return surreptitiously to retrieve bananas that he had spied but that the others had not yet seen. This innovative behavior obviated the ordinary necessity of sharing such a find. There is also indication in Goodall's observations of a kind of aesthetic resonance to natural phenomena, as in the "rain dance" that chimpanzees in the wild do at the first seasonal torrential downpour — tearing off branches and waving them in the air while rushing and jumping about. Finally, of course, we can add the controversial evidence of a proto-symbolic signing ability in specially taught higher apes, to be discussed in greater detail below.

Taken together, the co-emergence of these multiple indicators of self-referential symbolic cognition all seem to rest on or imply an underlying capacity for cross-modal translation. This seems most obvious with signing, where the proto-languages taught can be either visual or haptic. It also seems clear with spontaneous mirror behaviors and the kinesthetic "dance" to sudden rain. It is likely with recombinatory behaviors as well. In Köhler's crate-stacking situation it may be that it is a felt tension between what is seen to be the case and what is wanted kinesthetically that will resolve itself as the recombination of sight and movement in a novel pattern.

Reports of novel deceptive behaviors in parrots and some songbirds, as well as their sustained interest in games played with mirrors (Griffin, 1984), helps to suggest that the emergence of various components of a symbolic capacity can appear within other evolutionary lines than our own. To this we can also add the capabilities for signing and problem solving evinced by dolphins (Herman et al., 1984). If the basis of recombinatory and incipiently symbolic cognition rests in cross-modal translations, we would expect it to appear as an emergent possibility wherever specification in separate perceptual modalities has reached a sufficient point of differentiation to allow the beginnings of hierarchic integration.[5] Perhaps their lack of a manipulable hand ultimately restricts the active kinesthetic structuration available for cross-modal transformations in the songbirds and dolphins.

It is the research on signing behaviors in higher apes — especially chimpanzees — that has caused the greatest controversy within contemporary psychology and philosophy. On the one hand, a rationalist tradition has always argued that language is unique to *Homo sapiens,* and that all other symbolic forms and self-awareness itself depend upon it. From this perspective, there has been immense skepticism over the existence of a genuine proto-linguistic ability in higher primates and much puzzlement over its lack of natural expression in the wild. However, from an evolutionary perspective, as we have seen, we should be puzzled at a defining feature of our own mentality being totally absent in our nearest evolutionary cousins, the chimpanzees, with whom we share approximately 98 percent of our morphological DNA (Gould, 1977). That it might require special laboratory conditions to show proto-linguistic signing may also make sense on the view that an emergent cross-modal translation ability would set up a range of structural potentialities on an entirely new developmental level — one awaiting subsequent functional realizations depending upon the demands and possibilities of the environment.

It is probably fair enough that the earlier, more anecdotal research on signing in higher primates came under such heavy criticism — although not, as we will see, to the point of its condemnation as "pseudo-science" in some intellectual circles. This is all too easy an epithet to use against work that violates one's basic assumptions and so might actually break new ground. The early research in this area tended to concentrate on anecdotally observed instances of novelty in signing, as in one chimpanzee's describing her first encounter with watermelons as "candy drink" — combining separate signs never previously used together. As Seidenberg and Petitto (1978) point out, however, such novel signing, while clearly suggestive, is impossible to evaluate. The complete behavior protocols needed to judge the possibilities of a chance occurrence of such juxtapositions were never provided. Indeed, it does appear that the original behavioral records contain long strings of uninterpretable sign combinations and redundancies, and that many of the hand gestures of the apes were simply undecipherable. In addition, most of this early work measured spontaneous sign production only, rather than the less ambiguous behavioral execution of signed commands from the experimenter. Accordingly, it seemed to many that some combination of association learning and a strategy to keep on signing until the experimenter expressed satisfaction could account for the findings. Terrace (1985) also calls attention to the lack of any fixed syntax or sign order in this work,[6] along with the apparent absence in chimpanzees of the pointing and shared-attention behaviors that seem to constitute the "forms of life" out of which symbolic cognition emerges in human infancy. Chimpanzees are naturally acquisitive and competitive with objects of interest, so that "pointing" could only result in the loss of a potentially coveted object.

The more recent research of Susan Savage-Rumbaugh and colleagues (1983, 1986, 1988) and David Premack (1978, 1983) is, however, noteworthy for its elimination of these difficulties. Testing in this research is now based on chimpanzee behaviors in response to signed experimenter commands (both novel and ordinary), rather than on an open-ended production, and has included preliminary training in pointing, sharing, and joint referring. Savage-Rumbaugh (1983), for instance, developed a paradigm in which a chimpanzee in one room was required to provide the tool, based on signing, that would allow a chimpanzee in another room to retrieve and then share secreted food. Meanwhile, Premack (1978, 1983) described the simultaneous emergence of pointing behaviors, deception, and symbolic categories of "should" or "ought" in signing chimpanzees. The chimpanzees were separated by wire mesh from hidden food whose whereabouts they knew. They could only interact with individual experimenters searching for the food if they developed a capacity for pointing. In previous situations, one of these experimenters always shared food, while the other never did. The "good" experimenter elicited a spontaneous and accurate pointing, while the "bad" experimenter was systematically deceived. Similarly, these chimpanzees were shown videos of "good" and "bad" experimenters trying to solve various physical problems — including crate stacking. The videos were stopped short of resolution and the chimpanzees allowed to pick successful or unsuccessful video endings. They chose success for the "good" and physical disaster for the "bad" experimenters.

Savage-Rumbaugh's (1986, 1988) findings with pygmy chimpanzees (*Pan troglodytes* being the species used in most signing research) are the most startling and thorough in refuting critiques of the earlier signing research. Several pygmy chimps showed spontaneous pointing and gestural communication (twisting movements for opening a bottle) from an early age; and the chimp prodigy Kanzi acquired signing behavior entirely on the basis of his observations of his mother's laboratory sessions. Pygmy chimpanzees show equally accurate performance in novel signing tasks whether they see the lexigram for the object described or hear it pronounced — suggesting, in contrast to all other higher primates studied, a cross-modal ability that integrates hearing, at least to some extent, with sight and touch. In addition, and echoing Herman, Richards, and Wolz's (1984) related findings with bottle-nosed dolphins, these chimpanzees show an ability to use and follow a fixed syntax (agent-verb-recipient) entirely absent in previous studies. In ostensible demonstration of Mead's capacity to take the role of the other as basic to genuine symbolic communication, Kanzi is able to form three-word sentences in which he is neither agent nor recipient ("person x tickle person y"), which Savage-Rumbaugh points out has never been found in previous chimpanzee signing. Finally, in what seems to be the first stage of a capacity for internalized "inner speech" (Vygotsky, 1962), Kanzi goes off by himself with his portable signing board and spontaneously signs various unsuggested activities — such as "piling pebbles" or "hiding" — and then on his own initiative performs them.

We find in the higher primates — with dolphins and perhaps parrots — the seeds of self-awareness, empathy and deception, recombinatory problem-solving in physical and social situations, proto–sign language (at the least), and aesthetics. These cover what we might term the "horizontal" dimension of many of Gardner's fundamental symbolic frames. If we ask instead, however, what seems to be completely absent from higher primates that helps to define our own consciousness, we can begin to locate a missing "vertical" dimension. This would be anchored at one end by the "instinctual" and "driven" conflicts of Freud and at the other by "imaginative absorption" and spirituality.

I have already suggested that a full synthesis of the formal ratios of simultaneity to sequentiality in vision, vocalization, and touch-movement would, in addition to opening up a capacity for symbolic cognition, also fuse or coalesce need systems that are separate among lower mammals and tied to modality specific releasors. These remain separate even within the higher primates. For instance, the physical behaviors of human sexuality — both in foreplay as well as in the more striking sexual perversions — all show a fusion between behaviors generally kept distinct in other land mammals. Foreplay and sexual caressing involve a mixture of mating and nurturance behaviors, whereas kissing and touching are found in the higher primates chiefly in nonsexual affiliative contacts and originate in the mother-infant dyad. Correspondingly, sado-masochism reflects fusions of mating behaviors with those of territoriality or dominance, more than occasionally including predation, all of which are separated need systems "below" us. Finally, even though Goodall (1986) reported occasional instances of chimpanzees' "killing" a member of another band caught in their territory, not only does the final death seem to be a non-intentional by-product of the damage inflicted, but there is a conspicuous absence of the sort of "message," or just plain "fun," involved in the poking out of eyes or the castration that occurs in their human counterparts. Is it that chimps are not "smart" enough? They sign and recombine. They dismember their prey during occasional hunting activity. Perhaps they lack . . . imagination.

Freud's "drives" of aggression and sexuality, so visible in human politics and mythology, turn out to be amalgams of needs such as mating, nurturance, territoriality-dominance, and predation that are generally distinct and non-overlapping in other mammals (Eibl-Eibesfeldt, 1971). It seems most likely that modality-specific need releasors would themselves fuse into emergent recombinations with a cross-modal fusion that included vocalization and the full range of affect, along with kinesthetic and visual patterning. The result would be a "drivenness" and "conflict" based on need fusions that can neither be fully integrated nor fully segregated. These would constitute the species-specific human dilemmas that are the focus of both Freud's psychoanalysis and the various world mythologies of such interest to Jung.

The other "form of life" completely missing from accounts of higher primates in captivity or in the wild might best be labeled "imaginative absorption." Its cross-cultural development would appear as the shamanism of hunter-gatherer societies.

There is no sign whatsoever of individual apes spontaneously entering tonically immobile trances, after which they are especially nurturant or affiliative toward other apes, who would then respond with a temporary "state-specific" subordination or themselves become "absorbed" in turn. There might seem no reason in principle why this could not happen, especially given "regression" models of transformations of consciousness, but it does not. Higher primates sign, show self-awareness, recombine, and manifest the beginnings of an aesthetic sensitivity, but they do not go into spontaneous, nondefensive "trance."[7] We have already seen that the behavioral-physiological state of tonic immobility — as the setting in us for the fullest realizations of numinous or mystical experience — is also found prominently as part of the defensive behaviors of preyed-upon species. Higher primates, however, are more or less dominant within their ecological niches, so it is only the untoward predatory emergency that would find them tonically immobile. The puzzle is that tonic immobility is central to a human form of life, and we are the dominant species on the planet. We might expect, then, that our trance capability would reflect some transformation of the more concrete form of tonic immobility found in prey, and that this transformation would have something to do with the completion in us of a capacity for symbolic cognition only preliminarily emergent in the higher apes.

If we ask what the difference is between the human and higher-primate neocortex that might account for the absence of spontaneous imaginative absorption in primates, we arrive again at our more complete three-way cross-modal transformations. We add cross-modally based vocalization, which would be primarily responsible for opening out a dimension of sequential time ahead that ends in "death" — the unsayable as our symbolic "predator." The metaphors of "light" and "open space" would be the only structures of symbolic cognition open enough and inclusive enough to contain that dimension and reinterpret it positively. Indeed, strong evidence of the abstract symbolic basis of spontaneous tonic immobility in human trance states and deep meditation comes from its contrast with a more concrete form of tonic immobility that also occurs in human beings, as it does in all vertebrates, when they are physically endangered and overwhelmed — as in victimization by crime or war. This latter response is associated with feelings of numbness, sudden loss of emotion, and the absence of any sense of "infinity" typical of ecstatic trance. In addition, physically overwhelmed people and animals can both go into shock and actually die, whereas this does not occur with the "symbolic" death-rebirth experiences of deep meditation or LSD — no matter how "literal" that experiential cessation may actually feel. In short, our emergently human form of trance is symbolic unto its very foundations, which seem rather to reflect the symbolic reuse and reorganization of a more concrete tonic immobility.

William James (1902) insisted that the state of mind in mystical states was not just affective or emotional but specifically "noetic" — the conceptual aspect of its powerful felt meanings requiring the categories of abstract metaphysics for its expression. The reductionist view would be that these meanings constitute a "projection" of symbolic intelligence into a "lower" phenomenon of limbic discharge and tension release — part of an "anxiety buffer" function for religious experience. We will see later, however, that there is considerable evidence in support of the view that abstract cross-modal translations and metaphors are intrinsic to these states and not superimposed upon them.

Part III The Phenomenology of Consciousness

In telling again and again that something is frightening some one that one is convincing some other one that that one is frightened by that thing and it is a thing that would not be frightening any one, of that every one is certain. . . . This thing that is such a thing, this thing that is existing, that is a frightening thing to one, is a way of living of very many being living, a way of living of some who are being ones steadily working, who are ones steadily saving, who are ones paying what they are always needing to be paying that is enough to be ones going on being living. . . . This is certainly entirely frightening some one . . . some one is frightened by such ones being existing and is telling it again and again.
Gertrude Stein, "Rue De Rennes"

. . . and all the queer little streets and pink and blue and yellow houses and the rosegardens and the jessamine and geraniums and cactuses and Gibraltar as a girl where I was a Flower of the mountain yes when I put the rose in my hair like the Andalusian girls used or shall I wear a red yes and how he kissed me under the Moorish wall and I thought well as well him as another and then I asked him with my eyes

to ask again yes and then he asked me would I yes to say yes my
mountain flower and first I put my arms around him yes and drew him
down to me so he could feel my breasts all perfumed yes and his heart
was going like mad and yes I said yes I will Yes.
James Joyce, *Ulysses*

"Oh, so you're with them, you stinker! bastard! Oh... so you're with
them!"

And wham! slam!... *his skull again... square in the skull...* bam!...
what's he packing?... a hammer? wham!... *he passes out... he hasn't*
seen the monster... hasn't had time... who is it?

"I'm Charon, see!"

He comes to... he sees the being!... a giant!... really something: at
least three... four times my size!... built like a barrel... with a face...
that face!... like an ape... part tiger... part ape... part tiger... and
heavy!... the whole boat listed... wearing... he's still telling me his
story... some kind of frock coat... but a uniform frock coat... embroi-
dered with silver tears... but the most terrific: his cap... as big as he
was... an admiral's cap!... tall!... and wide!... embroidered with gold!

"You'll see him... his oar in your face... you'll see him!" A promise...

"He splits their skulls with an oar..."

"Oh?" I act surprised. Charon's oar he's talking about...
Louis-Ferdinand Céline, *Castle to Castle*

6 William James and the Stream of Consciousness: Metaphor Without, Mirror Within

The Idea of Phenomenology in James and Its Multiple Influence

William James, in his chapter in *The Principles of Psychology* (1890) entitled "The Stream of Thought," was probably the first western thinker and scientist to address ordinary lived consciousness as an empirical phenomenon in its own right. How curious that it is this recent. In so doing, he also addressed the relationship between consciousness and physical reality in ways which have not yet been fully assimilated. James's work informed subsequent schools of thought that are generally held to be antithetical — in psychology, functionalism and behaviorism as well as the Gestalt tradition; in philosophy, Wittgenstein as well as Husserl, Heidegger, and Merleau-Ponty. Since subsequent approaches to consciousness within psychology can in no sense be said to have "gotten past" James, we will need to engage his phenomenology of awareness as "streaming," to consider it as metaphor and as physical and neural reality. James becomes the fulcrum of this present endeavor, as well as its point of expansion into more contemporary approaches to transformations of consciousness and their relation to symbolic cognition.

In many ways, William James is one of our first modern thinkers. Within what he would help to establish as an emergent "science" of psychology, and writing in the wake of Nietzsche, he offers his own North American version of pluralism and the relativity of truth to human purposes. Niels Bohr mentioned his reading of James on consciousness as foreshadowing the principles of complementarity and indeterminism in quantum mechanics (Holton, 1968). Just as light becomes both wave and particles, consciousness is both substantive and transitive, both a pulsing and a continuous wave: "Nature is simple and invariable; makes no leaps or makes nothing but leaps; . . . what do all such principles express save our sense of how pleasantly our intellect would feel if it had a Nature of that sort to deal with?" (James, 1890, vol. 2, p. 672).

From his early writings, where he emphasizes the continuous "flow" of awareness, to his later discussion of its moment-by-moment "pulsing," James describes how the one feature is always found within the other. In "The Stream of Thought," he distinguishes within a primary flow of consciousness the coexistence of both "transitive" and "substantive" aspects. There are no thinglike units or elements in awareness, he says. "Images" and "feelings" are the relatively substantive lingerings and circlings of awareness. They reflect the slower parts of the same stream whose more rapid, transitive flows give our self-aware consciousness its sense of direction and relation. The transitive side of our experience consists in the "halos" or "fringes" that Gendlin would later term "felt meaning" — the impalpable sense giving birth to more explicit "thoughts." The very attempt to capture this flow of consciousness in our introspective awareness, as with the later indeterminism of subatomic physics, transforms the flight of awareness ever past itself into the sensory-imaginal "smears" of laboratory introspectionism: "As a snowflake crystal caught in the warm hand is no longer a crystal but a drop, so, instead of catching the feeling of relation moving to its term, we find we have caught some substantive thing. . . . The attempt at introspective analysis in these cases is in fact like seizing a spinning top to catch its motion or trying to turn up the gas quickly enough to see how the darkness looks" (James, 1890, vol. 1, p. 244). We know how much contemporary physics has learned from just such attempts in its own sphere, however, and we have already seen how systematic introspection actually elicited altered states.

The William James of *A Pluralistic Universe* (1912) might at first seem to have shifted his ground and to be recasting a continuous flow in terms of its moment-by-moment drops or pulses. Our experience, he says, comes to us in drops — as does time itself. Yet the drops that James says come whole or not at all from the bottle spout are also merged within the bottle into a single fluid medium that bears no trace of its pulselike manifestation. Indeed, James insists that each pulse or moment of awareness has within it the same transitive streaming of his earlier analysis: "The concrete pulses of experience appear pent in by no such definite limits as our conceptual substitutes for them are confined by. . . . The tiniest feeling that we can possibly have comes with an earlier and a later part and with a sense of their continuous procession. . . . Every smallest state of consciousness, concretely taken, overflows its own definition" (James, 1912, pp. 256, 258). In both early and later James, our self-referential consciousness is simultaneously momentary and continuous — pulses within wave, waves within pulse. Again, James foreshadows here the later physics of light as both particles and waves.

Something very similar, and presumably the perceptual template for James's self-referential stream, has already emerged from Gibson's ecological array. On the one hand, perception is a continuous asymmetrical flow. On the other, there are the periodic symmetrical loomings of surfaces into which it is transformed under the aspect of recognitive needs. The patternings of surfaces and edges are transformed by locomotion into an encompassing envelope of whence-whither gradients of flow, which simultaneously locates the creature within its "there." At the same time, but under the influence of organismic need, specific surfaces must be made to loom up or recede, expanding or contracting symmetrically in the context of approach or avoidance. On other occasions, however, when need does not predominate, these very same surfaces are rendered part of the asymmetrical flow envelope, as the organism slides on past them. Just as James found drops within waves, and vice versa, Neisser's recognition of significant pattern and Gibson's "direct perception" are coexistent organizations within immediate sentience. It is not for nothing that Gibson cited James with respect to the "streaming perspective" of perception (Gibson, 1979; Reed, 1988). I will consider later (chapter 13) whether this duality of perception would itself be the deeper template for the complementarity and indeterminism of modern physical theory.

What was entirely new in James, and to an extent in Henri Bergson (1889), is the attempt at a descriptive, empirical phenomenology of immediate consciousness. This requires what Edmund Husserl, so influenced by James, would later term a "bracketing" or suspension of the common-sense assumptions that would confuse consciousness as an encompassing medium with the world that it is "of" and "about." Hegel's *Phenomenology of Spirit* (1807) remained a purely abstract hypothesis of what would later be termed transpersonal development. Meanwhile, most of Husserl's writings set forth formal structures that themselves remained "about" the idea of a phenomenology, rather than the sort of direct descriptions of experience put forward initially by James and then found again in Heidegger (1927) and Sartre (1939). Not that James always maintained this radically descriptive intent, separated from both common sense and scientific assumptions about what consciousness should be like. For instance, he supports his demonstration of a flow that is sensibly continuous yet constantly changing with secondary and doubtful justifications from his understanding of neural processes. These latter, he says, constantly change, yet overlap, because some brain processes are always dying out while others come to the fore. Hence, consciousness must do the same. Rather than assuming such a direct translation from neural networks to ongoing experience, we might better "explain" these features of our self-referential symbolic consciousness by the primary flow of perception on which it is based. There is no reason for us to assume, with James, that the line between consciousness and brain can be crossed without considerably more speculation than a "radical description" should allow.

Yet a descriptive phenomenology of consciousness does emerge here as a distinctly modern possibility, requiring specialized terms for variations in consciousness and subjective states not in place until late in the nineteenth century (Hillman, 1971). Perhaps, with Heidegger (1977), the triumph of "objectivity" and "utility" had left consciousness over as its nonrational remainder — and so ripe for its own "discovery" as a separate realm by modern individuals, autonomous to the point of isolation. Yet to dismiss the enterprise begun by James and Bergson as simply the projective expression of a normative narcissism would be too facile. We will see (chapter 9) that the empirical terms for mind in Greek and Sanskrit originally referred to an embodied vitality, heart, flowing blood, and breath. All these usages had in common a streaming based on metaphors derived from the qualities of water, air, and fire. Whatever the underlying alienation beneath the various formulations of consciousness and subjectivity in this century, they are connected to an ur-phenomenology that lies implicit within classical usage.

The later James captured this sense of consciousness as always vitally embodied and present in the physical world — so central to Heidegger, Merleau-Ponty, and even Gibson. He discusses the body as the unique point of intersection between an objective and subjective series of facts based on the world and our experience of it: "Sometimes I treat my body purely as a part of outer nature. Sometimes, again, I think of it as 'mine,' I sort it with the 'me' and then certain local changes and determinations in it pass for spiritual happenings. Its breathing is my 'thinking.' . . . Everything circles around it and it is felt from its point of view. The word 'I,' then, is primarily a noun of position just like 'this' and 'here' " (James, 1912, pp. 80, 90). It is certainly testimony to the dilemmas of our modernism and postmodernism that Varela, Thompson, and Rosch (1992) are still calling for a view of human cognition as embodied and vitally present in the world. James's "stream" already presupposes and includes this inseparability of consciousness and world, mind and body.

The Stream of Consciousness as Self-Transforming Dialogue

Several features that James ascribes to the ongoing stream of awareness can seem contradictory: the stream is subjectively imposed and involuntary, yet always feels personal and "mine." It constantly changes and transforms itself, but is sensibly continuous. These ostensible contraries, however, all follow from the self-referential, recombinatory, and cross-modal bases of symbolic cognition — which will finally stand forth more clearly in the study of transpersonal states than in the more daydreaming consciousness of James and related stream-of-consciousness novelists.

James begins his analysis in *The Principles* by calling attention to the way that consciousness, once noticed as such, simply "goes on," independent of our own volition. He says, in a way certainly familiar to all scientists and artists who have felt that their best ideas come to them as if from outside, that it would be more descriptively accurate if we said "it thinks" or "feeling happening now," in the same way that we say "it rains." Simultaneously, each moment of the stream feels "mine," with a sensed "hereness" at the core of our feeling of personal presence. Any implied contradiction is resolved, however, when in his next chapter, "The Consciousness of Self," he points out that there is no phenomenal "I" in immediate consciousness. As further developed by G. H. Mead, consciousness itself is the only possible source for any spontaneous originating "I." Each of its successive moments wells forth in the form of a me-you dialogue that has more to do with multiple personality and its incipient normative roots than with our more common-sense notion of a central self: "The passing Thought then seems to be the Thinker; and though there *may* be another non phenomenal Thinker behind that, so far we do not seem to need him to express the facts. . . . It is this trick which the nascent thought has of immediately taking up the expiring thought and "adopting" it, which is the foundation of the appropriation of most of the remoter constituents of the self. Who owns the last self owns the self before the last, for what possesses the possessor possesses the possessed" (James, 1890, vol. 1, pp. 339, 340, 342). Faced with this curious impersonality of our ongoing personal awareness, and at the same point where Hindu thought posited a transcendent self (Atman) and Buddhism the no-self, James opts for the latter route — with "I" as nothing other than the ongoing streaming itself.

What James calls attention to here is what I have referred to as the dialogic organization of human consciousness (chapter 2). Consciousness feels as if imposed by an "other" precisely because, in order to observe it as an empirical reality in its own right, we must take up a role toward it. As in any conversation where we choose to remain still and observant — or meditatively and aesthetically "open" — the one who would have a dialogue with us must thereby take the active role and show us more and more of itself. In meditation and systematic introspection, the "other" is ultimately the deepest and most implicit levels of our own mind. This other will culminate in the abstract felt meanings and spontaneous transformations of nonverbal presentational states. On the more immediately accessible level of ordinary daydreaming and fantasy, many an original thought — indisputably "mine" once understood — has first been provided by some imagined interlocutor. This is the principle that was explicitly developed in Jung's "active imagination," the core of his therapeutic technique, based on deliberate imaginary dialogues with fantasy figures.

Our immediate consciousness just comes to us, finished and imposed. We now say that the "other" which so addresses us with our own sentience is "brain" or "unconscious." We miss the empirical phenomenology of an ongoing dialogic structure that is given as the immediate form of our experience and which equally allowed other cultures to see consciousness as "done" by heart, spirit, or deity. Both the modern and ancient leaps toward explanation have actually occluded this dialogic organization, which requires some account in its own right. How much of the intuitive plausibility of our view of the brain as "cause" of everything psychological is itself an unwitting elaboration of just this implicit phenomenology?

One of the most striking illustrations of the self-referential dialogic organization of immediate consciousness comes from what are often referred to as Schneider's "first-rank" symptoms of schizophrenia and acute psychotic onset (Mellor, 1970). These can be considered an intensification of forms of experience always present in all of us but ordinarily not noticed as such. Patients complain of "thoughts out loud," "made" thoughts, feelings, and volitions, and involuntary insertions and withdrawals of thoughts. In the first instance, these phenomena seem to reflect a greater-than-ordinary, if involuntary, introspective sensitivity to the actual dialogic features of our awareness. But in the withdrawn and highly stressful context of psychotic onset, these phenomena are not recognized as such and so are unwittingly projected outward onto an imagined external agent—and eventually one of increasingly magical powers (Hunt, 1985a; Hoffman, 1986). Initially, however, the actual thoughts inserted or made do not seem to differ in form or content from the ordinary experience of James's introspected stream, except that it is not ordinary to notice these ongoing features in their own right. Daniel Paul Schreber's (1903) minute analysis of the annoying peculiarities of his auditory hallucinations will actually sound quite familiar to any reader of Vygotsky (1962) on the incomplete, agrammatical organization of "inner speech." Freud (1933) even suggested that paranoid delusions of being continuously observed reflect an accurate introspective or "endopsychic" awareness of the self-observational core of the superego. What is unusual in these experiences is not their form but the involuntary introspective sensitization that makes them conscious and felt as unwanted intrusions.

A more constructive version of this same sensitization to the dialogue of ongoing awareness comes from the observations of Herbert Silberer (1909, 1912), later extended by Wilson Van Dusen (1972), on the spontaneously "autosymbolic" nature of certain forms of visual imagery. These can be especially obvious at sleep onset and, I might add, in meditative practice. Silberer noted a number of different categories of such autosymbolism, all of which self-referentially depict aspects of the person's immediate situation or state. In his "material" category, the ongoing content of one's verbal thinking is immediately translated into an imagistic form—as, when thinking about Kant's notion of transsubjective shared judgments, Silberer suddenly sees a large, translucent circle with the heads of numerous people held within it. In "functional" autosymbolism, it is the ongoing mode or form of cognition itself that is self-depicted — as when, on his trying and failing to remember a particular idea while falling asleep, an image appears to Silberer of a sullen office worker who refuses to hand over a needed "file." Especially interesting, if cross-modal kinesthetic translation is essential to all metaphor (Hunt, 1985a; Lakoff, 1987), are Silberer's "somatic" autosymbols. Here, it is one's immediate bodily state or position that is translated into visual imagery — as when a burning headache is transformed into a hypnagogic image of wooden matches standing upside down with their heads pressed together.

Van Dusen (1972) concluded that such imagery and spontaneous presentational states in general illustrate this most fundamental tendency of the mind to represent or show itself self-referentially. Jung (1944) similarly followed Silberer's (1917) earlier lead in viewing mythological systems, especially medieval alchemy, as "constructive" or "anagogic" self-depictions of the cognitive and emotional organization of mind. These depictions go beyond what could be captured in the linguistic formulations of our explicit self-awareness. All this "goes on" as an imposed dialogue in the form of spontaneous imagery and metaphor. The imagery itself is an unwitting introspection.

We move to James's view that consciousness is always changing, never giving exactly the same streaming twice, yet also sensibly continuous and without any genuine divisions. This was the core of his stream metaphor. Streaming water, and for that matter air currents (Schwenk, 1965), shift their flow constantly while endlessly repeating the same eddies and turbulence. Thus, James can emphasize both continuous change and the tendency of our awareness to synthesize and fill in any incipient division — from the visual blind spot to the automatic merging of the night-before with the morning-after upon awakening. Synthesis is a key attribute of sentience on whatever level, but James's description of a continuous recombinatory novelty would seem to rest on the self-referential organization of human consciousness. A consciousness referring inherently to itself, dialogic in all its manifestations, will change itself immediately as a result of self-scrutiny on the moment before — this being the introspective version of Gödel's mathematical incompleteness and Mead's self-transforming I-me dialogue. In general, James's attributes of consciousness would seem to follow if we posit a self-referential consciousness that reuses the whence-whither, here-there dimensions of Gibson's flowing perceptual array, combined with the immediate manifestations of the cross-modal transformations constituting that reuse.

James speaks of a transitive whence-whither flow of the stream of thought, which Gibson (1979) even credits as the model for his more primary flow envelope of perception. The more rapid, transitive aspects of James's self-conscious stream are the intrinsically vague "halos" or penumbras of felt meaning, in full and unrepresentable flight between the more "substantive," slower, and so more specifiable points of conclusion and consolidation. Transitive states include "feelings of relation," as in the sensed meanings of "and," "if," and "but" that Werner and Kaplan (1963) would later describe and draw as physiognomies of gesture. James also discusses "feelings of tendency" or "direction," which would in turn figure so prominently among the Würzburg impalpables. Thoughts are given moment by moment in a characteristic rhythm that always contains their entire felt meaning, but differently emphasized within each moment. We think, "The pack of cards is on the table," and at the moment where felt emphasis has shifted to "cards" there is still the dying echo within it of "pack of" and the vague anticipation of "on the table."

Gertrude Stein (1951) was James's student at Harvard, which had its influence on her later "stream-of-consciousness" fiction. She saw every person as having their own "bottom nature" — a characteristic pace and rhythm of emphasis and repetition that was their personal organization of flowing consciousness. The later laboratory research of Jerome Singer (1977, 1978) and his colleagues (Klinger, 1978, Starker, 1978) can be seen as a development of the notion that there would be characteristic individual differences in emphasis within the features of James's stream and that these would appear as the various styles of daydreaming. These researchers distinguish three varieties of intense daydreaming, overlapping into styles of nocturnal dreaming as well. It does seem that each style of ongoing consciousness shows a differing configuration of James's features, as illustrated in the samples of stream-of-consciousness fiction that stand as epigraphs to Part Three. First, there is the "guilty-dysphoric" manifestation of consciousness — negative in tone, obsessive in its endless repetitions, and certainly well illustrated in Stein's own experimental writing. The ruminations in her excerpt repeat like backward flowing eddies in a stream, circling back on themselves slowly, yet gradually shifting their emphasis as they proceed. Molly Bloom's final hypnagogic soliloquy in James Joyce's *Ulysses* offers the best version of Singer's "positive-vivid" style — rushing ahead, wish-fulfilling, and insistently hedonistic. As surely, the carefully crafted delirium in Céline's later writing well represents the pulses and bursts of the "anxious-distractible" or "mind wandering" style — with its intrusive bizarreness, rage and fear, and confusional qualities. In the latter, the more impersonal aspects of James's stream come most to the fore. This is reflected in the imagery research of Foulkes and Fleischer (1975), who found bizarre daydreaming imagery to be separate from its more mundane narrative expressions.

Our paramount concern here will be to develop "flow" as the metaphor that best characterizes ongoing consciousness and then consider its various manifestations in physical nature. But we note in passing how the more abstract forms of experience in presentational states involve a direct awareness of the general features of James's stream as such, relatively independent of its more practical, personally preoccupied expressions. Csikszentmihalyi (1990) characterizes direct experiences of feeling immediately present in the moment, closely related to Maslow's (1962) spontaneous peak or ecstatic experiences, as the direct awareness of "flow." Correspondingly, the later James (1912), in a manner reminiscent of both Heidegger and Buddhist meditation (chapter 11), describes "pure experience" as the sense of "that" prior to awareness of any specific "what."

The "object" of experience in these states is the direct sensing of existence — an abstract symbolic reconstitution of Gibson's "here." "Pure experience" in this sense is well illustrated in James's earlier account of the experience of a patient emerging from anesthesia: "During the [anesthesia] there is absolute psychic annihilation, the absence of all consciousness; then at the beginning of coming to, one has at a certain moment, a vague, limitless, infinite feeling — a sense of *existing in general* without the least trace of distinction between the me and the not me" (James, 1890, vol. 1, p. 273). It is the formal features of ongoing consciousness that turn out to be the "content" of at least one dimension of transpersonal or spiritual states. This will make considerable sense if we understand these states as expressions of a self-reference for its own sake (presentational), in contrast to the subordination of our self-referential capacity to the representational symbolisms of a more practically preoccupied "everyday life."

Stream as Metaphor—Stream as Reality

The Later James on the Inseparability of Consciousness and World

In 1904 James wrote an essay entitled "Does Consciousness Exist?" (in James, 1912). His answer, after so many years of wrestling with the issue, was "no" — at least not as an entity in its own right, with any uniquely defining characteristics that are separable from what it is of, about, and for. There is no inherent duality between consciousness and world. Rather, they are different organizations of the same underlying stuff or "thatness," a view remarkably resonant with Buddhism. The contrast, he says, is like paint in the pot as opposed to paint spread on the canvas. Or, just as a point can be simultaneously present on two lines where they intersect, the "that" of our existence is the point of intersection of a subjective series radiating out of our bodily "here" and of an objective series of outward facts. The room we are in, he says, is alternately a fact of consciousness and a fact of world, depending on how it is "taken."

The question James leaves for us, then, is how we are now to "take" his empirical descriptions of consciousness. Is it a continuous streaming or a moment-by-moment pulsing? Has "flow" in all its aspects merely become one physical metaphor among the many that could equally illuminate our experience? The physical world offers a myriad of such metaphoric mirrors, such that we could as well rewrite James's famous chapter as "The Winds of Thought," "The Fire of Awareness," "Diamond Thoughts," and so on. Would this make all our self-knowledge, to the extent it must rest on natural metaphor, relative and arbitrary? Or, perhaps there is something about flow — among other possible metaphors — that is not arbitrary but reflects the actual organization of perception as resonant to the moving physical surround. After all, in evolution we begin in a liquid, flowing medium, which is reconstituted for the mammalian embryo. Now, air currents surround us with an identically organized, encompassing medium (Schwenk, 1965). Water, air, and fire, as the major metaphors for the formal qualities of awareness, all have in common the properties of a turbulent flow in constant transformation. These same properties are central in mythology, philosophy, and the etymologies of words for "mind" in all languages, and they have now become the focus of contemporary nonlinear dynamics. Perhaps our self-awareness and the perception that it reorganizes is patterned in terms of flow properties "mirrored" in from the most fundamental features of the physical surround for living, motile organisms. If so, then James's stream is both a self-referential metaphor and a mirror of the physical reality most adjacent to the life-world.

Metaphor

Vico (1744) was probably the first to point out the seeming necessity of using the forms of physical nature as metaphors in order to refer to our own experience. He also called attention to the etymological origins of the comparatively few words in all major languages that are devoted exclusively to psychological reference (for example, emotion, anxiety, and happiness). Their original usages had an exclusively physical and so metaphoric reference (physical movement, being caught in a narrow defile, and chance, respectively).

Within a more cognitive tradition, Solomon Asch (1961), the anthropologist Claude Levi-Strauss (1969), and, as we shall see, Jung (1944) on alchemy have principally developed this notion that any differentiated representation of our own experience — personally and collectively — will rest on a largely unwitting utilization of physical processes as the necessary outer mirrors for self-reference. As both Levi-Strauss and Jung pointed out, this places the animism of native mythologies in a very different and nonprimitive light. They become systematic organizations of a metaphoric self-reference, the key to which we may well have lost. Asch demonstrates how we would lack any adequate vocabulary for self-awareness without the "double-function" words that refer to both physical properties and human experience. We say that someone faces a "hard" decision, or that someone is "deep" or "shallow," "colorful" or "rigid." We "carry" thoughts and feelings "in" the mind, hopes are "kindled," and insight comes in "flashes." Indeed "depth" psychology, in seeking a naturalistic account of our "inmost" reality, speaks of "splits" in a primal self and their potential "fusion." Arnheim (1969) picks up this same point on the metaphoric and so perceptual bases of all self-reference: "Profundity of mind . . . is named in English by a word that contains the Latin *fundus*, i.e. bottom. . . . Depth is not merely a convenient metaphor to describe the mental phenomenon but the only possible way of even conceiving of that notion. Mental depth is not thinkable without an awareness of physical depth. Hence the figurative quality of all theoretical speech" (Arnheim, 1969, p. 232).

I suggest that it is the initial organization of self-referential knowing in the mother-infant mirroring situation, generalized into the cross-modal translation of perceptual dimensions, that finally allows us to locate these more inaccessible and abstract features of our own experience. They are reflected back in all the phenomena of nature that flow and pulse "outwardly" in the same way that we do "within." Clouds, hearth fires, and tumbling mountain streams have always been sources of a fascinated absorption within which we seem to find ourselves. This is an exteriorized version of Silberer's and Van Dusen's autosymbolic imagery reflecting back our ongoing experience in sensory-imaginal structures. It is hard to see how we could understand the cognitive processes involved in such metaphoric self-reference other than as a cross-modal visual-kinesthetic synthesis. What is seen without resonates to abstract-expressive kinestheses within. Correspondingly, it becomes more plausible why models of mind shared by ancient Greece and India (Onians, 1951) would picture what we now call "consciousness" as contained not within the brain, but rather directly within the moving breath or blood — since these flow in the same way as the currents of air and water in which we have always found our consciousness as stream.[1]

Jung's fascination with alchemy becomes more understandable here. In his later writings — *Psychology and Alchemy* (1944), *The Psychology of the Transference* (1946), and *Mysterium Coniunctionis* (1963) — Jung engages in an initially bewildering mixing of his own psychological terminology with the language of alchemy. He sees alchemy as a metaphoric system for systematic self-awareness that may go deeper "within" than the more imprecise abstractions of modern psychology. Many of the alchemists themselves understood the processes of dissolving, sublimating, and mixing of mercury and sulphur as the chemical analogues of water and fire, and the resulting expansions, congealings, and flowings into diverse patterns, as a spiritual and meditative enterprise of personal transformation. For some, attaining the philosopher's stone not only required a corresponding purification of the soul of the alchemist but was actually seen as an attempt to reconstitute the Anthropos — the primal human condition before the fall of Adam and Eve.

For Jung and James Hillman (1978), there is an imagistic precision of psychological reference in these operations of the alchemist, in contrast to our more conceptual and removed psychological language. Jung argues that alchemy was as much an incipient system of psychology as it was a proto-chemistry. This is brought home by the image of the Uroboros, a major symbol of the alchemical process, portrayed as a serpent consuming itself — a powerful depiction of the transforming self-reference of consciousness pursued for its own sake. Similarly, the *prima materia* to be dissolved in the initial *nigredo* was often described in obviously projective terms as including substances such as menstrual blood, semen, feces, and animal fetuses. Its initial dissolution is sometimes described as "burning the salamander," an image reminiscent of the phylogenetic regression metaphors of both LSD experience and MacLean's "triune brain."

Alchemy is also, and not coincidentally, a precursor of the current interest in nonlinear dynamics. The alchemists, like some contemporary workers within chaos theory, were interested in the way that patterns or form constants from all of nature would "self-organize" out of the cross-flows of dynamic turbulence. Consider the following alchemical observations, quoted by Jung and resonant with both nonlinear dynamics and the psychology of transpersonal and psychedelic states:

> Take common rainwater a good quantity . . . preserve it well sealed in glass vessels for at least ten days . . . place in a wooden vessel . . . and set it in the sun about midday in a secret or secluded spot. When this has been done, take a drop of the consecrated red wine and let it fall in the water, and you will instantly perceive a fog and thick darkness on the top of the water, such as also was at the first creation. Then put in two drops and you will see the light coming forth from the darkness; whereupon little by little put in every half of each quarter hour, first three, then four, then five, then six drops . . . and you will see with your own eyes one thing after another appearing . . . on top of the water, how God created all things in six days and how it all came to pass, and such secrets as are not to be spoken aloud and I have also not power to reveal.
>
> They say . . . that different names are given to the stone on account of the wonderful variety of figures that appear in the course of the work . . . just as we sometimes imagine in the clouds or in the fire strange shapes of animals, reptiles, or trees, I found similar things . . . when the body is dissolved, then will appear sometimes two branches, sometimes three or more, sometimes also the shapes of reptiles. (Jung, 1944, p. 235, 237)

We could say that chaos theory, along with related interests in the self-organization of forms, is the direct historical continuation of these early alchemical preoccupations, otherwise so outside our mainstream scientific tradition. From the perspective of nonlinear dynamics, the alchemists were correct in their assertions that they were "present at creation." In this sense their descriptions and pictorial images call attention to the emergent self-organization of the same form constants at all levels of physical reality that is again of such contemporary interest. They also exemplify the flow dynamics of complex cross-modal cognition, since the alchemist will kinesthetically feel what he or she sees. Under it all, and the secret of its fascination, will be the fluid dynamics of the envelope of flow that is the perceptual array of all motile organisms.

Reality

It becomes apparent that the streaming and flow with which James characterizes self-referential consciousness, and Gibson the ecological array, are not merely arbitrary metaphors. Asymmetrical flows, meanders, and spirals are among the most fundamental form constants on all levels of physical reality, "self-organizing" out of the dynamics of turbulence. Meanwhile, the more symmetrical forms resulting from explosive "bursts" and their more contained manifestation as branching or filigree patterns are equally basic in nature (Stevens, 1974). We have already seen that these latter forms must also be basic to the explosive symmetrical looming of recognized surfaces during locomotion. Similarly, flow gradients are the key constituents of Gibson's moving ecological array. We can now go further and see, in particular, that the "stream" of James and Gibson directly mirrors the principles of organization of the level of physical reality most directly adjacent to the sentient life-space. This can be seen both in the actual features of water currents, as the original ecological niche for all sentient creatures, and in the very bodily shapes of motile sentient beings.

Keeping in mind Gibson's observations on the lamination of textured surfaces during locomotion, it is interesting to find the same phenomenon within physically flowing water itself. The surrounding resistance created by embankments causes a backward eddying termed "laminar flow" (Schwenk, 1965). Here the edges of the flowing main current continuously circle back and then forward again — creating the backwardly flowing currents of such fascination to children following the seemingly paradoxical course of a floating stick along the edge of a stream. Thus every flowing current creates its own backward streaming lamination, much like Gibson's array. When the resulting turbulence of these cross-currents is great enough, either from laminar flow or physical barriers within the flow, these backwardly spiraling eddies create vortices, or open funnels, within the turbulent cross-flows.

This brings us to the physical shapes assumed by primitive motile creatures, which directly reflect these same liquid dynamics. D'Arcy Thompson (1961) was perhaps the first to show how simple organisms actually look like the flow dynamics of vortices, drops, and splashes. For instance, ink dropped in water, or oil dropped into paraffin, makes patterns strikingly like the shape of jellyfish (fig. 3), and freeze-frame photographs of splashes look like polyps (fig. 4). In figure 5 we see the identity between colored jets of water forced into a surrounding watery medium and the basic forms of plant and bud growth. The single celled stentor, attached at its stalk, literally assumes the shape of a permanent vortex (fig. 6) and thereby fits

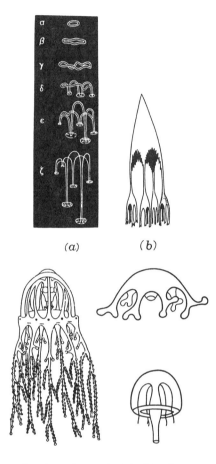

Figure 3. Liquid drops and medusa shapes. (top) *Falling drops:* (a) *ink in water,* (b) *fusel oil in paraffin.* (bottom) *Various medusoids. From* On Growth and Form © *1961 by D'Arcy Thompson, Cambridge University Press. Reprinted with the permission of Cambridge University Press.*

perfectly within the shape of the currents spinning around it. Theodor Schwenk (1965) takes this one step further with several demonstrations of how simple barriers placed in flowing water create permanent shapes in the resulting eddies that look strikingly organismic — often like horseshoe crabs or squid (fig. 7). His most intriguing illustration comes with the protozoan-like shapes created by allowing a source of water to discharge upward into the middle of a stream current, with a sink immediately behind it that allows the new water to descend again beneath the surface. The resulting shape — an enclosed flow within a larger streaming — is remarkably lifelike and exquisitely sensitive or resonant to changes in the surrounding flow (fig. 8).

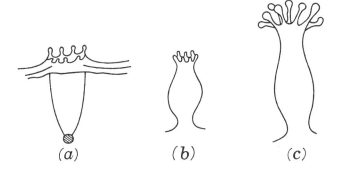

(a)   *(b)*   *(c)*

Figure 4. Splashes and polyps: (a, b) *phases of a splash;* (c) *a hydroid polyp. From* On Growth and Form © *1961 by D'Arcy Thompson, Cambridge University Press. Reprinted with the permission of Cambridge University Press.*

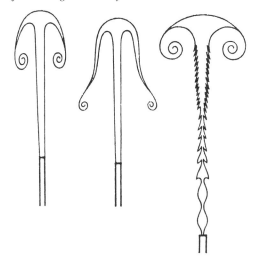

Figure 5. Liquid jets as organic shapes. From On Growth and Form © *1961 by D'Arcy Thompson, Cambridge University Press. Reprinted with the permission of Cambridge University Press.*

Earlier we located a perceptual template for "taking the role of the other" in Gibson's propriolocation given back by the particular flow of a perceptual array. Now, we find its deeper reflection, in turn, in a physical "taking the shape of the array" manifested in the very forms of motile sentient bodies. This "taking the shape of the other" seems the exact physical analogue to the mutual mirroring of a laminar "there" and a proprioceptive "here" in Gibson's array.

In water the surfaces of the forms that are created by flowing movements are unbelievably sensitive. But it is a sensitivity that is not based on any nervous system, [it]

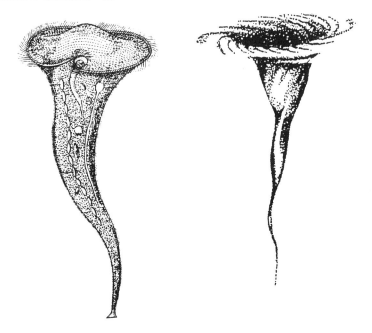

*Figure 6. Stentor and vortex. (*left*) From* On Growth and Form © *1961 by D'Arcy Thompson, Cambridge University Press. Reprinted with the permission of Cambridge University Press. (*right*) From* Sensitive Chaos © *1965 by Theodor Schwenk. Rudolf Steiner Press, Bristol, England.*

arises purely out of the interplay of forces. . . . Surely here Nature reveals one of her secrets by anticipating sensitivity in flowing movements without needing a nervous system! Does she not already incorporate in the substance of the nerve-sense organs in living creatures the sensitivity already present as a function in fluids? At a primitive level the amoeba, with the sensitive surface of its body, is an example of the principles of source and sink. It does not solidify into a fixed form but remains in the flowing, constantly changing fluid state. (Schwenk, 1965, p. 63)

When ellipsoid objects are drawn through water, they create their own characteristic contour lines and eddies in the surrounding medium, also quite similar to electromagnetic currents. The intersection of these contour flow lines with the actual cross-flows of the surround specifies a unique pattern of interference as the direct physical analogue and ultimate source for the coalition of array and proprioception in Gibson. We could say that sentient perception is a more differentiated and still more sensitive version of a resonance already reflected in primary body shapes and their movements. Just as thought reuses and reorganizes the structures of perception, perception is an elaboration of the cross-flow dynamics of its primary surrounding envelope of physical streaming. The array mirrors back the position of

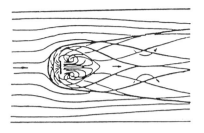

Figure 7. Barriers and flow. (left) Water flowing round an obstructing plate or slab. (right) If water flows round a fixed plate, a dividing surface arises in the water. From Sensitive Chaos © *1965 by Theodor Schwenk. Rudolf Steiner Press, Bristol, England.*

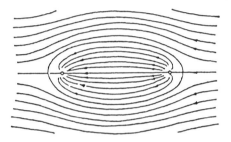

Figure 8. Organic shapes in flow and water. An enclosed dividing surface arises in the interplay of a source, a sink, and a direct current. From Sensitive Chaos © *1965 by Theodor Schwenk. Rudolf Steiner Press, Bristol, England.*

the organism perceiving it, while the body bears the direct imprint of the physical principles to which it is most immediately subject and out of which it originated.

There are some still more specific levels on which we can trace out the ubiquity of streaming and spiral form constants—first on the organs, limbs, and body proportions of more complex organisms and second, now directly mirrored within self-aware sentience, in some of the principles that organize interpersonal judgments and aesthetic response.

As Schwenk says, "The organ of the higher animal may be regarded as solidified movement" (p. 49). This obtains in the structure of the semicircular canals of the ear (Schwenk, 1965), in the embryological formation of multiple organs and limbs (Thom, 1975), and in the spirals of seashells and antelope horns (Thompson, 1961). Many of these forms also embody the "golden-section" ratio. The golden section is a proportion found throughout organic growth, with the latter's emphasis on asymmetry and odd numbers, and is based on the Fibonacci series (1, 1, 2, 3, 5, 8, 13, 21, etc.), by which the ratio of any two consecutive terms comes progressively to approximate .62 as the series proceeds. This "curve of life" (Cook, 1914) represents the ratios at which trees put out successive branches and the spiraling axes of pine cones and seashells (Stevens, 1974). It also holds for the proportions of body segments and limbs in most vertebrates. The golden section is found between successive body parts from fishes and frogs to the bones of the human hand (Doczi, 1981). It also appears in the overall proportions of that "ideal" adult human body of such fascination to the artists of the Renaissance (Ghyka, 1946; Huntley, 1970).

On the cognitive psychological level, golden-section ratios have been found to characterize the proportion of positive to total (positive and negative) interpersonal judgments (Benjafield and Adams-Webber, 1976; Adams-Webber, 1979; Adams-Webber, 1990). They match the proportions of aesthetically preferred rectangles in research going back, interestingly, to Fechner. Lefebvre (1990) has asserted that the golden-section ratio will emerge as the average proportion from a three-level structure of cognitive reflexivity ("I know that I know that I know x"), in which each level has a fifty-fifty probability of a positive or negative valuation. Lefebvre, Lefebvre, and Adams-Webber (1986) were able to use this three-tiered model to predict the precise ratios (golden section and non–golden section) of positive and negative judgments of self and others in diverse evaluative contexts. This work helps to establish a curvilinear mathematical organization for interpersonal judgment, of which the golden section would be but one expression.

Lefebvre's thesis will also follow from Mead's and Laing's versions of an interpersonal primacy for self-reference — "I (+−) know that he (+−) knows that I (+−) know x." The assumption here is that personal reflection is an internalized version of "taking the role of the other" toward the self. In Laing's examples (cited in chapter 1), self-reference must repeat in cycles of three and five phases, the latter being the probable practical limit of our cognitive capacity. These cycles would approximate a golden-section ratio on both Lefebvre's model and the Fibonacci series. In keeping with Lefebvre's view that the golden section and related proportions are ultimately nonverbal, being found in both the geometries of visual preference and western musical intervals, it is worth recalling that I have located the first manifestation of this three-layered reflexive structure in mother-infant facial mirroring — "I see you seeing me . . ." or "I am you being me. . . ."

Whereas golden-section and related asymmetries will predominate in naturalistic artistic traditions, intricate symmetrical geometric designs are a cross-cultural characteristic of sacred art (Seligman, 1976; Malraux, 1960), psychedelic and meditative visualizations (Fischer, 1975; Govinda, 1960), and Jung's (1950) descriptions of spontaneous mandala designs often experienced by persons at times of profound life change and personal crisis. In general, spontaneous visual imagery in presentational states will follow a logic of simultaneity and symmetry, condensing multiple meanings into single expressive forms, in contrast to the bipolar asymmetries underlying language. It makes sense that cultures oriented toward naturalism, like classical Greece and the Renaissance, should have an art imbued with golden-section ratios, if for no other reason than their preoccupation with the human body in action.

Certainly, it cannot be maintained that the golden section is somehow the "curve of life," while symmetry is the essence of the inorganic and crystalline. After all, golden sections are found in some spiral galaxies and in certain crystals (Pauling, 1989), and D'Arcy Thompson stressed that organically they are most commonly present in the frozen, "dead" residues of previous growth, such as animal horns and shell designs.[2] Meanwhile, fascination with the semantics of complex geometric symmetries is as central to sacred art and hallucinatory visions as it is to mathematics. We seem to have a dual aesthetics, based on the differently valued reflections inward of asymmetrical flows and the symmetrically looming pulses that punctuate them. What can be said is that the dual aspects of perception itself, direct perception and recognition, reflect the asymmetrical and symmetrical form constants that "self-organize" as the physical world "without." Spirals, meanders, symmetrically radiating explosions, and branchings are the very stuff of physical world, neural connectivity, and perception "within."

Inward and Outward Reflections of the Dynamics of Flow and Turbulence

The nonlinear fluid dynamics of water and air currents constitute the outer husk of the experienced life-space, what Lewin (1936) would call its "foreign hull." These nonlinear physical processes "hold" the diverse life-worlds of sentient creatures as their most adjacent envelope. It is these dynamic processes, mirrored inward, that inform the organization of immediate sentience — especially an ambient perceptual array more or less common to all motile creatures. Not itself alive, this dynamic hull reflects its organization inward to shape the "is like" of immediate perception. As both Schwenk (1965) and Skarda and Freeman (1987) point out, so close is this mirroring that the language of professional meteorologists referring to the dynamics of storms and cyclones is full of organismic metaphors of adaptation, survival, and intention. Even though these nonliving systems finally lack an immediate proprioceptive responsiveness to the consequences of their "actions," they do provide us with deeply resonant outward mirrors for the organization of our experience. Surely these isomorphisms between consciousness and the dynamics of the surrounding physical world place us, with Heidegger, very much in-the-world, and not somehow outside it.

We can now begin to outline a Leibnitzian series of mirrored levels from without-in and within-out that will reflect a similar dynamics. The nonlinear dynamics of flow and turbulence as the outer husk or hull of the life-world is most immediately reflected in the body shapes of the simplest creatures and in the embryological forms of more complex creatures. This level of physical resonance is also preserved, or with D'Arcy Thompson "enshrined," in the golden-section proportions of the bodies and limbs of adult vertebrates. On the actual level of the organization of perception we have Gibson's envelope of flow gradients, simultaneously specifying array and position, with a horizonal openness of ostensible turbulence out of which "the next" continually self-organizes. On the level of a symbolic self-reference reusing the forms and dynamics of perception, we find an open-ended, cross-modal flow and mutual transformation between the specific flows and looming pulses of the perceptual modalities. Later, I will focus more directly on the synesthetic form of presentational states in which these cross-modal flow dynamics are most visible and so available for study.

Moving from "within" back "out," we could consider the membrane polarizations in neural functioning as electrochemical instantiations of these sentient, proprioceptively locating, cross-flows of perception — especially since we have found the same electrochemical flow as the basic "mechanism" of motility/sensitivity in single-cell aneural organisms. It seems noteworthy that spontaneous firings of the single, experimentally isolated axon of the squid form "phase space" patterns that are based on chaotic or strange attractors (Aihara and Matsumoto, 1986; Rapp, 1986). In effect, the most basic physical expression of the transduction of the environment into motility/sentience mirrors the nonlinear dynamics that I have located in both "foreign hull" and ecological array. The very interconnectivity of more complex neural networks shows these same dynamics of cross-flow and turbulence. Thus, Freeman (Skarda and Freeman, 1987; Freeman, 1991) found chaotic-attractor patterns in the resting electrical activity of the olfactory lobes of rabbits — to be replaced by more regular cycles when the animals are exposed to recognizable odors. Skarda and Freeman's (1987, p. 171) statement that "chaos provides . . . a deterministic 'I don't know' state within which new activity patterns can be generated" suggests that nonlinear dynamics are involved in the organismic attunement to horizonal openness.

Similarly, on the level of neocortical symbolic cognition, it appears that the alpha-theta rhythm of the electroencephalogram is also organized in terms of a chaotic attractor (Friedrich, Fuchs, and Haken, 1991). Of course, it is these alpha-theta rhythms that are enhanced and generalized across the neocortex in the meditative cultivation of openness. Travis (1994), in addition to locating alpha-theta enhancement in meditation and some forms of lucid dreaming, has found brief manifestations of these same rhythms at all points of transition between the waking, sleeping, and REM states. This suggests that what we could call an attunement to openness (horizonal and symbolic) and what the meditative traditions call "pure consciousness" would be the background state beneath all more differentiated neo-cortical organizations.

What first appeared as "metaphor" in James now seems reflected back at us from every level of analysis relevant to the organization of experience. If it can be said that each species constructs its own life-world, it would do so by means of the same organizing principles that also inform its most immediate physical surround.

Archetypes of Experience: Metaphor or World?

These multiple resonances between consciousness and world are closely related to what Jung, based on his interest in these same processes of turbulent flow in al-chemy, termed the "psychoid" nature of the archetype. This refers to his notion that the organizing principles of mind and physical universe are ultimately identical — that the archetypes of experience so prominent in mythology and presentational states are also "outside" in the world. In his later writings, this view allowed Jung to bypass his more questionable hypothesis of a "collective unconscious" that some-how contains memory traces of the pre-human and evolutionary past. Instead, for the later Jung and for Hillman (1975), cross-cultural similarities in mythology and self-referential metaphor are the result of physical phenomena and processes com-mon to the environments of all people — water, air, and fire. These are pre-attuned for use in metaphorically based self-reference. Extrapolating from the archetypal-imagination perspective of Hillman and Paul Kugler (1982), Jungian psychology becomes a theory of the cross-modal bases of self-referential physical metaphor.

Let us consider from this perspective a related attempt to locate a fundamental structuralism of the mind that, along with the early Jung, similarly misses the possibility that imagination and metaphor are rooted in the perception of the physi-cal order. In R. D. Laing's (1976) late work *The Facts of Life*, in an uncharacteristic move toward a classical reductionism, he attempts to explain the cross-culturally common themes in mythologies of the journey of the hero in terms of the template supposedly laid down by the embryological journey of the zygote down the uterine canal to implantation in the endometrium. Grof (1980) has made an analogous attempt to reduce certain transpersonal experiences to memories of birth and pre-birth states. Although some psychedelic experiences produced by high dosages of psychotropic drugs actually take these forms, both Laing and Grof missed the possibility that their explanations may be based instead on metaphors provided by common principles of dynamic flow. These natural form constants would organize both ongoing perception and the life processes of embryological development. The ostensible arbitrariness of the connection between presentational states and, for instance, embryological development, combined with the seeming exactness of fit which so struck Laing, can thus be resolved by the common fluidic dynamics that self-organize all biological processes.

The journey of the hero has always been most purely and immediately available, not to the embryologist, but to any child engaged in floating a stick down a mean-dering woodland stream and following its dramatic adventures. The dynamics of flow and its various subregions do all those things to the insentient stick that are enacted in the various structuralisms of organismic behavior — including the course of embryonic implantation so intriguing to Laing. The stick is now assimilated, now accommodated, incorporated, retained, and expelled, and its encompassing region and progress are repeatedly intruded upon as it itself intrudes upon its surroundings. Now it shoots forward, then eddies back, spins in place, and finally finds itself lodged within a vortex or a labyrinth of cross-flows created by rocks and riverbank. The child here learns firsthand everything of importance about the role of the Homeric gods as he or she intervenes to rescue and restart the stick again and again, or else sees to it that the stick is repeatedly frustrated and stymied. Were the stick to respond directly to all this with the same sensitive patterns of inclusion and accom-modation as are done onto it in the turbulence of the stream, we would have more than simply the compelling illusion of a life's journey. All that would be needed is for the stick to act as responsively and immediately as the water does, and we would have exactly the coalition of array and propriosensitivity basic to Gibson's version of the streaming perspective of perception.

What I have begun to raise here is the issue of the nature and basis of metaphor. What is representing what among alchemy, contemporary nonlinear dynamics, James's stream, Gibson's array, and the child with the stick? Does chaos theory offer simply another occasion in the history of science in which research on the physical universe makes available new potential metaphors for consciousness and mind? Clock, steam engine, telephone switchboard, computer, light, and nonlinear dy-namics would be part of the list of constructed and natural physical entities that can be reused as metaphors for our own functioning. Or, does the development of a physics of nonlinear dynamics, and perhaps even relativity and quantum fields, betoken instead a largely unconscious turn within modern science? Perhaps we are now increasingly in search of just those levels of physical reality, in marked contrast to Newtonian mechanics, that *do* actually mirror the qualities of sentience and of our own increasingly problematic existence. As Schwenk (1965, p. 11) says, "Through watching water and air with unprejudiced eyes our way of thinking becomes . . . more suited to the understanding of what is alive. This transformation of our way of thinking is . . . a decisive step that must be taken in the present day."

Perhaps, in the sense of D. W. Winnicott (1971), we are now collectively looking for the structures that will mirror and contain our turbulent and increasingly isolated "consciousness" so that it can become more truly at home in the world. If — with

Heidegger and Jung, among others — we are, at our most fundamental level of self-characterization, Being seeing itself, then the closer our science approaches to the dynamic organizing principles of the physical universe, the closer we must also come to consciousness as the process of immediate resonance to these same principles. The stream of James turns out to be a self-referential metaphor that is also, and not accidentally, directly accessible to us as the most immediate organization of our physical reality.

Part IV The Imagistic Bases of Consciousness: Ordinary and Nonordinary, Contemporary and Ancient

What can be heard can at the same time be brought into view, if think-ing views with an ear and hears with an eye. . . . The concealed unity of bringing-into-view and listening determines the essence of the thinking that is entrusted to us humans who are thinking beings.
Martin Heidegger, *The Principle of Reason*

*The process of composition is essentially the same for any composer.
. . . You don't hear it at first. You perceive it first. You* are *it. . . . You conceive what is consecutive simultaneously. There's no hearing, no feeling. It's a structure . . . as the layers peel off from this soundless sphere, the sound enters. . . . You have to unroll it, unfold it. . . . In Mozart's case . . . he peeled off an entire movement in an hour. In my case, I peel off a section at a time.*
Phil Lesh, bassist for the Grateful Dead, *Berkeley Monthly*, July 1987

I can see the whole of it at a single glance in my mind, as if it were a beautiful painting . . . in which way I do not hear it in my imagination at all as a succession . . . but all at once, as it were.
Wolfgang Amadeus Mozart, quoted in William James, *The Principles of Psychology*, vol. 1

7 Synesthesia: The Inner Face of Thought and Meaning

The Würzburg Controversy Resolved: Thought as Synesthesia

The idea that synesthesias show the inner side of a cross-modal translation capacity at the base of symbolic cognition offers a solution to one of the oldest disagreements in cognitive psychology — the Würzburg controversy over the underlying nature of thought. The debate is still very much with us in the contrast between those who understand thought as a propositional logic (Pylyshyn, 1984) and those who posit its basis in abstract visual-spatial imagery (Shepard, 1978; Lakoff, 1987; Johnson, 1987).

The story is well known — perhaps a little too well. The two most prestigious introspectionist laboratories of the early twentieth century, Würzburg under Külpe and Cornell under Titchener, undertook to extend introspection into the more complex processes of symbolic thought and reasoning. Külpe's observers found . . . nothing. Thought just comes. It is an impalpable awareness, definitely there as an introspectable *something* but not further specifiable. Titchener and his colleagues suspected the Würzburg observers of "stimulus error" and themselves reported myriad sensory-imaginal qualities during thought, although they agreed that these often seem irrelevant to its ostensible topic. The scientific world recoils in horror: obviously, if the same method leads to such different results — thought as an impalpable state, thought as imaginal — the method must be flawed. Psychology as science shall henceforth pursue only outwardly measurable behaviors. Surely nothing so unseemly could happen with maze learning in rats! Enter Tolman and Spence.

There is real irony in the tendency of most textbooks to ascribe psychology's "flight from subjectivity" in the 1920s to the Würzburg controversy. First, this was the era that saw the introduction of complementarity and indeterminism within the very physics that psychology was supposedly trying to imitate — a physics influenced by none other than James on consciousness, as we have seen. In other words, the fact that the attempt to study something necessarily changes it (consciousness introspected, subatomic particles) and that a subject matter must be understood from more than one theoretical perspective simultaneously (thought as proposition, thought as imagery; light as wave, light as particle) could no longer be taken as scientific disqualification. Second, for psychology itself, the further irony, aside from the later ending of animal learning literature in total controversy, is that the standard textbook summaries are wrong: the two laboratories used *different* methods.

The Würzburgers looked at consciousness during complex problem solving under relatively natural conditions: "Give the superordinate category for whale," "Can the atomic theory of physics ever be proven untrue by any discovery?" The Cornell studies by Helen Clarke (1911) and Edmund Jacobson (1911b), on the other hand, were based on simplified tasks of semantic recognition (words and letters). In these studies ready identification was deliberately delayed or derailed by verbal satiation (Jacobson) or tactile letter forms presented to blindfolded subjects (Clarke), so that normally masked sensory-imaginal processes could appear within ongoing consciousness. Kakise (1911) even managed to produce both kinds of report from the same observers. Impalpable knowings appeared where his observers took a more active, pragmatic attitude, whereas imagery fragments predominated with the more passive, detached attitude that both Titchener (1912) and Spearman (1923) considered central for systematic introspection.

The supposedly devastating functionalist criticism (Humphrey, 1951) was that one could not tell from the descriptions of the imagery alone in these studies what their ostensible meaning could be — making such states an irrelevant by-product (Woodworth's "sparks struck off," Wittgenstein's "mental doodling"). But this was actually a source of considerable pride to the introspectionists around Titchener. It was what they were looking for. It showed that they had truly avoided the "stimulus error" and had described ongoing consciousness in its own right and independent of what it referred to in the world. There was much imagery in the Würzburg protocols as well, which they dismissed for its ostensible irrelevancy. Indeed, it *is* difficult to derive from the supposed imaginal vehicles of thought in Clarke's (1911) protocols what attitudes and thoughts these states are supposedly "of." It is impossible to guess, for instance, that "kinesthetic sensations in the back of the mouth," "a complex of sensations on the top of the head," and "visual image of people walking" could stand for, respectively, "I consciousness," the attitude of "wondering," and the word "individuals." It is possible to see metaphoric links and associational allusions between these states and their referents, but it is decidedly post hoc. On James's model of the scrutinized snowflake melting on the scientist's hand, these are indeed not so much functional thoughts as modality-specific "image smears." Yet Titchener's counterclaim that such sensory-imaginal "reflections" or "sparks struck off" nonetheless provide evidence of the normally unconscious processes of thought has not been refuted.

Correspondingly, although Külpe's student Narciss Ach (1905) had focused his observers on the moment of insight in problem-solving tasks and they had found no specifiable content whatsoever, all agreed that these "impalpable awarenesses" were nonetheless definite states — something in their own right and not merely an absence, lack, or emptiness: "Imageless thought . . . is not a logical abstraction. It is an apparent fact of introspection. . . . It would not be fair to call these moments pale and featureless; they are precisely the moments when a thought presents itself most definitely for what it is . . . though brief they are the real highlights of consciousness" (Woodworth, 1906, p. 702–705). Karl Bühler (1908) finally gave up and termed these moments "thoughts," by which *he* meant definite states with attributes of clearness, vividness, and intensity and which he classified as "consciousness of rule," "consciousness of relation," "intentions," an so on. Yet they lacked defining patterns of imagery in the sense of concrete depictions that would somehow "carry" these meanings.

So we still have a mystery — or at the least a disagreement over method — but hardly one to disqualify the original participants. What we have then is an unknown, "x," which stands for the actual processes of thinking. On the one side of this unknown we find the impalpable states of contentless awareness. On the other side, artificially enhanced by the derailments produced by systematic introspection, we find a series of concrete image fragments, related to their topic by, at best, an indirect metaphoric or associational link. The solution for "x" comes if we substitute in place of this unknown the full range of synesthesias, as a broad series of related states that link the two poles of empty proposition and irrelevant image. Not only will we thereby resolve a very old debate, still at the center of the cognitive psychology of imagery in relation to thought, but we may locate in the process the felt "inner" side of a cross-modal translation capacity basic to all forms of symbolic cognition.

At the outset, it is important to emphasize that the phenomenology of synesthesias is far broader than the cross-modality translations reflected in the most widely researched and relatively simple example of "color hearing," where each vowel may give rise to a characteristic color. Indeed, that phenomenon is relatively stereotyped, with "a" generally experienced as red or blue, "e" as yellow or white, "u" as brown or black (Marks, 1975, 1978). However, color hearing is a relatively routinized form of a much wider series — one so broad and inclusive that it is easy to miss as such. For instance, the color and dynamic-form synesthesias occurring for some people with music (Critchley, 1977), and which are probably implicit in all music appreciation, show the polysemy, complexity, and openness that one would expect in symbolic cognition. In psychedelic states there are also the so-called "complex synesthesias" (Klüver, 1966), in which tactile-kinesthetic patterns are experienced as fused with rapidly shifting geometric designs, all this inseparable from felt meaning. These fusions of body image and geometric form are directly manifested in the mandala and chakra experiences of psychedelic drug and meditative states. They also seem to be more vivid and explicit versions of the abstract visual imageries that Arnheim (1969), Shepard (1978), Lakoff (1987), and Johnson (1987) have come to see as the "deep structure" of all conceptual thought — verbal and nonverbal.

Persons who are commonly aware of spontaneous synesthesias insist that these states are not adequately described as either specific *sensory* effects or *associations* of one modality with another. Rather, synesthesias are paradoxical and ineffable — as one might expect with states reflecting the core of symbolic cognition prior to its more pragmatic articulation in word and image. These more spontaneous synesthesias, which tend to be noticed and reported by subjects with a high capacity for imaginative absorption (Ramsey and Hunt, 1993), are described as emergent processes of cross-flow and fusion which resist further description. They are felt to be one's actual manner of thinking, a kind of directly sensed alternative to inner speech.

James Hillman (1977) has suggested that all functional imagery contains these cross-modal fusions, although normally they are implicit and not easily identified as such. Their cross-modal basis, however, is easily confirmed if we think to look for the more plastic, incipiently tactile aspects of concurrent visual imagery. It would be these largely implicit synesthesias that confer the physiognomy or referential "feel" in imagery, the loss of which is equivalent to semantic satiation in verbal expression. Raymond Wheeler and Thomas Cutsforth (1921, 1922ab; Cutsforth, 1924, 1925), along these lines, reported a series of studies of the synesthetically based thought, emotion, and semantic recognition in Cutsforth himself (blind from the age of 11) and other subjects especially aware of prominent synesthesias. The synesthesias described were astonishingly complex, ranging from color hearing, in the more standardized fashion demonstrated by Marks (1978), to both thoughts and verbal comprehension occurring in myriad color complexes of rapidly shifting hues. These color configurations simply *were* felt meaning for these synesthetes, with direct verbalization a distinct and often difficult stage of further expression.

Something of this broader phenomenology of synesthesia is reflected in Eugene Gendlin's (1978) clinical development of his concept of felt meaning through a technique he refers to as "focusing." Focusing is a means of "making the unconscious conscious." It begins with a vague and inchoate mood pressing on the subject, who is then encouraged to concentrate on his or her immediate bodily sensations until a specific place and "feel" has been located within the body to match the mood. The subject is then encouraged to allow a visual image to emerge that will spontaneously express this tactile-kinesthetic pattern. This can be either an abstract visual physiognomy or a more concretely depictive image. The final step is to allow a verbal phrase or word to appear which will finish the translation of this felt synesthetic complex. The full cross-modal articulation of the initial mood commonly results in what Gendlin terms a "felt shift," a sudden giving way of the stasis of the initial mood along with an increased clarity and sense of understanding.

In more formal cognitive studies, Lawrence Marks (1978) has shown how what we might term "simple synesthesias," based on felt cross-modal fusions in terms of single sensory dimensions like brightness or intensity, are a major source for poetic metaphors. This is well illustrated in such phrases as "silver-toned chimes" and "cold so bitter." McKellar's (1957) demonstration of the rarity of simple synesthetic translations in which tactile or visual stimuli trigger an auditory effect in laboratory-based studies of synesthetic induction, whereas all other combinations among touch and the other senses are reasonably common, suggests that the missing categories may correspond to the forms of language and music. The prominence of these latter forms of expression would presumably block more spontaneous expressions of audition as the end point for spontaneous synesthetic translations. We have already seen that in its starkest simplicity language itself is a sort of complex synesthesia, cross-translating vision, vocal sound, and articulatory and gestural kinestheses, while painting entails complex synesthesias involving kinesthesis and visual patterns.

Most important for establishing synesthesias as a continuous series connecting impalpable awareness, on the one hand, and modality-specific imagery, on the other, are reports from the early experimental literature (summarized in Werner, 1961) of both "positive" and "negative" synesthesias. The former are the more commonly described in the literature — an explicitly felt fusion of identifiable perceptual modalities into an emergent amalgam. Negative synesthesias are states that are triggered in synesthetes by externally presented visual and auditory stimuli that will often elicit recognizable positive synesthesias, but in these instances induce an amodally felt "sense," usually brief, during which the subject can literally not tell what modalities have actually been stimulated. Werner describes these experiences as including a "vital" or kinesthetically embodied sensation that amounts to a contentless sense of significance — a kind of amodal physiognomy which will turn momentarily into the positive synesthesias that constitute semantic recognition for these subjects.

If we follow through on the hypothesis that all such subjective states must reflect cognitive processes latent within everyone, we begin to see that in the continuum between positive and negative synesthesias may lie the key to the strange duality of our own introspective experience of thinking as both impalpable and imagistic, yet somehow neither. Just as James says of the transitive, rapidly transforming aspects of the "stream," these states of felt meaning are especially difficult to recognize for what they are. They can as easily be labeled "amodal synesthesias" as "impalpable awareness" or "imageless images" or, with Titchener, "general kinestheses." In short, they are paradoxical states, an impalpable sense of significance combined with an imagery texture that resists further specification.

In my own case it took some time, despite carefully reading Heinrich Klüver (1966) on complex geometric synesthesias and the tendency of many synesthetic subjects to label their experiences as "thought," to realize that my experiences of an indescribable "sense" that I sometimes noticed as I fell asleep were *both* "felt meanings" *and* synesthesias. At the time I knew of Werner's negative synesthesias, in which subjects simply could not tell which modalities were involved, but I had not realized that it might not even occur to one to ask. Once I did, then on successive occasions I could begin to see the states in question as emergent wholes within which at one moment I "saw" geometric structures, the next felt a kinesthetic embodiment, then became aware that all this was also a thought awaiting articulation, then noticed more concrete depictive imagery or inner speech, and so on.

I was thus led by experience, theory, and research to the idea that thoughts are emergent synesthesias. If not disrupted, whether by sudden insight, introspective intent, or altered states, they will be experienced as "empty" — the impalpable sense of significance also noted with negative synesthesias. Once noticed as such, they range back and forth between these impalpables, kinestheses, positive synesthesias, and the imagery fragments whose pictorial specificity has some associational or metaphoric linkage to the more vitally embodied core of felt meaning. Synesthesias, in their actual range and transformations, constitute the missing "x" that joins Würzburger impalpables and Titchenerian imaginals, propositional thought and semantic imagery, within a single natural series of continuously overlapping states.

In further support of their connection to recombinatory symbolic cognition, there are a number of indications that synesthesias are, indeed, dynamic processes of hierarchic fusion and flow between modality-specific patterns. They can, accordingly, be constitutive of the novelty of symbolic thought, rather than being merely mechanical or static associations. Cutsforth (1925) observed that when his own synesthetic felt meanings suffered "semantic satiation," he was left with only meaningless and desaturated color imagery, minus what he termed the "parent process" that animated his ordinary imagery with an "inner movement" or "vitality" which he related to kinesthetic embodiment. Similarly, Zietz (cited in Werner, 1961) found that in order to induce synesthetic experiences in the laboratory he had to make his color stimuli dynamic and unstable by means of 100 millisecond tachistoscopic exposures. Only when rendered suitably labile and ephemeral would visual patterns interact synesthetically with concomitant tones, such that they momentarily became the tone and the entire complex was felt throughout the body.

The most striking demonstration of the importance of apparent movement or flow in the experimental induction of complex synesthesias comes from a study by Zaparoli and Reatto (1969). They found that only when there was a delay of 100 milliseconds, the same time that is optimal for the phi phenomenon of apparent movement and Michotte's causal launching, could they obtain complex synesthetic transformations between pairs of light flashes and auditory tones, in which one was experienced as turning into the other. Their subjects described complex and unexpected effects that included a feeling of movement through a tunnel of light, which might grow longer or shorter as the sound passed through it. One hundred milliseconds is also the same time frame for visual masking and assimilation in semantic recognition studies with the tachistoscope, as well as the minimum phase for the scanning of semantic memory (Blumenthal, 1977). This suggests that the experimental study of semantic recognition and induction of synesthesias would share common underlying processes.

That cross-modal translations involve dynamic fusions across complex modality-specific patterns is also shown by their first manifestations in childhood. A study by Wagner, Winner, Cicchetti, and Gardner (1981) looked at cross-modal matching capacity in eleven-month-old infants. These infants did not show cross-modal translation based on static, single-dimension differences between dark and light colors, long and short lines, or loud and quiet tones. Such would have to be the prediction of those who see synesthesias as a primitive capacity based on sensory dimensions that are preliminary to the differentiation of specific perceptual modalities — such as brightness-darkness or intensity. Instead, these infants demonstrated the cross-modal transfer of interest from a stimulus in one modality to a stimulus in another only when the patterns involved were complex dynamic forms. Thus, broken or continuous lines, jagged or smooth circles, and arrows pointing up or down could be transferred to a pulsating or continuous tone, or to a tone ascending or descending, but not to a simple high or low tone. This suggests that from very early on, cross-modal translation is a process of hierarchic integration occurring *across* dynamic, modality-specific shapes, not a pre-given correlation along separate single "dimensions" common to the various modalities and based on something like brightness-darkness. Something of this dynamic basis is, of course, strongly implied by the first emergence of cross-modal translations in the facial-mirroring games between infant and mothering one. Here, indeed, we find an emergent cross-flow between dynamic visual and kinesthetic patterns.

Since simultaneous stimulation in different perceptual modalities actually lowers the recognition thresholds for both (Blumenthal, 1977), we could also speculate that more "interior" cross-modality fusions could also have something to do with the proverbial "speed of thought." In combining different modality patterns, symbolic cognition would also accelerate the processes involved in perceptual recognition. In addition, Bühler's typology of impalpable awarenesses — consciousness of direction, consciousness of causation, and so on — would also follow if the separate modality patterns flowing together as felt meaning actually interacted in the same ways observed with tachistoscopic research on semantic recognition. Accordingly, we would expect these multiple-modality patterns variously to mask, causally launch, release, or fuse with each other — and this on every level of their imaginal-perceptual microgenesis. If the cross-modal processes of thought are so exteriorized by both the empirical range of synesthesias and tachistoscopic research on the microgenesis of perceptual recognition, we have located a key commonality between phenomenology and cognitive process — so frequently elusive in psychology.

This may be a good point to deal with what we might term the Helen Keller objection to this cross-modal, synesthetic model of the mind. Namely, if this were true, how could Helen Keller have had one? After all, the only perceptual modality available to her as the substratum for her slowly developed symbolic abilities was tactile-kinesthetic. If, however, we consider the basic patterning of the different perceptual modalities as primarily consisting in their different ratios of simultaneous to sequential information flow, it becomes possible to see that with a neocortex already potentially divided into overlapping tertiary areas, complex flow patterns between relatively simultaneous and relatively sequential tactile-kinesthetic patterns might substitute for the more optimal and dynamic cross-modal syntheses. Helen Keller's description of her experience of breakthrough into symbolic realization (in Werner and Kaplan, 1963) emphasizes the sudden felt confluence between the movement of her teacher's throat while saying "water" and the simultaneous flow of running water over her other hand. This illustrates a within modality fusion of a relatively active but demarcated patterning (throat movements) with a more passively imposed and continuous sensation of liquid flow. From the present perspective it would be the distinct differences in simultaneity and sequentiality across the separate perceptual modalities that would, in normal development, afford the optimal distance for a novel emergent interaction based on a dynamic cross-flow. In principle, however, there should be analogous interactions, if less optimal, within tactile-kinesthesis alone, falling as it does midway between the relative simultaneity of vision and the relative sequentiality of audition.

At least such an approximation would be possible with a neocortex already differentiated so as to allow cross-modality flows in the first place. I have already cited evidence (Sacks, 1989) that signing in the congenitally deaf is localized in the same temporal-lobe areas normally involved in vocal language, except that more of the parietal (spatial) tertiary zone seems to be included for exclusive signers. Hypo-thetically, such a parietal involvement would be still greater for those born without sight as well — while the same cross-flow between dynamic patterns that are rela-tively simultaneous and relatively sequential would obtain in all cases. It is the very structure of the human neocortex, with its tertiary (symbolic) zones at the con-vergence of the association areas for vision, touch-kinesthesis, and audition, which shows that the original potentiality for symbolic cognition must rest on cross-modal integrations, whatever the developmental potential for substituting the patterns from one modality across this multiple-modality template.

The Counterposition: Synesthesias as Pre-Symbolic

Any evaluation of the theory that synesthesias exteriorize the implicit structure of thought, as the inner side of Geschwind's cross-modal translation capacity, must also address an opposing view. Instead, synesthesias might reflect an evolutionarily primitive, pre-symbolic matrix of sensory dimensions that is actually preliminary to the differentiation of separate perceptual modalities. On that view, synesthesias would not reflect a hierarchic integration across differentiated perceptual modali-ties, but a preliminary matrix common to all modalities and out of which they would have differentiated in the course of evolution. We will see that this more reductive model only works by ignoring the more dynamic, complex synesthesias and falsely limiting synesthesia to the commonalities of simple sensory dimensions.

One version of this more reductive approach comes from the neurologist Rich-ard Cytowic (1989). He agrees that felt meaning rests on synesthesias but sees both as pertaining exclusively to a more primitive affectivity centered in the limbic region. Synesthesias are accordingly prototypically mammalian and not symbolic. They are the level of experience common to mammals that learn by association rather than being anything relevant to recombinatory symbolism. Thus, people whose ongoing consciousness is predominantly synesthetic, along with the artists whose experiences, he agrees, emerge out of synesthesia, are regarded as a kind of evolutionary throwback. Subjects like those studied by Wheeler and Cutsforth and Cytowic himself are "living fossils." Although such a model is consistent with the argument, considered earlier, that cross-modal matching is based in the limbic areas and related to associational capacities, we have already seen that a cross-modal *translation* capacity, as exemplified in language, the arts, and complex synesthesias, is basic to the emergent symbolic capacity.

Cytowic uses his own research showing reduced blood flow in the cortex of subjects while experiencing synesthesias to argue that the capacity involved must be subcortical. However, he finds this reduction of blood flow to be greater in the left hemisphere than in the right — leaving it open whether, instead, we should conclude that synesthesias involve the capacities of presentational symbolism generally more localized in the right hemisphere. Without EEG data we have no way of knowing whether the lower blood flow levels would actually approximate the findings of alpha-theta predominance in both meditative (Alexander et al., 1990) and creative (Whitton, Moldofsky, and Lue, 1978) states. In that case, it would be better to speak of a cortical enhancement of presentational intelligence by means of either greater balance between the hemispheres or right-hemisphere predominance. Cytowic emphasizes the importance of synesthesias in the arts, even mentioning that the golden section appeals to the limbic brain's sense of beauty and pleasure, but he misses the point that aesthetics is as surely emergent on the specifically human (and so neocortical) level as is mathematics and language. Certainly, aesthetics, deep meditation, and the felt meaning common to all symbolic frames must also engage the limbic pleasure centers and associational processes in general, but it is hard to see how limbic functioning could be the source of such capacities — unless one is committed to an older and ultimately computational model of mind that would regard the arts as primitive.

Earlier studies by Erich Von Hornbostel (1927) and his student Walter Boernstein (1936) set the tone for the primitivity models of synesthesia by arguing that these experiences are residues of lower evolutionary stages in which the senses had not been separately differentiated. We have here a model not of hierarchic integration but of preliminary globality and undifferentiation. Von Hornbostel demonstrated that subjects could consistently match colors, sounds, tastes, and odors on dimensions of brightness-darkness and intensity, which he interpreted in terms of such an undifferentiated unity of the senses. Von Hornbostel's common-matrix model has had a pervasive influence on subsequent cognitive approaches to synesthesias and has tended to be explained in terms of properties of muscle tonus that would be shared across these basic sensory dimensions. Such approaches are exemplified in the work of Osgood (1964), Hayek (1952) and Marks (1978).

Perhaps the tour de force for this perspective, although not beginning to explain the full range of synesthesias, comes from the somewhat stark research of Boernstein (1936, 1967, 1970). On the one hand, he showed that the contraction of the retinal cones in the eyes of frogs, caused by exposure to light, could also be induced in dark-adapted frogs by odors rated as "bright" but not "dark" by human observers. Moreover, he found that the melanophores in the skin of frogs — smooth muscle fibers that change pigment with light or dark adaptation — also change if dark-adapted frogs are exposed to "bright" odors. In a clear demonstration of the ultimate "physicality" of this effect,[1] he found that pieces of frog tissue floated in the blood of other frogs sacrificed during light adaptation showed a "brightness shift," but not those floated in dark-adapted blood. Finally, he reported that the blood from light-adapted frogs, rabbits, and people, when injected into the eyes of the dark-adapted frogs, also resulted in retinal cone contraction. There can be little argument, then, against the existence of an undifferentiated matrix common to perceptual modalities and out of which each differentiates with its own modality-specific qualities. The question is whether synesthesias, with their clear relations to aesthetics and poetic metaphor, should be understood as a throwback to such a primitive matrix. Or are they, instead, the immediate reflections of a hierarchic integration of perceptual modalities that might also reuse such a common matrix, but only as part of a much more complex cross-flow between modality-specific patterns?

Influenced by the earlier classificatory work of Hartshorne (1934), Charles Osgood (Osgood, Suci, and Tannenbaum, 1957; Osgood, 1964) suggested that both "simple" synesthesias and the essentially similar cross-modal matches made by nonsynesthetic subjects were based on three fundamental dimensions common to all the senses — brightness-darkness, intensity, and activity-passivity. These dimensions are understood as motoric and based on affect. They later became the dimensions of his "semantic differential" — evaluation, potency, and activity as the categories underlying all connotative or affective meaning. He called attention to the similarity between these semantic dimensions and Wundt's earlier tri-dimensional classification of emotion in terms of pleasantness, strain, and excitement. In so doing, Osgood carefully separated connotative or affective meaning from a more conceptual, denotative thought, in an approach that would have considerable influence on Lawrence Marks (1978). It is just this separation that Arnheim (1969), Lakoff (1987), and Johnson (1987) would replace with their view of an abstract imaginal and synesthetic core for all thought (chapter 8). For Osgood, however, synesthesias are purely connotative expressions of emotion, with their roots in the motoric response system rather than in the perceptual modalities. The senses have common underlying dimensions that provide the sources for a lower connotative meaning because they are rooted in the common dimensions of motoric responsiveness — which Osgood speculated might be located within the reticular formation.

What these earlier perspectives on synesthesias miss is, as above, the very existence of geometric-dynamic synesthesias. These involve patterns that are modality-specific (visual mandalas, kinesthetic flows) and so demonstrate a genuine integration, not some common pre-sensory template. Because these authors restrict themselves to the more easily researched "single-dimension" synesthesias involved in color hearing, they have overestimated the stereotypy in these phenomena and underestimated their potential creativity. Marks (1978), for instance, concludes that the synesthetic linkages expressed in so much Romantic poetry are too stereotyped and limited in their possibilities to allow synesthesias to be the actual source of poetic metaphor — being rather its more concrete, perceptual precursor. Yet Marks's own research also demonstrates that experimental subjects will match visual stimuli ranging from bright to dark with auditory tones based on either pitch or loudness, depending on the subject, the task, and the experimental set provided. This suggests that even synesthetic matching on single linear dimensions, let alone more dynamic-structural patterns, is open to the sort of plurisignificance that Werner and Kaplan (1963) made critical to a creative symbolic capacity.

Perhaps we could consider the structural-dynamic complex synesthesias as reflecting the relatively simultaneous aspect of cross-modal translations, with the more discrete simple synesthesias, based on variations in linear dimensions, reflecting more their sequential side. If we consider the eight configurations based on all possible combinations of the bipolar dimensions of brightness, intensity, and activity suggested by Osgood as the common dimensions for simple synesthesias, and then add all other possible combinations based on first one and then two of these dimensions being neutral, we end up with a twenty-six-pattern "alphabet" of expressive units, or what we might term "Osgood pulses." Surely such an array is complex enough to be strung together as the sequential, communicative side of symbolic expression. Something like this analysis was attempted by Marshall Edelson (1975) in his approach to the sound-based meanings of poetry. He showed how the juxtaposition of the specific phonetic sequences of poetry with the semantic meanings of the words creates a sense of either ongoing congruence or contradiction. This potential for synesthetic resonance, while largely suppressed within ordinary language usage, is correspondingly developed in poetry and released as such as part of the immediate impact of instrumental music. Rather than see this successive, recombinatory alphabet as some sort of evolutionary throwback, it makes far more sense to regard it as the direct manifestation, within presentational symbolic cognition, of the "pulsar," "substantive," or "drop-like" organization of our consciousness. These pulses could "spell out" the more expressive side of the structures created by geometric-dynamic cross-modal translations.

A series of studies by Marks and Robert Melara (Marks, 1987, 1989; Melara 1989ab; Melara and Marks, 1990ab; Melara and O'Brien, 1987, 1990) offers extensive experimental evidence on the question of whether cross-modal interactions are best interpreted as perceptual-sensory or semantic. Initially, Marks (1987) found that a high-pitched tone resulted in greater accuracy and quicker reaction times for identifying a bright light as opposed to a dim one, lighter versus darker colors, and a sharp geometric shape versus a rounder one. He interpreted these findings in terms of common neural coding features in the sensory analysis of audition and vision. Melara and O'Brien (1987), however, found faster reaction times to a dot positioned high or low in a visual display, depending on whether an accompanying tone was pitched high or low. These results were not affected by temporal delays of up to half a second or the placing of the sound source in relation to the dot. This is harder to reconcile with a strictly sensory effect, as is the related finding of Walker and Smith

(1984) of more rapid recognition times for the words *bright, sharp,* and *happy* if they are pronounced in a congruent "bright" tone of voice rather than in an incongruent low tone.

Subsequent studies (Melara and Marks, 1990ab) found that the same congruence and interference effects could be obtained whether the interacting stimuli were sensory or semantic. Appropriately pitched tones improved reaction times to the visually presented words *hi* and *low,* with similar findings if the words were presented in congruent spatial positions or spoken in a congruent tone, or if arrows pointing up and down were used instead of words. Although it is logically possible to interpret these findings, with these researchers, as engaging two separate processes of cross-modal interaction — one in terms of sensory redundancy and the other on a semantic level — it is most parsimonious to conclude, on the basis of identical statistical results, that the entire phenomenon is semantic and symbolic. It emerges from Geschwind's cross-modal capacity. We would also have a demonstration of the way in which cross-modality congruence speeds even quite simple levels of semantic recognition.

More generally, and to conclude my argument that synesthesias are part of symbolic cognition, we have already seen how the capacity to delay a functional semantic response — in systematic introspection, meditation, and tachistoscopic exposure — allows the development of synesthetically formed states of felt meaning. It makes no sense to ascribe synesthetic consciousness to nonsymbolic animals, since they lack a capacity to cultivate sensitivities for their own sake, that is, aesthetically. Moreover, there could be no possible use for such beings in having experiences that entail an inability, however brief, to tell which modality has been stimulated or the spatial-temporal location of its source. The aesthetically rich properties of these subjective states are the clue that we are dealing with a capacity fully emergent only on the symbolic level. Finally, of course, the significant correlations between questionnaires measuring the proclivity to synesthetic experience and both metaphoric ability and imaginative absorption (Wicker and Holahan, 1978; Rader and Tellegen, 1981; Ramsey and Hunt, 1993) are most consistent with such a symbolic-cognitive interpretation.

There is certainly the possibility, albeit exceeding parsimony, that a more primitive template of sensory commonality, based on motoric response, is being reused on a symbolic level and so taken up into a hierarchic integration of the senses. However, the emergence of both complex and simple synesthesias as explicit forms of consciousness imbued with felt meaning can be nothing other than human. Higher developmental forms will always be guided both by their own emergent possibilities and by any pre-existing organizing template, without being thereby reducible to the latter. The phenomenology of the full range of synesthesias, as they merge imperceptively into the impalpable, unclassifiable "thatness" of our here and now consciousness, shows the direct exteriorization of the inner organization of presentational self-consciousness.

Cross-Modal Fusions in the Geometric-Dynamic Patterns of Imagery and Gesture

Here we approach more directly the "complex synesthesias" that seem to underlie physiognomically expressive imagery and gesture, as well as presentational states. The very geometric-dynamic nature of the shapes fused in these phenomena bespeak a hierarchic integration rather than any reuse of a more primordial common matrix for the senses.

We begin with Werner and Kaplan (1963) and their illustrations of the cross-modal physiognomic expressions involved in pictorial depictions of emotion, sound symbolism, and even sentence structure. Their student Iritani (in Werner and Kaplan, 1963) investigated the cross-modal properties of thirty-five nonsense words and found that subjects showed consensus in assigning 75 percent of these along multiple sensory and affective dimensions. *Zeca* and *taki*, for instance, were labeled as small, angular, bright, moving, and happy, while *voag* and *huoh* were large, round, dark, static, and sad. Jakobson and Waugh (1987) have similarly portrayed such symbols in sound as a key element in linguistic meaning, relatively suppressed in ordinary usage and emerging in their own right in poetry and in the spontaneous linguistic creativity of young children. Mary Foster (1980) has extended the implications of these coordinations between sounds and expressive visual-spatial patterns in an attempt to reconstruct a "primordial" language that would originally have been based on the metaphoric similarities between the movements of the mouth and aspects of the environment thereby represented. Thus, the sound "pl" or "fl" — with lips initially protruding and then a pulling back of the tongue — appears in several languages in words describing things that are extended and broad. Examples in English would be *fly, field,* or *flood.* Bolinger (1989) has also stressed how articulatory patterns can mimic sensory-based semantic features--such as the "gl" sound for the radiating, visual features in *glitter* and *glow* or the "udge" sound for events that are heavy and sticky, as in *trudge, grudge, sludge.*

Lest such sound symbolisms seem too stereotyped to afford the polysemy and openness to reorganization required for symbolic cognition, it should also be noted that Werner and Kaplan's research subjects could also easily give sound patterns that expressed strong consensual meanings a very different emphasis by means of vocal pronunciation — thereby transforming their more average meanings. For instance, one can draw out and deepen the pronunciation of *taki* as "taaakeee," so as to render it large, round, dark, static, and sad. Or consider the expressive line patterns in figure 9 (after Kohler, 1947). Most subjects will agree, provided with the alternatives, that the one on the left is best called *ulalah,* and the one on the right

Figure 9. "Ulalah" and "zekite."

zekite. Correspondingly, in figure 10 the one on the left is most commonly taken as representative of "arrogance," while the right is more readily physiognomized as "modesty." However, something of the openness necessarily involved in all symbolic cognition—what Wittgenstein termed its capacity for "seeing as"—comes through here as well: *ulalah* can be enunciated in a harsh, angular, abrupt way, just as *zekite* can be drawn out and softened, reversing their more consensual physiognomies entirely. Meanwhile, the jutting "teeth" of the "arrogant" figure can now be seen just as well as modesty "covered" by the top shielding line, and the sweep and two lines of the other figure as easily become a gesture of disdainful dismissal.

Werner and Kaplan demonstrate how felt meanings can be exteriorized in abstract line patterns akin to the actual gestures we make while speaking and to selective phonetic emphasis during pronunciation. The next step in inference would be to suggest that these phenomena reflect an abstract cross-modal imagery that is the template out of which all understanding unfolds. Wittgenstein (1953) had stressed that the meaning of a word or sentence never rests on some inner subjective state or feeling, but that the use of language does involve a physiognomic quality which, Wittgenstein says, is like the expression with which a piece of music is played. By itself it is nothing and cannot exist apart from the musical performance, yet without it the music is not genuinely animated and meaningful. He says of such expressive physiognomies that they are "arbitrary yet instilled." The same verbal meaning could, indeed, be expressed by a very different physiognomy in Werner and Kaplan's examples. Yet without some such form of spontaneous animation—synesthetically based—we are, in Wittgenstein's terms, "meaning blind."[2] Especially interesting in this context is Werner and Kaplan's (1963) experimental demonstration that ongoing semantically relevant gestures can appreciably delay the subjective loss of meaning in verbal satiation. Thus, the word *push* can be repeated to the point that it becomes a raw, meaningless sound, but the onset of this loss is delayed by either a pushing or a pulling gesture, but not a lifting one.

Although it has seemed tempting to many to regard Werner and Kaplan's physiognomic designs for conceptual meaning as somehow ephemeral to the real business of cognition, as an inconsequential by-product or special trick, research by David McNeill (1985, 1992) on spontaneous gesture during speech has extended

Figure 10. "Arrogance" and "modesty." From Symbol Formation © *1963 by Heinz Werner and Bernard Kaplan. John Wiley and Sons, Inc. Reprinted with the permission of the publisher.*

Werner and Kaplan's pictorial designs into a general theory of the microgenesis of sentence construction. He shows that when gesturing we are engaged in drawing something very like these designs in the air, not as a mere by-product, but as a significant, functional component of verbal conversation. By gesture McNeill does not mean culturally specific emblems like *OK,* but rather the "beats" that mark emphasis and the logical relations like *if, and, but,* as well as the "icons" that metaphorically depict either the actual topic of thought or more abstract syntactic relations. A gestural component of language meaning directly contradicts the orthodoxy of a purely arbitrary relation between sign and referent, in that the meaning of a gesture cannot be conveyed without describing its actual form. McNeill's videotape studies show that gesture is not a separate system that intersects with language as it develops toward articulation, but rather a key stage of the actual organization of sentences — externalizing their otherwise implicit spatial design. Gestures actually slightly anticipate the spoken words and relations they depict. They disappear in cases of semantic aphasia and begin to come back at the recovery stage where inaccurate paraphrases predominate, at which point the gestures accurately depict the speaker's intentions even when the actual word choice is inappropriate.

In what might initially seem a contradiction of the above, Krauss, Morrel-Samuels, and Colasante (1991) have shown that in forced-choice situations subjects can match gestures with their actual sentence contents only about 60 percent of the time. Including or omitting gesture from spoken communications had no discernible effect on the information gathered. These authors concluded that gestures do not serve a major communicative function. Such a view, however, is actually quite consistent with McNeill's demonstrations that gestures are a key part of the initial construction phase of verbal thought and syntax. The fact that it is difficult to go from hand gestures alone (as also from Werner and Kaplan's physiognomic pictures, and Clarke's accounts of ongoing imagery) to reading off the ostensible conceptual topics they express has too often led to their dismissal as irrelevant to cognitive function. What it shows, rather, with McNeill, is that these phenomena are not primarily communicative but are part of the inner microgenesis of meaning construction — which reaches its full communicative form only in the outward media of the various symbolic frames, including language. Symbolic cognition could no more "be" without its inward genesis as a cross-modal stream of self-aware sentience than it could without its outer social communication.

Similarly supporting their relation to functional aspects of symbolic cognition, McNeill finds that gestures are especially frequent in anticipating those points, potentially present in every sentence, that show some degree of novel departure from a presupposed background. On the notion that every sentence contains some novel implication, these points would constitute the reason for the sentence in the first place. This, of course, is quite consistent with Geir Kaufmann (1980) and others on the functional role of visual imagery in the expression of novelty.[3]

The conclusion must be that the very conceptual thought which cognitive psychology has made its "frame of frames" actually entails multiple levels of cross-modal translation involving visual-spatial structures. Even syntactic structure itself must be animated by dynamic-geometric forms as the plan for the forthcoming sentence. Especially those points of unfolding syntax that carry novelty will be kinesthetically embodied and metaphorically envisioned. Language is a synesthesia, and this many times over.[4]

The White-Light Experience and Related States: Cross-Modal or Pre-Sensory?

Although I will deal in detail later with the complex geometric-dynamic synesthesias found in chakra and related mediative states (chapter 10), it is important to emphasize here that mandala and chakra patterns, and especially the "white-light" experience of classical mysticism, entail patterns specific to the organization of vision. Without such a demonstration it might seem more plausible to regard the "light" of the mystics, especially, as a sort of regression to the simple brightness dimension of Osgood and Von Hornbostel — to a primitive and nonsymbolic common matrix for the differentiated senses. On the contrary, these states reflect a cross-translation and transformation between the modality-specific properties of the tactile-kinesthetic body image and the visual field. Accordingly, they would exemplify an intensified form of the hierarchic integration across modalities that is basic to all symbolic cognition.

This is clear enough with Jung's mandala imagery and the closely related geometric synesthesias of the chakras, as visualized body-center experiences in meditation. These latter are generally regarded as preliminary to the more complete experiential integration of the "white light" experience. Jung's (1950) geometrically complex circular mandala patterns, which he took as abstract self-referential metaphors, are clearly visual. Yet there is some indication from the literature on LSD experience (Leary, 1962; Fischer, 1975) and meditative states (Govinda, 1960) that these patterns gain their sense of felt meaning precisely from a felt fusion with the tactile-kinesthetic experience of the body. Subjects feel that in a sense which is difficult to describe they have somehow "become" what started as an abstract visual pattern. Its shape is now indistinguishable from the shape of their own body or, in chakra experiences, regions of their body. It is this phenomenon of sensed embodiment that distinguishes these states, as full of an abstract, if ineffable, portent, from the merely sensory effects of the visual phosphenes and simple geometric forms that are also common in these states.

The complex synesthesias involved herein appear to be multiply determined. On the one hand, there is the tendency of mandala and chakra designs to be divided symmetrically, generally by two intersecting lines into fourfold structures. Given the predominance of odd-numbered divisions in the floral patterns of nature, which do bear a considerable resemblance to Jung's (1950) examples of mandalas, it seems likely that these fourfold symmetries reflect a synesthesia with the four limbs of the body image. If, in addition, we add the central axis of the trunk, this would create the less common sixfold division also prominent in Jung's sample designs. On the other hand, there is evidence from the descriptive literature on meditation (Chang, 1963), schizophrenia (Angyal, 1936a) and classical introspection (Schilder, 1942) that the body image is a kind of ambiguous gestalt that can undergo a potential reversal from the predominant sense of a solid substance into a direct experience of the body as a hollow container. This pattern can appear, under more contemplative conditions, because tactile sensitivity is actually confined to the periphery of the body. There is no differentiated sensation from the interior of the head and torso. Accordingly, the "hollow body" of meditative chakra experiences, as well as the vortex or tunnel experience in drug and near-death accounts, can be understood as a complex synesthesia between this "hollow" tactile structure and the symmetrical funnel or cone of the visual field itself.

A similar cross-modal fusion of what are in fact modality-specific forms also seems to be involved in the so-called "light-of-the-void" experience in deep meditation. I have already discussed the possibility that it is the luminosity of the first stage of visual microgenesis — incipiently "containing" all more differentiated visual qualities that can emerge out of it — which provides the perfect metaphor for a similarly all-inclusive "totality" or "absolute." Indeed, on the present approach, if this "open" visual pattern is to become felt meaning, it must undergo a cross-modal fusion with tactile-kinesthesis. This will entail a transformation of the body image into a "form" as open and expansive as luminosity itself. Such a cross-modal translation would amount to the subjective annihilation of the ordinary body image. This would be the reason for the descriptions of a vivid sense of cessation, dying, disappearance, and void by both mystics and some schizophrenics (Boisen, 1936; van Dusen, 1971; Hunt, 1984). Such accounts of body cessation and felt mergence with the horizonal openness of visual space become part of the evidence, then, that mystical experience involves a complex synesthesia.

The main indication, however, that these states are based on a hierarchic cross-modal integration rather than an amodal brightness matrix common to all modalities comes from the specificity of reference to formal properties of the visual field both in these experiences and in related introspectionist research. Meditative accounts of the white-light experience and introspective studies of the development of visual luminosity with tachistoscopic exposure are remarkably similar. The introspectionists (Bichowski, 1925; Dickinson, 1926) described two stages in the microgenesis of light. First, there is a diffuse grayish glow, spread over the screen in a way that is neither two- nor three-dimensional — identical to Titchener's (1929) pre-dimensional spread as the basic quale of vision and perhaps related to Marr's (1982) two-and-one-half dimensionality. Then there is something the introspectionists described as a "kick of light" or "explosion" shooting out from the center of this diffuse glow until it becomes the two-dimensional screen surface. Margharita Laski (1961), in her review of accounts of mystical and peak experiences, similarly distinguishes between an "intensity ecstasy," with luminosity effects that are explosive and fiery, and the more subtle diffuse glow of "withdrawal ecstasy." It is striking that both the introspectionists and the Tibetan Buddhists have likened this softer spread of luminosity to the first faint glow in the sky just before dawn.[5]

It is interesting in this regard that tachistoscopic research on advanced meditators by Brown, Forte, and Dysart (1984) found specifically lower thresholds for double-flash discrimination but no differences from nonmeditating controls for the detection of rapidly exposed letters and words. This implies that advanced meditation makes the properties of the visual field, specifically, more accessible to direct experience. This would fit well with the present view that these structures have become available as potential metaphoric vehicles for "openness." In addition, these researchers report some very unusual subjective descriptions of these tachistoscopically exposed light flashes, which were not found at all in the nonmeditators. Not only did the meditators show an ability to detect gradations in the appearance and disappearance of the separate flashes, which would be totally subthreshold for most subjects, but their experiences of these simple light flashes involved kinesthetic, and so synesthetic, transformations:

> Sometimes it's more out "there" like looking at a picture screen. Other times my body and the seeing of the light are together, somehow connected. . . . My mind becomes the screen of flashes which happen upon it, but not "out there." . . . You can go into it. I can touch it, have influence over it. I can touch the flash. . . . When I touch it there is a

vortex created, a very concentrated vortex. It can have a form, even like a cross — or a sun, very bright with light radiating out from the sun. The image is made out of very, very tiny points. I can go into any one of them. The small points have form, different texture. (Forte, Brown, and Dysart, 1985, p. 331, 334)

Meditative accounts of the light-of-the-void experience emphasize a paradoxical unity of light and "shining darkness" present simultaneously, which Longchenpa (Guenther, trans., 1976, vol. 3) likens to the "sheen of brocade." Similarly, early experimental introspectionist accounts of luminosity and luster effects (Bixby, 1928; Kreezer, 1930) describe an inseparability of light and dark points mixed up together in a surface that is not further localizable and which they often refer to as indescribable: "(Zinc) the surface is streaked with alternate light and dark points, like pinpoints, and it is as if there was a light behind and shining through. . . . (Shell) the luster comes as a soft, glowy mass of light that at the same time contains within itself a diffuse darkness" (Bixby, 1928, p. 139, 142). These are not Osgood's simple linear dimensions of brightness-darkness, intensity, and activity. They are simultaneously light *and* dark, intense *and* weak, and so on. Accordingly, the meditative experience of this "light" would involve the metaphoric reuse of the actual, paradoxical features of a specifically visual luster.

The qualities of the light-of-the-void experience, then, are specific to vision — but vision metaphorically and synesthetically transformed. They are not pre-modal or a-modal. Their participation in a felt synthesis of modalities strongly suggests that the resulting presentational states are a manifestation of symbolic cognition, as with the cross-modal translations underlying language itself. It may be the open horizon ahead, out of which appear the flow properties of visual space, that provides the only metaphoric pattern which can allow a correspondingly inclusive realization that the actual multiplicity of our more specific feelings and thoughts is potentially contained, held, and allowed within a unified reality.

8 The Multiplicity of Image: Phenomenology and Some Limitations of Laboratory Research

Before proceeding further in exploring the varieties of presentational states and their relation to cognitive theory, we must consider the more ordinary forms of visual-spatial imagery and their place in that wider context. After all, it was the initial attempts at empirical laboratory research on visual imagery that were heralded as a "return of the ostracized" (Holt, 1962) — the beginning of modern psychology's renewed interest in consciousness. Holt, among many others, hoped for a cognitive theory that would include the full range of phenomenological and clinical studies of imagistic states along with a laboratory science of imagery. That is not exactly what happened.

Cognitive research on imagery developed rapidly into two competing camps — both of which ignored the various phenomenologies of ordinary and nonordinary imagery that were available. Instead of seeking to expand the definition of image beyond the concrete or mimetic picture of a specific situation into a fuller range that would include abstract-geometric imagery in scientific thought, the arts, and altered states, laboratory researchers continued their debates within the narrowest possible confines. On the one hand, concretely depictive imagery was considered a direct reuse of perception; on the other hand, it was treated as an epiphenomenal by-product of linguistic-propositional thought. In effect, the Würzburg controversy was rejoined on a more sophisticated methodological level, but one that eschewed phenomenology with a paradoxical, if not defensive, intensity that prevented any placing of both positions within the fuller range of imagistic states.

In fact, as we shall see, there was soon ample experimental evidence for both of these views of imagery. Nowhere else in the current experimental literature in psychology has there been more sophisticated research that ends up supporting all of the positions under contention. Perhaps this does reflect, with Anderson (1978), a sort of indeterminism and complementarity that must be at the heart of any science of our own mind. Then it *would* be ultimately impossible for a self-referential being to determine its own *lingua mentis* (Juscyk and Earhard, 1980). How would *we* know whether thought is ultimately propositional or imagistic — we are too busy doing whatever it is and so can have no independent observational stance from which to judge. Or, perhaps these disputes are more positive and call attention instead to an actual multiplicity and pluralism within the phenomena of imagery. The implication would then be that imagery is far too broad and fundamental a phenomenon to be restricted to but one of its forms or to one area of the cortex.

Certainly there is no other area in contemporary cognitive psychology that poses more starkly the point raised by Ulric Neisser (1976) concerning the very real trade-off in psychology between the precision and control of laboratory research and the loss of "ecological validity" entailed by ignoring the actual manifestations of whatever we study in the ongoing experience of persons in the world. The latter, as a genuine scientific problem, may only be approachable through the use of descriptive phenomenology, based on interview and verbal protocol. As the cognitive psychologist Ralph Norman Haber states: "Psychologists in general, and perception researchers in particular, have invested enormous energy in developing methodologies in which we never have to trust what the subject says. . . . But when we believe that we can discover and understand all the rules of perception by treating the subject as a null indicator, then we must fail. The study of visual imagery is perhaps the clearest case of this failure" (Haber, 1979, p. 594). It is this "fear of phenomenology," in Haber's terms, that has left the experimental psychology of imagery disconnected from its "natural series" of presentational states.

Just as we needed to expand the usual definition of synesthesia to see its full implications for a cognitive theory of symbolic cognition, our concept of imagery must go beyond its usual limitation to voluntarily generated "mental pictures" of concrete events. In particular, we need to add the spontaneous abstract-geometric patterns that may be as central to conceptual thought itself as they are to the imageries of meditation and psychedelic drugs. Only these abstract imageries, supposedly impossible from the traditional definition of image in western thought, will establish the full range of imagistic states and their connection to synesthesias. Only then do we gain a description of consciousness in its presentational aspect with sufficient detail and grain to provide direct evidence of its underlying cognitive processes.

Imagery as Perception or Proposition: A Debate Won by All Sides

The first laboratory research on visual imagery, after its "return," seemed to indicate a direct reuse of perceptual processes. A series of studies by Sydney Segal (1971) demonstrated a specific competition between voluntarily generated imagery in a given modality and the threshold for perceptual detection in that same modality, but not in other modalities. Imagining oneself listening to a song raises one's auditory threshold but does not have a similar effect on visual sensitivity. Shepard and Metzler (1971) found that subjects asked to choose the pictorial view of a complex three-dimensional object that would match it correctly after it had undergone an imagined rotation took longer for rotations that would require the traversing of more angles in a real object. They concluded, in what is still regarded as the most powerful demonstration of this view, that such imagery works on the basis of a direct analogue with real physical transformations — rather than on some propositional or digitalized recasting of physical shape.

Somewhat later, Stephen Kosslyn (1981, 1983) and Ronald Finke (1980) extended this model of imagery as reconstituted perception by showing that subjects scanning an imagined map took longer to make judgments about points that were further apart on the originally perceived map, and were also able to make more rapid judgments about larger imagined objects than smaller ones. Such findings, along with demonstrations of negative after-images, contrast effects, and color mixing in vivid images, seemed to establish imagery within an emerging cognitive science as an ability that operated along the lines of the perceptual processes it directly reengaged. This combination of competition and sharing between imagery and perception in their underlying processes also extends into general spatial orientation as well, in addition to the above modality-specific effects. Thus, Kerr, Condon, and McDonald (1985) found a specific interference effect for memory for spatial information while standing in a physically unstable position, but none for analogously complex recall tasks based on purely verbal information. It would appear that spatial symbolic abilities engage the underlying schemata of posture and balance.

This perceptual analogue model of imagery has been opposed in cognitive science by a more traditional propositional theory. In psychology this has been represented by Zenon Pylyshyn (1973, 1981, 1984) and in philosophy by both the analytic (Ryle, 1949) and phenomenological (Sartre, 1940; Casey, 1976) traditions. From these perspectives the ostensibly sensory qualities of imagery reflect a mere surface array whose deep structure is propositional — with some uncertainty whether the latter is predominantly linguistic or mathematical-logical. Imagery here is rather like the illustrations to a novel. It can only express what is already in the "text," what the person already knows. Imagery alone can never produce new knowledge — despite the claims of many scientists and inventors that this is exactly how they proceed. Imagery may seem to present strikingly new material, but on

inspection its semantic content would derive from previous propositional knowledge. For Pylyshyn (1984), Kosslyn's and Shepard's tasks are not to be explained in
terms of any direct read-off of imagery. Instead, such imagery is "cognitively
penetrable." In other words, it is a secondary expression of propositional knowledge translated into an imagined form and open to subsequent modification as a
result of changes in that knowledge. Pylyshyn argued that Kosslyn's imagery research always involved the tacit suggestion to do the imagery task as you would do
the perceptual one in real life, making the perception-like results a product of the
demand characteristics of the tasks. He also tried to show that subjects' solutions to
imagined situations, such as dropping heavy and light weights simultaneously,
dropping a weight while running, or picturing the properties of fluids in containers,
depended not on what happens in physical reality but on the subject's beliefs about
what would happen.[1]

In somewhat analogous work, Neisser and Kerr (1973) found no differences
between memory performance in subjects asked to imagine various objects as
attached to each other in suggested ways as opposed to physically inside each other.
This implied that such imagery tasks are more related to descriptive knowledge than
to any direct reuse of perception, since that should have made the "inside" condition more difficult. Similarly, Neisser (1972) reported no statistical relationship
whatsoever between questionnaire measures of the vividness of subjective visual
imagery, presumably reflecting the sensory side of imagery, and subjects' actual
performance on Shepard-type imagined-rotation tasks.

Research by Martha Farah has provided results, albeit with a very simple form of
image generation, that are consistent with both the perceptual and propositional
models of imagery. First, Farah (1985) offered evidence that single imaged letters
do directly engage some of the same processes that are involved in actual letter
perception. Imaged letters speed recognition of the same letters flashed tachistoscopically, but only if the imaged version is exactly the same in size and position as
the actual one. Evoked potentials with such imagery were found in the same area of
the occipital cortex associated with response in actual perception (Farah, 1988;
Farah et al., 1988a).

On the other hand, Farah (1986) also found significantly better performance on
the image-priming task with tachistoscopic presentation to the left hemisphere over
the right. Studying neurological patients who complained of a loss in voluntary
image generation, she discovered that the damage tended to be located in the left
hemisphere rather than in the right, supposedly "spatial" hemisphere, previously
assumed to be associated with imaginal abilities (Farah, 1984). The occipital area
involved, at least for such volitional imagery, is adjacent to language areas. This is
much as Pylyshyn might have predicted. Farah (1989) completed this series of
experimental findings by showing that subjects' increased ability to detect real dots

that fell on an imagined letter, as opposed to those not on the imaged letter, did not stem from any lower threshold of perceptual sensitivity, as the perceptual model might predict. Not only was there no similar effect if the letters were actually seen, and not imagined, but the finding reappeared if two letters were shown at once and the subjects were asked to report only the dots falling on one or the other. Here imagery seems to be more a matter of attending and intending, not of changed sensory threshold.

It might appear then that voluntary imagery is a left-hemisphere capacity and best regarded as an attentional or anticipatory state — which does actually reengage perceptual-recognitive processes at some later point in its development. Yet other laboratory research on imagery shows a still broader phenomenon. Justine Sergent (1989) finds a definite right-hemisphere superiority for rotation of imagined shapes, reconstructing fragments into wholes, and recognition of physiognomic shapes. Although Charlot et al. (1992), using blood flow measures, found Farah's left-hemisphere dominance in a task involving examination of an imagined map, there was a right-parietal predominance during resting conditions for those subjects who were rated as highly vivid imagers.

Meanwhile, Kosslyn (1987, 1988), on the basis of both tachistoscopic and neuro-logical-damage studies, extended these localizations to distinguish "what" from "where" aspects of imagery task performance. Shape recognition and imagery were located at the juncture of the occipital and temporal areas in the left hemisphere, with a left-parietal localization for more spatial relationships such as "above" or "below," and a right-parietal localization for "near" and "far." Farah et al. (1988b) even located a neurological patient who, despite specific impairment in imagery tasks based on shape, color, and size (the sort used by Kosslyn and Finke to demonstrate the specifically visual nature of imagery), showed no decrement on the imagery scanning tasks often used to argue for the more general spatial bases of imagery.

We are left with the suspicion that different forms of imagery — volitional versus spontaneous, concrete versus abstract, form recognition versus spatial relations — can be differently organized and differently related to linguistic-propositional processes. The probable hemispheric basis of such different forms of imagery may itself reflect different possible "roles" within a dialogic structure of consciousness. Volitional imagery, constructed and maintained piece by piece, reflects an active "sending" attitude, while a more spontaneous dynamic and holistic imagery emerges as incipient answer in a more passive, "receiving" stance.

Visual Images and Gestalt Reversals: Crucial Test or Different Forms of Imagery?

Nothing would seem to pose the issue more sharply of whether imagery is more like perception or more like thought than the debate over whether the *images* of ambiguous or reversible figures can actually undergo reorganization. Can they shift predominant organization in the same way as actual perceptions of the Necker cube, Wittgenstein's duck-rabbit, or Kohler's vase-face? Gibson's (1979) own model of imagery was broadly propositional. He insisted that images are constructed on the basis of a pre-existent interpretation, so that they will not impart new information on the basis of direct inspection. This led Deborah Chambers and Daniel Reisberg (1985) to predict that it should not be possible for subjects to mentally reverse images based on ambiguous perceptions, at least where the second organization had not been detected prior to the later imagery recall condition. This was exactly what they found — a total failure at image reversals with a range of ambiguous figures, and this despite subjects being able to experience such reversals by inspecting their own drawings of their recalled images.

Meanwhile, in the fashion now typical in this research literature, Finke, Pinker, and Farah (1989) fired back with a study that showed that novel interpretations of images could occur based on the suggested recombinations of separate parts or segments — as in taking a "D," rotating it so that it is flat side down, and placing that side on the top of a "J," making . . . an umbrella. They suggested that spontaneous reversals of whole patterns, as opposed to imaged reorganizations of parts, may be difficult because the actual reversal of perceived ambiguous figures is involuntary, once the subject has fixated on the appropriate area. Yet these experiments elicit requested images that are necessarily voluntary. Voluntary imagery would be much more likely to be based on Farah's discovery of a left-hemisphere "Pylyshyn center" for image formation. It might simply lack some of the figure-ground properties of more spontaneous, involuntary imagery.

Kosslyn's (1983) research, as well as anecdotal accounts of deliberate visualizations in some meditative practices (Govinda, 1960), shows that volitional images are built up and fade segment by segment. Accordingly, the parts of the imaged ambiguous figures which are not crucial for the alternative, not-yet-seen shape will be more likely to undergo fading during the imagery condition. This would make a direct imaginal inspection, at the crucial spot needed to encourage reversal, difficult or impossible. This latter possibility fits well with the greater difficulty that subjects have in recognizing changes from the original stimulus drawing in later drawings, precisely in the areas in which attention would induce reversals in actual perception (Chambers and Reisberg, 1992).

The breakthrough in this curious debate that for a time seemed to constitute the crucial test between image as percept and image as description came with studies by Reisberg and Chambers (1991) and Peterson et al. (1992). They developed an earlier observation on shape recognition by Rock (1983), who found, consistent with the idea of recognitive perception as specific to spatial orientation, that subjects generally could not recognize the shape of Texas if it was rotated ninety degrees from its ordinary position. Reisberg and Chambers (1991) found that subjects could not identify a visual image of Texas in its rotated form if they were told to transform its orientation by a certain number of degrees during the imaginal task, but they could if they were told to make the appropriate side into the new "top."[2] The authors concluded that such imagery is more descriptive than perceptual, although something like a perceptual "scanning" of imagery is also clearly involved.

Meanwhile, Peterson et al. (1992) were able to report a 40 percent reversal rate with classical ambiguous figures if imagers were given similar "reference frame realignment" instructions, leading them to regard certain areas of the shape as its new "top" or "front." This jumped to 83 percent with images of more simple ambiguous figures, whose reversals did not require any shift in gaze in order to make them reverse. We would seem to have in these studies ample evidence that recognitive imagery is based both on perception, in that an image's fading prevents its reversal, and on a process of cognitive description, since attentional direction to recognitive cues is crucial.

This picture is further extended if we do something that seems to cause many laboratory researchers the greatest difficulty and admit into consideration anecdotal reports of imagery experience. In particular, what is necessarily missing from the laboratory literature on reversing figures is the involuntary, preemptory imagery that is so conspicuous in persons of high imaginative absorption. There are reports of eidetic images of Necker cubes being easily reversed (Haber, 1979), and George Gillespie (1989) describes a vivid hypnopompic grid-like pattern which on scanning could undergo repeated reversals from a two-dimensional lattice to a three-dimensional dome. The Poetzl effect in dream and imagery research (Erdelyi, 1985) shows that an initially undetected form can later influence the thematic and pictorial content of subsequent experience, again implying that imagery can undergo its own spontaneous reorganizations and subsequent development. This is also the phenomenon that Roger Shepard (1978) finds basic to much scientific discovery and invention — where anecdotal accounts of more abstractly patterned involuntary imagery stress its potentiality for spontaneous reorganization. Here individuals do seem to learn something new from the image itself, which leads to insights beyond previous propositional knowledge. The addition of phenomenology to an already eclectic research literature shows still more clearly that there is more than one variety of image — a lesson brought home as well by a brief review of the imagery of dreams and the now-familiar debate about its various relations to perception, language, and abstract visual-spatial cognition.

The Stuff That Dreams Are Made On: The Multiplicity of Image in Dreams

Not surprisingly, the contrasting views of imagery as secondary to propositional knowledge and imagery as autonomous reuse of perception are well represented in research on dreaming. For Foulkes (1985), we dream not as we see the world but as we know it to be. Foulkes and Schmidt (1983) find a comparative paucity of new characters, settings, and objects in later phases of dream episodes, suggesting to them that once the narrative-linguistic plan of the dream is laid down, subsequent imagery would be largely subservient to it. Notably absent here were the sort of unexpected intrusions that would be predicted if dream imagery had a spontaneous autonomy. Similarly, Kerr, Foulkes, and Schmidt (1982) found that the partially blind dream as they know their current surroundings to be, not as they actually see them. These subjects described a visual detail in their dreams notably lacking in their actually dim and vague perceptions. From this perspective, imagery is a propositional description and relatively independent from how things actually appear.

On the side of dream imagery as perceptual and spatial, however, and potentially independent of propositional knowledge, we have the demonstration of a direct carryover of red-tinted goggles, worn for several days, into the reported colors from REM-state dreams, but not into the more daydreamlike imagery of non-REM awakenings (Roffwarg et al., 1978). The powerful impact that a blood pressure cuff inflated during REM dreaming has in increasing dream reports of flying, spinning, and other forms of spatial bizarreness (Nielsen, 1993) demonstrates how dream content can be directly influenced by purely spatial processes.

My own research finds significant correlations between high degrees of dream bizarreness, including unusual dream forms like lucid dreaming and archetypal-mythological dreams, and measures of good physical balance, high performance on block design tests (a measure of abstract spatial reasoning), and proclivity to physiognomic imagery (Hunt, 1989; Spadafora and Hunt, 1990; Hunt et al., 1992). The fact that such correlations do not obtain with more normative dream samples, however, is certainly consistent with the view that much of ordinary dream content is propositionally rather than spatially controlled. Perhaps the most striking evidence that people will at times dream both as they perceive and as they know comes from a study of dreaming immediately following limb amputation (Shukla et al., 1982). This is a remarkably specific test of contrasting hypotheses, since these patients know intellectually that they have lost a limb, but phantom limb sensations provide perceptual evidence of its continued presence. In fact, about half of the patients dreamed of a normally present limb, and half dreamed what they knew to be the case.

The fact that voluntarily generated imagery is typically associated with an absence of scanning eye movements, while REM dreaming is defined in terms of rapid eye movements ostensibly scanning the dream array, might seem to be clear evidence that the envisioned content of dreams is closer to perception than to daydream or thought. Here again, however, we find a new version of this continuing debate, and a notable absence of any concession to the complementarity and pluralism that might offer the most parsimonious and even rigorous solution. Thus, Herman et al.

(1987) showed that the ostensible differences between waking scanning and REM-state eye movements, in terms of the latter's greater roundedness and smaller range, did not really distinguish the two states, since they were also found in waking eye movements in darkened surroundings. This does leave open the hypothesis of a dream scanning of percept-like imagery. On the other hand, Aserinsky (1986) has shown differences between the two forms of scanning that do not seem so easily resolved — with a regularity in REM-state saccades that is notably lacking in waking. This, along with the preservation of some eye movements in the REM states of kittens blind from birth, points to the view that REM-state eye movements are part of a discharge process based on vestibular overactivation. They would have nothing to do with any actual looking at the scenes of a dream. Here again, however, a superimposition of the high vestibular activation in REM sleep leading to more automatic eye movements (Aserinsky) over an actual, empirically demonstrated scanning function (Roffwarg) leaves plenty of room for both models. Finally, the absence of REM-state eye movements in the direction of attentional neglect in brain-damaged subjects, who nonetheless show waking saccades in these areas, implies that dreaming eye movements may even be more controlled by attention and orientation response than is usual in waking (Doricchi et al., 1993).

Recent research on both hemisphere involvement during ongoing REM dreaming and the impact of brain damage on dreaming and/or dream recall confirms an ostensible pluralism in the imageries of dreaming. Initial reports of an apparent loss of dreaming with aphasia (Epstein and Simmons, 1983; Foulkes, 1985) might seem to fit well with Farah's (1985) finding that a reported cessation of dreaming, along with the ability to generate voluntary waking imagery, is sometimes associated with damage to the left hemisphere center for imagery. This would be consistent with a Pylyshyn model of dream imagery as ultimately dependent on a left hemisphere propositional capacity. Yet both Geschwind (1981) and Critchley (1953) have observed that the hallucinatory anomalies of spatial perception that are most like the extreme forms of dream bizarreness are associated with right-hemisphere parietal and temporal damage. Schanfald, Pearlman, and Greenberg (1987) shed considerable light on this matter in showing that long-term work with patients complaining of dream loss with either left- or right-hemisphere damage led to some dream recall in most subjects, which, however, never occurred with damage to both hemispheres.

It would make the most sense to postulate a right-hemisphere form of holistic, spontaneous imagery and a left-hemisphere imagery based more on volition, analysis, and propositional control. Damage to the left hemisphere would lead either to a loss of the narratively cohesive forms of imagery studied by Foulkes or to a loss of ability to intentionally recall actually occurring dream experience, or both. Evidence from EEG studies showing enhanced hemispheric coherence in the REM state, in contrast to wakefulness, reinforces this more pluralistic picture of dreaming consciousness (Armitage, Hoffmann, and Moffitt, 1992). Subjects who show the greatest degree of hemispheric coherence during waking cognitive tasks actually have more eye movements during REM sleep and better dream recall (Lavie and Tzischinsky, 1985; Bertini and Violani, 1984).

It would seem that on cognitive, phenomenological, and neurophysiological grounds the forms of imagery involved in dream experience are at least as broad as those in waking symbolic consciousness — perhaps weighted in highly bizarre dreams more toward autonomous, holistic imagery forms. These appear as such only in the more presentational states of waking consciousness. Yet the evidence from dreaming has been largely ignored by cognitive researchers on imagery. The vast majority of laboratory-based cognitive research on waking imagery has been confined to imagery that is concretely pictorial as well as volitional. Of course, deliberate manipulation is the great strength of the experimental method in psychology, if also testimony to its potential lack of ecological validity. So it is not surprising that the sort of image studied has been specific, controllable, and responsive to task demands. Yet the inevitable bias in our understanding of imagery, and so of the presentational side of consciousness in general, seems obvious enough. What has been largely ignored is the descriptive evidence that would demonstrate a more abstract and geometric form of spontaneous imagery, central to creation in science and art and directly manifested in the geometric-dynamic imageries of presentational states. It is the further consideration of the latter, especially, that leads to a rejection of the view, found from Freud (1900) through Allan Paivio (1971) and well beyond, that imagery is necessarily a concrete and so more primitive form of thinking — one that would give way with development to abstract conceptual structures only possible with language. Imagery can become abstract and cross-modal all on its own.

Abstract Imagery: A Heterodox Revolution

We have already discussed visual microgenesis, as manifested in tachistoscopic exposures of recognitive patterns and directly experienced in spontaneous presentational imagery. It provides the geometric dynamics that would be central to an abstract cognition conceived as broadly imagistic and nonlinguistic. It would be the disassembling of visual patterns along the lines of their normally unconscious, ultrarapid microgenesis that would both allow the speed of thought and extract the abstract lattices, spirals, flows, and bursts that are implicit within every optic array. These would not be discernible as separate phases within navigational perception at all, but would be released by cross-modal translations as the most likely medium for a simultaneously given structure of thought.

Rudolph Arnheim (1969, 1974) has provided the major illustration of how such abstract imagistic processes might operate in aesthetics, with his demonstrations of how tachistoscopic and stroboscopic exposures bring out the expressive structures of painting. Whether outwardly naturalistic or abstract-expressionist, the felt meanings of visual art are most immediately conveyed by what Arnheim termed the abstract "visual dynamics" or "skeleton of forces" embedded in the painting at the most basic level of figure/ground differentiation. These abstract shapes and incipient dynamic flows will stand out as such with stroboscopically induced pulsations ("gamma movements"). The rapid oscillation of the stroboscope does not give enough time for the identification of specific objects in the painting, but it does allow a fundamental dynamic shape to loom out as its most basic physiognomic or expressive structure. For instance, predominantly horizontal line dynamics will tend to convey stability and calm, verticals more excitement and upward striving, and diagonals greater degrees of tension (Bang, 1991). The complexity, dynamics, and relation to symmetry of geometric shapes has also been pursued by Leyton (1992) in his similar analysis of visual art.

The artist Gordon Oslow Ford (1991) makes observations analogous to Arnheim's descriptions with the tachistoscope. His work demonstrates how extremely rapid drawing — permitting only briefly sketched lines, dots, or simple enclosed outlines, what he terms "Live-Line-Beings" — will approximate a speed of awareness basic to all creativity but normally denied direct access to awareness by the slower, more finished qualities of practical consciousness:

> At a certain speed of awareness ō elements fuse together and become Live-Line-Beings. We are all descended from Live-Line-Beings. . . . A spontaneous line is alive. It introduces a force along its length and can also cause a lateral wake in surrounding space that is sometimes visible, sometimes implied. . . . Awake and asleep we are in the Great Spaces whether we are aware of it or not. . . . Demons belong to the world of dream and myth and exist at a speed of awareness too slow to gain entrance into the inner-worlds beyond. . . . To discover the landscape of the muse, a language has to be found in lines, forms and colors. (Ford, 1991)

Such expressive visual dynamics are clearly synesthetic. In Arnheim's terms, they are "felt" as much as they are "seen." They are visual versions of McNeill's gestures. Such abstract spatial dynamics also seem to be part of the microgenesis of word recognition, as we saw in Werner's (1956) demonstration that subthreshold words, with meanings explicitly unidentifiable, could nonetheless be sensed as high, heavy, deep, expansive, and so on. This reflects ultrarapid live-line structures within language itself.

Whereas Arnheim (1969) stressed the importance of abstract diagrams and imagery in scientific discovery, it was Shepard (1978) who documented the extent to which physical scientists have claimed to think in spontaneous geometric-dynamic imagery. Shepard presents anecdotal accounts of the relation of such imagery to the discoveries of Einstein, Maxwell, Faraday, Helmholtz, Watt, Tesla, and of course Kekule, with his oft-cited serpentine spirals as the structure of the benzene molecule.[3] He also cites Jungian mandala imagery and spontaneous geometric forms in the hypnagogic state as spontaneous exemplifications of these structures of abstract thought, here released presentationally and for their own sake. Shepard quotes a passage from the astronomer and chemist John Hershel, written in 1867, on the implicit logic within such imagery:

> If it be true that the conception of a regular geometrical pattern implies the exercise of thought and intelligence, it would almost seem that in such cases as those above adduced we have evidence of a *thought,* an intelligence, working within our own organization distinct from that of our own personality. . . . In a matter so entirely abstract . . . as the production of a geometrical figure, we, as it were, seize upon a creative and directive principle in the very act, and in the performance of its office.
> (Quoted in Shepard, 1978, p. 181)

Arnheim himself argued that all thought, including the logical and linguistic, must ultimately rest on ultrarapid geometric-dynamic imagery. Contra Kosslyn and Paivio, imagery is not to be restricted to the concrete depiction of specifics, nor is it intrinsically subordinated to language. Only geometric-dynamic forms are, for Arnheim, complex enough, precise enough in their relational structure, and given rapidly enough to be part of a primary medium for conceptual thought. The morphemic or sound structure of language is too amorphous and purely sequential to be part of that organizing medium. Arnheim notes that these same visual dynamics appear in gestures during speech — a point developed by McNeill. For Arnheim, it is the structures of perception itself that are the ultimate template for all knowledge:

> This spontaneous use of metaphor [in gesture] demonstrates not only that human beings are naturally aware of the structural resemblance uniting physical and nonphysical objects and events; one must go further and assert that the perceptual qualities of shape and motion are present in the very acts of thinking . . . and are in fact the medium in which the thinking itself takes place. . . . Man can confidently rely on the senses to supply him with the perceptual equivalents of all theoretical notions because these notions derive from sensory experience in the first place. . . . Human thinking can not go beyond the patterns suppliable by the human senses.
> (Arnheim, 1969, pp. 118, 233)

I will return, in chapter 13, to the implications of this view that all scientific concepts are formalizations of principles already present in perception.

Arnheim provides many examples of how subjects can make geometric-dynamic drawings that reflect their actual understanding of various abstract, ostensi-

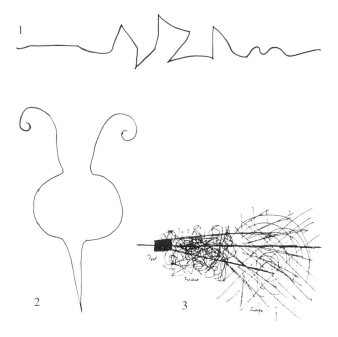

Figure 11. Pictorial representations of time. From Visual Thinking *by Rudolf Arnheim ©
1969 The Regents of the University of California. Reprinted with permission of the University of California Press.*

bly verbal concepts. Figure 11 shows several such examples of the concept of
"time" as drawn by different subjects. In the first, the individual seems to think of
time as a connected line: the present is everything, with past and future lacking its
specifying detail. The second subject sees time as a natural expansion outward from
a fixed past into an open present and still more open future, while the final subject
links an impenetrably dense past with a chaotic present foreshadowing a similar
future to come. Of course, such illustrations cannot prove that all thought operates
with such patterns on an ultrarapid, normally unconscious level. They can only
demonstrate that it is possible to translate the logic of semantic relations into an
abstract imagistic form.

It is true that if one walked into a classroom and saw just these unlabeled designs
on the blackboard, one would not thereby say "Oh, you're discussing time, aren't
you?" In other words, as with the functionalist critique of introspected imagery and
gesture research, there is no way to go from the supposed vehicle of symbolic
expression to its specific referent. What is absent from these drawings is the pointing that takes them beyond themselves and into the referent that is their meaning.
For Arnheim, this is the paramount function of language. The apparent lack of

communication in abstract dynamics alone shows that they reflect primarily the inner and microgenetic processes of felt meaning and less the conventional, culturally dictated codes for referential pointing. Yet even if we are not told that these diagrams "stand for" different versions of time, it is readily possible to see the structural and logical relations within them, to see how the various components of each drawing are related to each other. It would take these subjects many minutes to state verbally this inner logic of their understandings, here given at a glance and awaiting only the final labeling to achieve considerable communicative intent. What we can tell from Arnheim's sample drawings may not include their referents, but it certainly covers a great deal of the formal, logical structure implicit within all felt meanings.

The major subsequent development of Arnheim's theory of the basis of abstract thought in visual-spatial metaphor is to be found in the combined efforts of the linguist George Lakoff (1987) and the philosopher Mark Johnson (1987). In contrast to Pylyshyn, Kosslyn, and even Arnheim, they attempt to derive the actual organization of syntax itself from abstract imagery. Contrary to almost everyone who has written about imagery, except Shepard and Arnheim, they do not view imagery structures as developmentally primitive but rather consider them the actual *lingua mentis* of all symbolic cognition — extending as surely into logic and physical science as into daydreaming and fantasy.

For Lakoff (1987) and Johnson (1987), conceptual structure becomes meaningful because abstract spatial metaphors are kinesthetically embodied — a view quite consistent with the explicitly synesthetic model of symbolic cognition developed above. Basic perception would provide two kinds of symbolic structures, which these authors term "basic level structures" and "image schemas." Basic level structures are defined as the "convergence" of gestalt principles of perception, the forms of basic body movements, and the ability to form rich imagery. Included are properties like tall-short, hard-soft, heavy-light, and cold-hot, being essentially identical to what Asch referred to as the "double-function" terms of metaphoric usage. That these patterns would arise out of a convergence across gestalt properties and bodily actions obviously implies that they are precipitated as potential symbolic meanings by a cross-modal integration. We will see, however, that this concept remains underdeveloped within the theory to date.

Image schemas are somewhat more abstract forms found in ongoing bodily and spatial experience. They include container, path, source-goal, limits, balance, merging-splitting, and force, among others, as well as bodily orientations like up-down, front-back, near-far, part-whole, center-periphery, and full-empty. With respect to "force," for instance, Johnson (1987) points to many kinds of physical force readily expressed in imagistic terms, including compulsion, blocking, diversion, removal of constraint, enablement, and attraction. He goes on to suggest that the various parts of syntax gain their meaning through the animation of such patterns —

"must" resting on compulsion, "may" on the removal of constraint, and "can" on enablement. All logical relationships are rooted in the image schemas provided by perception. They are not per se propositions, but the template allowing propositional logic in the first place. Nor should these patterns be regarded as "mental pictures." They are not restricted to any particular modality, Johnson says, and cannot be drawn without making them overly specific.

There is the strong implication in both Lakoff's and Johnson's discussions, unfortunately not developed further, that image schemas are cross-modal translations. Both refer to them as "kinesthetic," which they define, somewhat strangely, as "independent of sensory modality," or as "general enough to have a kinesthetic nature." They also relate image schemas to Arnheim's earlier "visual dynamics," which Arnheim described as kinesthetically felt as much as seen. Like Jackendoff (1987), however, they opt for treating these basic perceptual forms as "amodal" rather than synesthetic, which ultimately leads them away from the cross-modal synthesis theory actually implied by their material. Since path, link, near-far, etc., are also the organizing principles of the behavior of nonsymbolic creatures, there must be a step beyond the manifestation of these structures in movement that is needed to raise them to the status of organizing spatial metaphors. Since these structures are part of the organization of all perceptual modalities, that missing step would be their abstraction for symbolic use by means of cross-modal translations and transformations. As cross-modal emergents, their structural complexity is located somewhere between simple synesthesias and the complex geometric synesthesias of hallucinatory states. They would be the fundamental structures out of which representational semantics and syntax could emerge, on the one hand, along with the more structurally intricate patterns of abstract conceptual thought and spontaneous presentational states, on the other.

Finally, Lakoff (1987) stresses that image schemas are as basic to the self-referential conceptualization of human experience as they are to representations of the structures of the external world. Here he makes a major contribution to the earlier demonstrations, from Vico to Jung, Asch, and Arnheim, of the etymological rooting of all words for psychological states in physical patterns that have been given a metaphorical usage. For Lakoff, we cannot even begin to describe our experience, or indeed to have it in the first place, without using image schemas. In a fashion that emerges even more directly in the presentational states of meditation (chapter 10), we sense our body as a container, "within" which we *experience* our emotions as fluidic energies that manifest different types of physical force. To illustrate, here is Lakoff's discussion of anger:

> The body is a container for the emotions.
> — He was *filled* with anger.
> — She was *brimming* with rage.

Anger is the heat of a fluid in a container.
— You make my *blood boil.*
— *Simmer* down!
When the intensity of anger increases, the fluid rises.
— His pent-up anger *welled up* inside him.
— We got a *rise* out of him.
(Lakoff, 1987, pp. 383–4)

Such usages utilize, and presumably not coincidentally, the same geometric-dynamic forces and forms involved in the direct experience of transpersonal states. Meditative consciousness, while especially enhanced and intensified, is also structured through and through by cross-modally based physical metaphor as its very fabric.

Some Implications of a Metaphoric-Imagistic Theory of Symbolic Cognition

We have already seen that any theory of the metaphoric roots of cognition as generated by cross-modal translation will imply an openness and novelty in all symbolic expressions, since there is no one way to "deconstruct" perceptual structures. Lakoff and Johnson echo Wittgenstein in the view that all our knowing is thereby indirect — a "seeing as" based on contemplating one situation through and by means of another. The basic structure of the situation we use as "lens" may consist in dynamically expressive visual imagery or in sound patterns utilized to bring out the same dynamics. We have also seen that the assumption that the metaphor comes from a domain somehow better known than its referent is a fiction. Rather, the lens or vehicle is treated *as if* it had a fixed and known structure, in order to cast light on an event or situation under explicit question. When we say "man is a wolf" or "anger is explosive" it is absolutely not the case that we really know more about wolves and explosives. Arnheim, McNeill, Johnson, and Lakoff locate the dynamics of such usage. They demonstrate how metaphoric vehicle and referent are, to use Werner and Kaplan's terms, "reciprocally rotated" so as to set up a cross-reference that will extract an illuminating common structure, or "shared face." This linking of symbol and referent is cross-modal — an inner kinesthetic embodiment fuses with Arnheim's abstract visual dynamics or Lakoff and Johnson's image schemas in order to bring out a meaningful pattern. The two patterns flow into each other in a manner which, experienced presentationally, is synesthesia, and subordinated to pragmatic reference is symbolic representation.

The interactions between linguistic and imagistic systems, of such interest to both Pylyshyn and Arnheim, albeit very differently conceived, would now be understood as secondary relationships between differently organized systems of cross-modal integration. Language has a maximally verbal-acoustic outer face, but one that is animated by visual-kinesthetic synesthesias at all stages of its development.

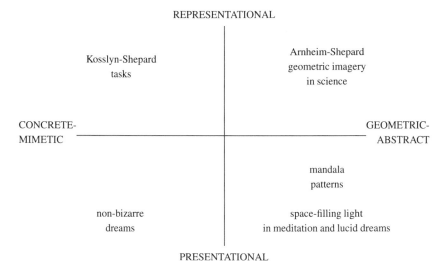

Figure 12. Dimensions of imagery.

Imagery has an outer face of visual forms, kinesthetically animated and so potentially penetrable at multiple stages by the linguistic cross-modal system. Imagery unfolds into speech as surely as speech is envisioned, and both forms share a common kinesthetic embodiment that can equally be informed by the maximum simultaneity of vision and the maximum sequentiality of audition.

Figure 12 summarizes and integrates the multiple forms of visual imagery, here represented in terms of two orthogonal dimensions. The first is anchored at one end by the more traditional concrete or mimetically depictive imagery. It is common to Kosslyn's and Shepard's imagery tasks, which reuse modality-specific structures, and to the content of realistic or nonbizarre dreams. At the other end would be the abstract geometries common to discovery in the arts and sciences and to visionary mandala patterns. The second dimension separates representational imagery, where the image points beyond itself to a denoted referent, from imagery best termed presentational--where a typically polysemic meaning emerges in successive layers only through an experiential "living" of the image itself. Ordinary, true-to-daily-life dream scenarios are depictive and presentational. Writing would be representational and geometric-dynamic, since, in Gibson's (1979) terms, forms seen for their own sake are assigned arbitrary meanings. Each quadrant could both penetrate and be penetrated by propositional-linguistic knowledge. This latter penetrability would be greatest for concrete imagery, where language can readily drive its content on associational and illustrative bases, and least for geometric-dynamic imagery. In turn, the latter would be required as part of syntactic structure itself.

There are two further implications of this mutual influence of a cross-modally based language on image and a cross-modal image on word. The penetrability of spatial-metaphoric processes by cultural knowledge and convention makes all the world a medium for the expression of our beliefs. Along these lines, Claude Levi-Strauss (1969) saw mythological systems as classificatory grids whose dimensions were anchored by the concrete particulars of the physical environment, which thereby constituted a version of the physical world as text. At the same time, the geometric-dynamics endlessly reorganized through the diverse symbolic frames are ultimately rooted in the properties of the physical order and the organization of perception. This also entails the conclusion that a symbolic consciousness based on perception must ultimately be shared and common. The structures of thought are directly given to all of us by the phenomenal organization of the world.

Finally, the imagistic-metaphoric rooting of thought does not mean that anything can be arbitrarily "seen as" anything else. To return to an example from the previous chapter, the predominantly chosen design for *zekite* cannot be turned into *ulalah* in any fashion at all. Its perceived structure must be respected and followed precisely for the emergence of its otherwise latent polysemies. Certainly, all our symbolic formulations may be thereby open to "deconstruction," but that will be less resonant with Derrida than with James Hillman. The opening out of text is explicitly guided by the polysemic image structures within words and their etymologies. The paths untaken are really there.

9 *Sensus Communis:* A History of the Cross-Modal Theory of Mind

The major alternative to a computational theory of mind has always been the view that self-referential consciousness emerges out of the dynamic synthesis of the senses. We can trace this alternative history of mind from Aristotle's *coeno-aesthesis*, as common ground of the senses and source of imagination, to the Roman *sensus communis*, closer to our common sense, to Romantic accounts of imagination, aesthetics, and ethical "truths of the heart," and even to Freud's system unconscious. It disappears and reappears periodically, based always on the placing together of the unity of the senses, self-consciousness, intuition, empathy, and creative imagination — in short, a view of mind centered on presentational consciousness.

Aristotle's first explicit formulation of this theory actually reflects a simplification and partial eclipse of a still earlier understanding of mind as emergent cross-modal fusion, implicit in both ancient Greek etymologies and the pre-classical stories of Homer and Hesiod (Onians, 1951). My own view of presentational consciousness is in fact a reassembling of a tacit model that can be traced back to both the ancient Greek and Sanskrit traditions. Following this history forward again, through Aristotle to Geschwind, Arnheim, Lakoff and Johnson, and this present account of symbolic cognition as synesthetic, locates a recurrent perspective that appears whenever phenomenology and self-referential metaphor are admitted as the primary evidence for the nature of cognition.

What periodically reappears is a heterodox view of human consciousness that does not separate thought from senses, or senses from world, imagination from empathy and community, language from feeling, or body from mind. The history that we are about to trace seems like a single struggle to bring something into a more clear and explicit focus. Its interruptions are analogous to a swooning and forgetfulness based on the periodic turning away from our actual experience of ourselves. With Heidegger (1942), we will find in this account that the true beginning often seems to lie ahead, in the clarity gradually approximated as earlier implications are made explicit. Specifically, we will see a single theory of consciousness appear in successively different lights as it is revived again and again in ever differing cultural contexts. The question for a psychology of consciousness, entirely analogous to Heidegger's version for philosophy, is whether we are ready again for the beginnings of the psychology of mind. Very often in development, whether organic, psychological, or cultural, it is the initial form of something, albeit hard to see in its essentials, that foreshadows the final form of its higher integration — once its multiply differentiated parts have been subordinated again to the originating template that only then comes into distinct view.

Aristotle and the *Sensus Communis:* Its Ambiguities and Fragmentations

For Aristotle (*On the Soul, Sense and Sensibilia, On Memory and Recollection, On Sleep and Waking*), reason (*nous*) is autonomous, as it was also for Plato. The price it pays for its embodiment is the necessity of imagery, "without which thought is impossible." *Nous* touches the body at the heart (*kradie, kardia),* which is both the source of imagery and the locus of the integration of the senses. It is the latter that names its function for Aristotle as *coeno-aesthesis* — later the Latin *sensus communis* and our common sense. Aristotle begins by distinguishing between objects that can only be perceived by a specific sense (color, sound) and the "common sensibles" — movement, number, size, duration, and, with important implications below, shape. These are the common ground of the different senses, since any object presented to any sense must have these features. Aristotle states that these common or root properties are perceived by a sense of "internal movement" — that we perceive size and shape by means of a more preliminary motion. This notion seems multiply determined both by the Greek root meaning of "sensation" as movement (Ross, 1959) and by the location of the *coeno-aesthesis* in the heart, as the organ in which the blood, in Aristotle's view, carried the impressions from the different perceptual modalities to their point of integration and coalescence. The integration of the senses in the heart was inseparable from the cognitive capacity for self-awareness, because, Aristotle argued, a sense modality could not know itself but could only be known by something other than itself that also shared in all the modalities. It is the flowing together of the senses that produces such self-awareness, as well as the images of memory, thought, and dreaming.

As an organ, the heart is characterized by movement, as in the flow of blood, and by heat, as reflected in the earlier Greek location of courage and strong emotion in the chest. In early usage this was the *thymus,* which originally referred to the smoke from thyme leaves burned in sacrifice (Onians, 1951). The brain, for Aristotle, was merely an organ for cooling the blood. The human brain is so large in comparison with those of other species because it has to cool our comparatively large and complexly driven heart, as the true seat of emotion and thought.

We need to stop here, briefly, if we are to see the phenomenology in all this, to ask what it was that Aristotle knew in a positive sense, as incipient phenomenologist, that allowed him to make just these mistakes. On the one hand, he locates the mind in the heart, but on the other, that heart ends up performing all the key functions of Geschwind's cross-modal fusion model of the neocortex. The answer would seem to be that the Greeks, along with most other traditional peoples, located consciousness — self-reflective and otherwise — in the chest because that is the area where striking changes in breathing and heartbeat are associated with our most intense experiences. Also, we may find some resonance between movement, as the primary quality of the common sensibles and the essential characteristic of blood, and Gibson's envelope of perceptual flow. Once experience is understood as "stream," it would be tempting indeed for a speculative physiology to locate it in the blood or breath, or both. Some such considerations must have inspired the Greek philosopher Empedocles, in this statement so reminiscent of James's stream of consciousness: "The heart dwells in a sea of blood which flows back and forth around it. That encircling blood is what men experience as thought" (Wheelwright, trans., 1966, p. 137).

Finally, Aristotle and other ancient thinkers cannot have been insensible to the way in which the perceptual modalities, located in specific regions on the periphery of the body, do actually fuse together in our immediate experience — in the same fashion noted by Gendlin as "felt meaning." The heart, attracting blood from the periphery to the center, flowing like experience itself, becomes the obvious candidate for such a fusion. In effect, there is an accurate, if tacit, phenomenology buried within all this erroneous anatomy. Its metaphoric resonance is still with us when we speak of something as "heartfelt" or of the "wisdom of the heart."

One might assume, then, that it is but a small step to link Aristotle's *coeno-aesthesis* with Geschwind's theory of the cross-modal bases of symbolic cognition. But this would clearly not be Aristotle's view. Instead, there is a major ambiguity in Aristotle's concept and its subsequent influence. *Coeno,* as well as the Latin *communis,* refers to a common or universal root, to "that which goes together as common or public" (*Klein's Etymological Dictionary*). Aristotle had in mind something more like Von Hornbostel's and Boernstein's "primordial unity" of the senses, rather than Geschwind's hierarchic integration. Notably absent in Aristotle's usage is the Greek root *syn* — as in *synthesis* or the nineteenth-century coinage of "synesthesia." Whereas most contemporary psychologists and philosophers would see the capacity for self-awareness as only fully emergent on the human level, this does not seem to have been the case for Aristotle. He regarded the imagistic core of imagination, memory, and dreams as present in lower animals. He never discusses *coeno-aesthesis* in the context of reason or soul or anything else he held criterial for human beings.

If our present connection between cross-modal synthesis, self-consciousness, and symbolic cognition is not strictly Aristotelian, it is also true that the various functions he ascribes to *coeno-aesthesis* do cover capacities we now feel correct in regarding as only fully emergent in human beings. Since the flowing together of the senses is what allows us to sense that we are seeing as opposed to hearing or tasting, Aristotle is clearly approaching that reflexivity which Mead, Neisser, and Hofstadter have all made basic to the human mind. If Aristotle is really describing a function that is rudimentary, in our terms phylogenetically primitive, it is surprising that he includes shape or figure as one of his common sensibles. Boernstein (1967) points out that shape or gestalt would never have received such emphasis in perception if psychologists had focused on the more labile and basic senses of smell and taste, rather than on the distance senses of such importance for a theory of mind. There are, moreover, implications in Aristotle that are consistent with a theory of human imagination as a hierarchic integration of modality-specific forms, and so contradict the idea of an undifferentiated sensory matrix. For instance, consider his account of dreaming, in which impressions from the day are carried by the blood and flow together in the heart during sleep, so that sudden activations in the blood during the night produce new amalgamations of previous experience as imaginative dreaming. This model clearly presupposes a cross-modal recombinatory activity that most contemporary observers would understand as human.[1]

The Roman *sensus communis* removes this ambiguity between "lower" and "higher" in Aristotle's account in favor of the latter. Cicero's version of the *sensus communis* (Bugter, 1987; Van Holthoon, 1987) combines Aristotle's own *koine aesthesis* (*coeno-aesthesis*) with the stoic *koine ennoia* — meaning socially common or shared ideas — into a concept that approaches our *common sense. Sensus communis* refers to the judgments shared by people and later, by the 1700s (Arendt, 1971), is represented in vernacular usage as having a "sixth sense" about something. The only difference between the Roman and the contemporary usage is that the former still carried with it the implication of a connection between thought and the fusion of the senses. For Aquinas, in the *Summa Theologica, sensus communis* is one of the "interior senses" and has multiple "sensitive powers." It is the root of the exterior senses, based on "quantity" as their common property, and the source of self-awareness, "as when someone sees that he sees" or makes a discerning judgment between the senses. It is also closely linked to fantasy and imagination, memory, and the "estimative" or "judgmental" capacity. At this point *sensus communis* has come very close, indeed, to being a kind of reason (Van Holthoon, 1987), with the clear implication that this self-conscious capacity rests on a cross-modal integration.[2]

It was not until the eighteenth-century Romantics, with their interest in aesthetics and empathy and their elevation of imagination over reason as the defining attainment of the human mind, that the full implications of the classical understanding of *sensus communis* could be developed. The next and most recent coalescence of these multiple strands of an alternative theory of mind comes, more or less independently, in the work of Geschwind, Lakoff and Johnson, and my own approach to transpersonal states. Meanwhile, our more mainstream psychology has tended instead to carefully separate a capacity of reason or computation as a purely "inner sense" from perception, body, and world. The commonality of the senses, lost as a dynamic-holistic concept, resurfaces, instead, in a more displaced and fragmented fashion, as the electrical basis of neuronal functioning, also identical across modalities and from periphery to cortical center.

The first step in putting mind "inside" and equally distant from senses and world came with the transformation of Aristotle's specific and common sensibles, by Locke and Galileo, into the distinction between primary and secondary qualities. All qualities that are specific to a given modality, as in colors, melodies, and taste, are now secondary, "subjective," and outside of what science can investigate "objectively." They become "mere experience." Primary qualities — size, shape, and above all quantity and motion — are the only properties open to quantification and science (Martinez, 1974). Primary qualities have a greater reality than our experience of the world since they are the very basis of the physical universe as measured by Galileo and Newton. Secondary qualities are cut off from a primary reality. They become the basis of our modern sense of consciousness as a separate and subjective realm. What had been, with Arendt (1971), a connotation of "felt reality" and "immediacy" in Aristotle's common sensibles — a being "in touch" with the "flow" of real events, a "thought of the heart" — becomes limited to whatever can be measured and calculated. Phenomenology will eventually cover whatever is thereby left over, which paradoxically includes our immediate experience of the world. This is now by implication "less real" than its invisible calculated atoms.

The next step, reserved for nineteenth-century physiology, was the transformation of primary qualities into a theory of peripheral nervous conduction. It is now from the binary quantitative pulses of nervous flow that the consciousness of secondary qualities must be reassembled — and at a considerable distance from "world." "Reality" is entirely quantitative within and without, leaving everything else as a construction and so as potential illusion — well open to Cartesian doubt and several steps from the reality defined by physics. Nervous conduction is based on motion and quantity as the core of Aristotle's common sensibles, but their connotation of "lived reality" and "heart" has been completely reversed.

On the philosophical side, soon to become basic to cognitive psychology, *sensus communis*, as the synthesizing capacity of mind, had already migrated inward as Kant's a priori categories, by which the outward chaos of sensation is somehow organized (Marks, 1978). Kant's categories transformed Aristotle's common sensibles of size and shape into "space," duration into "time," and quantity and motion into "causation." The discipline of psychology was thus left with fragmented and ill-fitting versions of the original *sensus communis*. A set of logical categories within a central nervous system, several steps removed from the world, must impose order on a cascade of incoming energy quanta. These interior categories had long since lost their original basis in an embodied felt reality or a common, sixth sense. But then so had the quantitative firings of neural conduction, as the side of *sensus communis* that had originally been both embodied and attuned to the surrounding world.

Further testimony to this loss of an earlier synthesis comes as we trace the quest in late-nineteenth-century physiology and psychology for a new sixth sense as the core of the more differentiated senses. There were several suggestions that actually reformulated aspects of the original *sensus communis*, now denuded of its earlier reference to imagination and cross-modal integration.

Hamilton, for instance, was especially, if ironically, successful in establishing "coenesthesis" as the new term for organic sensation or deep body sensibility (Boring, 1942). The concept is resonant with aspects of Aristotle in describing a sensibility that is highly general, interior to the body, and a common root of more differentiated sensitivities, although here exclusively tactile and excluding vision and hearing. This left the *syn* root for "synesthesia." That term was coined in the modern sense by Galton and Myers, as "vestiges of a primitive undifferentiated sensibility present when the hearing of an external sound carries with it the sensation of a form or a color" (*Oxford English Dictionary*), with a lost usage (from Ribot), completely consistent with the Roman *sensus communis*, as "agreement in notions between different people" (*OED*). Ironically, while Hamilton restricted the literal term utilized by Aristotle (*coeno-aesthesis*) to a sense of interior cutaneous pressure, the *syn* root — implying emergent, higher synthesis — was literally contradicted by the predominant definition of synesthesia in psychology as reflecting an undifferentiated and primitive root of the senses.

The second major candidate for a sixth sense in sensory physiology was "kinesthesis." Kinesthesis was understood as the "sense of motion" from muscular contractions and relaxations. It extracts "motion" from Aristotle's common sensibles, and also describes something primitive and foundational to the senses. Yet it was not long before Titchener and his colleagues at Cornell, generalizing from their introspective studies of problem solving, described thinking as a nonlocalized imaginal kinesthesis. By implication, they had added back into the original *sensus communis* its "higher" component related to symbolic cognition.

Finally, the self-awareness explicit within Aristotle's usage resurfaced again with Sherrington's "proprioception" — a potentially separate sensory capacity related to the immediate feedback from all sensory experience (Boring, 1942). Proprioception or reafferance is certainly basic to perceptual experience and preliminary to the symbolic self-reference of such interest to Mead. For Gibson (1966, 1979), however, the intrinsically self-locating aspect of all direct perception makes it unnecessary to posit proprioception as its own separate sense or ur-sense. Like kinesthesis, proprioception hovers as a sort of conceptual ghost in modern psychology — with the same ambiguity that we found in Aristotle concerning its relation to "higher" thought or "lower" perception.

"Thought of the Heart" in Romanticism: The Reassembling of *Sensus Communis* as Imagination

It was the inversion of value between reason and imagination in the Romantic reaction against the Enlightenment that rendered image, dream, and aesthetics as the highest expressions of the human spirit. Accordingly, the classical *sensus communis* became open again to a very different reading, although one always implicit in its earlier versions. Rather than being a lesser faculty, the blending of the senses creates mind in its highest imaginative and empathic aspects. I will trace two overlapping strands in this new view of mind — one focused on imagination and creativity, the other on community feeling and an empathically shared collective consciousness. Neither of these overlapping traditions of Romantic thought, however, gained any direct access to the mainstream of our psychological and philosophical tradition — disappearing instead into literary criticism, aesthetics, and nineteenth-century approaches to hypnosis and dreaming, and thence finally into Freud's dynamic unconscious.

I will term the first line of this revival "organismic associationism" to distinguish its preoccupation with imagination and aesthetics from the more mechanistic and better known associationism of Locke, Hartley, and Mill. Following here the account of James Engell (1981), we find a specific formulation of an emergent flowing together or coalescence of the senses that is to provide an explanation for the creativity exemplified in aesthetics, metaphor, myth, and intuition. Joseph Addison, writing in the early 1700s, conceived of imagination as a "blending of the senses" through a "common center," wherein each sense adds to the others and in turn changes them to create a "total impression" greater than its parts. Hutchinson and Akenside later suggested that it was this "internal sense" that also perceives beauty and an aesthetic harmony with physical nature. In the early 1800s, the literary critic and historian William Hazlitt brought these views to fruition in a theory of mind remarkably like Lakoff and Johnson's. He was part of a tradition of literary criticism that sought to formulate a theory of what the Romantic poets like Goethe, Keats, and Coleridge were actually doing in their works. Imagination, sympathy, and intuition were understood as related facets of a fluidic blending of the senses into a "total awareness" in which one modality-specific pattern passes into another, thereby creating new forms. Hazlitt's term for this inner sense was "gusto," from the Latin for "taste" — recast here as a generic intuition and common sense. Gusto was the central feeling exciting and recombining all the senses at once, integrating them as the hand does its five fingers.

The second line of articulation, with its preoccupation with empathy and community feeling, reflects the more Roman side of the classical *sensus communis*. Subsequently it was to be reflected also in C. S. Peirce's notion of a pragmatic common sense as the true core of abstract knowledge and of the immediate feeling or sense of reality (Peirce, 1905; Arendt, 1971). Following mainly the account of Hans-Georg Gadamer (1975), we begin with the Earl of Shaftesbury's view, in the early 1700s, of a *sui generis* inner sense of community as the spontaneous source of that morality explicitly denied by Hobbes and Locke. It is "imagination," today the most private of faculties, that allows us to put ourselves in the place of others. For Shaftesbury, imagination is *the* moral faculty. By the late 1700s the Scottish philosophers of common sense (Reid, Brown) argued that the "good sense" embodied in ordinary practical judgment comes from the ability of the mind to connect itself to the world by integrating the senses. Finally, with Oetinger, the Swiss Pietist, *sensus communis* is once again directly translated as "heart." A "thought of the heart" will, if we but let it, see through to the fundamentals of living. This view is perhaps best expressed by William Faulkner in his story "The Bear": "Truth is one. It doesn't change. It covers all things which touch the heart — honor and pride and pity and justice and courage and love. Do you see? . . . Courage and honor and pride, and pity and love of justice and of liberty. They all touch the heart. And what the heart holds to becomes truth, as far as we know truth. Do you see now?" (Faulkner, 1946, p. 329–30).

We have already encountered Giambattista Vico as a direct precursor of Jung, his archetypes, and their basis in physical metaphor. It was Vico's *New Science* (1744) that best synthesized the aesthetic and the communal sides of this transformation of *sensus communis* into imagination. "Uniform ideas originating among entire peoples unknown to each other must have a common ground of truth." (Vico, 1744, p. 22). There is a collective mentality, an "intuitive wisdom of all peoples," based ultimately on shared physical metaphor and the animistic use of the forces of physical nature to serve as "mirrors" for psychological and social realities. This principle was also reflected for Vico in the basis of etymologies for words referring to psychological states in physical metaphor. This "sublime poetry" results from our ability to transform ourselves imaginatively into the congruent aspects of a physical nature within which we can locate what would otherwise be the invisible core of our experience. The combination here of an incipient version of Jung's imaginative "collective unconscious" and Werner and Kaplan's expressive physiognomies is quite striking. We are left with the inevitable conclusion that the fascination with alchemy found in the later Jung, as the deepest and so truest projective psychology, actually represents one of the most complete modern restatements of the Romantic *sensus communis* — in both its psychological and incipient sociological aspects.

We cannot leave this tale of *sensus communis*, its periodic reemergence and occlusion, without taking note of how thoroughly, if implicitly, this ancient concept informs Freud's account of his "system unconscious." There is considerable irony in an original phenomenological theory of consciousness ending up as the structure of the unconscious. Surely this must attest to a kind of historical displacement if not outright repression. For Freud (1915ab), the process of becoming conscious, which is the most basic tendency of the unconscious, involves a "hyper-cathexis." This is the progressive fusion of modalities in which an initial gestural-kinesthetic core gains a visual cathexis, and that amalgam is in turn verbally cathected, so becoming fully conscious in a focal and communicative sense. Correspondingly, repression is based on a dissociation of the senses. First, the verbal cathexis is removed and replaced by an "anti-cathexis" that restrains any verbal formulation. Then, since in Freud's view feeling per se cannot be repressed, the visual image and motoric cathexis are separated. The image is then "repressed," while the motoric element is released as a "primary affective discharge" that can range from outward muscular tension and unwitting gestural expressions to panic. The necessity of affect being released motorically, in various forms, links Freud's account to the empathy side of the classical theory, for it means that Freud's unconscious, although by definition hidden from oneself, is with equal necessity shown to others. What we repress is directly available to the empathic abilities of others. This account of an incipient cross-modal cognition in Freud's unconscious makes it more intelligible how he could also speak of the therapeutic process as coming to know oneself as others do. It is what is most denied in ourselves that shows itself most insistently and repeatedly to others. To fully and completely "take their role" is to see ourselves as others do — which will gradually include what we usually show without full self-conscious awareness.

We can thus see an ever-present, if tacit, phenomenology within the more impersonal or "process" side of Freud's psychoanalysis. The only major psychoanalyst to see and develop this *sensus communis* concept within Freud's account of mind was W. R. Bion (1962, 1963). For Bion, symbolic cognition, as expressed in language, thought, dreams, and memory, is only possible on the basis of "alpha elements" — essentially identical to Gendlin's felt meanings. Gendlin's synesthetic core of felt meaning is what Bion had termed "alpha function" — the capacity to sustain organized experience on a cross-modal, symbolic level, in the face of that anxiety at the sense of the unknown which is the price of human cognition. Defensive splitting for Bion consists in the fragmentation of this alpha function, integrating the senses, into multiple "beta" elements. These are modality-specific sensations and images that have been denuded of any sense of significance as a result of their failure to fuse into the cross-modal alpha elements that make organized symbolic cognition possible. The collapse of alpha elements, as the semantic units of mind, is thus indistinguishable from clinical withdrawal, semantic satiation, and the modality-specific "sparks struck off" of introspectionism. We have already seen how Gendlin's (1978) clinical method of focusing, by which diffuse moods are first kinesthetically located, then given visual image and verbal expression, is the experiential version of Freud's process account of "becoming conscious." Bion explicitly understood his alpha function as a contemporary version of "common sense," whose cross-modal coordinations allow us some sense of felt reality and being.

The Original *Sensus Communis:* A Phenomenology of Consciousness in Ancient Greek and Hindu Thought

A Greek Phenomenology of Ordinary Mind

We turn now to evidence from the etymologies and usages in Homer's *Iliad* and the writings of Hesiod, following especially the work of R. B. Onians (1951), which will allow us to trace a still more inclusive prehistory for Aristotle's *sensus communis*. This earliest view sees mind as a fusion of thinking, feeling, and desire, based on a synthesis of the senses resulting from the mixing of their multiple "breaths." It is the breaths or winds produced by the peripheral senses, not blood in this earliest conception, that carries impressions inward towards their coalescence in the chest. Thus the lungs are the source of that unity of the senses which, again, Geschwind places in the tertiary neocortex. It is the same theory, with a different localization. In this most ancient phenomenology, however, there is also a second, "vertical" axis of experience, likewise based on a flow of liquid and air, and linking sexuality and spirituality as two poles of the same dimension. We will see below how close this vertical axis is to the yogic chakra traditions and Buddhist "mind as such." For now I emphasize only that Aristotle's "naturalism" is actually a simplification of this original system. Aristotle places it instead in the heart and blood, both promoting and separating reason (*nous*) into the vacated place of the earlier spiritual dimension in the head.

We have already noted that the etymologies of words for mind and experience in Greek and other languages were originally metaphors for the same flowing and coalescing properties of water, wind, and fire that have been the continuing sources for our "modern" phenomenologies of consciousness. These natural phenomena are pervasive and impossible to circumscribe in the same way as the flow of immediate experience for James. Constantly changing, flowing, and transforming, they take the shape of their surroundings and assimilate them in turn. The absence of any explicit differentiation between experience and physical metaphor means that this early usage will not have suffered our perhaps specifically Western separation of an autonomous consciousness from body and world.

Julian Jaynes (1976)[3] has traced the transition of the multiple Greek words eventually used exclusively for subjective experience from an original reference to properties of the physical world to a transitional instantiation in specific bodily organs. This "localization of function" was apparently based on the metaphoric fit between implied phenomenology and the physiognomies of the organs in question. Thus *thymus*, originally from the burning and smoke of thyme leaves during sacrifice, was localized in the chest as the seat of strong emotion and its burning heat. *Phrenes* first referred to air and wind, but ended in the lungs as the source of emotion, recognition, and speech — all these directly manifested in changes of breathing as the outward signs of experience. *Kradie*, or heart, as an organ that sees and knows and also beats loudly in situations of courage and fear, originally seems to have referred to any rapid motion — as in the quivering of a branch. The related *nous*, Aristotle's term for mind as reason, was originally anything physically shown in the world — thence to be located also in the heart as the capacity that sees, hears, and feels. *Nous* is described in the *Iliad* as a liquid that darts, rushes, and is restrained. I have suggested already that the coursing and rushing of blood and air through the chest becomes an obvious source of metaphoric resonance with the flow dynamics of perception in Gibson's "streaming perspective" and with thought in the flows of its cross-modal syntheses.

R. B. Onians (1951) organized these concepts, along with their implied phenomenology, into a hidden cross-modal theory of consciousness deducible from Homer and Hesiod and made explicit in Hindu yoga. All that we now refer to as symbolic cognition was localized in the *phrenes*. They hear, see, and speak. Indeed, the original meaning of *aesthesis* (sense) was "to gasp." The localization of *phrenes* as lungs is strongly implied in both the *Iliad* and ancient Hindu thought by the references to changes in breathing as a reflection of experience and the fact that they are described as "blackish" in the *Iliad*. *Thymus,* Onians concludes, must also refer to the flow of air in breathing. Although often linked to Aristotle's "heart," *thymus* is not described as fluidic like the later *nous*, but as vaporous and smoking. Its later connection to blood through their common "heat" is not conclusive, for Onians, because the early Greeks thought that blood was equally distributed through heart and lungs. The early Greeks seem not to have differentiated between these organs as the common source of air and blood. As courage, *thymus* was described as "breathed" into the heroes of Homer by the gods. There is even mention of the belief that flute players were of low intelligence, since they blew away the flowing source of mind.

The notion of perceptual and symbolic experience as based on flowing breath became more explicit in the later Stoic view that sense impressions are winds or breaths carried inward from the perceptual modalities to coalesce in the chest. It is further developed in Hindu thought, where all levels of consciousness, sensory, conceptual, and spiritual, are based on the *phrenes* and their channels. Hesiod's *Theogony* described men of wisdom as having eyes, ears, and mind that were especially deeply rooted together within the chest, thus being in our sense, and obviously theirs, "balanced" or "centered." Onians believes that this view of mind as cross-modal synthesis carried out in the lungs from the incoming breaths of the senses would have been suggested to the Greeks by the fact that the brachial tubes look like roots, with vessels from the heart also overlapping the lungs in a dense network. Taken as a metaphor for consciousness, this network itself implies a process of synthesis and integration. Geschwind, of course, followed this same logic in his discussion of neocortical zones of convergence.

Phrenes, thymus, nous, and *kradie* (along with *ker* as another synonym for heart) form a sort of horizontal axis for a more inclusive version of *sensus communis* that co-relates the coalescence of the senses, emotion, thought, and language, while refusing any separation between mind, body, and world. What we also find in this first version of *sensus communis* is an intrinsic relation between the flowing consciousness of breath and temporality, in the sense of "lived time." This gives Onians's account a remarkably existential flavor that goes well beyond Aristotle's inclusion of duration as a common sensible. In the *Iliad, kradie (cardia)* and *ker* are used interchangeably to refer to the heart as the source of courage and strong emotion, but *ker* is also closely related to *moira* or fate. It is the fates *(keres)* who bind the heart with threads, thereby determining the time of death — the point where the beating (and breathing) of the heart, basic to thought, feeling, and the flow of personal time, finally stops. This seems to be the first assertion of an inseparability between our sense of consciousness as flowing and a corresponding flow of time. Later (chapter 12), in the explicit phenomenologies of Bergson and Husserl, and of course Heidegger, we will see how this sense of consciousness and temporality as two sides of the same phenomenon comes again to the fore.

"Mind as Such" in Greece and India: A Vertical Axis of Consciousness Linking Sexuality and Spirituality, Time and Eternity

The ur-form of the *sensus communis* constituted a horizontal axis of experience embodied in the chest, where the senses coalesced to create thought, emotion, desire, and time as personal fate. It is supplemented in the prehistory of Greek thought, and especially in the Indian tradition, by a vertical axis, also based on the flow of liquid and breath, but here more interior to the head and spinal column. As *psyche* — its higher, sublimated form — it is the source of spirituality and life after death. In its lower, procreative form — *aion* — it is the seat of sexuality and vital energy in general. We are dealing here with a conceptual framework intriguingly common to Freud, Jung, and classical yoga, and one remarkably like the present attempt to relate transpersonal and cognitive psychology through their common synesthetic organization.

The Greek *psyche,* following Onians's account, was, like *phrenes-thymus*, originally a "breath" soul. In the *Iliad, psyche* is understood as a general life force located in the head. It leaves as a spirit at death from the mouth, face, or top of the head. *Psyche* has no function in ordinary waking life in this earliest literature. Its significance comes only with death or in the experience of "visitation" dreams from gods — the Greek form of archetypal or "culture pattern" dreaming (see Hunt, 1989a), in which the god appears as an apparition standing by the head of the sleeping hero. In the early Roman tradition, one's *genius* was similarly located in the head, seen as a snake or a flame in the dying, and represented by rays radiating out of the heads of the gods. For both the Greeks and Romans, the head was holy and the seat of life. One cannot help but wonder whether this account reflects a proto-phenomenology of out-of-body experience. Modern subjects do often describe a sensation of energy flowing up from the spine and out the head (Green, 1968b). The out-of-body experience is directly implied within the still earlier "flight of the soul" as the ubiquitous form of transpersonal experience in native shamanism (Eliade, 1964).

Of the later Greek philosophers, Alcmaeon of Croton was the first to locate the convergence of the senses or *sensus communis* in the head. Onians speculates that this shift upwards from the chest to the head may have been helped by the important place of *psyche* in the developing mystery cults, which in turn led to its use more and more in reference to thought and feeling in daily life. Whatever the basis, the Greek philosophical view of mind (*nous*) shows a gradual fusion between the *phrenes-thymus* axis and *psyche* into one system, with a long debate over its location in head or heart. Emotion was most obviously manifested in heartbeat and breathing, whereas reason was calm and cool — as in the actual liquifying brain tissues of the dead and in contrast to their "steaming blood." Accordingly, there was also the tendency to separate emotion and reason, locating only the latter in the head. Aristotle followed this shift, as well, but in spirit only. Higher reason is the closest he gets to a sacred principle, one forced to use the "lower" images of the heart. What we are tracing here is a process of secularization, common to many classical peoples, in which universal access to the gods and mythological realms through dreams and visionary states is gradually lost. By the time the naturalistic Greek philosophers began to construct a formal theory of mind, they did not need a separate dimension for the transpersonal.

We are also tracing, and not coincidentally, the beginnings of our own misleading separation of thought and emotion, so laboriously linked again by thinkers like Gendlin and Heidegger. We are at the first manifestations of the mind-body split that would fit so well into the Judeo-Christian era. *Psyche,* as vital soul, originally played no part in the ordinary consciousness of thought, feeling, and desire embodied in the chest, while *soma* similarly referred in its earliest usage only to the bodies of the dead — to corpses. The later secularized usage of these terms created a new division completely absent in the earlier Greek and Hindu accounts. There we find two interrelated axes of experience — one, *sensus communis,* treating mind and body inseparably, the other, *psyche,* a more abstract spirit or vitality itself. Both these axes crossed at the heart. By Hellenistic times *psyche* had come to convey most of what we now mean by mind, especially in its "higher," more specifically human aspects (Hillman, 1972). But the price was a division between mind and world, higher reason and lower senses, totally at odds with both the classical *sensus communis* and the earlier view of *psyche* as a transpersonal dimension — one bound up with an incipient vitalism.

In fact, the earliest references to *psyche* are inseparable from *aion (aeon),* which meant both one's own lifetime, as well as the vital fluidic principle of procreative seed. This latter the Greeks understood as descending from the head to the genitals. A primary indication of this downward descent was the appearance of genital hair at puberty. Where *psyche* was wind, flowing up and out with death, *aion* was liquid, flowing down — the early Greeks apparently instantiating this in the cerebro-spinal fluid.[4] The spinal marrow of the dead is described as going watery and flowing like a snake (Onians, 1951). The only body truly separate from the pre-classical *psyche-aion-phrenes* was the dead one. In the living body, on the contrary, vitality and spirituality were inseparable. In both the Greek and Indian traditions, retention of the life fluid through sexual abstinence will result in the prolongation of life. Later, Taoist sages would seek prolonged life and greater vital energy for spiritual practice by using penile rings to prevent seminal emission (Blofeld, 1973). Freud's own resort in old age to what is now termed vasectomy for the purposes of supposed rejuvenation attests to the durability of this notion, or more likely, perhaps, to the continued availability of bodily metaphors for a more general implicit phenomenology.

Further indication that this vertical axis is the ancient Greek version of transpersonal psychology comes from the coordination of *aion,* as the more personal flow of time, with *Okeanos* — the mythic ocean encircling the earth and surrounding the serpent *Chronos* (cosmic time). The world soul to which *aion* is coordinated is thus a serpent consuming itself, beginning with its own tail. This is the origin of the uroboros symbol of such importance in the imagery of alchemy and an obvious autosymbol for the self-referential nature of all symbolic cognition — perpetually turning around on itself, yet unable to get the whole into view. Both *aion* (personal time) and *Chronos* (its cosmic or spiritual aspect) are represented as serpentine and liquid. It cannot be a coincidence when contemporary phenomenologies represent both consciousness and the sense of temporal duration with the same imagery of flowing and streaming. Certainly, for Heidegger, the human sense of a transcendent reality at the basis of the mystical traditions rests on a direct attunement to time as an experienced flow out of an unknown source.

The Hindu and later Buddhist meditative traditions developed this vertical axis as both metaphor and description of transpersonal experience (Onians, 1951; Govinda, 1960). I will deal with the phenomenologies of these abstract synesthetic states in the next chapter, but it is worth emphasizing here that in eastern thought as well, ordinary mind is a sixth or inner sense located at the heart as the point of convergence of the perceptual modalities. The heart chakra, often depicted as red and associated with heat and fire, is the integrative center of most meditative traditions. It is also part of the vertical dimension that is specifically activated in meditation. In ordinary mind the winds (pranas) and drops (liquid vital seeds) descend from the head along the two side channels on the left and right sides of the body and linked respectively to the energies of sexuality and aggression. These side channels provide their energies to the sixth sense, which is equally thought, feeling, and desire. Meditative practice is understood as arousing the "cosmic" energies of the central channel, otherwise not part of ordinary mind. This activation of the central channel is variously termed the arising of the serpent power Kundalini, in Hindu thought, or Dumo heat, in Tibetan Buddhism. It allows the "drops" and "winds" of the brain to descend into the central channel. The final re-ascent of these coalescing, synthesizing streams back into the head chakra is associated with the white-light experience or with passage out of the head, on the pattern of the out-of-body experience.

Rather than treating such accounts as "explained" by what we can now see is a fantastic and erroneous physiology, it seems more plausible to regard such systems as an incipient, metaphorically based phenomenology of the varieties of presentational consciousness — unfolding for their own sake, or independent of the horizontal axis. This is explicit in Indian thought and implicit in the early Greek tradition. The "subtle physiology" of these traditions is partly based on the synesthetic patterns involved in transpersonal states, partly on the metaphorical similarities between internal organs and presentational experience.

Implications and Consequences: The Primacy of Experience and Its Periodic Recovery

As we have already seen in the close relation between Freud's system unconscious and *sensus communis*, the core of Freud's psychoanalysis is surprisingly archaic and classical in its implications and resonance. Just as *aion* animated the body from the head down, Freud's libido is initially bound up orally and narcissistically, thence descending along the cerebral-spinal axis to animate the earliest "body ego" and energize the erogenous zones of anus and genitals. Similarly, there is an ascending sublimation in Freud based on the containment of libido and the diversion of its energy as secondary narcissism, to provide the more differentiated energies needed for symbolic cognition (Freud, 1923).

It was this potentiality for sublimation that Jung addressed most directly. Both Freud and Jung agreed that the "building blocks" of spirituality came from bodily vitality, but they differed on how that should be evaluated (Hunt, 1989a, 1992). By sharing the classical *sensus communis* as the largely implicit source of their thinking, they had far more in common than Freud would have with the later interpersonal (Sullivan, 1953) and object-relations (Fairbairn, 1954) theorists. The latter were surely correct to attempt to operationalize psychoanalysis in terms of its actual empirical basis in the observation of relationships, but may have missed the descriptive phenomenology hidden within Freud's ostensibly impersonal language of intrapsychic processes. The irony is that many of us also ended up persuaded that Freud's libido model was the very essence of an outdated nineteenth-century mechanism and hydraulics, now to be safely discarded as without any basis in lived experience. Perhaps only a civilization as dominated by a disembodied reason as ours could miss the references embedded in Freud's discussion to a more classical, vitally embodied consciousness, whose sensed absence in contemporary life brings so many people, along with their "inner" narcissism, into psychotherapy (Winnicott, 1971; Kohut, 1984; Almaas, 1988).

Why has the deep resonance between the Greek view of mind and Freud generally gone so unremarked? In part we may miss the connection between libido and *aion* (and so with *psyche* as a spiritual-transpersonal dimension of mind) because, in Lakoff and Johnson's terms, our image schema of Freud misleads us. Freud is supposed to deal with the "lower," the body and not the head — as if the latter were still somehow separate and higher. It is thus easy to miss the fact that Freud's libido and narcissism also descend down from the head, for it is counterintuitive to our image of the "lower."

More generally, connections between *sensus communis* and contemporary psychoanalytic, cognitive, and transpersonal psychologies get lost because, as thoroughgoing materialists, we fixate on the misleading physiology of *sensus communis* and its *aion-psyche* axis and so miss the descriptive phenomenology of consciousness that lies within it. We mistake what can be nothing other than ancient metaphor for our modern notion of material explanation, and then reject the latter as hopelessly inadequate. Our brain-based theory of mind rules out the central hollow channel or chakras of the Indian tradition because it fails to distinguish between, on the one hand, the physical body of today and, on the other, the felt body — as in synesthetic states central to ancient systems of mind and the meditative practices that exteriorized them. The ancients were mapping an implicit phenomenology of consciousness onto bodily organs as both metaphors and felt sensations. If we can but step back from the "mistakes" in their physiology, so differently intended than our own, it becomes more obvious that Aristotle, the pre-Socratics, and most especially Homer were speaking primarily of "body image" as a lived aspect of all symbolic experience.

The consequences of our modern loss of this original system of metaphorically based phenomenology include a lack of balance in most modern accounts of mind and consciousness. We now enshrine and assume a split between mind and body, thought and feeling, senses and world. It is as if we took the two distinct axes of the ancient phenomenology of consciousness and folded them over into one single and artificially simplified dimension. Thought — cool reason — is now in the head, and thus privileged and "sacred," while feeling, sensation, and intuition (to use Jung's typology) are separated from thought as lower. The teeming sensations, drives, and feelings of the body are left unorganized and chaotic. They lack any connection with reason and so can only reverberate within a metaphoric heart. This is the "animal" within us that must be controlled and contained by reason alone.

The loss of a specifically spiritual dimension coincides with the promotion of reason to its new position in the head — now "brain." What goes with this is a corresponding inflation. Propositional thought usurps all other symbolic frames and makes itself the measure of all symbolic consciousness. Reason, and its primary expression in science, becomes the new religion, as Jung (1944) rightly pointed out. Heidegger (1959) also complained of the grandiosity and false omnipotence of a modern "calculative" thinking, which in its strongly idealized "coolness" and dispassion makes everything into a commodity — people and modes of experience as well as physical resources. The result is an essentially schizoid theory of mind in which faculties and frames become separated in the western tradition in a way that would have shocked our ancestors. Feeling is left as something unstructured and primitive — the heritage of Augustine's "bleeding heart" of Jesus (Hillman, 1981). Any attempt to show the cognitive symbolic structure of emotion becomes a major achievement. Similarly, James's insistence that the experiences of the mystics are essentially noetic becomes a strange and daring assertion, whereas it would be obvious in more traditional cultures. A culture that puts thought, separated from feeling and all traces of felt embodiment, in the place of soul might indeed be said to "worship" control and order — also the conclusion reached, through a very different route, by Foucault (1978).

On the other hand, it does appear that the *sensus communis* gets reconstituted wherever the primary evidence considered for a theory of mind is the stuff of immediate experience and its primary reflection in self-referential physical metaphor. Even when phenomenology is deemphasized, something of this *sensus com-*

munis, however displaced and distorted, can still be traced through the impersonal "processes" of reason's analysis of itself. From the perspective of *sensus communis,* just as thought cannot be separated from perception or from world, neither can a fully embodied symbolic cognition be separated from our direct sense of being in time. The sense of a lived time opening out ahead into an encompassing unknown is implicit in the classical and pre-classical understanding of "heart." The power of the explicit restatement of this relation between consciousness, world, and time in Heidegger's *Dasein* would seem to attest to a pervasive sense of loss of our own access to experience and a basic sense of aliveness. We have seen that the fullest versions of *sensus communis* include an explicit transpersonal dimension, in which the same dynamic processes that underlie practical awareness and the thought of the heart reappear as such in a dimension that links Jung's spirituality with Freud's concept of instinctual drivenness.

We have traced the periodic reemergence and recession of a synesthetic model of consciousness. As an ur-system it appears entire, if implicitly, within Homer and Hesiod. It is partially reconstructed but radically simplified in Aristotle's *coenoaesthesis*. The Roman and Stoic *sensus communis* reintegrates some of its earlier range once more, prior to a doubly enforced recession within the Judeo-Christian tradition (after Aquinas and medieval scholasticism). Well out of the mainstream now, it reemerges again within the Romantic rejection of a dominant mechanism and rationalism. This reconstitution once again approximates the more complete range and potential of the pre-classical *sensus communis*, through its emphasis on creativity and imagination. Subsequently, we find these insights at best displaced and implicit within Freud, Jung, and the cognitive psychologies of consciousness and synesthesia that were part of the European microgenetic tradition.

Starting roughly, and surely not coincidentally, in the 1960s, there is another spontaneous resurgence. In multiple areas and largely independent of each other, versions of *sensus communis* reappear yet again. Within neurophysiology, there is Geschwind (1965) and to some extent Luria (1972); within philosophy, Suzanne Langer (1972), Hannah Arendt (1971), and Martin Heidegger (1957); within cultural and media studies, Marshall McLuhan (1964); and among an eclectic group of psychoanalysts, clinical psychologists, and Jungians we find Bion (1962, 1963), Gendlin (1962, 1978), and Hillman (1975, 1981). Finally, within a holistic and heterodox cognitive psychology, we have Werner and Kaplan (1963), Arnheim (1969, 1974), Marks (1978), Lakoff (1987) and Johnson (1987), Haskell (1984, 1987), and McNeill (1991), along with corresponding perspectives on transpersonal states (Hunt, 1976, 1984, 1985ab; Globus, 1973; Fischer, 1975; Deikman, 1966, 1971). What all these views have in common is an approach to symbolic consciousness based on an explicit or implicit phenomenology, as reflected in the structure of self-referential metaphor and/or the empirical features of presentational states.

The belief that reality is or could be known is mistaken because reality is not something which lends itself to being known. It is impossible to know reality for the same reason that makes it impossible to sing potatoes; they may be grown, or pulled, or eaten, but not sung. Reality has to be "been." . . . The point at issue is how to pass from "knowing" "phenomena" to "being" that which is "real."
W. R. Bion, *Transformations*

We will have to ask about the relation between the unconcealed and space. Must we think the unconcealed on the basis of the essence of what is spatial, or is what is spatial and all space founded in the essence of [the unconcealed] as primordially experienced? . . . Because he has the word, man, and he alone, is the being that looks into the open and sees the open in the sense of the [unconcealed].
Martin Heidegger, *Parmenides*

the free animal
has its perishing constantly behind itself,

and in front of itself God, and when it moves it moves
in eternity, just as wells do.
Rainer Maria Rilke, quoted in M. Heidegger, *Parmenides*

The focus of expansion is the direction in which one is going, and the
focus of contraction is the direction from which one is coming.
James Gibson, *The Ecological Approach to Visual Perception*

10 A Cognitive Psychology of Transpersonal States

The Experience of Presence and Openness as Complex Synesthesias

We can now undertake a more formal cognitive psychology of the developed forms of transpersonal experience — for the ancient Greeks, the vertical axis of *psyche-aion*, in contrast to what I have termed the horizontal *sensus communis*. Just as *psyche-aion* was described in terms of the same processes of fluidic dynamics as the "thought of the heart," it also seems entirely plausible from a contemporary cognitive perspective to understand the range of experiences emerging with deep meditation and psychedelic drugs as cross-modal synesthetic translations across the more abstract or formal stages of perceptual microgenesis. In other words, these states manifest exactly the same cross-modal metaphoric processes as in all symbolic cognition. The difference is that transpersonal states show the structures of symbolic cognition unfolding presentationally, for their own sake. Accordingly, these states will show most directly the cross-modal, hierarchic syntheses normally hidden within the pragmatics of representational symbolism.

We have already considered the more inclusive and "impersonal" forms of mystical experience along these lines. In the "light-of-the-void" experience the glow of luminous open space, as the basic quality of the visual system, was understood as becoming, with cross-modal translation, the perfect metaphor for the openness of time. There is another, more "personal" pole of such experience, however, which we might term the sense of presence, or "I am." This experience of one's here-and-now being is very close to "peak experience" (Maslow, 1962) and "flow experience" (Csikszentmihalyi, 1990). All these terms describe a special sense of felt reality and clarity, with a concomitant sense of exhilaration, freedom, and release. Such experience is also involved in many accounts of lucid dreaming, where the sudden realization that one is dreaming entails a special attention to one's immediate here-and-now experience for its own sake and in a way that is rare not only within ordinary dreaming but in everyday life as well (Hunt, 1989a). This sense of vital presence is sought more formally as the "subtle" or "imaginal" body experience of the meditative traditions. We will see that it can also be identified as a cross-modal translation, here between a general kinesthetic sense of flow and corresponding visual-spatial and vocal patterns. We will see, too, that the set made by these patterns constitutes the meditative chakra experiences, and that these are also complex synesthesias.

The basis of "presence" and "openness" in cross-modal translations emerging for their own sake suggests that these realizations may reflect the fullest presentational expression of a specifically human intelligence. Nonetheless, there will also be reason to conclude that while the experiential capacity for such states must be specifically human, the forms of experience thereby reconstituted on a symbolic level are also basic structures of perception. As such, they are potentially shared by all motile organisms in terms of their orientation toward horizonal openness, on the one hand, and the propriolocation of specific position within the array, on the other.

The Subtle or Imaginal Body in Schizophrenia, Classical Introspection, Bioenergetics, and Meditation

I have suggested already that the geometric mandala imagery of such importance in Jung's active imagination, psychedelic drug experience, and meditative chakra experiences could be understood as the visual translation of the symmetrical body image — both vision and touch-kinesthesis sharing a common tunnel structure. There is considerable evidence that the most direct introspective experience of the body image is as a hollow container, with the kinesthetic pulls and pressures of muscle tension and relaxation potentially experienced as fluids moving inside a central body cavity. Such patterns would result from the synesthetic translation between the kinestheses of muscle tension and corresponding visualized flow patterns, which would normally be inhibited by our more functional image of how our body actually looks "from outside."

Some of the most striking evidence along these lines comes from an extraordinary, yet almost uncited, series of papers by Andras Angyal (1935, 1936ab, 1937) on the phenomenology and cognitive bases of somatic hallucinations in schizophrenia. We have already seen how the closely related first-rank symptoms of psychotic onset include examples of sophisticated, if involuntary, introspective sensitivity. Angyal's hospitalized informants described the sense that their bodies no longer hold together and are hollow — these suddenly noticed effects, of course, being given a correspondingly delusional interpretation:

> There is a definite impairment of the unity of the body. The patient often complains that "the body doesn't seem to stay together"; he feels "loose-jointed" or "falling apart." My patient says that "the head and the neck do not connect" . . . he has "no inside of the body but only a frame." He says that when he eats "the food is falling in a vacuum." "Behind the chest is nothing, only a big hole." "The inside of the skull doesn't feel at all, it is like air." "The stomach and the top of the skull are open." It is interesting to observe that patients having these disturbances complain about them in the same words, which shows that these are not random bizarre ideas but must have a common basis. (Angyal, 1936a, pp. 1041–42)

As Angyal points out, these complaints are very close to the early observations of laboratory introspectionists, who carefully avoided the stimulus error of what they "knew" about their bodily experience and sensed instead only what is given to immediate tactile-kinesthetic sensitivity (Schilder, 1924, 1942). If one sits very still with eyes closed and attempts to banish all one's concrete imagery of what one knows about the body and about how it looks, one's immediate somatic experience becomes strangely labile and unorganized. There are certain areas of sensed heaviness and density, at the base of the skull and in the lower part of the abdomen and upper thighs. Strictly speaking, however, there is no sensation from the inside of the torso and head. In radically descriptive terms, we are encased by an outer tactile-kinesthetic envelope within which we are "hollow." We will see shortly how this "container" image of inner hollowness is directly cultivated in some meditative practices and in the bioenergetic therapies of Reich (1949) and Almaas (1986a, 1988).

In addition, and closely linked to these introspective observations of hollowness, Angyal's patients described hallucinations of internal forces and fluidic substances moving inside the body. At times these are astonishingly like accounts of the somatic sensations accompanying out-of-body experience (Green, 1968b; Fox, 1962) and descriptions of Kundalini activation in Hatha Yoga (Krishna, 1967). Such experiences of hollowness with internal motion seem to constitute an alternative to the ordinary body image, rather like the ambiguous, reversing figures of gestalt psychology:

> The conditions responsible for the spontaneous sensation of lightness and elongation of the body or of parts of the body may give rise also to the impression of a light substance passing through the muscles and emanating from the body; it is as though another limb, or another body, made of a very light substance were leaving the body. This experience in my patient is common. "When I move I seem to lose, it seems that

the whole body leaves me. The spinal column or something passes invisibly through the flesh. As if somebody would be able to get hold on me, like an eagle, and draw my flesh and bones away." "They pull out another person from my body. I feel that my form leaves me; not exactly my form but a second form." . . . "When they take that out of me, it feels like a quick sensation, like a jar." . . . "Now, when I leaned back on the chair my body seemed to slide out of me. Not exactly my body, but another form like mine." (Angyal, 1936a, p. 1039)

That these experiences are part of the incipient synesthesias of felt meaning rather than merely sensory is confirmed by the fact that Angyal's patients tended to attribute these kinesthetic phenomena to "little people" inside them and often located their auditory hallucinations, as well, as coming directly from these inner body regions and movements. In short, we have a spontaneous, if idiosyncratically distorted, version of Gendlin's "focusing."

Angyal advances diverse evidence that such experiences of internal fluidic motion and hallucinatory elongations of the body image are based on an unusual sensitivity to kinesthetic sensations and after-effects. He notes how complaints of a light substance passing out of the gluteal region or from the bottoms of the feet directly followed the sudden cessation of muscle tension in these regions when patients stood up after sitting down for long periods or began walking after standing still. He was able to duplicate experimentally the sensation either of an actual elongation of the body or of an internal light substance passing out the top of the head, much like the early stages of out-of-body accounts. Angyal asked normal introspectors to observe their somatic awareness while a bucket of water held on their heads was surreptitiously drained of its contents. The chronically held tensions created by supporting the water were transformed into the sense of an impersonal force flowing upward. Schilder (1924) described similar transformations noticed by sophisticated introspectionists during elevator movement.

Angyal's suggestion that unwitting tensions and relaxations of major muscle groups can be directly experienced as the movement of inner forces and fluids also receives support from the earlier introspectionist literature. I have already noted (chapter 2) Nafe's (1924) observations that introspected pleasure, associated with relaxation and incipient approach movements, could be felt introspectively as an internal flow within and up the torso. In a fashion also reminiscent of out-of-body descriptions, this could sometimes be felt as emanating out beyond the outlines of the head and body image. Nafe's observers used the same words that Laski (1961) abstracted from accounts of classical mysticism and spontaneous peak experience, referring to upward direction, the inside of the body, brightness and light, and liquid flow. Laski stressed that these "quasi-physical" sensations of mystical ecstasy could range from overt hallucinatory experiences — as in levitation — to purely metaphoric, self-referential description — "I was uplifted." This continuum between metaphoric felt meaning and overt hallucinatory transformations, both organized in terms of the same perceptual patterns, helps to locate a kind of symbolism that directly reuses perception. It is difficult to determine, however, the extent to which basic patterns of perception are read directly into metaphor or a synesthetic cross-modal translation reorganizes perception in terms of emergent presentational symbolism. Doubtless, both forms exist.

Wilhelm Reich's (1949) "bioenergetic" therapy is based on the progressive relaxation or "de-armoring" of chronically contracted muscle segments that correspond to the classical chakras of Indian yoga. The experience of de-armoring is also associated with a very similar phenomenology of subjective streamings and flowings within the body image. These are clearly the subjective concomitants of the kinesthetic loosening of contracted muscle groups. The implication is that the classical meditative chakras or body centers would be synesthetic felt meanings fusing these same kinestheses with geometric form constants.

Reich held that chronic psychological conflicts were inseparable from unconscious chronic contractions in seven major muscle segments, varying with the kind of conflict involved. These segments were the eyes, mouth, throat and tongue, chest, diaphragm, abdomen, and pelvis. The loosening of contractions in these segments proceeds from the head down by means of an array of techniques including stimulation of the gag reflex, deep massage, and forced breathing of the kind now utilized by Grof (1988) for the induction of psychedelic-like states. The release of chronic tension in the first six segments eventually results in the spontaneous release of what Reich, in his early and very literal version of Freud, termed the "orgasm reflex." In fact, not only is the phenomenology of this diffuse motoric release not specifically sexual in Reichian accounts (Sharaf, 1983), but it seems identical to the spontaneous motoric relaxations and jerks that emerge out of very deep meditation (Bernard, 1950; Walsh, 1977; Kornfield, 1979). In turn, all of these phenomena are similar to the massive startles noted in the hypnagogic period and often associated with visualized energy release and internal bodily flow (Oswald, 1962).

There are many indications that what Reich is describing, as also in meditative chakra activation, is not merely curious kinesthetic sensations alone but synesthetically embodied felt meanings, like those of Gendlin's "focusing" but more formal and generic. First, the release of the sensations of streaming and melting through the body is often blocked by terrifying feelings of dissolving, exploding, or disappearing — which would appear to be cross-modally translated versions of the felt meanings associated with such letting go. Just as with chakra activation, de-armoring can be associated with sudden, involuntary "made feelings" related to anger, jealousy, grief, and so on. These not only attest to the emotional conflicts being held in check by chronic muscular contractions but also show the symbolic felt meanings involved in these ostensible "sensations." Finally, although Reich himself at first preferred an interpretation in terms of Freudian genitality, it becomes clear that the fruits of bioenergetic release involved enhanced feelings of vitality, presence, and felt reality — the opposite of the schizoid, narcissistic complaints of many of Reich's clients.

Reich's later discussions of the goals of his therapy are quite congruent with Maslow's "peak experience" and self-actualization, Csikszentmihalyi's "flow," and what A. H. Almaas (1988) refers to as "presence." That there was a transpersonal component to Reich's work seems clear from his final view, however misleadingly physiologized, that the fully open person would feel a direct resonance between his or her internally activated streamings and the streamings of energy in the physical universe. It is clear from Reich's descriptions of full "orgonomic functioning" that he was very close in his conception of the goal of development to the later work of Maslow and Almaas, although Reich himself falsely concretized this in terms of a physically measurable life energy — "orgone."

The chakras of the "subtle body" in meditation involve the cultivation of the hollow-body experience and imaginally directed experiences of energy streamings. They are actually complex synesthesias. The activation of the chakras, centered in the bodily areas that comprise Reich's tactile-kinesthetic muscle segments, also involve specific imagery of colors and geometric designs, physiognomically expressive vocal sounds or mantras (om, ah, hum, hri), as well as characteristic gestures, or mudras, made with the hands, and spontaneous emotional release similar, again, to that described by Reich. What we have, then, is something like Gendlin's synesthetic felt meanings, but developing in their own right, independent of particular circumstances and following an intrinsic sequence across the body image. By contrast, the felt meanings of everyday life, as developed within Gendlin's technique of focusing, reflect the same processes of cross-modal translation between kinesthetic muscle segments, visual patterns and colors, and incipient sounds, but constrained and guided by the person's specific interpersonal relationships. It is also striking in all this material how full self-reference entails the direct experiential realization of Lakoff's body-as-container schema, supporting the view that our consciousness is entirely structured through presentational metaphor.

I will develop these comparisons in some detail by considering the Vajra or diamond body practice of Tibetan Buddhism as one of the major cultural systems formalizing complex synesthesias as sequences of felt meaning. As with cross-cultural accounts of out-of-body and near-death experience, there is both enough overlap and enough variation in the versions of the subtle or imaginal body across the various meditative traditions, such as Tibetan Buddhism, Chinese Taoism, and Indian Yoga, to suggest that we are seeing a common set of states and processes unfolding in similar but culturally distinct ways.[1]

Visualization practice in the Tibetan subtle-body meditation begins with the cultivation of and attunement to the sense of the hollow body, followed by a visual-kinesthetic experience of its internal channels. These will be energized by the various winds and drops described in this tradition. The central channel is visualized and eventually directly sensed as very thin and extending from the crown of the head to the base of the spine. It is not part of everyday consciousness, and the whole point of these practices is its activation. On each side there is a white channel, associated with sexual energies, and extending from the left nostril to the genitals, and a red channel, utilizing and sublimating aggressive energies, and extending from the right nostril to the anus—a model certainly also in the spirit of early psychoanalysis.

From Indian hatha yoga (Bernard, 1950) it appears likely that these central and side channels have some basis in the muscles of the abdomen and diaphragm, as should be the case if these are the predominantly kinesthetic side of developing synesthesias. Thus there are physical exercises to make each channel stand out from the abdominal wall. The tactile-kinesthetic basis of this practice, rather than reflecting any interior physiology as has commonly been maintained, is also demonstrated by the fact that the activation of the Kundalini, or serpent power, normally latent at the base of the central channel, involves the deliberate contractions of these muscle columns—described as "milking the nalis" (Bernard, 1950). On Angyal's model of the kinesthetic bases of somatic hallucinations in schizophrenia, we would expect that such contractions, held within a state of meditative and introspective detachment, would feel as though they were being imposed by an impersonal force. Combined with the deliberate cultivation of other image modalities, the result would be the spontaneous synesthetic cross-flows that are the point of the practice.

To return to the Tibetan Buddhist account (Govinda, 1960; Chang, 1963; Longchenpa, 1976; Gyatso, 1982) the pranas or breaths would normally circulate through the side channels only, but in the subtle-body practice are to be visualized and felt as gathering at the base of the central channel. There are also multiple "drops"—or "seed syllables" with colors, sounds, and textures—which are the energy sources that are to be "melted" within the central channel. Thus, the white "Ham" drop of pure consciousness between the eyebrows and the red "A" just below the navel, when combined with the winds from the side channels, activate the central channel and its chakra centers.

These practices can be regarded as a systematic cultivation and mapping of the possibilities of complex synesthesia and related felt meaning. This view is confirmed by descriptions of the chakras (literally, "wheels") as energy centers located along the central channel, each of which has its own color, geometric pattern, body region, mantra, and mudra. Although there is considerable variation both within and between traditions in the number, order, and specific characteristics of these chakras, we will follow one of the more inclusive Tibetan accounts of one such system

(Chang, 1963; Gyatso, 1982). Here, and confining our summary to the visual, kinesthetic, and physiognomic aspects only, the first chakra is the "jewel" wheel at the genitals, a black triangle visualized as having eight curved spokes as energy conduits, angled upward. These face the square yellow abdominal center, associated with the element earth, and visualized with thirty-two spokes angled downward. The navel center, a white circular disc associated with water, has sixty-four spokes going upward, while the heart chakra, the red triangle for fire, has eight pointing down. The throat center is a green semicircular disc standing for air or wind, with sixteen spokes pointing upward towards the head chakra, which is a blue sphere depicting the open spaciousness of the sky, with its thirty-two spokes pointing downward. If we stand back and picture this total effect, we have Reich's major muscle segments. In addition, the outline made by the incipient meetings of the chakra spokes of the head and throat, heart and navel, and lower abdomen and genitals traces the three areas of diffuse sensation in the body image — head, chest, and abdomen.

The thousand-petaled lotus at the top of the head is, as we will see, only relevant to the more transcendental "ascending" practice that culminates in the white-light/cessation experience. It needs to be considered separately from the other chakras, whose activations are associated with more specific emotions and synesthesias. These lead to a sense of felt vitalization and bodily presence in the here and now and contrast with the more impersonal, transcendent qualities of the synesthetic experience of luminosity itself.

That is the system, but before considering its actual implementation in meditative practices, I should note that the chakras fit well with Shepard's and Kosslyn's approaches to an imagery based, at least in significant part, on the direct reuse of perception and initially constructed part by part. The imaginal symbolic side of these experiences seems clear enough from their multimodal nature and close relation to abstract felt meanings. On the other hand, that these synesthetic states directly engage perceptual processes is also shown in a number of ways. The initial arousal of Dumo heat in the navel (Tibetan) or Kundalini at the base of the central channel (hatha yoga) is associated with intense perspiration and with contractions in the muscles of the anus and lower abdomen, and can be aided by physical massage of the abdomen (Bernard, 1950; Chang, 1963). This certainly sounds perception-based. In addition, there are accounts of the autonomic arousal involved in these states inducing "trembling of the body" and involuntary "jumping about like a frog," along with such intense heat that the practitioner may need to be stabilized by repeated bathing in cold water (Bernard, 1950). That body temperature is considerably raised in these circumstances is attested by the widely cited Tibetan "contest" for aspiring monks in which, with Dumo heat aroused, they sit outside all night to see who can dry the greatest number of soaking-wet sheets by dawn (David-Neel, 1932).

Just when this begins to sound like a somatic trick that would have nothing to do with symbolic processes, there is the suggestion in Gampopa (eleventh century) that there comes a point in the course of meditative practice where the heat phenomenon will reach its maximum physical intensity and, simultaneously, the corresponding understanding of Buddhist doctrine will also reach its maximum attainment in terms of fully felt realization. This close connection between insight and the physical aspects of ecstasy, here part of an elaborate meditative practice, is really quite consistent with accounts of less systematized moments of creative ecstasy in the arts and sciences. People with sudden conceptual insights of creative importance may also leap about.[2]

To return to our discussion of the actual utilization of the chakra system, there are two sequences of practice in Tibetan Buddhism. First comes a "descending" sequence of activation, showing a striking resemblance to Reich's de-armoring and associated with states of emotional release and vital presence. Then comes an "ascending" sequence, the ultimate point of the practice, culminating in the light-of-the-void experience and the realization of emptiness/openness as the basis of consciousness. In the descending sequence, the meditator visualizes the red symbol "A" at the navel as a thin, narrow flame that spreads up the central channel and melts the white "Ham" symbol at the top of the head. The felt result is a downward melting or flow in which the aion-like fluid flows through the spokes of each chakra before descending to the next and the next. These "meltings" lead to successive relaxations of the respective parts of the body associated with each chakra and are accompanied by awareness of its color, shape, sound, and so on (Chang, 1963; Gyatso, 1982). This is very reminiscent of Reich's streaming and melting sensations of profound motoric relaxation and release, moving from the head down the torso.[3] Although such visualizations initially involve what we might regard as "guided imagery," it is clear from the descriptions of vitalization and energization that result from chakra activations that the aim of the practice is to have these visualizations culminate in spontaneous, involuntary realizations of the synesthesias being constructed.

The ascending sequence may then follow this descending pattern as its more transcendental counterpart. The pranas are visualized as gathered into the central channel, along with the heat and energy from the full activation of Dumo. These energies are visualized as going back up the sequence of chakras and finally activating the thousand-petaled lotus at the crown of the head. This seems to be very close to the powerful and overwhelming activation of Kundalini in hatha yoga and ends with the white-light experience as the maximum fusion of ecstasy and noetic insight. Something of the preemptory quality of such activation in the ascending sequence comes from the following account of a spontaneous Kundalini experience from the Indian yogic tradition:

A large tongue of flame sped across the spine into the interior of my head. It appeared as if the stream of living light continuously rushing through the spinal cord into the cranium gathered speed and volume. . . . Sometimes it seemed as if a jet of molten copper, mounting up through the spine, dashed against my crown and fell in a scintillating shower of vast dimensions all around me. . . . As far as I could look inwardly with my mental eye, I saw only a brilliant shower or a glowing pool of light. (Krishna, 1967, pp. 54–55)

The ascending sequence can also be practiced on its own as a series of visualizations of progressively more subtle and abstract felt meanings of the nature of consciousness as such, but without the above autonomic engagement. Following Govinda (1960), and illustrating a more simplified sequence of chakras than that reviewed above, one could start from a visualized yellow square, localized in the lower abdomen, representing all that is solid, impenetrable, and earth-like in one's immediate ongoing awareness. After a time, this is dissolved into a white disc in the diaphragm, to be directly sensed as exemplifying everything in one's experience that flows like water. This, of course, is James's "stream," symbolically concretized as part of a sequence of metaphors that will progressively approach an impalpable immediate consciousness and its unknowable, but clearly present, source. This synesthetic image is dissolved in turn into the red triangle in the heart, as all that is hot and fiery in our awareness, thence into the green half-circle of the throat chakra for the aspect of consciousness which is like wind. This is then felt as dissolving into the openness of space itself, visualized as a blue sphere located behind the eyes, with the quality of the clear blue sky, as the most indefinite and impalpable pattern of physical nature with which to represent the corresponding openness of consciousness. "There arises a cognitive capacity open and lucent, divested of all propositions about it. . . . Outwardly, the clear sky serves as an example; inwardly, there is experience as experience, the real sky, larger than the former" (Longchenpa, vol. 1, 1976, pp. 213–14).

Finally, the meditator lets the sky image, which is "only a symbol" (Evens-Wentz, 1954, p. 231), dissolve into a still more open, containing, and compassionate sense of the luminosity that fills all space. This may first be visualized as a translucent luminous sphere at the very top of the head, but eventually it disappears into an open, all-containing emptiness: "In its openness, [space] is an open-ended accommodating of various views, all welling up, floating, gathering within space. . . . Space is therefore not static, but is instead a serene explosion . . . filling all the eons of pasts and futures, without exhausting its openness or its capacity for exhibiting a further wealth of openness" (Tarthang Tulku, 1977, p. xl).

I have already discussed how luminosity welling forth, synesthetically translated as felt meaning, would entail both a maximally presentational sense of something all-encompassing and the synesthetically based dissolution of the ordinary body image. The openness of space constitutes the closest metaphoric approximation to the categories that representational self-reference can never fully encompass — consciousness, self, and time. For the cognitive tradition represented by Asch, Arnheim, and others, it is not at all clear that this concept of the openness of consciousness could be thought, let alone realized as felt meaning, without the metaphors afforded by the perception of sky, space, and glowing light. Indeed, it would be the synesthetic embodiment of these perceptions that would create the abstract states whose more noetic and conceptual side we will consider in the next chapter.

Realizations of Essence in A. H. Almaas: The Presence-Openness Dimension and Its Relation to Dilemmas in the Sense of Self

The "diamond-heart" approach of A. H. Almaas (1986ab, 1988) will help us draw together the above discussion of presence-openness as the two poles of transpersonal experience, or what Almaas would call "essence." His work echoes Angyal (1965) on the "universal ambiguity" of all experience (chapter 2) in emphasizing a double aspect within presentational states. Their optimal expression is found in states of metaphorically based felt meaning sought in classical meditation, but their impacted and conflicted forms comprise the narcissistic dilemmas described by the object-relations and self-psychology approaches within contemporary psychoanalysis. Almaas's work is based on an original theoretical and methodological synthesis of the meditative subtle-body traditions (especially Sufism), the Gurdjieff-Ouspensky tradition of self-remembering, contemporary psychoanalytic approaches to vulnerabilities in sense of self originating in the first two years of childhood, Reichian bioenergetics, and a guided-imagery approach broadly similar to Gendlin's focusing.

Almaas distinguishes between two aspects of essence — the sense of presence or "I am" and the more impersonal, felt transcendence based on the experience of openness and space. We have approached the latter in terms of the Buddhist meditative traditions described above, but "presence" has been less developed in the current literature on transpersonal psychology. Almaas stresses that the sense of "I am" emerges spontaneously whenever we feel our situation wholeheartedly and without internal reservation. It can be directly cultivated by methods of "self-remembering" that are largely Sufi in origin and were introduced in a modern context by Gurdjieff (1975) and Ouspensky (1949). In self-remembering, the subject cultivates an ongoing, nonverbal sense in the midst of ordinary daily involvements, akin to "I am here now in this place, doing. . . ." Success with this more "extraverted" form of meditation is marked by those moments, very much akin to the experience of lucid dreaming (Hunt, 1989a), when the person feels a sense of

presence and vital embodiment, with feelings of special clarity and freedom inseparable from one's involvement in the actual situation. The philosopher Mervyn
Sprung (1994) similarly describes an "aware behavior" as being fully and "viv-
ially" in one's present situation, where what is happening to one is exactly the same
as one's sense of what is happening.

In the Almaas work, consistent with my discussion of James's stream and the
necessity of metaphor in all self-reference, essence is experienced as an actually
sensed fluidic substance that is felt to fill "holes" or "gaps" in the body image.
These latter are related to Reich's observations on the selective deadening of sensitivity resulting from chronic muscle contractions. These sensed holes or gaps are
the outcome of a progressive loss, beginning in childhood and perhaps inevitable in
a secular culture, of the various aspects of essence that Almaas terms essential love,
strength, will, compassion, peace, and awareness — these being partly reminiscent
of Erikson on developmental virtues. To the extent that the subject can remain fully
open to the anxiety and despair associated with the direct awareness of these holes,
themselves closely related to Indian chakras and the Sufi lataif, they are experienced
as filled with a flowing substance and opening out into an expanded sense of
spaciousness.

Each sensed deficit in sense of self, as formulated by Winnicott (1971), Kohut
(1977), and Mahler (1968), when experienced as fully filled and open, has a specific
cross-modal physiognomy expressed in terms of characteristic texture, density,
temperature, viscosity, and color. The total system of centers and essential aspects
described by Almaas is intricate indeed. As examples, I will focus on essential
strength, located in the stomach, and "merging essence" or love, most often centered in the chest. The felt integration of these essential aspects is also central to
what Almaas calls "personal essence" and is understood as a reexperience and full
assimilation of the conflicts associated with Margaret Mahler's account of individuation and symbiosis in the first two years of life. Thus, essential strength is
experienced as red in color, hot, with a sense of body fullness, roundedness, and
expansion, as in the following description from a middle-aged man, with a predominant conflict over early maternal separation:

> I felt a very warm feeling in my solar plexus and in my back. I have been able to
> experience the heat many times before. I also remember that at first I thought I had
> some sort of fever, my whole body became hot. . . . I felt I had a blackish kind of lump
> or ball in my solar plexus, as big as a basketball. I felt this blackness peeling or
> dissolving to reveal some kind of beautifully translucent presence in the belly. As I
> talked with you this presence grew very quickly and filled me up enough to give me a
> sense of a full belly. When it went into my chest it strengthened my shoulders. I felt
> very pleased with myself, very happy, just as if something good had taken place. I am
> feeling stronger. (Almaas, 1988, pp. 207–8)

The full opening to merging essence is described as a felt sense of sweetness, honey-like flow, melting, and golden color. It is illustrated in the following account from a woman with a long history of conflict with her mother:

> I am beginning to see how much I identify with my mother. . . . Part of the reason I sell myself short is to try desperately to get her love; she did not want me to be me and do well. . . . I felt a large gaping hole around my heart and lungs as you spoke. I kept trying to fill it in various ways, one of which is trying to be my mom. . . . She has the love and warmth, and I am nothing without her. As we worked Saturday night I felt at some point a juicy, honey-like feeling or presence in my chest, where the wound is. It was sweet and warm and like nectar. . . . I feel strong and more myself than before. (Almaas, 1988, pp. 229–30)

Consistent with the cognitive theory of transpersonal experience as abstract synesthesias that express a self-reference unfolding for its own sake, Almaas describes the felt release of essence within the body image as a sense of a fluid substance that is clearly multimodal and synesthetic:

> Essence, when experienced directly, is seen to be some kind of substance, like water or gold, but it is not physical substance like physical water or gold. . . . Imagine that this water is self-aware, that each molecule is aware of itself and of its own energy and excitation. Imagine now that you are this aware substance, the water. This is close to an experience of essential substance. . . . Essence is self-aware. It knows itself, intuits itself, sees itself, hears itself, smells itself, tastes itself, touches itself. But all this is one act, one unified perception. . . . This phenomenon points to a very deep truth, that of the unity of the senses. (Almaas, 1986a, pp. 54, 80, 132, 133)

This account sounds like the self-awareness of James's stream combined with the Greek-Hindu *sensus communis*.

Certainly, if Asch (1961) and Lakoff (1987) and Johnson (1987) are correct about the dependence of all self-reference on physical metaphor, and Langer (1942) is right in her notion that presentational symbolism directly displays its felt meanings through the contemplation of the expressive medium itself, then the full self-experience of ongoing consciousness should come to feel exactly as described by Almaas. Experienced as such, presentational consciousness would feel like a sentient, self-aware fluid, its cross-modal patternings reorganizing continuously to yield different facets of felt meaning. The rebuttal that this is "merely" metaphoric, while certainly capturing the cognitive processes entailed, misses the fact that full self-reference must invoke suitable structures of perception that will be directly and vividly felt in a presentational symbolic mode. All classical cultures have described something very much like this self-aware cross-modal flow. It becomes prominent wherever people have paid attention to the actual phenomenology of what it feels like to be human—especially at those moments when we feel that we are most aware of our actual existence and most truly ourselves.

There have been other modern expressions of this sense of consciousness as an interior fluid substance. I have already discussed Freud's concept of libido and its close relation to Greek *aion* or "vital substance." In a fashion remarkably reminiscent of Plato's account of the incarnation of the soul, Freud (1914, 1923) describes the first organization of the libido as narcissistic and bound up in itself (in the head); then, on the model of an amoeba gradually putting out its pseudopods (object libido), the body is gradually cathected and animated. Whereas Freud's own account is only implicitly experiential, Reich's (1949) description of the internal streaming of orgone, as a life energy in resonance with the fluid dynamics of the surrounding physical universe, was based on phenomenological descriptions — however much he may have overly concretized his explanatory principles in physical terms. Not only does Reich's account echo Gibson's view that awareness is a direct resonance with the flow of the world, with the brain as localizing but not explaining this primary function, but it also constitutes its own version of *sensus communis*:

> "Orgonotic sensation" is a true sixth sense. Besides the abilities to see, hear, smell, taste, touch, there existed unmistakably in healthy individuals a sense of organ functions, an orgonotic sense, as it were, which was completely lacking or was disturbed in biopathies. The compulsive neurotic has lost this sixth sense completely. The schizophrenic has displaced this sense and has transformed it into certain patterns of his delusional system, such as "forces," "the Devil," "voices," "electric currents," "worms in the brain or in the intestines," etc. (Reich, 1949, p. 456)

Reich held that the actual source of mystical experience is the direct sensing of our vitally streaming aliveness. It was through the development of self-referential cognition that we became alienated and cut off from this direct sensing of flowing orgone. It is the sense of aliveness that is partially lost with the human symbolic capacity and so projected into the metaphysics of the spiritual traditions and the bizarre physical intrusions of delusional schizophrenia. We will see that if we understand Reich's reference here to the symbolic capacity as referring to representational symbolism but not symbolic presentational states, then it becomes plausible to link Geschwind and Gibson in an account of transpersonal experience that would be in keeping with Reich's intuitions on the vital core of mystical experience. Yet this will also uphold James's insistence that such states are intrinsically cognitive and so only experienced in symbolizing creatures.

The Presence-Openness Dimension and Its Relation to Symbolic Cognition and Gibson's Ambient Array

Higher states of consciousness or transpersonal experiences are, on the one hand, clearly and specifically human — based on the fullest possible presentational expression of the processes of cross-modal translation underlying all symbolic cognition and here manifested "as such." Yet these states also reconstitute, on the level of symbolic cognition, the primary structures of perception as understood by Gibson, and these are broadly shared across species, perhaps across all motile organisms. The experience of vital presence, as variously described by Maslow, Reich, Gurdjieff, and Almaas, follows the template of the here-there axis of Gibson's array, by which the specific gradients of flow "confer" on the organism its unique position within that array. The void-openness experience, metaphorized as glow welling forth, follows the template of horizonal openness. I have already discussed the horizonal openness of the next moment to which all sentient organisms must be attuned and which perpetually "gives" the differentiated whence-whither structure of the envelope of flow. Presence-openness would, indeed, not be experienced as such by simpler organisms. Their experience unfolds within this form but cannot include it as content. Rather, this dimension becomes the template for the hierarchic integration of differentiated perceptual modalities as their common organizing principle. Felt as such in presentational states, it becomes the metaphoric expression for an all-encompassing totality.

That said, it must be added that presence-openness is not some sort of psychological process, but an existential fact. We really *are* here, all of us sentient organisms. We really do face out into that which surrounds and opens before us. We do exist. On occasion, we self-referential beings realize this presence directly, and it is a highly characteristic and valued experience. I am proposing that presence-openness is the core of mystical experience, after we have stripped off the conceptual metaphysics partially encrusted around it by cultural traditions. Heidegger, as we will explore in the next chapter, finds the most basic "meaning" of presence-openness to be Being — the sheer "isness" of things and ourselves within.

Similarly, presence-openness is not, in the sense of the early Jung (1928) or Grof (1980), an archaic or phylogenetic memory, but rather the basic structure of sentience necessarily common to motile organisms. Nor is it a metaphor in the sense of one of many possible structures that can be abstracted out of perception. It is the basic organization of perception itself. In short, presence-openness is not *created* by cross-modal translation or transformation. Rather, these processes of symbolic self-reference serve to reveal a basic form already there. They do not cause it, any more than a telescope causes the stars.

Finally, the full presentational expression of consciousness is not "private," as the western tradition so much wants to believe, but rather doubly or even triply shared. Transpersonal states are truly social in the sense of being based on symbolic self-reference. They also have the potential of unifying members of a group or society in communal presentational states, since they are based on shared spatial-temporal metaphors. The perceptual structures on which these metaphors are based are necessarily shared cross-culturally among self-referential beings as the template organizing all awareness. They must also reconstitute, however, the form of all sentience within nonsymbolic organisms. Consciousness, always "of" and "in" a world, is as primordially and necessarily a "with."

Some Issues Still Pending: Critical Questions from the Perspectives of Cognitive, Psychoanalytic, and Transpersonal Psychology

Our discussion to this point gives rise to so many questions and potential challenges from such different theoretical perspectives that it might be useful to address these explicitly and together.

Are presentational experiences really just forms of psychotic experience that have gained some sort of cultural acceptance?

If there were not a crucial difference between meditative states and psychotic onset in terms of their overall organization or gestalt, with admittedly much overlap in the specific transformations of consciousness involved (Lukoff, 1985; Hunt, 1984), it is hard to see how certain psychiatric observers (Boisen, 1936; van Dusen, 1972; Bowers, 1974) would have noted spontaneous remissions in some hospitalized patients immediately after white-light experiences. Similarly, there would be no conceptual basis for the concerns of some traditional gurus (Kapleau, 1967; Krishna, 1967; Trungpa, 1973) that certain meditative practitioners might "go insane," owing to character flaws or the misuse of powerful chakra activation techniques. On the premise of the question, there would simply be no way to make such distinctions.

Considered most broadly, schizophrenic experience comprises a range of transformations of consciousness induced by chronic stress, however variously determined, often in persons already disenfranchised socially and incapable of sustaining socially shared activities or any sense of personal competence. Meditation, on the other hand, reaches toward specific transformations of consciousness that not only have been given a culturally shared or sanctioned significance, but require social participation in an appropriate group and sustained long-term efforts at concentration in deliberately achieved states of deep relaxation.

In chapter 2, I referred to the possibility of interpreting mysticism and schizophrenia as "positive" and "negative" organizations of the same level of experience (Angyal's "universal ambiguity"). I also cited findings that high levels of spontaneous experience of transpersonal-spiritual states are associated with superior visual-spatial skills, in marked contrast to schizophrenia (Swartz and Seginer, 1981; Gackenbach and Bosveld, 1989; Spadafora and Hunt, 1990; Hunt et al., 1992). Subjective accounts from schizophrenic and psychotic onset indicate that some of these patients are struggling to hold off something that sounds very much like the white-light/cessation experience, believing that it betokens personal death or cosmic catastrophe (Boisen, 1936; Chapman, 1966). More chronic and hebephrenic patients, rather than describing any of the above complex synesthetic states, seem to sink into conditions of apathy and withdrawal that may be linked to a defensive cross-modal dissociation, with concomitant loss of both felt meaning and any sensed openness of time ahead:

> Sometimes everything is so fragmented, when it should be so unified. A bird in the garden chirps, for example. I heard the bird, and I know that he chirps; but that it is a bird and that he chirps, these two things are separated from each other. There is an abyss. Here I am afraid because I cannot put them back together again. It is as if the bird and the chirping have nothing in common with each other. . . . The bird and the fact that he chirps, there is such a separation between them, perhaps because I have come to unite myself there, or something with time. In reality, there is no time . . . ; I did not know that death happened this way. The soul does not come back any more. I want to go out into the world. I continue to live now in eternity; there are no more hours or days or nights. Outside things still go on, the fruits on the trees move this way and that. The others walk to and fro in the room, but time does not flow for me. . . . What does the outside world have to do with me? Everything is the same to me — trees, images, or men. I only bump up against time. (Minkowski, 1970, pp. 285–86)

Does the meditative path exacerbate narcissistic and schizoid dilemmas in the sense of self?

That can be true. Jack Engler (1984) has noted that many contemporary western practitioners of the eastern meditative traditions can sometimes confuse their own, sometimes clinically pathological withdrawal, feelings of unreality, or sense of grandiosity with the states sought by these practices — actually occasioning much confusion on the part of their eastern teachers. Similarly, Ken Wilber (1984) has stressed that powerful transpersonal realizations, whether in long-term meditation or occurring spontaneously, can stir up what Maslow (1971) had earlier termed "meta-pathologies." These include withdrawal, emotional flattening, and personal inflation and grandiosity, along with the anxieties concerning disappearing, bursting, and fragmentation that Reich and Winnicott discussed. These complaints are also prominent in narcissistic-borderline disorders as described by Winnicott (1971), Khan (1974), and Kohut (1977), and which these theorists locate in terms of developmental difficulties in the sense of self beginning in the first two years of life. Thus, we can no longer follow the earlier Maslow (1962) and other humanistic psychologists in simply separating a "higher" self-actualization from the "lower" preoccupations of psychoanalysis.

It also makes sense that long-term meditative practices seeking wholeness and presence, not easily attained in contemporary society, would themselves create feelings of deficiency and inadequacy, and that these dilemmas, along with powerful transpersonal states affecting one's immediate sense of self, will stir up any unresolved conflicts and traumata from earlier development—residues of what Michael Balint (1968) termed "basic fault." It may well be that traditional western attitudes to very young children exacerbate these difficulties and make transpersonal practices in later adulthood more difficult. This is in part why Almaas (1988) and others have been developing a more direct integration of meditative and psychoanalytic practices. It seems clear that narcissistic dilemmas in sense of self must be addressed to some degree if any genuine development as outlined by the meditative traditions is to occur.

Does the form of mystical experience, as an encompassing totality that "holds" and compassionately "allows," show that the source of these experiences is the nurturing mother figure of infancy and so suggest that such states are ultimately regressive?

The abstract, geometric nature of the cross-modal translations that seem to be entailed in the states leading up to the white-light experience, and the metaphysical meanings ascribed to the latter as its noetic content, would seem to be utterly beyond the limited cross-modal translation abilities of the young child. It is true that the imagery of mystical experience is broadly maternal, as noted by both Freud (1930) and Erikson (1962), and that its potential association with syndromes of withdrawal and grandiosity, as miscarriages of meditative practices, fit well with Winnicott's view of a sense of being as originating in the mirroring relationship with primary maternal figures. This need not, however, follow from a regressive model but rather is consistent with a fuller consideration of the contrast between representational and presentational symbolisms.

In presentational symbolism the sense of meaning emerges directly from experiential absorption in the medium of expression. If the deepest structure of the symbolic capacity is a dialogic organization rooted in mother-infant mirroring, then maximum expressions of presentational consciousness will entail that this dyadic nurturant pattern becomes part of the actual form of awareness — not as a regression but as the internalized matrix for all symbolization. In the most abstract presentational states this most basic structure itself becomes a metaphoric vehicle for the felt meaning of an all-encompassing, nurturant totality that "holds" or "contains" the person and everything else within it. Of course, if there were major deficiencies and traumas in the earlier establishment of this matrix, then its direct presentational reemergence as potential metaphor must exacerbate these early difficulties. If the pattern to be translated into felt meaning was inadequately experienced in the first place, it will not be able to contain these powerful states.

What of the "mainstream" cognitive view of synesthesias and mandala imageries as reflecting a concrete, primitive mentality common in childhood and mostly disappearing with linguistic and conceptual development?

So Werner (1961) himself unfortunately thought, but we have already considered copious evidence that imagery can undergo its own development into abstract representational and presentational thought. In addition, there is no real evidence that eidetic imagery, synesthesias, and physiognomic awareness are more prominent in young children than in adults (Haber, 1979). This impression seems to be based mostly on individual cases where adults recall forms of experience no longer present in their lives, rather than reflecting a developmental rule. Also, if we could establish such a decline, it might as easily be understood in the way that Vygotsky (1962) interpreted the loss of egocentric speech in young children: it is not that these behaviors and experiences disappear, it is that they are internalized and automatized as the "inner matrix" for verbal, and here nonverbal, thought. Finally, and returning to the first point, if what we are tracing is the development of a presentational imagistic capacity, most fully developed in the aesthetic and religious traditions, then its selective disappearance in adulthood may reflect the general failure of our culture to support early spontaneous forms of a major symbolic frame. That would make it appear that language (and mathematics) took over from imagery, when this shift is actually a by-product of western-style education and its tendency to ignore the nonverbal.

What of the "pre-/trans-" fallacy, and is it being committed here?

Wilber (1980) developed a linear model of transpersonal experience considered as the culmination of all human cognitive development, rather than one line of development open to a symbolic frame or, better, meta-frame, as in the present treatment. From Wilber's perspective, the occurrence of altered states of consciousness in childhood is a conceptual problem, which he resolves by distinguishing forms of experience that are regressive, or *pre*-ego, from the genuine spiritual development of adulthood, as *trans*-ego and *post*formal operations in Piaget's sense. Wilber criticizes what he sees as a common confusion of the pre-ego primitivity of synesthesias, geometric imagery, and bizarre dreams with the genuinely transcendent experiences of the meditative traditions.

Whether in the area of history, art, or spirituality, no one would want to mistake early stages of development for later ones. One should not, however, allow that concern to obscure the actual continuities in any line of symbolic development — even if a line based on presentational states unfolds over a lifetime and, as in western culture, with striking interruptions. If one's development along a certain line — here presentational states and "spirituality" — is typically interrupted or fixated at an early (primitive) stage of its unfolding, then its later reemergence is not a regression but the return to a road untaken. Almaas (1988) has argued that the continuity of being or presence in most of us is disrupted in childhood through the inevitable failure of the adult environment to mirror our early spontaneity and wholeness. Spontaneous presentational states in adolescence and adulthood would begin to reanimate what Winnicott referred to as this lost "true self," without making these imagistic phenomena into something regressive, primitive, or pre-ego.

But is not the focus of this discussion on the "lower" forms of sensate mysticism rather than on its noetic goal?

It is certainly true that all of these complex synesthesias, geometric images, chakras, and lights, as imagistically based felt meanings, are preliminary to the often ineffable intuitions of ultimate reality or mind in classical mysticism (Underhill, 1955; Deikman, 1982). Such noetic realizations are preceded, however, by these sensate, presentational patterns, from which they unfold as culmination. Accordingly, it is just these more specific presentational states that provide the only available evidence for the cognitive processes that would underlie this entire line of development. On the view that *all* experience points or refers beyond itself as part of the very nature of intentionality, then the sensate stages of meditative realization are like the learning of any new language — here an abstract imagistic one. One learns lexicon and grammar to the point that their use becomes relatively internalized. Only then can the new language be used to refer fully beyond its materials. What the study of these presentational states has already shown us is not only the cognitive processes hidden within their more developed forms, but the way in which this entire line of development rests on the same cross-modal and metaphoric processes in all symbolic cognition. The meditative traditions often emphasize that ordinary mind and mind-as-such are two aspects of the same capacity, a view surely supported by the demonstration, in terms of contemporary cognitive psychology, that they exemplify the same processes.

Is it ultimately reductionistic to give a cognitive account, however supposedly holistic and phenomenological, of human spirituality?

If the sense of transcendence, even if given to us by an absolute spiritual reality or Being, comes through the human mind, which it clearly does, then that must be mediated by cognitive processes of some kind. These can then be researched without that being automatically reductionistic. My own strategy (Hunt, 1984, 1985ab, 1986, 1989b) has been to reason back from the descriptive phenomenology of presentational states to the sort of mind that might have such experiences. This allows us to see how that mind would be related to general principles in cognitive theory. By itself, such an approach is agnostic with respect to whether the mind thus revealed is thereby prone to just these sorts of illusions, or whether instead it constitutes just the sort of telescope needed to see spiritual truth. The reader is, of course, free to choose either alternative, the former clearly reductionistic and the latter possibly veering into what James termed "over-belief." It is true that I see a greater danger for our present era in the former than in the latter.

To follow the lead of Nietzsche, James, and Jung, if the higher spiritual traditions of humanity might actually refer to something important and thus need to be preserved and carried forward in some fashion within our predominantly scientific and utilitarian civilization, then some sort of account of how they could occur as an expression of the structure of the human mind will be necessary. That need not be reductionistic, and indeed the alternative has been to explain away such states as merely the residue of a primitive, nonrational mentality which we have supposedly left behind. Surely the pluralism of contemporary society will ultimately require a similar pluralism in our theory of mind. We need to understand how these practices and states could be expressions of the same mind that, in its other frames and forms, gives us language, logic, and science itself. In making judgments about the supposed validity of one of these frames, we may unwittingly be making the same judgments about them all.

11 Heidegger, Mahayana Buddhism, and Gibson's Ambient Array: A Logos of Sentience

We have been dealing with the cognitive processes that underlie experiences which we have variously termed higher states of consciousness, transpersonal experience, or presentational states. These have been understood as a reconstitution on the level of symbolic cognition of presence-openness as the basic structure of perception in motile sentient creatures. Horizontal openness and the flow gradients of the ambient array are "real," "existent," and inherent to the structure of sentience, but would only be realized as such, as felt meaning for its own sake, on the human level. Presence-openness emerges into presentational symbolic cognition through the synesthetic translation of the spaciousness and glow of the visual surround, as its "there," and vital kinesthetic embodiment as its "here."

Now we need to look less at the process side and more at the noetic "point" of such experiences in order to attempt some broadly naturalistic and descriptive understanding of what these states are about. From this perspective there are two related accounts of the realizations involved in presence-openness that are especially congruent with our discussion of its holistic cognitive psychology. First, the later writings of Martin Heidegger portray the experiential realization of openness or "unconcealment" as the sense of being at the core of all spiritual traditions. Then, in Mahayana Buddhism, ostensibly the same characterizations used by Heidegger for the sense of "isness" emerge as the meditative realization of the voidness or openness of "mind as such." Both these traditions of thought see a recurrent loss of these felt realizations or attunements, which must follow from our embeddedness in practical social reality, along with their ever-present potential for reawakening.

This coordination of the experiential realisms of the later Heidegger and of Mahayana Buddhism is aided, in particular, by Herbert Guenther and his decision in editing and translating primary sources in the Tibetan Mahayana Buddhist tradition to render Sanskrit and Tibetan usages by means of the terminology of the later Heidegger as their closest western equivalents. (See Longchenpa, *Kindly Bent to Ease Us*, vols. 1–3; Guenther, *The Life and Teaching of Naropa, Matrix of Mystery,* and *From Reductionism to Creativity.)* For Guenther, Heidegger's increasingly poetic and metaphoric attempts to "say" Being clearly intend the same meaning as the Buddhist practices. This would represent the first point where our own tradition approaches close enough to eastern meditation to afford a genuinely adequate translation. The translations and commentaries that result are both controversial and quite striking. It is as though one were encountering the Tibetan Buddhist tradition as it might have been rewritten by Heidegger himself, and this not as interpretation but as direct translation. Suddenly, the distance between eastern meditation and our own realism and naturalism seems considerably lessened.

Jung (1954), however, has certainly not been alone in concluding that, although eastern meditative traditions offer important parallels to western spiritual traditions, they could not be fully practiced by westerners. The ways of life and background assumptions are just too different, he insisted, to be more than superficially imitated by westerners. There is no denying the problems of mutual misunderstanding. Yet, if Guenther is correct, then without any awareness of the eastern traditions during the crucial early years of his writings, Heidegger's attempt to re-present the spirituality of Meister Eckhart as part of a phenomenological description of *Dasein* (Caputo, 1986) has resulted in a view of lived experience with significant parallels to Buddhism. Since Heidegger's intentions were descriptive and phenomenological, there is much fascination in the possibility that his later thought "says" what meditative practice "shows".[1]

In the discussion to follow, we will first consider Heidegger (early and later) and Tibetan Buddhism (especially as presented by Guenther) in parallel, then pursue their areas of overlap and difference. The addition of Gibson's ecological array to Heidegger's presence-openness completes the latter in a way that increases both its distance from the western tradition and its agreement with Buddhist views on the commonalities of humans and animals — views that Heidegger himself did not share. There is no intention, then, to provide a reading of Heidegger that is "strict" or "purist." That would ill repay the importance of the issues he raises. I will leave for later (chapter 13) my own version of Guenther's (1984, 1989) related attempts to tie his Heidegger-Buddhism interface into the language of nonlinear dynamics. It will appear more fundamental to show how all these systems — phenomenologies of lived experience and nonlinear dynamics — might be rooted in the first instance in a primacy of perception. As sentient creatures, it would be perception that offers us the template for both the most inward and the most outward of human realities.

The Later Heidegger and Mahayana Buddhism: Parallel Phenomenologies of Being

Heidegger

I have already mentioned the preoccupation of the early Heidegger in *Being and Time* (1927) with what he took as a characteristically western loss of the sense of "isness" or Being — the capacity for wonder that the world and ourselves *are* at all. It is our potential awareness of our own existence, and the implicit structures of the latter allowing such awareness, that for Heidegger is the key to regaining our sense of being. Because we are the being that can potentially question itself, human existence (*Da-sein* — literally, "being there") is uniquely coordinated to Being (*Sein*). In particular, our experience of time is an "ecstasis" of past and present into future and so into the nonbeing and incomprehensibility of "death." It is this openness of our temporality that provides, in Heidegger's term, the "horizon" for our direct experience of Being as such. For the early Heidegger, the awakening of this potentiality for "authenticity" rests entirely on our courage to see and bear an ontological or intrinsic "dread" as the sign of our facing into this uncharacterizable openness of lived time. This experience of time ahead and the attendant wonder at Being is specifically human, and absent in lower animals.

However, a "forgetfulness" of Being — the loss of our ability to be struck by immediate isness — is *also* intrinsic to human existence. It is the burden of much of Heidegger's analysis of *Dasein* in 1927 to show how we must, for much of our lives, fill in the openness of temporality with the "busy-ness," "chatter," and "projects" of everyday life. This Heidegger terms "inauthenticity." All these everyday concerns are treated as if they were matters of life and death precisely so that we do not have to notice the ever-present death and life opening out directly before us. The very intensity of our "care" betokens our potentiality for the sense of an encompassing transcendence that is continuously implied within our experience of time. The sudden sense of strangeness when we notice that, just as surely as we now are, we must someday not be, is the "call of Being." Whereas the early Heidegger sees only dread and the uncanny as the marks of this openness, later he will emphasize chiefly the wonder, gratitude, and "releasement" or "letting be" that brings him closer to the meditative traditions.

The ever-renewed potential for the loss of isness that follows from the preoccupations of everyday life in all cultures and times is, on Heidegger's analysis, especially intensified within our western tradition. For all its worship of scientific "fact" and "reality," we seem to have rendered Being as something merely utilitarian. Our "calculative" and functionalist thought has turned everything, most especially our own existence, into a commodity or resource to be mined for whatever use we can extract from it — very much as if there were nothing outside our narcissistic humanism that could "matter" (Heidegger, 1947). This leaves the "subject" as simultaneously the master of the universe and a nonrational residuum, marked by a "consciousness" that already attests to its epiphenomenal and derivative status.

Being and Time is the most thoroughgoing attempt to articulate a potentially cross-cultural structure for human existence (Dreyfus, 1982, 1991). As such, its major contribution may be Heidegger's assertion that it is this sense of isness that constitutes the common felt meaning within all traditional metaphysical and spiritual traditions. This felt sense is what Heidegger seeks to release from its encrustation within the rationalistic metaphysical systems of western thought. Its ongoing experience is the immediate source for any expression of a transcendental dimension within human life — whether that is defined as deity or the would-be utopias of science.

It is interesting that one of the major thinkers of our factual, scientific, and materialistic age would locate isness or existence as the core of the human capacity to sense transcendence. It might seem easy in reading the early Heidegger, let alone his later more experiential and metaphoric expressions, to conclude that this is the stuff of a subjectivism and neo-Romanticism. Yet what could be more realist or scientific than making a fascination with isness the core of our experience? Is Being not "factual" and a "fact"? Is that not what this age now worships? Is it not true that all of us do forget most of the time that we exist and that this is proven by the highly characteristic shocks of realization that occur when we "self-remember"? At the very least, Heidegger's version of this hidden "sense" behind all metaphysical and spiritual traditions is fittingly "empiricist" and "realist." There does not seem to be any way to conclude that the sensed "isness" and presence at the core of transpersonal and peak experiences is somehow an illusion — that it somehow "is not."

What is most striking about Heidegger's later writings, especially from the late 1930s until his death in 1976, is his diverse pursuit of Being as something to be sensed or felt everywhere — in art and poetry as much as the concepts of metaphysics, within the immediate experience of nature more than in the temporality of *Dasein*. These are the writings that, in the words of John Caputo (1986), best show the "mystical element" in Heidegger's phenomenology of experience.[2] It is here that Heidegger conveys the sense of isness within metaphors so remarkably resonant with Mahayana Buddhism that Guenther could essay his translations of the latter into a Heideggerian phenomenology. Being is no longer present only by implication and indirectly, to be approached through the "horizon" of something else. Instead, it is directly sensed through multiple natural metaphors for luminosity and flow.[3]

Being now "shines forth." The thinking that senses it is equally a "thanking." In a manner especially reminiscent of the Buddhist notion of a voidness/emptiness that "gives" all experience, Heidegger, in *The Question of Being* (1956), actually writes Being as B̶e̶i̶n̶g̶, to convey his sense of an isness that wells forth beings while simultaneously withdrawing behind them as "Nothing." In many of these writings, "Being" is simply replaced with words like "presencing," "shining," "glowing," "opening," "clearing," "giving," "allowing," "releasement," and "unconceal-ment" (Heidegger's translation of the Greek *aletheia* as "truth").[4]

In order to see how closely the later Heidegger comes to the meditative path of Mahayana Buddhism, we turn now to Guenther's rendering of the Tibetan tradition.

Mahayana Buddhism as a Phenomenology of Human Existence

Buddhist meditation seeks directly experienced realizations of the presence-open-ness basis of mind — of an emptiness/voidness welling forth with all the specifics of our experience. Mind or consciousness as such is uncharacterizable and ineffable. In Sanskrit this appears as *shunya* in the sense of emptiness. Guenther stresses that this emptiness or nothingness is not a negation in the sense of privation, but rather a felt fullness — very much in the spirit of Heidegger's B̶e̶i̶n̶g̶ that simultaneously wells forth and withdraws:

> Shunyata is a highly positive term. . . . In . . . popular language, if a glass had no water in it, it could be called shunya. But this is not at all the sense of shunyata in Buddhist philosophy. . . . When we perceive, we usually attend to the delimited forms of objects. But these objects are perceived within a field. Attention can be directed either to the concrete, limited forms or to the field in which these forms are situated. In the shunyata experience, the attention is on the field rather than on its contents. By "contents," we mean here those forms which are the outstanding features of the field itself. . . . This openness is present in and actually presupposed by every determinate form. Every determinate entity evolves out of something indeterminate and to a certain extent also maintains its connection with this indeterminacy; it is never completely isolated from it. Because the determinate entity is not isolated from the indeterminacy and because nevertheless there is no bridge between the two, our attention can shift back and forth between one and the other. (Guenther and Trungpa, 1975, pp. 26–27)

This account is quite similar to some observations on the phenomenology of perception by Mercedes Gaffron (1956). She describes the effect of shifting one's manner of attending to the visual surroundings from the "surfaces" that are usually the focus of our typically "recognitive" gaze to the spaciousness "behind" these surfaces and from which they loom. When we deliberately look behind objects into their background, we do experience the world differently. Objects become dynamic and fluctuating. They seem to well forth from an indefinite and dynamic background. Gaffron's interest was primarily in a different mode of visual appearance, but her accounts, considered as an exemplification of a more general attitude, fit with both Buddhism and Heidegger on the ways that forms dynamically emerge out of an uncharacterizable source.

Realization within Tibetan Mahayana Buddhism has multiple aspects, which in one form or another we have already touched upon: *Dharmadatu* refers to the inseparability between forms and emptiness, such that each implies the other. This is illustrated above in Gaffron's phenomenological version of the figure-ground relation in perception and is also reflected in Heidegger's discussion of the way in which B̶e̶i̶n̶g̶ "gives" beings. *Dharmakaya* is the inseparability of emptiness (openness) and clarity, also consistent with Heidegger's discussion of isness in terms of the metaphors of shining, lighting, and glow. Finally, *Bodhichitta* refers to the inseparability of emptiness and compassion, conveyed by the metaphor of an open spaciousness that allows an infinity of possible perspectives within it. Compassion here seems clearly resonant with Heidegger on the giving and letting of isness — a giving that retreats behind what is given. The realization of compassion comes on two levels. "Relative" compassion results from the empathy that the meditator who has realized the uncharacterizable openness of all experience comes to feel for those who cling to their experience as definitely "this" or "that." "Absolute" compassion is the fully embodied realization that the openness or voidness of all experience is itself the primary expression of compassion, since it allows all specific things that can occur to appear unstintingly within it. The meditator who completely embodies both levels of compassion is termed a bodhisattva within the Mahayana Buddhist tradition, and has pledged continual rebirth as a teacher until all sentient beings have realized presence-openness as the basis of their experience.

As we have already seen, the full experience of openness as the glow of empty space is especially attuned to lived time, since luminosity welling forth is the only spatial metaphor encompassing and nonrestrictive enough to "match" the openness of time ahead. This full realization in meditative practice elicits a metaphorically based felt meaning in which anything that happens to one is already sensed as an expression of that glow:

> With the realization of the realm of free space in which all things are identified, anything which enters experience is known to be unborn in its origin. This is the attainment of the ultimate refuge. . . . Detached, without any tendency to slow the natural progression from unitary totality to the intimately related flash of the following moment, no . . . fear arises to begin the process of action-reaction producing attraction and aversion. . . . Rather there is a continuous sense of amazement at the ineffable beauty and sublimity of the being in life and understanding. (Tarthang Tulku, 1973, p. 106)

No wonder, then, that the mood of Heidegger's discussion of temporality shifts from anxiety to one of calm with the appearance of the metaphors of "shining" and "gift." This seems to be exactly the sense of the following Buddhist passage as well, in which the felt meaning emerging from open space as metaphor is described as taking the sting out of time and ultimately out of death itself:

> By allowing a gap, space in which things may be as they are, we begin to appreciate the clear simplicity and precision of our lives. . . . Patience also feels space. It never fears new situations, because nothing can surprise the bodhisattva — nothing. Whatever comes — be it destructive, chaotic, creative, welcoming, or inviting — the bodhisattva is never disturbed, never shocked, because he is aware of the space between the situation and himself. Once one is aware of the space between the situation and oneself, then anything can happen in that space. Whatever occurs does so in the midst of space. (Trungpa, 1973, p. 167, 175)

In Longchenpa's *Kindly Bent to Ease Us*, so painstakingly rendered into Heideggerian by Guenther, the relation of meditative realization to the immediacy of isness seems clear enough. Ordinary experience is finally to be sensed as a sort of "wizardry" or "magic show" since, although having no fixed essence, it nonetheless springs forth continuously and in endless generosity. Longchenpa describes the fully realized sense of presence-openness as like a dream, and this, again, on two levels. In ordinary dreams, as in everyday life, we take things as having a fixed and determinable significance, whereas when the dream becomes lucid — a specific goal of Tibetan dream yoga (Chang, 1963) — we realize that what we took to be fixed is intrinsically open and ephemeral. At a further level of practice, the attempt is made to regard the here-and-now experience of everyday waking life as itself a dream. This leads to a transformation of our experience akin to that which occurs with lucid dreaming and self-remembering during wakefulness — with the increased sense of clarity, immediacy, and freedom also described by Maslow as part of peak experience:

> When you are not separate from the idea that
> Whatever is present, whatever is being done and
>   whatever is being thought about is all a dream,
> Then you train yourself in absolute non-subjectivity
>   (by realizing that your dream)
> Has no truth-value, is but something flimsy, something
>   ethereal something evanescent,
> Something fleeting, something faint. . . .
> After having had this experience in which what is
>   present is not held to be this or that,
> Whatever presents itself arises in primal openness
>   having no root whatsoever.

This is the experience of Being in its actual primordiality.
(Longchenpa, vol. 3, 1976, pp. 44–5)

If at this very moment you were to seriously consider your current circumstances as a dream, then whatever else that entailed, you would have to turn to the moment-by-moment here and nowness of your unfolding experience with a specific attentiveness and fascination very similar to that sought by the self-remembering waking meditations of Gurdjieff (1975) and Almaas (1986a). You would sense the immediacy of all that was welling forth around you with the same wonder that Heidegger locates within the similar "gift" and "mystery" of isness.

Much of this language common to Buddhism and Heidegger may seem like truism and playing with words, but what is conveyed most directly thereby is not conceptual analysis but an evoked phenomenology latent within ordinary experience. It does seem to be true that what we experience at this very moment is continuously emerging out of a "nothing" that we cannot identify or know as such, since it is always already ahead of itself toward the next and the next. Our consciousness is clearly given yet not known apart from these ongoing unspecifiable moments of continuous welling forth.

Presence-Openness in Heidegger and Buddhism: A Confluence

We are now in a better position to see the similarities between Buddhist meditation, even without Guenther's insightful assistance, and the later Heidegger's search for ways to "say" the sense of Being. Heidegger's descriptive metaphors, liberated from the static abstractions of western metaphysics, are the same as Buddhist metaphors used to convey meditative realizations. Both traditions are resonant with descriptions from classical introspectionism as well, as we shall see.

In "Time and Being," a lecture given in 1962, Heidegger develops a play on words with the German *es gibt* — ordinarily translated as "there is." Instead of our saying "there is" Being, "there is" time, he suggests a return to the more literal meaning, "it gives." Being and time are both "given" or let be by an "it" that withdraws into concealment in the very motion of its giving forth. This "it" is both nothing and a continuously renewed fullness. Here we are close to the Greek notion of truth, understood by Heidegger as an "unconcealing," a showing forth that simultaneously conceals itself: "A giving which gives only its gift, but in the giving holds itself back and withdraws, such a giving we call sending. According to the meaning of giving which is to be thought in this way, Being — that which It gives — is what is sent" (Heidegger, 1972, p. 8).

Time is no longer conceived as the "horizon" of Being, but in terms of its sense of a continuous welling forth. The "It" is like the source or head of a stream that gives the flowing water behind which it is invisible as such: "The giving that gives time is determined by denying and withholding nearness. It grants the openness of time-space and preserves what remains denied in what has-been, what is withheld in approach. We call the giving which gives true time an extending which opens and conceals. As extending is itself a giving, the giving of a giving is concealed in true time" (Heidegger, 1972, p. 16).

Another term Heidegger uses for this "it" is "appropriation" (*Ereignis*), as the inner structure of "event" or "happening" (the latter being the usual translation of *Ereignis*). Appropriation is understood as a giving that takes itself back. Both time and Being are now understood as resting on a common appropriation of a "region" or "clearing" out of nothing. "Something" replaces or "takes" the "nothing" that would otherwise have been, and that something unfolds as a continuous unity of past and present, present and future. We say "everything *takes* time." Presencing for Heidegger is the immediate exfoliating of time out of itself, a perpetually renewed giving: "Appropriating makes manifest its peculiar property, that Appropriation withdraws what is most fully its own from boundless unconcealment. Thought in terms of Appropriating, this means: in that sense it expropriates itself of itself. Expropriation belongs to Appropriation as such. By this expropriation, Appropriation does not abandon itself—rather, it preserves what is its own" (Heidegger, 1972, pp. 22–23).

The sense here is reminiscent of the realizations emerging from "anaesthetic revelation" with nitrous oxide, from William James: "The Revelation is . . . the one sole and sufficient insight why, or not why, but how, the present is pushed on by the past, and sucked forward by the vacuity of the future. . . . The real secret would be the formula by which the 'now' keeps exfoliating out of itself, yet never escapes. What is it, indeed, that keeps existence exfoliating?" (James, 1902, p. 351). James and Heidegger seem to notice very much the same thing about experience, namely, its inseparability from sensed temporality.

There is a key similarity between Heidegger's characterization of presencing as like the source of a stream and the introspectionist Titchener's (1929) attempt to describe the basic givenness of temporality in immediate consciousness during his later, more phenomenological phase. He describes this ur-sense of time as a "pre-temporal welling forth," while Heidegger locates welling and flow as inescapable spatial metaphors for the temporal dimension of experience.

Also reminiscent of Titchener is Heidegger's attempt to capture the experiential quality of space and its openness with terms like "regioning" and "clearing." It is only within a clearing or region that events can shine forth. It is the clearing in the woods that lets the shining be within it. The clearing is hidden behind and emerges through this "gathering" of light.[5] This approach to Being as nothing in itself requires metaphors that become more and more subtle. Where Heidegger refers to the clearing as the primordial experience of the openness of space around us, the later Titchener (1929) similarly describes the ur-quality of space as "pre-spatial spread." This is an expanse or spreading, neither two- nor three-dimensional but prior to both, that can be experienced with the tachistoscope and in introspective studies of luster and sheen (chapter 7). It seems of genuine interest that these two gifted observers, who were jointly concerned with the primacy of ongoing experience, would characterize lived time as a "welling forth" and the expansive opening of space as "clearing" and "spread."

To complete this comparison of the later Heidegger and Mahayana Buddhism I return to Guenther's translations of key words in Longchenpa's *Kindly Bent to Ease Us* by means of Heidegger's terminology and metaphors. Indeed, both traditions rely fundamentally on the metaphors of "shining," "glow," "radiance," "welling forth," and the image of the source of the stream ever-present but invisible within its outpouring. Mind-as-such (*sems-nyid* in the Tibetan text), as opposed to our everyday grasping of things as "this" or "that," is inherently responsive to a pure facticity (*ngobo*), which has a characteristic and defining openness (*stong pa*). Consciousness and world are co-emergents from a common ground or source (*gzhi*) that is not characterizable at all other than as a compassionate emptiness to be evoked by metaphors of open sky and empty luminous space. The most immediate experience of this ground, which like *Dasein* is neither subject nor object, has a self-presencing clarity (*rig pa*) that is attuned to pure there-ness (*dag sang*). Felt as such, this attunement is experienced as an actuality (*rang bzhin*) and as a radiancy or lucency (*gsal ba*):

> Insofar as Being involves experience, it is already an "objective" continuum of meanings that in its presence is pure, an open dimension, defying any propositions about it. It also is lucent and radiant without its radiance being concretely tangible, and it is equally cognitive without there being the necessity to resort to concepts. By way of analogy it is like the clear autumn sky and, since experience is directly involved and cannot be detached from it, it is encountered by the cognitive capacity in a state of utter composure. (Longchenpa, vol. 3, 1976, p. 15)

At various points, and depending on the context, Guenther translates as "Being," or treats as synonyms of Heidegger's Being, *gzhi* (ground), *ngobo* (facticity), *rang bhzin* (actuality, immediacy), *stong pa* (openness), *snang ba* (thereness), and *chosku* (dharmakaya, or the inseparability of emptiness-openness and clarity). This reflects a remarkable confluence in the history of the attempted mediations between East and West. If Guenther is right, and the metaphors common to both traditions do support his decision, then the emergent coordination of Being, as the experiential core of western metaphysical thought about "isness," and consciousness-as-such, as the openness and compassion of experience in meditative realization, must mutually illuminate each other.

Some Differences between Heidegger and Meditative Buddhism, with Gibson as Mediator

The Place of History

Apart from these later attempts to convey the immediacy of "isness" as "it gives," Heidegger's writings, not surprisingly, retain a distinctive western character. This is especially visible in the importance he ascribes to history (Caputo, 1986; Galka, 1986). For Heidegger, the "regioning" of Being is a historical process, in a way that would seem strange indeed in the context of the meditative traditions. Human beings, as the being uniquely attuned to Being, are intrinsically historical. The different historical epochs and civilizations can be understood as different ways in which Being shows itself. Our modern history mirrors the "it gives" of appropriation in a process that Heidegger terms "enframing." In a manner later developed more specifically by Foucault (1970), each historical epoch is based on a set of tacit assumptions concealed within their more outward cultural expressions. Thus, Heidegger traces a fundamental shift in the felt sense of truth from "unconcealment" in the early Greeks to a progressive loss of this attunement to the "it gives" in our later metaphysics of reality and reason, where truth becomes "correspondence" or "accuracy," and finally "commodity." Our era of technology offers its own unique version of Being within the very sense of uncanniness that emerges when we contemplate our historically unique efforts to control and dominate both ourselves and our world (Heidegger, 1962).

It would not occur to a Buddhist to examine history for clues to the nature of presence-openness. Its realization emerges only when one steps back from all versions of everyday reality (*samsara*) in order to appreciate the nature of our immediate experience through meditative practice. Some historical eras make that easier to undertake than others, but otherwise what we call history is not of focal interest. For Mahayana Buddhism, time comes in two forms: one's personal life course, of such prominence also in Heidegger's early analysis of *Dasein*, and vast eras termed *kalpas*. While each such period of cosmic creation and annihilation has its own Buddha and manifestations of Buddhist teachings, what is important for individuals in all ages is the attunement to openness-compassion as the emanating source of all experience.

The Relation of Human Beings to Presence-Openness

In Heidegger, consistent with the Christian Scholastic tradition of such powerful influence on his early thought, it is Being that addresses the human being, revealing or concealing itself. Heidegger uses locutions such as Being "turns away," or "only a god can save now," implying that the most that modern people can do in response to their loss of "isness" is to orient themselves to the gap left by its absence and await its return. While this is, of course, consistent with the phenomenology of the numinous, in which the great mystics insist that "it has you, you don't have it" (Otto, 1923), the meditative traditions emphasize our inherent potential responsiveness to presence-openness. Human beings have the intrinsic ability, by means of meditation, actively to prepare the way for such experiential realizations.

This difference is clearly a matter of degree, since the later Heidegger does begin to discuss our approach to Being. First, he urges the cultivation of a "meditative thinking," in contrast to our predominant mode of calculative or computational cognition. Meditative thinking entails *Gelassenheit* — an attitude of "calm abiding" or "releasement" that opens to the "mystery" of that which "regions" (Heidegger, 1959). Second, the fullest development of thinking shows it to be a "thanking" for the "it gives," again something we ourselves can actively cultivate (Heidegger, 1954). Finally, in a fashion similar to Suzanne Langer (1942) and developed in turn by Hannah Arendt (1978), Heidegger (1959) makes a distinction between "representational" thinking and the "presentational" thinking that is directly responsive to "isness." In poetry and art, thinking "shows," "allows," and "gives" in a way that directly mirrors the "it gives" of Being: "To say means to show, to make appear, the lighting-concealing-releasing offer of world" (Heidegger, 1959, p. 107).

We have already seen that from a cognitive perspective meditation itself can be understood as the maximally abstract development of a presentational symbolic capacity. The basic structures of ambient perception reappear in meditative realization as inclusive metaphors whose contemplation releases presence-openness.

The Place of Animals: The Ambient Array as Template of Presence-Openness

For both the early and later Heidegger, it is only the human being that can experience presence-openness. In the Parmenides lectures (1942) Heidegger insists that only symbolizing, self-referential beings can become attuned to openness as such. In *Being and Time* (1927), of course, the openness of time ahead is specific to *Dasein*. Human existence, through its openness to time ahead, is the "horizon" for any sense of transcendence. Nonsymbolizing animals are simply not "ahead of themselves" into the future. Heidegger must reject the Buddhist view, here supported by our treatment of Gibson's array, that the "form" of openness lies within all sentient beings. In Mahayana Buddhism all sentient creatures have *bodhichitta* — the unity of openness and compassion — as a "seed." The importance of human existence is that only on our level can this seed be developed and fully realized by means of meditative practice. Such a view is quite close to the present cognitive perspective in which presence-openness is the background structure of perception common to all motile organisms. Experienced as such, in presentational symbolic form, it reemerges as the primary metaphoric vehicle for transpersonal experience.

Heidegger, however, cleaves instead to the more traditional western tendency to separate man and animal. This is somewhat ironic, given his strong critique of that tradition and his otherwise striking parallels with Mahayana Buddhism. In his introductory lectures on metaphysics from 1929/30 and repeated in his Heraclitus seminar of 1966/67, he says: "The stone is world-less, the animal world-poor, and the human world-forming" (sometimes also translated world-building) (Heidegger and Fink, 1979, p. 146). Only we are in-the-world in such a way as to be attuned to presence-openness. In the Parmenides lectures Heidegger is especially critical of what he sees as the romanticizing and humanizing of lower animals by the poet Rilke, citing in particular the passage also quoted at the beginning of Part V. Animals, Heidegger insists, cannot respond to openness as such with the fascination and wonder that things are at all.

What Heidegger missed was the possibility that presence-openness appears in simpler, nonreflexive organisms precisely as "seed." The ambient array of motile sentient organisms has two dimensions that reappear as the inner structure of human transpersonal experience. First, there is the co-specification in all versions of the ambient array of the "here" (presence) uniquely given (afforded) by the particular "there" of the surround. Second, the array of any moving creature has a whence-whither pattern of flow that emerges out of the indefiniteness of a horizonal openness always ahead. This flow, as Gibson states and Rilke echoes, has its focus of expansion in the direction in which the creature is moving, and its focus of contraction in the direction from which it comes. Contrary to Heidegger (and to Bergson, 1907) the ambient array of motile organisms is the very opposite of anything static and fixed, such that a genuine temporal dimension could only be added on the human level. Rather, the openness of time ahead for us rests already on the symbolic recasting of a here-there, whence-whither openness intrinsic to the array. In an important sense, as we have already seen, what it is "like" to be a bat is what it is "like" to be human. An array of specific gradients opening out ahead of us gives us a specific presence within a surround of possibilities, just like the bat. Certainly, we alone can notice this structure as such and find it expressive of meaning, but Heidegger was as surely incorrect not to carry his "structuralism" into perception itself.[6]

As one would expect, given the centrality of metaphors based on space and light in Heidegger, he does come close to the position outlined here, although he ultimately rejects it. In his later writings, as well as in *Being and Time,* he develops the notion of horizon as openness. In *Discourse on Thinking* (1959, pp. 63–64) he speaks of "the horizon which encircles the view of a thing — the field of vision," but then renders it as the structure made possible by our human way of being: "We say that we look into the horizon. Therefore the field of vision is something open, but its openness is not due to our looking." In his 1929/30 lectures[7] he specifically mentions Von Uexküll (chapter 5) on the way in which the surround opens out around animals — "their opening upon the stimuli with which they encircle themselves" (translated in Olafson, 1987, p. 236). There he rightly insists that these stimuli are not experienced as "things," that is, noticed in their "isness," since they are restricted to serve as the releasers of fixed drives. Again citing Von Uexküll, Heidegger noted that the stimuli that engage organismic needs are thereby "set aside" or eliminated by the satisfaction of the need. They are made to go away and so cannot be appreciated in fascination and wonder for their sheer "isness." From the present perspective we can agree with Heidegger that animals lack an aesthetic sense and are incapable of presentational states, without having to deny the presence-openness structure of their array.

Gibson's discussion of his ambient ecological array is full of echoes of Heidegger's being-in-the-world as a unique opening around and for sentient beings:

> The mutuality of animal and environment is not implied by physics and the physical sciences. The basic concepts of space, time, matter, and energy do not lead naturally to the organism-environment concept or to the concept of a species and its habitat. Instead they seem to lead to the idea of an animal as an extremely complex object of the physical world. . . . This way of thinking neglects the fact that the animal-object is surrounded in a special way, that an environment is ambient for a living object in a different way than a set of objects is ambient for a physical object. (Gibson, 1979, p. 8)

Contrary to the models of tension reduction in traditional animal psychology, motile organisms seem also to be engaged in a spontaneous exploration of their array. In this sense "curiosity motivation" would be the need system associated with the array, while tension reduction behaviors, Heidegger's exclusive preoccupation when it came to animal behavior, would be restricted to the recognitive sphere. Heidegger's notion of being-in-the-world as successive concealments and unconcealments seems especially resonant with Gibson's progressive deletions and additions of surfaces in moving through the array.

Heidegger does not take the step that is otherwise strongly implied by the entire corpus of his writing, of finding the source of the openness of our experience of time and being in a presence-openness structure within the array itself. Thus, he is held back from any understanding of our human concern with transcendence and our capacity for the numinous as a reconstitution within symbolic self-reference of the most basic structures of perception. This is remarkably close to the Mahayana Buddhist view that all creatures contain presence-openness as seed, but only human beings realize it as such. It is of interest that something like this intimate relation of human and animal is also axiomatic within the shamanic traditions of hunter-gatherer peoples — where the soul, on death, may be understood as returning to the animal or plant spirit that was its source.

Similarly missing in Heidegger, although also implied throughout, is any real sense that "world" is shared in terms of the most basic structures of perception as co-given in mutuality — both between people, his discussion of "being-with" not-withstanding, and especially between humans and animals. In part his early grounding in the Christian theology of Aquinas and Eckart, and his attempt to restate this tradition as a phenomenology of Dasein, doubtless favored the separation of human existence from all "lower" soul-less forms. In addition, I suspect that his extremely conservative political values tended to exaggerate his sense of the separateness among different cultural groups. His dismissal of the "primitive" *Dasein* of native peoples, all too typical for the times, would make it still harder for him to see any fundamental commonalities across all of human experience, let alone with still "lower" beings. This exaggerated separation between human beings and animals has made it especially difficult to see perception itself as a "consciousness-with."

Heidegger's reluctance to follow out the more radical implications of his phenomenology of experience is perhaps the major reason why he has not come to be regarded as the key philosopher of a contemporary ecological consciousness. His juxtaposition with the meditative traditions, on the one hand, and with Gibson, on the other, would certainly allow for that possibility.

Presence-Openness as Compassion: Projective Animism or the Self-Awareness of Being?

It remains to ask whether the experiential realization of presence-openness, as the fullest development of presentational symbolism and based on the most fundamental structure of perception, is in an important sense of the term "true" — a contemporary, naturalistic version of a very traditional self-understanding. Or is it a projection, ultimately "primitive" in cognitive-developmental terms, of our own humanness onto an alien surrounding universe? In both Heidegger and Mahayana Buddhism are we perhaps really dealing with a sort of abstract animism, in which the "holding" that Winnicott locates as the most fundamental template of our earliest interpersonal dependence is *arbitrarily* joined with the openness of the ambient array and thence projected onto the more inclusive properties of the physical universe?

We have already seen that something like the realization experiences common to the major meditative traditions are intrinsic to the development of the presentational side of our cognitive capacity. Indeed, if self-reference entails the use of physical metaphor as "mirror," with the more basic perceived forms providing the more inclusive metaphors, and if the presentational side of symbolic cognition must be experientially felt to be fully meaningful, then the way in which the horizon opens toward us and "allows" us to be present before it must have the felt meaning of "gift" and "compassion." The question then becomes the status of presentational symbolism. Is the truth status of our self-referential knowledge intrinsically different from the various developments of representational symbolism in physics, astronomy, and logic? Would it be a case of certain symbolic frames, using the same

cognitive processes as all the others, having a different truth value? It seems un-
likely, or at best intrinsically cumbersome in the argumentation needed to support it.

Heidegger (1936), in his comments on the pantheism and nature mysticism of
Schelling, recasts this traditional debate over animism and anthropomorphism. He
questions how *we* would establish what is human and what is not if our symbolic
capacity itself necessarily rests on physical metaphor and so on perception in the
world:

> The "anthropomorphic" objection immediately exposes itself to the most pointed
> counterobjections. . . . Behind it stands the conviction which it doesn't explain further
> that everyone, of course, generally knows what man is. . . . Does a humanizing of
> everything cognizable and knowable follow without further ado from the fact that man
> remains the "criterion" in this sense? . . . Does it not rather follow primarily that *before*
> everything the question must be asked who is man? . . . Does man not exist in such a
> way that the more primordially he is himself, he is precisely not only and not primarily
> himself? . . . If man, as the being who is not only itself, becomes the criterion, then
> what does humanizing mean? Does it not mean the precise opposite of what the
> objection takes it for? (Heidegger, 1936, pp. 163–64)

Heidegger offers here his own version of a cognitive epistemology extending from
Vico to Jung, Arnheim, and Lakoff and Johnson. We can only know ourselves by
embodying and dialoguing with what is *not* us. How could such a being really know
where it ended and "otherness" began, whether in the relation of the language of
mathematics to the physical universe (Bronowski, 1971) or in the relation of openness-compassion to Being?

For Heidegger the dialoguing nature of all *our* experience necessarily extends
into the structures of whatever physical reality *we* can know. This means that as a
species we will perpetually find ourselves in otherness, and otherness in ourselves.
In *The Basic Problems of Phenomenology* (1982) he states, "*Dasein* finds itself
primarily in things. The *Dasein* does not need a special kind of observation, nor
does it need to conduct a sort of espionage on the ego in order to have the self;
rather, as the *Dasein* gives itself immediately and passionately to the world, its own
self is reflected to it from things. This is not mysticism and does not presuppose the
assigning of souls to things. It is only a reference to an elementary phenomenological fact of existence" (Heidegger, 1982, p. 159). Heidegger continues this thought
in *The Question Concerning Technology:* "It seems as though man everywhere and
always encounters only himself. . . . *In truth, however, precisely nowhere does man
today any longer encounter himself i.e. his essence.* . . . He fails to see himself as the
one spoken to, and hence also fails in every way to hear in what respect he ek-
sists, . . . in the realm of an . . . address, and thus *can never* encounter only himself"
(Heidegger, 1962, p. 27).

Put in a somewhat different form, our existence has emerged out of the physical universe and most immediately and adjacently out of the niches or "clearings" in some sense "afforded" or "allowed" by the nonlinear media dynamics that surround all living forms. If so, it cannot be intrinsically wrong to look for our reflected "face" and "structure" within the physical systems that at various levels have generated our being. The question becomes, rather, where should we look to find our own structure outside ourselves and how do we recognize it?

The life-worlds of sentient beings must be in some sense afforded by their physical surround. Gibson has described the way in which the experienced ambient array for any motile being "gives" its specific presence and immediate possibilities for locomotion. The terms *we* have to describe this phenomenon come, inescapably, from our social existence and our relation to nurturance. For as long as a creature is alive, it is afforded, allowed, let be, held, contained by its array, much as the mothering one affords and holds the infant's growing responsiveness and sense of its own being. If this is not done sufficiently, that infant's spirit dies as surely as the fish out of water — only more slowly.

On level after level of reality it would appear that we are somehow "allowed" or "let" — from the cosmic asymmetries following the big bang, to nonlinear dynamics, to ecological niches, to the ambient array, to the nurturance of mammalian young, to mother-infant mirroring. If we describe this as "gift" or "compassion," is that necessarily projective anthropomorphism? The structure of being "given" and "afforded" is, of course, prior to and separate from how we judge this gift, or what then happens to us. But it does appear to be difficult to get away from the language of nurturance when we look at the place of sentient being within the broader surround of nonsentient nature. If we find that the fullest expression of our presentational symbolism involves a realization of presence-openness as compassion, then an obvious conclusion would be that such awareness rests on our capacity to "take the role of the other" and that, rather than being an illusion or regression, it is as accurate as anything else we do with our minds.

I said earlier that within the human sciences there was no reason to conclude that "explaining" experience and behavior thereby invalidated the rather different mode of "understanding." Understanding and explaining are two different cognitive attitudes that meet, and at times collide, both within everyday life and in the multiple disciplines that seek knowledge of our own nature. Of course, our century has seen unprecedented developments in the "explanation" of the physical and biological universe. Yet I am aware of no reasonable arguments that would show the expressions of the humanities to be some sort of mistake in contrast to the representations of the physical sciences. Indeed, the latter now wrestle with the relativity, complementarity, and indeterminism that have always been intrinsic to all expressive self-reference. "Religion," on this view, would be nothing other than the transformation of physical reality — at whatever level it is known and explained by a given culture — into self-referential metaphor. The difference between ourselves and traditional cultures is that the sudden expansion and continual reorganization of our knowledge of the universe has only haltingly been followed by the corresponding and inevitable attempts to "understand" it as, ultimately, our home. The same structures, then, face either "in" or "out" — with a necessary ambiguity, following Heidegger, as to which is which. "Out" is the special extension of perception that constitutes physical science, and "in" is the metaphoric mirror afforded by a nature so conceptualized. Why would one of these directions be "true" and the other "false" in a symbolic being whose world is based on dialogue with — and taking the role of — "the other"?

Such an analysis, of course, does not entail any view that the giving-allowing of the physical universe is in any way intentional or purposive — as in the stronger forms of the anthropic principle in recent scientific speculations. Nor does it mean that the structures of the physical universe that form the most immediate outer envelope to life-worlds are themselves "alive." Demonstrably, they are not. It does mean that we cannot begin to fully "think" our relation with the physical universe without tapping into — wittingly or not — the general patterns of sentient perception and of being a mammal. The point is existential and even epistemological, not scientific *or* theological.

The current separation of transpersonal psychology, with its understanding of "higher states of consciousness," and existentialism, especially Heidegger's phenomenology of being-in-the-world, is unfortunate and misleading — although generally endorsed by both perspectives. On the contrary, the presentational metaphors of meditative realization just *are* the felt meanings of the basic structures of human and sentient existence, as located more or less independently by the world mysticisms, descriptive phenomenology, and Gibson on perception. These forms are "just there," and their synesthetic embodiment as felt meaning seems to be as close as *we* can get to the full exercise of our presentational intelligence. It seems to be as close as we symbolizing beings can get to our actual situation. In the nexus common to both Heidegger and Buddhism, the full experience of presence-openness also seems to release us from the need to grasp and fix what is open anyway. Consciousness is an open system. The formal system or logos of sentience is openness — always around and ahead as long as awareness continues.

Part VI Consciousness and Reality

The work of Einstein, Schrödinger, and others seems to have led to the realization of an ultimate boundary of physical knowledge in the form of the media through which we perceive it. It becomes apparent that if certain facts about our common experience of perception, or what we might call the inside world, can be revealed by an extended study of what we call, in contrast, the outside world, then an equally extended study of this inside world will reveal, in turn, the facts first met with in the world outside: for what we approach, in either case, from one side or the other, is the common boundary between them.
G. Spencer-Brown, *Laws of Form*

Thought and reality are made of one and the same stuff, which is the stuff of experience in general.
William James, *Essays in Radical Empiricism*

Life itself is the consciousness of space and time.
René Thom, *Structural Stability and Morphogenesis*

12 Consciousness as Time

We have begun to consider consciousness in terms of its "with" — as the socially shared forms of awareness in self-referential symbolic beings. In addition, since symbolic cognition reuses the here-there, whence-whither dimensions of the array, this human "with" extends into the envelope of flow shared by all sentient motile beings. It remains to turn our attention back toward the "in" of consciousness. Human consciousness is inseparable from a being-in-the-world. The life worlds of sentient creatures are also "in" the physical universe as understood by modern physical science. Accordingly, we would expect the being of sentient creatures to be broadly consistent, at the very least, with the principles of organization of those aspects of the physical universe most adjacent to life forms. We have seen how the ambient array of sentient creatures in some sense mirrors the nonlinear dynamics of its most adjacent "foreign hull." We can now begin to look more generally at the extent to which the basic organizing principles of physical science are reflected and located in some way within perception. Does perception have, in Merleau-Ponty's (1964) sense, a "primacy" as the most basic template and ultimate source for all our knowledge?

If so, then the current excitement over parallels between the organization of "higher states of consciousness" and basic principles of modern physics is somewhat misplaced. The source of these correspondences is perhaps not so esoteric but closer to home. A demonstration that all forms of human experience have their template in perception would have implications opposed to recent speculations about the quantum basis of consciousness. We will consider the role that Gibson's array might play as the originating template for competing models of time in physical science in the first part of this chapter, leaving a more extensive discussion of the modern physics of space and matter for the next chapter.

David Bohm (1980) has suggested that the organizing principles of modern physics — space/time relativity, complementarity, indeterminism, and, we can add, nonlinear dynamics — reflect a progressive approximation of our mathematical constructs to the underlying organization of perception itself. Rather than modern physics abstracting itself further and further away from experience, as is usually held, its major breakthroughs would follow from its closer and closer approximation to the principles of the ambient array. This point has been generally missed precisely because the more traditional categories of space, time, and causality are actually the misleading and static simplifications of perception. Modern physical theory and the phenomenology of consciousness, then, become conjoined attempts at the liberation of our thought from false abstractions. They are both, in a curious sense, *experiential*.

Perception and the Arrow(s) of Time: Pulsations and Flow, Appearance and Disappearance

Time is generally considered an asymmetrical dimension flowing through a present from past into future. There has been considerable debate about whether this "arrow" runs through all levels of physical reality as understood by modern science or whether it only emerges as such with the more complex dynamics adjacent to the level of living organisms. On the one hand, the second law of thermodynamics — the tendency inherent in physical systems to move toward conditions of low organization and high entropy — has often been regarded as the very basis of a universal physical time. It has become part of popular consciousness to understand entropy as a sort of principle of "death" within the physical order. This view of a uniform tendency toward the dissipation of all energy formed much of the inspiration for Freud's mythic version of *thanatos* — an "instinct" of death leading toward the dissolution of all living systems.

On the other hand, works by the physicists Roger Penrose (1989), Stephen Hawking (1988), and Peter Coveney and Roger Highfield (1990) have suggested that the mathematical representations of the "big bang" of cosmic creation and the second law of thermodynamics are in principle not temporally asymmetrical — that they operate in either direction equally well, from past to future or future to past. Add to this the possibility that the big bang may someday be followed by a big crunch, during which entropy would actually decrease, and we see why for these authors the "arrow" of time may rest on what are actually temporary asymmetries of the physical universe. Time might then be understood as open to reversal. This hardly fits with *our* living experience of a temporal streaming that flows inexorably in one direction only. Surely, on the level of organismic reality, time is an inevitable flow against which all living beings move by virtue of their being alive.

Coveney and Highfield (1990) seek the actual beginnings of this asymmetrical flow of time in the realms of complex nonlinear systems immediately adjacent to the organizing principles of life-worlds. Roger Penrose (1989) follows the opposite strategy of searching for a "quantum gravity" force at the level of subatomic reality that would ultimately confer an intrinsic temporal directionality on all levels of physical reality. Be that as it may, it is certainly the case that by the time we reach the properties of nonlinear self-organizing systems we seem to have more than just an analogy to the temporal asymmetry of living experience. At least within certain fixed temporal spans, nonlinear systems, animate and inanimate, self-organize against and in the face of entropic dissipation. From chemical cycles like the Belousov-Zhabotinsky reaction, oscillating from ostensible chaos to emergent spirals (Prigogine, 1984), to the "life spans" of hurricanes and weather systems, we find a sensitivity to feedback and initial conditions that makes these inorganic systems unique and nonrepeatable in a fashion usually associated with organic behaviors.

In point of fact, however, the "seeds" of a self-organizing, pattern-increasing temporality *and* of a linear entropic time are both directly present within the temporality intrinsic to perception in sentient organisms--thus providing a template within perception that would allow the discovery of both principles.

With respect, first, to the temporality of self-organization, Henri Bergson (1907), in a fashion echoed by the physicist Roger Penrose (1989), located the characteristic temporality of living systems within the inseparability of their capacities for motion and for sensitivity to their surroundings: *"Wherever anything lives, there is, open somewhere, a register in which time is being inscribed. . . .* We perceive duration as a stream against which we cannot go. It is the foundation of our being, and, as we feel, the very substance of the world in which we live. . . . In vital activity we see, then, . . . *a reality which is making itself in a reality which is unmaking itself"* (Bergson, 1907, pp. 20, 45, 270). Sentient creatures accumulate energy from multiple sources in order to dissipate it in the periodic convulsive discharges underlying movement. The result of these discharges, however, is to organize and reorganize the complex flowing gradients of a life-world. The envelope of flow, texture gradients, and repeated surface occlusions and deletions that constitute the array of all sentient beings create continuously transforming patterns that are the very opposite of anything entropic.[1]

Both Bergson and the early Heidegger made the mistake of concluding that a "lived time," as the source of human transcendence, had to be added to an otherwise static spatial perception characteristic of lower organisms, although Bergson at least saw duration as an evolutionary continuum. Edmund Husserl (1905; Miller, 1984) also understood the anticipatory "protentions" and past "retentions" of temporality as added to a "horizon" of partial and inadequately given perspectives. All the early pioneers of radical descriptive phenomenology missed Gibson's location of a unitary space-time in the here-there, whence-whither flow of the perceptual array itself.

This shared failure to see horizonal openness welling forth the envelope of flow as the key to the human sense of duration would seem to stem from two sources. Given the penchant of European culture earlier in this century for exaggerating the division between human beings and all other life forms, let alone between cultures, it is not surprising that the understanding of perception itself finally arrived at by Gibson would elude observers who also, and rightly, located part of the essence of the specifically human mind in its capacity to experience duration *as such*. And although Bergson was much more open to positing a continuity within the "freedom" of all motile life forms, even he, with Heidegger and Husserl, was held back from Gibson's breakthrough by the Kantian separation of space and time as logically distinct categories. If "duration" is separated from "extension," it must indeed leave the latter static and frozen, just as the former becomes impalpable and empty. In this regard, the relativity of space-time to the events within it, although first outlined by Einstein, can be as readily located within Gibson's ambient array — supporting Bohm's (1980) contention that modern science returns us to the features of ordinary experience.

Gibson (1975) himself suggested that time is nowhere other than the flowing array of events undergone. A Gibsonian rewrite of Kant would understand space, time, causality, and self as codetermined and inseparable aspects of a single, seamless, ecological array. As soon as we posit a creature in spontaneous motion through its array, we have a space made up entirely of properties of sequential, asymmetrical flow, which also self-locates that creature within its array and creates a field of if-then sequences of surface appearance and deletion. Once we make sentience-movement the "constant," analogous to Einstein's speed of light, then all other ur-forms emerge as relative to the specifics of that flow.

We can also locate the seeds of a very different entropic temporality within a primacy of perception. Bergson was convinced that only an artificial intellectual analysis spatializes the elan of lived time and turns it into a succession of static instants. It becomes clear, however, that a temporality based on successive pulsations of discrete moments is to be found within any account of perception that adds Neisser and Rock's recognitive mode to Gibson's ambient array. We have already seen that the recognition of organismically significant forms requires momentary "glimpses" of symmetrically presented surfaces. In addition, the needs so engaged, such as mating, territoriality, nurturance, or predation, are broadly "entropic." In other words, these needs invoke behaviors whose outcome is the elimination of the rapid, successive cues that triggered them. Recognitive perception exists on the animal level first and foremost to make things go away. If a principle of entropy had not been discovered within thermodynamics, it could also have been derived from the contemporaneous formulations of a tension-reduction principle in animal behavior. It is also true, of course, that the centrality of physical metaphor in human and behavioral sciences makes the actual "entropy first" historical sequence far more likely, if not intrinsic. The question here is one of logical possibility, implying, perhaps, that what we discover without must first be mirrored within.

Organismic temporality is a fusion of both the self-organizing flow, engendering curiosity and readiness, and the tendency to release energy and abolish structure inherent in drive reduction behaviors. The temporalities of flow gradients and moments of discharge are clearly codetermined within organismic behavior. Gibson's flow can only be produced by an organismic locomotion rooted in the repeated, dissipative "explosions" of successive limb movement — here subordinated to the envelope of flow created once the array is thus set in motion. This structure of pulsation also appears within sentience in the often brief "moments" of recognition afforded by symmetrically looming surfaces. Fully adequate response to these significant forms abstracted out of the flowing array generally entails their disappearance. This is in marked contrast to an array that must continue to well forth ever new, complex dynamics as long as movement continues.

The Co-Dependent Origination of Lived Time and Self-Consciousness within Symbolic Cognition

Phenomenology: The Common Flow of Time and Consciousness

We move back now from the grounding of competing physical accounts of time in perception to the inseparability of "consciousness" and "lived time" within our self-referential "turning around" on perception. These dimensions seem distinct only until we attempt their description.

We have already seen that the openness of temporality so central to Bergson and the early Heidegger is intrinsic to perception itself and not specifically human. Heidegger in *Being and Time* correctly called attention to the temporal openness ahead as the most immediate horizon for our sense of being as such. In rejecting consciousness as an artificial and misleading concept, however, Heidegger risked a similar hypostasizing of temporality. His later, more experiential explorations of the sense of presence-openness found it in all aspects of the human world and thought. Heidegger's early tendency, however, to substitute temporality for the more traditional role of consciousness in philosophical idealism does highlight a special relation between *self-referential* consciousness and our sense of time. Such a relationship was also essential to Husserl's (1905) earlier treatment of consciousness and time as the inner and outer versions of the same "flow." To notice consciousness is to notice time, and vice versa. We will see that this follows for both their flows and their pulsations.

Husserl (1905), as discussed by Paul Ricoeur (1988), insisted on the phenomenological co-givenness of consciousness and temporal duration. This would go beyond the common metaphor of "flow" seemingly necessary to each, since that could merely indicate a mutual ineffability and impalpability. Rather, we cannot sense one of these flows without immediately finding the other as co-given. To attempt to express the passage or flow of time as such is to find oneself attending to the immediacy of the present stream of consciousness as it flows past. To attempt to notice immediate consciousness entails the sense that in so doing we can only become aware of its passing moment just "before" our "now." William James (1890) also noted this same co-givenness of consciousness and duration. He explains both our sense of time and the differences between transitive and substantive aspects of immediate consciousness in exactly the same terms. Both are derived from the varying amounts of overlap among neural processes fading away, present, and anticipatorily welling forth in one's immediate situation.

This inseparability of Husserl's "constitutive flux" of consciousness and felt duration leaves it indeterminate whether one could be said to originate from the other. It can be presented in either fashion: sensed duration just is the result of our awareness of the flow of consciousness; *or* our human ability to sense passing time as such creates the opening for what we call consciousness. Their co-givenness, along with the cognitive research on temporality in altered states of consciousness, to be reviewed below, actually implies that neither could be the source of the other. It does seem that both our sensed consciousness and our sensed duration are equally the results of our capacity for a self-referential turning around on the primacy of perception. As the result of a cross-translation between the space-times of different modalities, perception becomes self-aware and open to both analytic and experiential observation, which must also include both the whence-whither dimension of the array, considered up to now, and the successive pulsings of recognition. Flows and moments, once abstracted from the array, become equally constitutive of our consciousness, our temporality, and our recombinatory, creative thought. As we have seen, this "turning" within symbolic cognition allows us both our striking uniqueness as a self-aware species and our commonalities, potentially sensed as such, with the life-worlds of all sentient beings.

Cognitive Research on the Consciousness of Time: Time as Moment, Time as Flow

James said of consciousness that it streams, within each flow being myriad drops and within each drop a further streaming. Not surprisingly, this fits quite well with the twin preoccupations of the cognitive psychological research on time perception — sense of duration and the psychological moment.

To begin with the latter, Stroud (1955) was perhaps the first to propose a fixed psychological moment within which all ongoing cognition would be integrated in non-overlapping pulses. On the basis of various studies, Stroud suggested a limit of between 50 and 200 milliseconds for such moments. Of course, some such model had been assumed within the microgenetic-perception tradition of Werner and Schilder, where the flow of awareness is understood as a phenomenal fusion of successive microgenetic bursts. Allport (1968) amended Stroud's model to suggest a "moving window" or "travelling-moment" model that would synthesize in successive bursts and allow more redundancy and so continuity in the events so integrated. The growing consensus for such a moment of integration, whether discrete or overlapping, became about 100 milliseconds. Since this coincides with the cyclicity of the alpha rhythm, it has led to a cortical scanning model for such successive integrations (Block, 1979, 1990; Patterson, 1990).[2]

Arthur Blumenthal (1977) has collected copious evidence of this approximately 100 millisecond "unit of synthesis" for both perception and symbolic cognition. Apart from several demonstrations that memory scanning proceeds at about 100 milliseconds per recovered node of information, this is also the optimal stimulus separation to induce the masking of a stimulus by one immediately following, the phi phenomenon of apparent movement in successively flashing lights, the trill threshold for auditory tones, and Michotte's phenomena of perceived causation. We have already seen that the 100 millisecond period is important in cross-modal integration effects, as with the research of Zaparoli and Reatto (1969) on the visual-auditory synesthesias created by alternating visual and auditory stimuli at this interval. In terms of the temporal dynamics of spontaneous image formation, stroboscopic light flashes of ten per second are optimal for the "photic driving" that induces hallucinatory geometric patterns and image scintillation effects (Smythies, 1959; Glicksohn, 1986). Finally, Varela et al. (1981) found that the visual phi phenomenon can be abolished if the stimuli are made to fall on either side of the 100–150 millisecond periodicity of the alpha rhythm, offering further support for the idea of a central scanning hypothesis for the synthesis of successive psychological moments.

The 100 millisecond moment is not part of ordinary awareness, but it does emerge within the presentational microgenesis elicited by the tachistoscope and stroboscope (chapter 2) and in the introspective sensitizations entailed by various altered states of consciousness — especially those achieved through psychedelic drugs and meditation. Under more ordinary conditions these moments are themselves synthesized into longer periods of felt continuity — much as James suggested for the successive nesting of drops and flows in his final discussion of consciousness. Ernst Pöppel (1988) provides evidence of a three-second "now" for the synthesis of perceptual and conceptual "units" of experience that is more readily accessible to functional awareness. Thus, his subjects could not induce any perceived rhythmic emphasis in metronome beats if these were separated by more than three seconds. This is also the average period for spontaneous alternation of the Necker cube. Moreover, Pöppel calls attention to the three-second pauses apparently common among all spoken languages, with the same period for "beats" in poetry and shifts in classical music. Of course, other longer spans of periodic synthesis are quite possible. James (1890) suggested a twelve-second "specious present," a composite of lesser pulses and obviously potentially open to its own further integrative flow.

This brings us to some mention of the rather different research on the perceived duration of time — its relative rapidity or slowness when directly sensed as a continuous flow. Here we deal most explicitly with the whence-whither continuity of lived time, its perceived speed, and the circumstances that determine whether we notice it at all. It does appear that when we are most fully engaged in events, whether external or intense internal scenarios, we do not notice the passage of time any more than we notice the qualities of our immediately ongoing consciousness. When such a situation is over, we may then be amazed that so much happened in that given amount of clock time, although, phenomenologically speaking, we were then "outside" any sensed temporality.

James (1890) was perhaps the first psychologist to note that the basis of our sense of time passing quickly or slowly differs depending on whether we are within the ongoing situation or recalling it afterward: "In general, a time filled with varied and interesting experiences seems short in passing, but long as we look back. On the other hand, a tract of time empty of experiences seems long in passing, but in retrospect short" (James, vol. 1, 1890, p. 624). Ornstein (1969) confirmed this experimentally in a study in which subjects inspected simple and complex geometric figures for thirty-second periods. The same objective time spent in inspecting the simple figures felt longer than for the complex figures, if subjects were asked immediately at the end of the task, but the finding was reversed if subjects were asked some time later for the same judgments of felt duration. Ornstein suggests that whereas more complex objects are more interesting at the time, which then seems to go relatively quickly, remembered duration will vary directly with the complexity of the information being retrieved.

The Experience of Time in Presentational States

I have been suggesting that our experience of temporality is inseparable from our self-referential attunement to the immediate flow/pulsation of consciousness. We only seem to notice an *ongoing* passage of time spontaneously when we are less engrossed in our situation and so come to notice features of our ongoing state of consciousness. This implies that as we start to notice aspects of immediate consciousness, its "is like" rather than its "is for," we must also sense temporal flow and duration. Boredom, of course, is a "state" — the state of noticing one's awareness in a situation in which nothing of interest is happening. Characteristically, when we are bored we notice the passage of time as such and sense its comparative elongation. However, this state conspicuously lacks the enhanced absorption in the immediate moments of consciousness which will transform both our ordinary awareness of consciousness and our ordinary awareness of time.

It is noteworthy that the full range of altered states of consciousness, which we have already seen must entail an induced introspective sensitization, shows striking changes in the experience of time as a seemingly invariant feature. Transformations in temporality may be invariant features of presentational states, but they are also the most subtle and difficult to describe. Accordingly, they have been far less researched than the more easily characterizable changes in feeling, thought, and imagery.

If the sense of time is ultimately based on the whence-whither flows and pulsations of perception, and if self-referential symbolic cognition is, in turn, based on the reuse of perceptual dimensions as metaphoric vehicles, then it would follow that any change in the form or level of the basic structures of perception appearing in our awareness, as in the introspective awareness of microgenesis, for instance, must also entail transformations in lived time. In other words, since the symbolic cognition of everyday pragmatic awareness reuses the structures of perception, that self-referential cognition will also generate our ordinary sense of lived time. Alterations in the flow and microgenetic level of these perceptual structures, if reflected within presentational consciousness, will necessarily transform that experience of time. This is exactly what accounts of the various altered states show.

The co-givenness of transformations in the organization of consciousness and changes in temporality is well illustrated empirically. One of the most interesting demonstrations of their ostensible inseparability comes from the observational research of Bernard Aaronson (1966, 1968, 1971). He suggested specific changes in the sense of time to a small number of high-absorption hypnotic subjects, in order to trace what sorts of other, nonsuggested transformations in consciousness would also occur. Direct suggestions that time was passing more rapidly or more slowly produced a relatively predictable sense of manic excitement or relative dysphoria, respectively. He also found that the hypnotic suggestion to eliminate the sense of one's immediate present produced the flattening of affect, cessation of spontaneous movement, loss of depth perception, and derealization that are part of the experience of psychosis. Of course, these changes are also consistent with our earlier discussion of cross-modal dissociations in chronic schizophrenia. Correspondingly, the suggestion of an expanded present and heightened being in the moment elicited reports of meditation-like tranquility and even bliss, with an expanded sense of depth and color.

If self-referential consciousness and the sense of temporality are co-determined, we might also expect that so-called "consciousness-altering drugs" should be associated with characteristic transformations in temporal awareness. Indeed, they are. Reports from the use of psychedelic drugs like LSD and heightened-arousal producers like amphetamines describe a sensed elongation of felt duration (Block, 1979). Ordinary activities, remarkable in their newly discovered complexity, seem to take longer than usual, and subjects will usually be very surprised to learn how little clock time has actually passed while they were so absorbed in the details of ongoing awareness. William James, from an era far less constrained than our own, made the following observations:

> In hashish-intoxication there is a curious decrease in the apparent time-perspective. We utter a sentence, and ere the end is reached the beginning seems already to date from indefinitely long ago. We enter a short street, and it is as if we should never get to the end of it. . . . If our discrimination of successions became finer-grained, so that we noted ten stages in a process where previously we only noted one . . . the beginning of our sentences would have to be expressly recalled; each word would appear to pass through consciousness at a tenth of its usual speed. The condition would, in short, be exactly analogous to the enlargement of space by a microscope; fewer real things at once in the immediate field of view, but each of them taking up more than its normal room, and making the excluded ones seem unnaturally far away. (James, vol. 1, 1890, pp. 639–40)

Short-term memory is being asked to handle not only the sentence spoken but also the separately felt physiognomies of each and every word and all the associations thereby triggered.

Such induced introspective sensitization can be contrasted with the opposing effects of tranquilizers and sedatives. Here, most subjects seem to report time passing very quickly (Block, 1979). They are surprised when they notice that hours have passed in what seemed to be minutes. However, in contrast to the similar effect on felt duration when we are caught up in interesting ongoing events, the subject may have been sitting in a chair the whole time without very much "going on" subjectively.

Possible explanations for these twin transformations of time with consciousness-altering drugs follow if we take each to its extreme. To begin with the continuum of sedation, actual anesthesia produces the impression of an ultrarapid passage of time. We simply cannot believe that the operation could already have happened and actually be over. Or as young children, we are incredulous that the end of nap time could have arrived when we had only just reluctantly closed our eyes, convinced it was all a sham and that sleep would not come. This suggests that without *any* ongoing stream of consciousness available for self-reference there is no felt duration at all. It seems to be exactly as James says about the absence of any "gap" in the stream of consciousness: when we awake in the morning after a deep dreamless sleep, the last moments of recalled awareness from the night before and the ongoing morning flow of experience join seamlessly, if entirely implicitly and without conscious noticing of the fact.

Extrapolating back to the rapidity of time with tranquilizers, it would appear that our dulled attention to the fine grain of ongoing awareness makes for "gaps" that function a bit like mini-sleeps, so that the moments of experience, now fewer than normal, fuse together as usual and leave the subject with the sense of a not-much-happening that goes very quickly. Although the alteration in arousal level makes consciousness noticeable as such, there is actually less consciousness to notice.

From the perspective of James's approach to consciousness as drops or pulses, foreshadowing as it did the microgenetic tradition, awareness comes in moments separated by gaps across which our awareness naturally melds — much like the flicker/fusion effect with the stroboscope. In the self-reflective consciousness produced by lowered cortical arousal these gaps may actually widen; but with the enhanced introspective sensitivity produced by arousing and psychedelic drugs, we become absorbed in the finer and finer details of these moments, to the point where the pulsating structure becomes noticeable as such. Observers describe these distinct moments as emerging out of a diffuse light into an expressive visual geometric form and then into more representational content, only to disappear again into geometry and light before the next burst (Schilder, 1933, 1942). These observations are common to the meditative (Goleman, 1972) and microgenetic (Brown, 1991) perspectives, as well as the psychedelic-drug literature (Fischer, 1975). With increasing absorption these moments become predominantly experienced at earlier and earlier stages of perceptual and imaginal microgenesis.

I have suggested that self-referential cognition needs access, albeit ordinarily unconscious, to the expressive dynamics of perceptual microgenesis as part of the cross-cultural genesis of the vehicles of metaphor. In presentational states these expressive patterns can appear as such in ultrarapid expressions of incipient felt meaning. These have been referred to as image "scintillations" (Horowitz, 1970) — rapid bursts of barely distinguishable patterns welling forth at up to ten flashes per second (Siegel and Jarvick, 1975). The forms of this imagery can be at any level of microgenesis, from brief flashes of concretely depictive content, to the more abstract visual-dynamics of Arnheim, to the variously gradiated luminosities of mystical experience.[3] The elongation of felt duration that seems to follow from increasing absorption in these moments would result from the increasing detail available within shorter and shorter objective time periods. This phenomenon of an extending sense of duration within the expanding moment is well described by one of Titchener's star introspective observers, Elizabeth Möller: "I localize these [immediately introspected] qualities . . . 'out there' in a field which I realize now is restricted, but at the time experienced seems all of existence. . . . There is a going-on-ness about them, as if they existed forever" (From Burnett and Dallenbach, 1927, p. 427).

We come, then, to the most extreme transformation of duration associated with LSD and deep meditative accounts — the sense that this absorption in the immediate "now" extends out into an eternity or timelessness. The felt absorption in eternity in classical mysticism and in these related presentational states may turn out to have lasted only a few seconds in clock time. In cognitive language, we could say that as the state of absorption deepens into the microgenesis of luminosity and glow, to the point of becoming so subtle that it is indistinguishable from the gaps between these pulses, the structure of each successive moment — as glow welling forth — has become identical. In other words, the dynamic variation across successive microgenetic moments normally provides us our sense of building transitions and resolutions in experience, so well described by James with respect to his transitive and substantive aspects of the stream, and which is directly utilized in the rapid dynamic transitions of music. When experience has become glow welling forth, however, this sense of dynamic change and transformation ceases, while ongoing self-referential consciousness, synesthetically translated, yet continues. At this point the whence-whither flow of immediate experience, and its sensed elongation within the details of each moment, is composed entirely of more and more subtle pulses of light — each at an identical and incipient stage of microgenesis. The future has become identical to the present and to the immediate past — all being the same glow, synesthetically animated as sense of "source," "totality," or "Being." This sensed annihilation of the flow of duration, with none of its ordinary building and declining of felt tension, would elicit the experience, so often described, of the immediate "now" as paradoxically timeless and eternal. Future has come to equal past, and succession equals simultaneity. Each moment, fused with all other moments ultimately as "glowing darkness," continues to well forth, based on a "structure" we have identified with the openness of the horizon. The corresponding sense of presence would also be a felt openness and extension through a vastly elongated present. There is nothing else this phenomenon could "mean" except the metaphoric expression of the mystic "one" — spatially infinite and open, temporally eternal.

The Near-Death Experience and Eternity: The Pragmatist's Tale

This would be the point to bring together this analysis of the inseparability of temporality and consciousness with our general cognitive-phenomenological approach to presentational states and apply them to the current fascination with reports of near-death experience (Moody, 1975; Ring, 1980; Sabom, 1982; Greyson and Flynn, eds., 1984). Near-death experiences become an important focus for some of the fuller implications of integrating the third-person functionalism of modern psychology with the first-person phenomenology where we all also live.

On the one hand, the commonalities of experience described by some near-death and resuscitated patients, often independent of their previous religious beliefs, have been taken by some as empirical evidence or even proof of a literal afterlife. On the other hand, a more traditional psychiatric point of view holds that we would have evidence here, instead, that at least some of us — women more than men, probably those generally highest in imaginative absorption regardless of sex — die in the midst of a hallucinatory, psychotic state. Both of these views appear to be somewhat overwrought, and both stand in dire need of a more cognitive and phenomenological mediation. We have just seen, for instance, that the relative brevity in "objective" clock time may not tell us much about the felt duration of an experience, which, in turn, does not tell us anything of its nature or validity. The question becomes, what is it that is undergone in these states?

With respect to the account preferred by various spiritualist traditions, I have already cited James's well-known dictum that no experiential state can by itself establish the objectivity or truth of a belief. Not only do we know of near-death experiences only from those who are not dead, however physiologically "dormant" they may have been for a time, but all the basic elements of these reports can also appear within the naturalistic states created by psychedelic drugs, the hypnagogic period of sleep onset, and deep meditation. Thus, the out-of-body perspective and attendant somatic transformations, experiences of light and bliss, the more occasional "hellish" encounters, traveling through a tunnel, meeting spiritual guides, loud roaring noises (probably based on sudden myoclonus in the muscles of the inner ear), and a life review in the form of ultrarapid image scintillations are all commonly described in these other altered-state settings. Even Moody's (1975) descriptions of approaching a boundary of some kind just prior to being resuscitated — a visionary field or road or stream, for example — are found in Silberer's (1918) accounts of functional autosymbolism as self-depictions of the change in organismic state just prior to awakening from ordinary sleep.

There are also indications that the various features and stages of near-death accounts vary systematically with the outer circumstances of the near-terminal situation, including sociocultural setting. This suggests we are dealing with a self-referential presentational state broadly dependent on natural conditions. For instance, Carol Zaleski (1987) has demonstrated both overlap and considerable variation in medieval, Tibetan Buddhist, and modern accounts. Kenneth Ring's (1980) research locates the basic elements and frequencies within contemporary reports, ranging from sense of peace and acceptance, reported by 60 percent of the subjects describing some sort of retrospective awareness, through the out-of-body pattern, entering a tunnel, seeing some sort of light, and entering the light—the last as the least common, at 10 percent. (Entering the light rarely seems to mean a felt mergence or dissolving into the light as described in some drug states and deep meditation, but rather entering an area sensed as sacred, such as a celestial city or visionary temple.) Although 40 percent of all near-death patients studied report at least some of these transformations of consciousness, they do vary significantly with outer circumstances.

Near-death reports in general are significantly more likely if the patient has been unconscious more than thirty minutes and if medical resuscitation efforts are made (Sabom, 1982). This shows that the experience is more likely if there is a natural and prolonged setting that affords the real time it needs to develop, and if there is some effort made to "sample" that awareness. It is also more likely with long-term illness than with sudden accidents (Sabom, 1982). This is consistent with the view that a longer anticipation of one's possible death primes self-referential awareness to form these appropriately expressive presentational states. Indeed, when such experiences occur with sudden accidents, as in mountain climbers falling off a cliff (Noyes and Kletti, 1976), then an explicit life review phase is significantly more likely to occur than in longer illness. Apparently, the life review can be accomplished in a more "ordinary," less compressed awareness, when sufficient time is available. Accounts from long-term illness are much more likely to mention an encounter with light, again, as if more preparatory time gets one further into the state.

We might also consider the puzzle of why the majority of near-death accounts do not include descriptions of the "hellish" phantasmagories that we already know can easily appear in high-dosage LSD experience and acute schizophrenia, but emphasize instead bliss, acceptance, and compassion. Of course, it may be that such negative experiences, along with a defensive dissociation of cross-modal synthesis that would lead to schizophrenia-like "blocking," do occur much more frequently, but that they interact psychosomatically so as to make later recall or even medical resuscitation itself less likely. On the other hand, even more than in very deep meditation, the state resulting from actual physiological cessation must eventually entail a very profound muscular relaxation and release. Assuming that one were able to maintain a continuous consciousness into this deep "letting go," the eventual experience must become one of deepening calm, detachment, and acceptance —very much like the effects of deep meditation. The fact that actual dissolving into the white light and elongation of the immediate "now" into sensed eternity, as described by the classical mystics, does *not* commonly appear in these near-death reports strongly suggests that most resuscitations occur short of this developmental point. Accordingly, the still more subtle experiences of nonresuscitated dying could well include such expansions of consciousness into openness as such, with its correspondingly sensed "eternity."

We are left then to face the opposite argument that has been brought to bear on near-death experience — that it reflects a hallucinatory and ultimately illusory form of awareness. A cognitive-phenomenological perspective will rescue us from this extreme, as well. We have already seen that presentational states such as appear in both classical mysticism and the near-death experience show the basic structures of abstract intelligence reflected in a presentational, imagistic mode. Thus, we have geometries and luminosities as metaphors for an encompassing totality, the out-of-body perspective as the imagistic expression of Mead's "taking the role of the other," an extremely pervasive self-referential capacity that synthesizes one's major life events into rapid image scintillations, and the synesthetic cross-modal translation capacity basic to all symbolic operations. The actual situation of physically dying, or being about to die, would favor a presentational mode of symbolic cognition over a verbal-analytic one because imagery is more immediate and emphasizes the sense of wholes over parts. The situation of dying occurs with potential rapidity, exceeds our ordinary conceptual ability, and raises personal and ultimate questions, all favoring presentational over representational symbolism. From a cognitive perspective, near-death experiences represent our self-referential intelligence operating at its maximum within an imagistic-intuitive mode — to achieve a last look at what it has all amounted to, in a sort of illustrated crash course in metaphysical/spiritual thought applied to one's own life. We saw earlier how difficult it would be to show that the maximally abstract development of one of our symbolic frames is "illusory" while the others are "true."

To return to the James of the *Varieties*, mystical experience may not be able to establish its own truth for people who do not share it, but it is necessarily personally decisive for those who have it. The "facts" of our experience may be "merely subjective," but that is ultimately where we all live anyway — within our ongoing experience of this world. All our objectivities and logicalities must be sensed and felt first in order to be known at all. If the letting go of tension and muscle contraction while dying is at all similar to that occurring in deep mediation, then it would lead to more and more subtle experiences of light and a synesthetic merging with that light. This would be felt as a compassionate "letting" or "allowing." It would, as we have seen, necessarily involve a corresponding transformation in our sense of time, with the elongating moments of microgenetic glow expanding into a sensed eternity. This is, indeed, a kind of psychological "last judgment" made in an imagistic mode. When and if it occurred, there would be nothing else to compare it with, offset it, or contradict it. Accordingly, it would meet any and all pragmatic criteria for truth.

What it would amount to is that as long as there is any experience at all in the form of a self-reference for its own sake, then at its most fundamental levels it *would* have the structure of openness-compassion-eternity. In the most abstract presentational states, based on synesthesias across the most basic forms of perception, we will experience the felt meaning of horizonal openness. If, from an "objective" point of view, we conclude that any such experience of eternity must in fact cease with final brain death, it would also be the case that at levels of glowing darkness welling forth, that cessation would not be noticeable in first-person terms. The "next" would become ever more open and eternal and compassionate with attunement to an ever more subtle glow.

Perhaps some physician of the future could "time" the actual neuronal manifestations of near-death experience with a stopwatch and declare that it lasted, say, five or ten minutes. The point surely is that in such states first- and third-person criteria have long since gone their separate ways and can no longer meaningfully cross-reference each other. From the perspective of the present cognitive psychology of consciousness, and curiously consistent with various spiritual traditions, death turns out to be a third-person phenomenon only.[4] From the first-person perspective, specifically enhanced in presentational states, we really cannot die. Either we would cling and struggle and "pass out" into a state based on blocking and cross-modal dissociation, or else, at least with immediate awareness retained or reappearing, we would become one with eternity. The doctor's watch at such a point would become completely irrelevant, as it is for the similar "moments of eternity" in deep meditation.

Pragmatically speaking, with respect to that primacy of experience out of which each of us must live, there is a potential afterlife. To label it illusion presupposes that it is given to us to stand outside our own being and intelligence and make such judgments. In the end, either we respect our basic experience of this world or we don't.

13   Consciousness as Space: Physics, Consciousness, and the Primacy of Perception

A number of investigators from both sides of the interface between physical theory and consciousness have called attention to some intriguing parallels between various aspects of modern physics and eastern meditative traditions (Bohm, 1980; Capra, 1975; LeShan, 1969; Grof, 1980; Wallace, 1986; Wolf, 1990). Vedanta and aspects of Buddhism picture a "unified field" comprising physical reality and consciousness, both of them based on minute particle energies in vibration. The difference, of course, is that even the most speculative of physicists, who understand consciousness as a subatomic quantum reality, are nonetheless deriving mind from the principles of the physical universe. This contrasts with the traditional idealism of mysticism, which would derive quantum reality itself from a still more fundamental "cosmic consciousness" or "universal mind."

Capra, LeShan, Wallace, and Grof, in particular, see the possibility of a direct attunement of consciousness to the realities of modern physics, especially in reports from deep meditation or high dosages of LSD. Such subjects, often ostensibly unaware of the concepts of modern physics, will describe experiences of a vibrational field which seem congruent with physical formulations of space-time relativity, complementarity, and indeterminism. Accepting, provisionally, the apparent correspondences in such claims, the question must become *how* mystics would be able to know the realities of contemporary physics.

One possibility is a direct intuition of consciousness into cosmos, possible because the latter is somehow made out of the former. A second possibility is that consciousness itself is rooted on a quantum level of reality, so sentience and cosmos share a common structure. The latter has had the greatest appeal, not surprisingly, in the recent speculations from physical science about consciousness, which will be my initial focus. On the one hand, consciousness would have a material base in the reuse of quantum events indeterminate and complementary enough to match the mind. On the other, it has seemed tempting to some thereby to explain extrasensory perception in terms of conjoined quantum fields.

There is a third possibility, more modest and in the end more parsimonious. Consciousness and physics may share, instead, a primacy of perception necessarily underlying both traditions. What mystics and physicists would share, along with the rest of us, is a common set of metaphors. Since the metaphoric patterns underlying symbolic cognition are ultimately derived from the perceptual array, we find ourselves faced with the possibility not only that all thought rests on perception, but that the still not fully discovered principles that organize ambient perception contain or imply or mirror various aspects of the organization of physical reality itself. It is the shared structures of perception that would return both mystics and physicists to their common experience, however differently mediated and developed. That "source" must "mirror," with varying degrees of directness and clarity, the physical surround of sentient beings — the very physical universe that "permits" us to be.

Consciousness and Quantum: Some Competing Versions

There are several extant versions of the idea that consciousness is either fundamentally attuned to the quantum field level of reality or is actually based within quantum events as part of its very existence and operation. The physicist Roger Penrose, in his challenging integration of physics and psychology, *The Emperor's New Mind* (1989), makes much of the fact that a single photon can in principle activate a receptor in the retina of the frog. This suggests to Penrose the possibility that neuronal functioning could actually be influenced by subatomic events, especially, by implication, within neuronal regions less involved in immediate sensory-motor coordinations. Penrose is thus led to a theory that is somewhat analogous to the function of cross-modal integration. Since both quantum reality and consciousness are equally noncomputable, he speculates that thought might operate on the model of a "quantum computer." A quantum computer would instantiate multiple algorithms simultaneously within the probabilistic waves of quantum fields. If the brain operated in this fashion, consciousness would be the collapse of simultaneous probabilistic waves of network conduction into a single outcome. In the same way, within contemporary quantum theory, the measurement of one parameter of a particle/wave collapses the total phenomenon down into one dimension and eliminates what would have been other possibilities originally open to measurement.

Penrose points out that both neuronal networks and quasi-crystal growth patterns are examples of phenomena, on a more molar level of reality, that work on the same principles as such a hypothetical quantum computer. At first, he leaves it open whether he is advocating the view that thought is based on neural nets being "played" by subatomic particle fields, or whether we are speaking rather of different levels of physical reality which may become organized in terms of analogous principles — here complementarity and indeterminism. Subsequently, Penrose (1994) has speculated that it is the microtubular structures in cells, small enough to conduct electrons, that would locate such a parallel quantum computer. Entirely within cytoskeletons of neurons, this tiny network would "collapse," finally, into depolarization. Problems appear as this theory becomes progressively more definite. Consciousness and quantum particles may both be examples of indeterminism, but that does not necessarily make them the same — especially across such widely separated levels of concept and reality. Microtubules are part of the chemical-message functions within all cells and are present in the neurons of creatures not capable of the self-referential symbolic cognition that Penrose seeks to explain. In short, Penrose's speculations remain both logically possible and curiously ad hoc to the problems of the emergence of sentience — which, as we have seen, are better addressed via the commonalities of depolarization in neurons and protozoa.

Right away we can see that physical scientists are allowed to have much more fun than psychologists, especially in speculative excursions into other fields of knowledge. They are able to dispense with Occam's razor if the joining of disparate realms be but audicious enough.[1] While in that sense their efforts are admirable, some of the difficulties inherent in such quixotic speculations are further illustrated by the theories of the neurologist John Eccles (1986, 1990) in his very different appropriation of quantum mechanics to posit a dualist basis for mind-brain interaction. Eccles suggests that if mental activity, "acting analogously to a quantal probability field," could modify the secretion of neural transmitters and inhibitors for even a single synaptic vesicle, thus modifying the probability of firing in the adjacent neuron, then we would have a way that an immaterial mind could influence a material brain. Eccles seems to think that it will be easier to make the causal effect of consciousness on brain more plausible if he selects a small enough and probabilistic enough spot for such proposed interactions. What may have been illustrated instead is that if a literal dualism of consciousness and brain cannot even work on the level of a single photon, it will not work anywhere.

Unless, of course, consciousness itself is a sort of emergent particle field — a quantum radiance of some kind. This is a view that clearly tempts many, although it bypasses, as Penrose (1989) points out, how such processes would preserve their functional integrity in the midst of molar physiological and physical fields based on much more powerful forces.

On this more general level we can return to Penrose's account, so reminiscent here of Bergson's philosophy. Penrose suggests that, in some sense at least, consciousness moves against the second law of thermodynamics toward a level of organization formally lower in entropy and higher in organization than the physical processes that generate it. Living systems take solar energy from the earth's surface and transform it in two directions — first, into an entropic release of energy associated with the maintenance of metabolism, and second, "up" into a complex patterning associated with the experienced life-world. In Prigogine's (1984) terms, we could say that sentience reflects the output of a self-organizing "dissipative" system, since it breaks down and degrades other structures in order to sustain its own emergent generation of pattern. Or, we could say that neuronal activation is a phenomenon higher in entropy than the patterning of sentience that is emergent from it.

It is not, however, as Penrose would have it in his interpretation of Libet's research on the delay of sensation following cortical-evoked response. We do not see "backward" in time, except in the purely formal sense that cosmological time tends to move in a direction toward lower organization and higher entropy, whereas sentient creatures resonate to a continuously renewed patterning. Consciousness may be more complex than its neural substrate precisely because it does, as Libet shows, take longer to form than the cortical manifestations that "launch" it. In itself, this relation between neural substrate and emergent sentience does not make consciousness material or nonmaterial, causal or epiphenomenal. It only says that consciousness reflects a resonance with the ambient ecological array that is formally on a more complex level than the "dissipative" electrochemistry of neural nets. Lamination, occlusion, and texture, continually renewed out of horizonal openness, are lower in entropy than the physiological events that support and maintain them. So far, we seem to have a version of Sperry's "emergence" in a somewhat different vocabulary.

We thus arrive at an interesting choice point, and a rather fateful one at that. On the one hand, the above analysis could lead us toward a physics of consciousness. Consciousness could be a sort of "physical radiance," literally reconstituting a quantum field in its move toward high energy organization — albeit facing all the problems with such a view, as discussed above. If consciousness itself, as opposed to its temporally antecedent neural substrate, is a physical field of some kind, then it would be emergent from the molecular level of processing in the nervous system. Consciousness, with Wallace (1986), becomes part of a "unified field" of subatomic composition linking all levels of physical and psychic reality. Accordingly, consciousness would quite literally be a kind of rarified substance that flows and pulses.

Meditation would release consciousness from its ordinary subordination to ongoing resonance with the array, to gather and focus it in a way that could "explain" both personal and collective extrasensory coordinations of mind and reality. For good or ill, this "radiance" is quite reminiscent of Reich's orgone, Reichenbach's od, and Anton Mesmer's still earlier magnetism. Such a quantum radiance would be in principle physically measurable, but not with any methods presently available. As we have seen, the same energy fields that today would prevent its measurement would nonetheless somehow have to permit its existence. It could preserve its integrity within microtubules, perhaps, but these prove gratuitous to the core of what is to be thus explained — sentient motility.

The alternative view, more modest and actually open to psychological research, is that the ecological array of Gibson and the potential unified field of contemporary theoretical physics are similarly "open" systems. The isomorphism between consciousness and physics is one of organizing principle only — quantum reality and consciousness sharing low-entropy, high-organizational dynamics, but on very different levels of physical reality. Following the model of David Bohm's (1980) holomovement, in which all aspects of reality are enfolded within each other, or Leibnitz's similar monadology, the organization of perception would be formally similar to complex levels of physical reality — which becomes the condition for our knowledge of the latter.

Most commonly, "perception" has been seen as the limiting principle of modern science, transcended or undercut by the new realities of the material universe which supposedly can only be understood when we give up the biases and intuitions of ordinary perception. Perhaps, however, it is our notion of perception itself that has been distorted and simplified by Newtonian mechanics and Kantian categories. In seeking a more parsimonious account of the ostensible commonalities between consciousness as such and modern physics, the question becomes to what extent the latter is already "mirrored" into the flowing gradients and pulsations of perception. If that should turn out to be one hundred percent, then the most parsimonious view would be that perception is the template for both the modern developments of physical science and the meditative development of consciousness as such. If both these most outward and most inward of cultural traditions are reorganizations and transformations of the same perceptual template, then their coordinations are not as remarkable as some have thought.

Physics and Consciousness: Metaphor and the Fluctuating Line between Consciousness and World

I have argued that cross-modally constituted metaphors are at the basis of all symbolic cognition and are themselves abstractions and elaborations of the properties of perception. It would follow that such metaphors will face in two directions simultaneously. First, they point outward. If we can in fact derive the basic principles of modern physics from the perceptual array, then all physical knowledge becomes an extension of perception. Second, if we can only know ourselves through the metaphoric transformation of the properties of physical reality, then not just with native animism but continuing into the realities revealed by modern physics, any feature of the world becomes a potential metaphor for our own consciousness. With Jung (1944) on the alchemists, what had seemed inanimate and nonhuman and alien suddenly reflects back aspects of our own nature of which we had been hitherto unconscious. From this perspective, mysticism and physics are coordinate because they are elaborated out of the same structures. In each case, knowledge is based on a reconstitution of more and more basic principles of the perceptual array.

In the passage that begins Part VI, G. Spencer-Brown (1969) suggests that the world outside reveals the world within, and the study of consciousness in turn must tell us something real about the world without. All human knowledge, he says, reflects our approach to this shared boundary between animate and inanimate and, we can add, a continual oscillation across it. Spencer-Brown's comments are intriguingly resonant with Freud (1919b) on what elicits the sense of the "uncanny" — our capacity to become fascinated and absorbed in the eerie and strange. Basing his analysis on fairy tales, mythology, and the literature of the supernatural, Freud points out that we feel a sense of uncanniness where the ordinary line between animate and inanimate undergoes a shift. If what is not alive and not human suddenly behaves as if alive and sentient, or if people and animals behave in ways typical of mechanical and purely physical processes, we become fascinated and full of an ambivalent mix of wonder and terror. But we have already seen that metaphor itself entails the abstracting of structures from the physical world and their potential use in self-reflection, so that we find our feelings and states within the streams and glows of the physical world. This implies that the very basis of symbolic cognition in our ability to see one of these realms in terms of the other entails the potential sense of the uncanny. Our thought moves back and forth across the line between the living and the dead.

We ask about the nature of the physical world and about what it is like to *be* in that world, but we seem to address one question always in terms of the other. Historically it has not been possible either to drive these questions definitively apart or put them definitively together. From traditional cultures to our present "scientific" one, the location of a common boundary of fascination between these two realms has shifted. It began with animism, in which the structures of the physical world are directly felt as conscious and so as mirrors for consciousness. The modern era was defined by a shift to "mechanism," where we have extended our own will and capacity for motoric control into the physical world as though they were its sole and inmost principle. Heidegger expressed a concern that all aspects of our modern lives ultimately would become commodities to be similarly controlled and used — a fear not so easily dismissed if the causal principles of the material world are really our own.

It would appear that although the line between consciousness and world changes continuously across cultures and times, our preoccupation with it does not. Some now seek to "understand" the big bang of cosmological creation by identifying it with the explosion of light in mystical states. Others seek to "explain" religious experience as dissipative seizure. I have suggested that the current interest in non-linear dynamics already reflects an increasing interest in the levels of physical reality closest to being alive and sentient. It is as if we have turned back again to look across the line in a new direction — from and via world toward consciousness.

Richard Rorty (1979) also argued, but to very different effect, that we have overstated the differences between the understanding-interpreting disciplines of the humanities and the explanatory disciplines of the sciences — their separation being merely an historical accident. Indeed, traditional native societies and classical civilizations have not made any absolute dichotomy between spirit and nature. Instead, there is only a reciprocal mirroring between "microcosm" and "macrocosm," with the same patterns organizing each domain. But traditional societies understood nature as the elaboration of spirit. The western shift to mechanism involved, instead, the extension of our own motoric power and manipulation out into physical nature and then back again to ourselves. This shift that characterizes modernity has profound implications, since we then come to derive ourselves from a nature so dominated and enslaved. Rorty misses the fact that even if we should end up with the same categories of thought in both the physical and social sciences, the intent of each discipline is still distinct. This remains true even if the categories of this mutual crossover shift from classical Newtonian forces to nonlinear dynamics. After all, in the humanities we seek what it is *like* to *be* — wherever we take our metaphors and whether they are explicitly derived from physical theory or only implicitly reflected.

If Bohm (1980) is correct that the most basic concepts of contemporary physics reflect a progressively closer and largely unconscious approach to the organization of immediate perception, perhaps civilization is trying to recover what it is to be alive, sentient, and present in the world. The major developments in modern physical theory — from relativity theory, to quantum mechanics, to the cosmology of universal expansion out of singularity, to nonlinear dynamics — have stimulated an extraordinary popular fascination and have lent themselves to "imaginative identification" on a level that many scientists explicitly reject as "mystic." If, however, we have evolved out of the dynamics and structure of this very universe, and if its principles are indeed reflected within the perceptual array of sentient creatures in diverse forms and levels, then our turning around on these structures must similarly illuminate both universe and consciousness.[2] With all aspects of the universe in some sense implicate within each other, the most parsimonious view of the source of our knowledge of these relations would be in the myriad metaphoric patterns afforded by perception. It is necessary, then, to explore provisionally just how far "down" we can locate modern physics within the principles of the perceptual array — a view of cognition that brings us back to the primacy of our sentient being-in-the-world, and away from all things "extrasensory."

The Space-Times of Perception as the Origin of Modern Physical Theory

We have already seen how Bohr's notion of complementarity and Heisenberg's uncertainty principle were partly inspired by James on the stream of consciousness and have located competing views of temporality in the perceptual array. I have also sketched a possible derivation of complementarity from the alternate organizations of perception as envelope of flow in Gibson's ambient array and as the symmetrical loomings and recedings entailed in rapid recognition. The same surface pattern would either be "recognized" as having specific significance for the organism or become part of the envelope of flow, but never both simultaneously. A surface either flows past, as part of a total lamination, or is abstracted out of that array as potentially stationary. Both these processes are "perception," and of the "same" thing, so the analogy with the physical complementarity of light as wave or particle seems exact. Theoretical parsimony would dictate that the physical theory comes out of perception as its ultimate template or source, even if it might be the theory itself that has first sensitized us to the duality of that perception.

Something very much like a principle of uncertainty or indeterminacy — in which the observation of one parameter so changes the situation that other parameters become unobservable as such — is also present in the interface of ambient array and recognition. The array affords a locomoting creature multiple pathways along which to proceed, but these are not reversible in the fashion of logic. To select one path and proceed partway down it will not permit the organism, if it returns to the original choice point, to proceed down another path in the same manner and to the same effect as it would have, had that path been chosen initially. In the meantime, the regions ahead have changed as a direct result of the time taken for the first choice and also as a result of the organismic significance of the events transpiring there. From the point of view of an event-centered life space, the organism proceeds down a different path both when it returns and rechooses and if it proceeds down the "same" path on successive occasions.

The "parallel-universes" model (Wolf, 1990) would solve quantum indeterminacy by positing that all possible particle trajectories coexist in parallel to the point of an infinity of multiple diverging realities. The complex mathematics of those formulations may, nonetheless, be rooted in a fundamental feature of Gibson's array, as formulated by Terry Swanlund (personal communication). The specific array as given to a particular creature proprioceptively defines that creature's unique position and path of locomotion through just that array. This implies that an array itself can ultimately not be defined other than as the simultaneous collection of all possible positions and paths from which it can be given — for a life-world can only be in its multiple givenness to the resonating beings that equally and collectively bring it forth, as it in turn allows and affords them. If the sum total of the possible positions within it constitute the array, this implies a "multiple worlds" given in parallel as already intrinsic to perception itself.

Bohm (1980) suggested that the relativity of space-time to the nature and momentum of the events within it, although a crucial departure from the Newtonian universe, actually represents a progressively closer approximation to ordinary perception. Rather than thinking in terms of abstracted "points" in space, "the basic element [becomes] a *moment*, which, like the moment of consciousness, cannot be precisely related to measurements of space and time, but rather covers a . . . region which is extended in space and has duration in time" (Bohm, 1980, p. 207). Our consideration of Gibson (1979) and Von Uexküll (1934) has shown how the array unfolds out of the totality of the movements that a particular creature of a particular size, shape, and speed can make within it. The result is that "this room" is an utterly different space-time event for different species — myself, my dog, a moth on the curtain. Yet each such world will be unfolded on common organizational principles in which "spread" and "welling forth" are a function of the events so unfolded — much as the water of a stream makes a characteristic space-time envelope around a rock in its way, and, in turn, large astronomical masses "bend" the space-time around them in Einstein's universe.

I have also discussed Freeman's (1991) research showing that the electrophysiological activity from the resting olfactory lobe of the rabbit approximates a chaotic attractor, whereas specifically recognizable odors elicit more regular spiraling patterns. Nonlinear dynamics now offers a mathematics of self-organizing systems that appear to be on the borderline between living organisms and nonliving media. The question becomes whether the self-organization of dynamic flow out of ostensible chaos is already part of the organization of Gibson's array. Nonlinear dynamics pertains to flowing and turbulent phenomena. Freeman demonstrates that these properties of nonlinear flow can be located within the functioning of neural nets. From Gibson's point of view, however, these neural nets must constitute patterns of resonance to the flow envelope of the array. The mathematical structure of neural nets is thus ultimately explainable by the structure of lamination and not the other way around. The rabbit's olfactory lobe would thus either recognize a regular "olfactory surface" or resonate to a nonrecognizable turbulence of a more general readiness in the midst of flow. Nonlinear dynamics are in principle discoverable within perception, quite apart from weather systems. In what follows, we will also see how the attempted spatial representation of the formal aspects of perception and experience may require some of the principles of nonlinear dynamics.

Drawing Experience: Some Mutual Limitations in Theoretical Physics and Theoretical Psychology

I have tried to show how the formal properties of perception could be regarded as the source not only for mystical experience but for the basic principles of modern science. Whereas presentational states have always been based on spontaneous cross-modal reconstitutions of the essential structures of perception, the development of modern physics reflects an ever closer approach to the formal properties of presence-openness and the whence-whither flow of perception.

The traditional view, of course, has been that modern science undercuts the properties of ordinary perception, which can only mislead us in our thinking about the newly discovered realities of the physical order. This view of the gap between science and perception has been linked to a related argument that has stretched through twentieth-century physics. As aptly summarized by Arthur Miller (1984), there has been considerable debate over the possibility of any full visualization or spatial representation of the key concepts of modern physics. Miller suggests that as physics removed itself progressively from the classical worldview, the imagery of scientific thought underwent a corresponding abstraction. Only the most selected and abstracted relations could be depicted in abstract pictorial representation, which was now utterly removed from anything related to concrete perception. A common view has been that modern physics is too formal and too abstracted from ordinary perception to be drawn at all, without misleading distortions based on the inappropriateness of the pictorial medium itself. It would also appear, however, that prior to Gibson and the closely related phenomenologies of perception in Heidegger and Erwin Straus (1963), our "picture" of perception was itself entirely artificial and based on a classical Newtonian mechanics projected over the place where our contemporary phenomenologies have so haltingly emerged.

The debate over whether modern physics can be fully presented in abstract pictorial diagram may not reflect so much its progressive remove from perception but the very opposite. The point is that experience, and most specifically perception, cannot be "drawn" either — at least not without the same abstractions, simplifications, and distance from its immediate reality. If we consider Gibson as having supplied us with our most complex "picture" of perception as envelope of flow, how vastly different this is from the traditional naturalistic schools of painting. None of the western techniques of perspective and illusion begin to show us what perception is in Gibson's terms. We can draw anything — any object or person or complex feeling state — often via the very abstract expressive forms of such interest to Arnheim and Werner. But we cannot draw the structure of experience as such and in itself. Modern physics and phenomenology share precisely the problematic status of any diagrammatic representation of their fluid, turbulent space-times. As we turn now to some attempts in psychology to "draw" the abstract structures of experience, we will see that perception and the physical universe resist more traditional representation in characteristically similar ways.

Topologies of the Life Space: Incommensurabilities in the Pictorial Representation of Experience

Lewin's Topological Psychology and Its Limitations

The most ambitious attempt to draw the formal properties of experience was made by Kurt Lewin, widely acknowledged as one of psychology's geniuses. Lewin (1936) appropriated the mathematical topology of his day — a qualitative mathematics of regions and their properties — as a psychological language to represent the structure of experience in the specific "life space." Although this project was quickly and widely dismissed as a failure, or at best an instructive curiosity, the nature of this failure has not really been explored. Selected aspects of Lewin's diagrams are still used instructionally, but taking Lewin's intentions as seriously as he did shows with unique clarity the problems inherent in such an enterprise. It does appear that the dilemmas of representability being faced by the new physics in the 1930s were being equally engaged by Lewin.

Lewin wanted an abstract depictive language that could convey what a skilled novelist does, but on a purely formal level that would cut across the more specialized languages of the subdisciplines of psychology. What was sought was a representation of the first-person perspective in terms of what the subject understood, at a particular moment, as psychologically possible in his or her unfolding situation. Each region in one of Lewin's famous life space diagrams is supposed to represent a felt psychological reality, whether depicting goals, activities, barriers, mental states, or the like. Regions are related in terms of nearness-remoteness (a goal being anticipated in the immediate or more distant future), fluidness-rigidity (regions felt as easy or difficult to pass through on the way to other regions), and the thickness-thinness of psychological boundaries (regions can be sensed as easy or difficult to enter or leave). Since the life space at a given moment must be depicted as a static pattern, Lewin added a separate "vector" psychology to depict energy gradients that would determine which pathways of locomotion will be chosen, in terms of the needs of the person and the experienced valuative "charge" or "valence" of the various regions.

This representation of the person's experience of their situation cannot, however, include certain factors that nonetheless have an influence on its outcome. These various "external" factors might pertain, for instance, to facts of neurology, social structure and social class, and even geography (in a pending earthquake). They are either not actually part of the person's ongoing experience as such or at best indirectly reflected within it. These are represented in what Lewin terms the "foreign hull" surrounding the life space on all sides. Our experience is always influenced by nonpsychological factors, without their necessarily being directly or adequately reflected in the life space — as when a rock coursing toward the head of a picnicker is seen out of the corner of the eye as a butterfly, or not seen at all.

Figure 13 shows a typical and relatively simple Lewinian life space diagram. Following the convention of a felt temporal dimension moving from left to right, we see here the structure of a lived situation in which a person experiences himself or herself as located in a particular region (mood or activity or simply waiting). This is separated from an anticipated resolution section by intervening regions, represented here as entailing an anticipated choice or alternative. Resisting the temptation to burden the reader with the concrete specifics of the situation so represented, we can see that one of these intervening choice regions is experienced as easy to enter and pass through but difficult to exit (thickness of the final line). The other is hard to enter and difficult to pass through (density of medium) but is felt to permit an easier final access to the "goal" or "outcome." (The thinness of the line connecting the two choice regions indicates that the subject experiences this situation as permitting a possible change of mind — that the alternatives might be easily exchanged once under way.) The foreign hull, then, includes all those factors that will influence this passage but of which the person is unaware or which are only indirectly reflected in experience. Here we have all the unanticipated earthquakes, stray bullets, unappreciated factors of social class and accent, unknown opinions of others about us, misperceived social practices and customs that will determine our experience as it unfolds, as much or more than our construals.

The standard criticisms of Lewin's topology of the life space can be set aside fairly quickly (Hall and Lindzey, 1970). Its solipsism and failure to represent the mutual co-givenness of "world" is doubtless the most serious, but it is shared with the rest of mainstream cognitive theory — with the exception, in potential at least, of Gibson. It is also true that Lewin's method is more like a formalized description than the more traditional explanations and predictions that we psychologists are taught to value. It has never been clear, however, whether explanation can play the role in the human sciences that it does in natural science. Lewin's failure is rather more profound and instructive than the criticism that he offers only description. What an achievement it would be, were it possible, to describe psychological reality in abstract topological terms that are fully adequate to its materials. How interesting if we could replace Lakoff and Johnson's loose collection of the physical metaphors

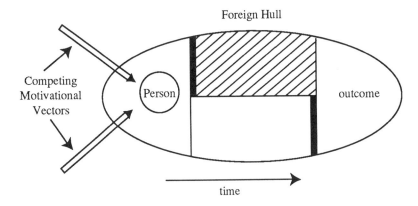

Figure 13. Lewinian life space.

used in self-reference with formal mathematical regions and forces. But neither seems to be possible.

Dynamics of Change in the Life Space and Catastrophe Theory

Consider first the inability of Lewin's language to represent the dynamism of change in the life space, by which one's situation is continuously dissolving or about to dissolve into another totally different organization. How long does a life space last? How do we represent that, as well as its "readiness" to reorganize?

The separation of the vector psychology of dynamic need from the topology of life space regions means that Lewin can never address the actual relativity of the psychological moment as his true unit of analysis. He is, of course, keenly aware of the problem. Lewin (1936) states that the life space in general, along with its regions, must be subject to moment-by-moment reorganization depending on the impact of successive experiences and rapidly changing motivational dynamics. There is no way, in principle, to determine the actual amount of time to be covered by a life space diagram. Whether a life space is to cover a brief instant or a period of weeks can only be determined by the tensions and tendencies that will yield the next resulting psychological situation and its own relative stability or instability. In everyday life the total life space can change several times a second, as we construe and reconstrue a complex, rapidly changing situation. On the other hand, the general structure of a life space could be maintained more or less unchanged for much of a lifetime — all this depending, of course, on the level of abstraction and the psychological factors that we choose to represent. In this context, Lewin mentions the importance of "the velocity of the mediating processes" in determining the "length" of the life space as a "differential time section," but he is not able to represent any of this in formal terms. A true depiction of the life space as "unit" should reflect the actual dynamic structure of situations, as if they were breaking waves caught at their crest of "realization" — a bit like James on the movement of emphasis through "the-pack-of-cards-is-on-the-table."

In his review of the use of topology after Lewin, Kurt Back (1992) sees René Thom's (1975) and Christopher Zeeman's (1976, 1977) "catastrophe theory" as the major subsequent development of Lewin's attempts to represent the vector dynamics of conflict situations that are about to undergo qualitative reorganization. Thom sought a formal language with which to represent sudden discontinuities and departures from symmetry in biology and experience. On the basis, ultimately, of the properties of breaking waves, he located seven "elementary catastrophes" or sudden forms of reorganization. These differed in the number of variables involved, but all were based on two underlying wave forms — breaking cusps or hollow elliptics. Zeeman applied Thom's cusp template to bifurcation events such as the point at which an aggressively barking dog suddenly turns and flees, or a frightened one attacks, as well as sudden shifts in stock markets, attack versus surrender in military strategy, the anorexic-bulimic cycle, the moment of neuronal firing, and even the point at which a bridge girder will buckle under pressure.

One of the most interesting extensions of catastrophe modeling has been the proposal that it can be used to represent qualitative, stagewise shifts in cognitive development (Van Der Mass and Molenaar, 1992). Longitudinal data showing some combination of bimodality, sudden jumps, regressions to previous performance levels, slowing or accelerating of change, and anomalous variance can be taken as indicating the abrupt qualitative shifts in organization posited by catastrophe theory. On more microgenetic levels of development, all these indicators will also describe the fluctuations and sudden reorganizations in perceptual recognition with the tachistoscope, as well as the discontinuities and intrusions of bizarreness in dream formation.

Catastrophe modeling does allow a representation of the formal dynamics of psychological moments or developmental stages poised between multiple attractors, repellors, limits, and separators (Abraham and Shaw, 1988). It does so, however, at the price of depicting the formal properties of only that aspect of the phenomenology of experience in artificial isolation. A full *logos* of experience as sought by Lewin, Gibson, and Heidegger eludes us in Thom's and Zeeman's diagrams, as it did in Lewin's. Although the mapping of sudden reorganizations of the life space on the model of breaking waves does pertain to the "is-like" of immediate experience, it does so in the same abstracted fashion of diagrams in modern physics (Miller, 1984), by a combination of convention and highly selective emphasis. Catastrophe models formalize Lewin's "velocity of mediating processes," but in so doing they sacrifice any broader phenomenology. We are "in" our experience as surely as we are "in" the physical universe, and it may be that we cannot "draw" either one without pretending to occupy a fictional platform outside ourselves that must inevitably both distort our view and render it incomplete.

The Boundary between Life Space and Foreign Hull as Double Torus

A similar lesson emerges from considering another feature of Lewin's life space drawings that must also misrepresent the broader phenomenology of our experience. In this instance, however, neither Lewin nor his major critics seems to have noticed.

If we keep in mind that *all* drawn boundaries are supposed to reflect "psychological reality" as experienced by the subject, it becomes apparent that there is a crucial difference between the boundaries between the various interior regions of the life space and the overall boundary between life space and foreign hull, in terms of their relation to descriptive phenomenology. To draw the life space/foreign hull boundary as a definite line should mean that I *experience* it as a barrier or region in its own right. To be consistent with the lines of the interior regions, if I draw that line as very thin, then am I saying that I sense my immediate situation as especially open to "foreign" influences that I cannot specifically anticipate? (If I could anticipate them, they would become interior regions.) If I draw it very thick, am I saying that I sense nothing else outside my "world" or that I actually feel positively protected from the unexpected? However, the boundary that encloses the life space and separates it from the foreign hull is normally not experienced at all. Lewin's boundary around the life space has a totally different experiential and conceptual status than the regions whose boundaries and densities show our actual experience.

Presumably, the life space "ahead" has something of the horizonal openness of Gibson and Heidegger — sensed as such to varying degrees in various situations. Lewin states that the life space is "open" and "unlimited," but he always (and necessarily) draws it as closed. How do we draw "no boundary" — and that as a variable parameter? Some of his critics (Allport, 1955) have pointed out that Lewin has great difficulty in fully realizing the logical separation between psychological and physical space, even though he is continually preoccupied with the problem. In the present example, it is as though he sets out to depict first-person "space" (which is open with "possibility," as we have seen) but can only derive it from a third-person view that must see the other as a circumscribed and fixed entity — closed. At its "perimeter" the life space should be represented as opening out into an indefiniteness that cannot be fully circumscribed. Lewin (1936) can say this, and does, but he cannot draw it in the same way that he draws the genuinely phenomenological interior regions of the life space.

In order to address the representation of the boundary of the life space, we must approach it in a similarly selective way, separating these issues from Lewin's finely nuanced regional depictions of the sensed flows and barriers of the life-world. Freely speculating, we can approximate a spatial modeling of the boundary between life space and foreign hull by means of a torus or solenoid shape — a potential chaotic attractor that can collapse multiple cycles of oscillation together into a single dynamic constant. Here again, however, while something of the "is-like" of sentient experience may be captured, it is at the price of any more complete *logos*.[3]

I have already discussed the view that the life world of sentient beings is based on two very different systems, direct perception and recognition, variously superimposed over each other within all organismic moments (chapters 3, 6). Direct perception flows out from horizonal openness. This is also implied by Lewin's notion of the representation of felt possibilities ahead, which, although actually sensed, are not to be explicitly represented as a closed boundary. Gibson depicts this openness by means of a "visual cone" emerging out of an indefinite horizon onto the point of observation and welling forth lamination and texture. We can consider direct perception in terms of this funnel or vortex as open at each end, in topological terms, because the openness of the horizon ahead leaves the position of the subject similarly open to sudden reorganization. Within this formalized system, "energy" flows from the horizon into the laminating surfaces that move past the subject. Since this cone of perception is continuously renewed and reorganized as we locomote and change direction within it, we can see it as a sort of vortex whose edges can never complete a fixed or stable funnel. It is an open system somewhat akin to a cyclone.

The recognitive system, correspondingly, is also a continuously renewed and shifting vortex but facing in the other direction. Although occupying ultimately the "same" space as direct perception, it is based on its own cycle of need-based energies. It seeks an orientation to object surfaces that must loom symmetrically in approach or recede symmetrically in flight. Thus it is representable as a variable vortex that closes down toward the recognized object but still remains open, since objects so recognized can easily evanesce like bursting bubbles with continued approach or avoidance. As Von Uexküll shows, it is not just for humans that getting what you want can be full of surprises — at minimum the object changes, at maximum it is gone. The broader base of the funnel is also open, since it represents the sensed space within which the creature will maneuver in terms of the changing motile possibilities of approach and avoidance. As we have seen, energy in the recognitive cone follows a more entropic order than the cone of direct perception, since it is based on the dynamics of specific need satisfaction.

Whereas subject and object are normally considered logical opposites, from this view of the life space as superimposition of direct perception and recognition, they are not psychological opposites. Rather, "subject" is coordinated with the array that positions it, while it is need and object that are at the opposite ends of the recogni-

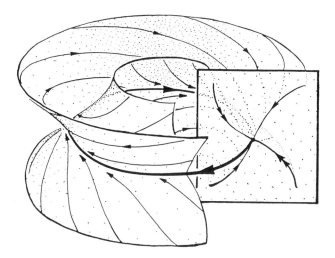

Figure 14. Double torus. From Ralph H. Abraham and Christopher D. Shaw, Dynamics: The Geometry of Behavior © *1992 by Addison-Wesley Publishing Company, Inc. Reprinted by permission of the publisher.*

tive dimension. Perhaps the interactions between subject and need, object and array, constitute "strange attractors" on a level of analysis more molar than that considered by Freeman (1991). Subject and object are then not truly contrastive opposites, since each is a dynamically interactive system in its own right. Subject becomes the dynamic and shifting amalgam of position and desire, whereas object is the fusion of significant surfaces and ambient surround. No wonder the contrast between "subjective" and "objective" has caused such confusion in psychology.

If we now pictorially superimpose these two vortices, since their differently organized systems do cover the "same" life space, we get a double vortex with a saddle point at their areas of cross-section. This constitutes the organizing strange attractor for a single dynamic system, one very similar to the double-torus shapes presented in Abraham and Shaw (1983, 1984) (see figure 14). Oscillations around such a saddle point turn this double vortex into a solenoid or torus pattern containing alternating superimposed cycles (figure 15). It is this double-torus shape that would be a candidate for the formal depiction of the outer hull or husk of the life space of a motile creature. Such a solenoid will reorganize continuously in terms of which vortex, recognitive or navigational, is dominant at a given point in time, although both, by definition, are always present to maintain the self-organizing dynamism of the life space within. For good or ill, this is also the four-dimensional pattern created as the waves of receptor potential, depolarization, and reactive hyperpolarization move along the neuronal membrane, as discussed by Yasue, Jibu,

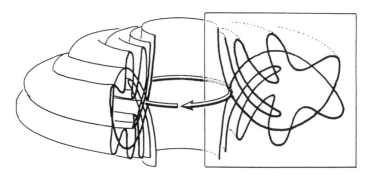

Figure 15. Double torus as chaotic attractor. From Ralph H. Abraham and Christopher D. Shaw, Dynamics: The Geometry of Behavior © *1992 by Addison-Wesley Publishing Company, Inc. Reprinted by permission of the publisher.*

and Pribram (in Pribram, 1991). We have already seen that neuronal activity is best modeled as a protozoan in motion through its surround.

The double torus is certainly not the full life space. Only on the most abstract level does it reflect anything of that "is-like" — perhaps in the sensed openings out and contractions of one's "world." Primarily, this design represents the outer husk of the life space and the portion of the foreign hull most adjacent to, and directly shaping, the life space. Lewin's life space can be drawn inside this husk, with its sensed possibilities and diffuse needs now extending out into the open ends of the torus and reflecting the differently sensed opening and narrowing of both systems. The torus reflects the outer shape or hull of the life space, just as, with D'Arcy Thompson, the spiral seashell is the outer record of a previous course of organic growth.

Perception, World, Universe

We face exactly the same problem in diagramming experience as we do in mapping the "unseen" realities of modern physics. It can be done only by an abstract geometric depiction of selective organizing principles that will then seem to have little relation to the concrete specifics of either realm. Consciousness is about as hard to "draw" as space-time relativity or waves/particles, perhaps because they come from the same place. The possibility that all of the formal organizing principles of modern physical science can be applied as well to the most general properties of the life space and ambient ecological array is most consistent with the view that these conceptual structures have been abstracted out of a "primacy of perception" in the first place. Outwardly, these structures are found in the physical order and then redirected metaphorically at ourselves in the service of self-reflection. But this redirection is hardly arbitrary. The organizing principles of world are instead being returned to their most probable source in the organization of perception — a source mirroring the properties of the physical universe in diverse and multiple ways, direct and indirect. If we consider the question most parsimoniously, how else could we successfully know the universe and even mathematicize it, if its principles were not derivable from perception itself, as the ultimate template of thought?

If the structure of perception in motile creatures is the ultimate lens for all knowledge, it has been treated with an astonishing contempt by western scientific and religious traditions — whose originating template it must nonetheless remain. This failure to study the nature of life-world, not to mention its "eliminative" reduction to physical systems of higher entropy and less complexity, constitutes a parallel within the theory of knowledge to our global ecological crisis. It is as though our contempt for perception as the lens for knowledge matches our contempt for the ecosystem of the earth as the only place we have to stand and be. Wherever this discussion leaves us, it is at home in our surround — a considerable step past the more traditional, and more than faintly schizoid, alternative. To recover from this blindness we must overcome our traditional insistence on the separation of nature and man, and man and animal — since the organization of perception as the root of our physical and spiritual representations seems to be more or less common across motile creatures. The basis of all our transpersonal and scientific experience becomes our alive, shared, sentient presence in the world.

Part VII Concluding Sociological Postscript

Collective consciousness is the highest form of the psychic life, since it is the consciousness of the consciousness. . . . If the communication established between [individual consciousnesses] is to become a real consciousness, that is to say, a fusion of all particular sentiments into one common sentiment, the signs expressing them must themselves be fused into one single and unique resultant. . . . The life thus brought into being enjoys so great an independence that it sometimes indulges in manifestations . . . for the mere pleasure of affirming itself. . . . This is often precisely the case with ritual activity and mythological thought.
Emile Durkheim, *The Elementary Forms of the Religious Life*

When there was no dream
of mine
You dreamed of me
R. Hunter/J. Garcia, "Attics of my Life," © 1970 Ice Nine Publishing Company

14 Consciousness as Society

The Double Crisis of Meaning in Contemporary Life

Throughout the twentieth century social scientists have portrayed western civilization as in fundamental crisis. The foundational figures of both psychology (James, Freud, and Jung) and sociology (Durkheim and Weber) built their disciplines around the assumption of such a crisis in value or spirituality — a crisis to be understood both in its own right and as offering the beginnings of a revised conception of humanity. The dilemmas of modernity, and now postmodernity, have, however, been conceived in very different terms.

From the perspective of psychology, the crisis is in our sense of personal meaning and purpose in living. The sociological perspective, on the other hand, sees a loss in sense of community and shared social allegiance of any kind. From our earlier discussions of the social organization of self-referential consciousness and its shared perceptual template, we might expect that these views of crisis are really two faces of the same loss. We have seen that transpersonal experiences, as the maximum expression of presentational states, are structured dialogically. The very existence of a "sociology of religion" attests to their corresponding potential for a powerful societal impact.

James, Jung, and contemporary transpersonal psychology understand our crisis as a loss of "soul," "inwardness," or "sense of meaning" — the loss of a sense of being and felt reality of equal concern to Heidegger's analysis of culture and to the psychoanalysis of Winnicott. Common also to the pioneers of sociology, however, was the description of a progressive secularization of what Max Weber termed "charisma" and Durkheim "mana" — the social expression of Rudolf Otto's numinous. Weber (1915, 1922), his associate Ernst Troeltsch (1931), and Durkheim (1912) all saw secularized mass society as increasingly dominated by an ethic of radical individualism, and thereby ripe for a spiritual renewal in the more ostensibly experiential forms of mysticism. Weber posited a long-term cyclic relation between rationalization and charisma. After a period of maximum disconnection between a traditional church and the changing socioeconomic conditions of everyday life, charisma is reborn in one of two directions. These move toward prophetism or mysticism, depending on general social conditions and the group from which the resultant "radical salvation movement" first emerges. Later it may spread across the entire society as an orthodoxy of its own.

What Weber termed "asceticism" or "prophetism" tends to emerge out of the lower middle and artisan classes (Christ as carpenter). Its characteristic form of religious experience involves a "possession" by a theistic divinity, with emphasis on hallucinatory voices that address the importance of ethical conduct in everyday life. Such conduct will qualify the believers, who themselves may not hear these voices, for a future utopia that will follow either after death or at the "end" of history and time. Prophetic religions entail unending ethical struggles between good and evil to be played out in the theater of daily social conduct. In specific contrast to the more personally and psychologically centered mysticisms, it is prophetism, in Weber's view, that can bring about revolutionary social changes, especially since the commandments heard by the prophets are generally obvious projections of the concerns of an oppressed class or social group. The modern era reflects the final phase of secularization of the prophetical Protestant ethic, leaving the middle and upper classes in their present condition of collective disenchantment, civic cult of the individual, and ripeness for a shift toward the mystical. Meanwhile, we see a counterreaction in the worldwide revival of various prophetical fundamentalisms among the more disadvantaged classes and peoples.

Whereas prophetical possession is clearly the form of religious experience that can have the most obvious political impact, mysticism has the deeper psychological impact — albeit equally shared and socially expressed. This is because the direct phenomenology of the numinous is more fully explored in mysticism. Mysticism, for Weber, seeks the unitive experience of an all-encompassing, "timeless," and compassionate openness. Cross-culturally, mystical movements tend to appear first in the artistic and aristocratic classes (Buddha the prince), where it is not so easy to blame one's radical discontent on social conditions. One's search is accordingly "within," by means of more specifically psychological techniques such as meditation.

Both Weber and Durkheim forecast the development of an "inner-worldly" mysticism (to use Weber's terminology) within the educated middle classes of the twentieth century to replace our overly secularized, predominantly prophetical Christianity. Whereas "other-worldly" religious movements, mystical and prophetical, break away from mainstream society in specially segregated communities, inner-worldly forms seek to encounter the numinous while continuing to live within ordinary society. A contemporary leaning toward an inner-worldly mysticism would be reinforced at least twice over. First, some form of a more directly experiential mysticism becomes the potential direction for a renewed "sense of meaning" because our educated, predominantly middle-class society has increasingly modeled itself on more traditional aristocratic values of self-expression and inward cultivation. Even with tightening economic pressures, radical unhappiness in this large segment of modern society will tend not to be blamed on outwardly controllable circumstances, and so must be addressed within. Second, the progressive secularization of a Christian inner-worldly prophetism (Weber's "Protestant ethic") has left us, as a people, perhaps uniquely centered on the concrete social and material order as what "matters." Our predominant commitment to the here-and-now material order will lead us toward an "inner-worldly" orientation in any renewed search for meaning.

Aside from periodic expressions of a western "counterculture" of inner-worldly mysticism in early Gnosticism, the Renaissance, and Romanticism, there have been several resurgences of such a tendency, more naturalistically understood, over the past hundred years. Starting with Nietzsche and his call for the "yea-saying" overman and Kierkegaard's forays into the "aesthetics" of experience, before his final return to the "ethics" of Christianity, this more dissident interest resurfaced in the spiritualism and theosophy and drug experimentation of the late 1800s, the interest sparked by Jungian self-actualization beginning in the 1920s and 1930s, the LSD and eastern-meditation movements of the 1960s and 1970s, and "new-age" interests in shamanism and out-of-body and near-death experience. It would include much of the interest in more naturalistic studies of imaginative absorption and transpersonal psychology.[1] Indeed, their psychological conception of religious experience makes James, Jung, and contemporary transpersonal psychology both the beginnings of a "science" of what is traditionally termed "soul" and the outward expressions of this sociocultural shift toward inner-worldly mysticism. The search for a holistic cognitive psychology and neurophysiology of the transpersonal can be seen both as a genuine extension of the science of mind and as an expression of incipient social collectivity. This is also the view reflected in Durkheim's expectation of a new "religion of man," which, in its insistence on direct experience, would be closer to the attitudes of modern science than to the Judeo-Christian tradition of "belief" (Campbell, 1978; Westley, 1978).

This shift toward inner-worldly mysticism, and its attendant concern with personal meaning, has often been portrayed, misleadingly, as a major contributing factor to the second great crisis in modern life as delineated by contemporary social science — the loss of a sense of "community" within a culture that seems increasingly "narcissistic." The sociologist Robert Bellah (1985), the cultural analyst Christopher Lasch (1978, 1984), and the neo-Jungian James Hillman (Hillman and Ventura, 1992) have all described a loss of commitment to the civic ethic of maintaining the actual fabric of everyday society. They associate this loss of community with radical, secular individualism, which they see as culminating in a private ethic of psychotherapeutic "growth" and "self-actualization."

Initially, it may well seem that the current interest in all things mystical must be part of that loss of community. Bellah et al. (1985, p. 246), speaking of these contemporary leanings toward inner-worldly mysticism, describes "its inner volatility . . . , its extreme weakness in social and political organization, and above all its particular form of compromise with the world — namely, its closeness to the therapeutic model in its pursuit of self-centered experiences and its difficulty with social loyalty and commitment." Earlier, Weber (1922) had mentioned the specifically "broken" quality of the inner-worldly mystic in relation to the social order. Indeed, to cultivate mediative openness in the midst of everyday social commitments that are, in their turmoil, the very antithesis of the "states" being sought is to invite a continuing narcissistic injury and pain. We have already seen how deficits in the sense of self — all too common in modern society — must be stirred up to some extent by direct transpersonal experience anyway. Thus, the outward behavior of those drawn to contemporary mysticism often does appear "withdrawn" and lacking in more specific social commitments to community and profession.

Yet the full realization of presence-openness as the fundamental existential reality shared by all sentient beings is the very opposite of anything withdrawn and asocial, as we have seen. So we arrive at something rather puzzling. While it often seems that contemporary "new-age" activities are part of a "culture of narcissism," the realizations being cultivated are generally based on an egalitarian sense of oneness and identity among all human beings and, indeed, all sentient beings.

Further, the meditative traditions have their own developmental roots in the shamanistic practices typical of hunter-gatherer peoples and integral to the latter's sense of community and group identity (Eliade, 1964; Bourguignon, 1972, 1973). There is no hint in these societies of our very modern separation of consciousness and community. In fact, it appears that trance states and archetypal dreams in these "dream-centered" societies, the specialties of the shaman but potentially open to all, are central to the actual sense of everyday group unity. Such dreams are almost always also performative, requiring some communal social enactment after waking. They also have significance for shamanic healing, and may provide sacred names and guidance for individuals in vision quests during key life stages (see Tedlock, ed., 1987; Hunt, 1989a).

The communal basis of such dreams, since their scenes and characters are defined by collectively shared mythologies, means that the further an individual in such a society goes "within," toward what we would term the archetypal or imaginative absorption, the more common, shared, and socially directed the resulting state. These dreams and related waking visions are the very opposite of what we now call narcissism. Indeed, the out-of-body states cultivated by the shaman involve journeys to this same collectively defined realm of the gods, so that the resulting experiences will tend to support and complement each other. Not surprisingly, the discussion of dreams and visions, and instructions for what to do and look for in such states, begins in early childhood. Significant dreams are generally told to the entire group and discussed in terms of their personal and social implications and performative consequences. In these societies, at least, the more consciousness as such is cultivated, the more shared it becomes, not the less.

Perhaps our own radically isolating individualism is more the secularized residue of the Protestant Reformation than something newly created by an ethic of psychotherapy and meditation. These latter, after all, appeared as responses to that isolation, whatever their mixed impact on it. With its initial concentration on the outward marks of the grace of God and now on the various material rewards of a mass society, our cult of the autonomous individual sits ill with the potentially shared searches of inner-worldly mysticism. Meditative practice involves a direct and often group-based cultivation of a shared structure of presence-openness, understood as potential within all. The contemporary narcissism of much "self-actualization," which is surely undeniable, may follow instead when we take transpersonal experiences in a more traditional fashion as the mark of individual merit. If so, contemporary social science may have equally misjudged both the nature of consciousness cultivated as such and the basis of our sense of commonality with others, precisely by virtue of their separate treatment.[2]

Durkheim on Collective Consciousness

Only Durkheim (1912) and his expositors (Tiryakian, 1962; O'Keefe, 1982) have attempted to provide a theoretical basis for the role that communally shared transpersonal experiences and related ritual practices and mythologies play in maintaining the most basic sense of community and group identity. The function of presentational states in intensifying a sense of community follows as the empirically researchable consequence of Durkheim's more extreme and unnecessarily reductionist claim that experiences of "mana" are nothing other than the members of a society directly sensing the social bond itself. In Durkheim's "sociologism," people first become aware of the numinous as an "effervescence" from group activities and then subsequently symbolize it in the emblems of group identity and allegiance. Society itself stands in relation to the individual as the source of the felt meanings of presentational states, namely as a superior and encompassing entity, immortal in comparison to the life span of the individual, and providing a shared symbolic cognition upon which the individual must remain utterly dependent. For Durkheim, as summarized by Edward Tiryakian (1962, pp. 33, 35), "Religion is not something illusory; on the contrary, it has an existential reality, for it is grounded in the reality of collective life . . . arising from the psychical excitement generated by the collectivity on special occasions. . . . When the faithful believe in a moral power upon which they depend and from which they derive their best aspects, they are not deceiving themselves: such a power — society — does exist. . . . God is Society worshipping itself."

Durkheim's concept of an emergent collective consciousness, most directly expressed in the shared unity of presentational states, bears an intriguing resemblance to Sperry's notion of individual consciousness as the holistic emergent of neural processes. Durkheim (1912) states that just as individual consciousness is more than a simple "efflorescence" of the nervous system, since it obeys laws not necessarily reducible to specific neural events, so the collective consciousness of society cannot be reduced to individual consciousness. Indeed, once launched, it exerts just the kind of "downward control" on the individual that was posited by Sperry between individual consciousness and brain. The difference, and the problem from the present perspective, is that Durkheim seeks to reduce the existential reality of our experience of being as presence-openness to something supposedly more fundamental, of which it is but the outward expression.

As self-referential beings whose symbolic capacities rest on the metaphoric reuse of the forms of perception, consciousness as such comes to feel presence-openness, the most fundamental structure of perception, as the potential metaphor for an encompassing "totality." That totality will match anything we choose to conceptualize as encompassing us. Accordingly, it will "fit" society, but no better or worse than it does the physical universe itself or traditional metaphysical absolutes. Locating presentational states in the presence-openness of perception stays closest to the actual phenomenology of experience. We thus avoid the various reductionisms of sociology, psychoanalysis, and neurophysiology. There is no particular virtue in explaining away fundamental features of living, especially in the name of "human science."

That said, however, there is no question that the empirical side of Durkheim's equation of presentational states and society is correct and important. Presentational states, based on a dialogic self-reference, are inherently social in structure and potential effect. Moreover, since they are directly responsive to the most basic structures of perception, their experience will create the fullest possible sense of group identity and joint community among those who directly share them. This is why, hunter-gatherers aside, most meditative traditions stress the importance of group meditation. It quite palpably enhances the depth and power of the individual's meditative practice. It also follows that when shared access to these states ceases on the level of an entire nation, under the pressures of increased socioeconomic complexity and secularization, people will feel less in touch with each other on a deep level — less "one." This level of deep commonality, and its potential for direct experience "as such," is still latent within more complex social orders, as demonstrated by the periodic resurgence of mystical radical salvation groups.

Whether the separation of individual and collective consciousness that has come to characterize modern societies is inevitable must remain an open question. Certainly Durkheim thought that a complex-enough social order could become open again to the level of collective consciousness that I have argued was conferred by sacred dreams and presentational states among hunter-gatherers — a speculation that reappears in a related form in McLuhan's (1964) "global village." At present, I will merely stress that it is no longer so obvious that the mystical is intrinsically pitted against community feeling and commitment. They have gone together periodically in ways that have enhanced and intensified both.

The idea that the further one goes "in," the more shared and common the resulting state, has been with us for a very long time. We have already seen that the classical *sensus communis* underwent a joint and coordinated development. On the one hand, in its relation to synesthesia it emerged as the creative imagination of Romanticism. On the other, it appeared as the empathy and community feeling implied by the Roman "common sense." For both the Romantics and traditional hunter-gatherer peoples, imagination seems to have been *the* social sense. Similarly, one of the most persistent complaints against Freud's psychology of the unconscious, endlessly circling around Oedipus, is the alleged monotony and impersonality of this, our most supposedly private and idiosyncratic life. The "inner" side of our outward individual diversity became a psychic pain curiously and universally shared. If everyone in this culture of radical individualism has essentially "the same" oedipal complex and, with Winnicott and Kohut, the same shared deficits in sense of self, then the psychoanalysts have paradoxically discovered society "within."

The similarity between Jung's "collective unconscious" and Durkheim's "collective consciousness" makes this point still more obvious. Jung's later version of an "objective psyche" was his attempt to move away from earlier speculations about a collective unconscious based on biological and racial inheritance. Instead, he ends by positing a level of experience that, while based on imagery and metaphor, feels absolutely objective and all-encompassing (numinous). Spontaneous mythological themes more or less common across cultures are the most obvious outward expression of this level of mind and are understood as based on common metaphors available from the natural order. Accordingly, Jung's objective psyche is absolutely collective and open to conscious realization in much the same way as Durkheim's collective consciousness — itself most fully revealed in presentational states, ritual behaviors, and mythologies.

The empirical study of Durkheim's collective consciousness has unfortunately been centered largely on research on public opinion in complex societies. More relevant is the notion of pervasive social cycles of optimism and pessimism (Tiryakian, 1962). These would be shared by all members of a society as communal felt meanings and indirectly reflected in various composite measures of social existence, such as crime rate and global economic indices. What seems to have been bypassed is Durkheim's own assertion that the fullest access to a collective consciousness will be through the maximum development of the very presentational states that modern society has come to regard as the most inward and subjective. For Durkheim and his major commentators, shared religious experience is the fullest possible manifestation of collective consciousness.

Can we find any empirical reflection of this level of Durkheim's collective consciousness within the efflux of mysticisms in contemporary society? It should be the case, for Durkheim, that those segments of society that are cultivating states of imaginative absorption and meditation should thereby also be connected to the social collectivity in some demonstrable way, even if they are unaware of this linkage as such. Meditative states themselves should be ways of attuning the individual to the felt meaning of the entire society. Whatever else they do, our cognitive approach to these states as dialogic should entail that they are also the most direct way of tapping into a shared "social field." We will see that such a view is supported by a sociological reinterpretation of some recent parapsychological research. It will appear that our most ostensibly inward and subjective moments are the points where we actually, if often unwittingly, are the least alone.

A Sociological Reinterpretation of Parapsychological Research

The "Maharishi Effect" as Social Field

The Vedic-based Transcendental Meditation (TM) movement has been responsible for most of the formal psychophysiological research on the effects of meditation and related states (Alexander et al., 1987; Gackenbach et al., 1987; Travis, 1994). Our concern here, however, lies with a much more controversial side of TM research based on the suggestion of their leader, Maharishi Mahesh Yogi, that a large-enough number of meditators, gathered in a given geographic region or even worldwide, will causally influence basic social conditions for the better, as in diminished crime and improvements in various economic and public-opinion indices. They believe that such changes would be empirically measurable whenever the number of persons practicing in their group meditation sessions exceeds 1 percent of the local population or the square root of 1 percent of the population in the case of more advanced practitioners. Starting in the mid-1970s, this hypothesis was tested in an extraordinary series of studies focusing on different cities and regions within the United States, the country as a whole, and a series of international areas of chronic warfare and strife (Aron and Aron, 1986; Wallace, 1986).

These researchers interpret their consistently positive results in these studies in terms of a causal effect that communal meditation would have on society, which they term "the Maharishi Effect" and which they interpret on the hypothesis of a unified physical field operating on a quantum level that would include consciousness. This, of course, is just the kind of theorizing rejected in the previous chapter as lacking in the most basic considerations of parsimony. The question will not be whether something replicable has been located, for the results are indeed broadly and consistently significant, but rather what this data has actually measured. Does it show the causal influence of meditative practice on a unified physical field that would also encompass social consciousness? Or, more parsimoniously, have these studies been unwittingly attuned to the widely shared cycles of optimism/pessimism that express Durkheim's collective consciousness? Such an interpretation would indeed be consistent with Durkheim on the relation between collective consciousness and presentational states, reflected here in periodic decisions to cultivate them communally.

The initial studies in this series (see Wallace, 1986) compared U.S. cities having the requisite percentages of TM meditators with control cities matched on such dimensions as population, education level, stability of residence, and unemployment. They found on the average an 8 percent decrease in crime rates in the TM cities, and these changes were maintained over several years despite the steady increases in crime in all the control cities. On the national level, it was found that communal meditation at Maharishi International University by seven thousand advanced meditators at the end of 1983 statistically anticipated upturns in the stock market, reductions in traffic accidents and air flight fatalities, reductions in infectious disease and crime, and, strangely enough, an increase in patent applications (since one would assume a rather lengthy period of gestation for the latter) (Wallace, 1986). Subsequent studies based on spontaneous fluctuations in the number of meditators attending these communal meditation sessions found that attendance predicted changes in levels of crime and other socioeconomic indices over the next several days (Orme-Johnson and Dillbeck, in press).

On the international level, Orme-Johnson et al. (1985) found reductions in United Nations ratings of hostile actions and increases in cooperative activities in

multiple world "hot spots" visited by groups of TM meditators (including Nic-
aragua, Israel, Thailand, Syria, and Cypress). International studies of major cities
were further extended and replicated in Dillbeck et al. (1987). In their most prominent study, published in the *Journal of Conflict Resolution* with editorial comments
praising the methodology and rejecting the theory, Orme-Johnson et al. (1988)
described a two-month study in Israel ending in September 1983. Using time series
analyses and controlling for expectable fluctuations in terms of holidays, temperature, weekends, and so forth, they found decreases in automobile accidents, fires,
crime, and war deaths in Lebanon, and rises in the stock market index and the
national mood (based on newspaper ratings), whenever the number of meditators
attending the group sessions exceeded the predicted threshold number during their
stay.

Although one must be impressed with the noble intentions behind these studies,
and with their relative immunity from standard methodological criticisms (Schrodt,
1990; Orme-Johnson, Alexander, and Davies, 1990), their general failure to ran-
domize the timing of their attempted social interventions leads us to a more conservative conclusion than the demonstration of a unified physical field causally
influencing society. More plausibly, they have unintentionally attuned themselves to
anticipatory fluctuations within collective society in a way that amounts to a kind of
"Durkheimian surfing." For instance, the U.S. cities matched on socioeconomic
variables in these studies were not matched for broader and probably more relevant
cultural indicators, of which the increase in TM meditators will have been but one
part, such as artistic activities, number of psychotherapists, and especially the quality of local colleges. The failure to determine the timing of group travels and
fluctuations in the number of meditators by means of randomization procedures
leaves out the key control required in all parapsychological research (Irwin, 1989;
Alcock, 1981). The risk is that these researchers have automatically fallen into step
with similarly nonrandom fluctuations in the optimism/pessimism cycles of society
as a whole. In the Israeli study, for example, the meditators were struck by what a
good mood the taxi drivers were in on the days of high spontaneous attendance in
group meditation (Aron and Aron,1986). This might rather suggest that the daily
attendance decisions of the meditators were already part of a much broader social
cycle equally affecting the entire society.

It is true that some of these studies had to be planned months in advance and
were restricted to predetermined time periods. If, however, cycles of the depth and
pervasiveness posited by Durkheim are present in national and world society, the
nonrandom selections of location and time risk unconscious attunements to extremely broad social indices, some of which might be present months in advance in
terms of diffusely felt mood. Indeed, the most impressive replications of the Maharishi Effect occurred during the artificial economic boom of the 1980s, along with

the decline of the Soviet Union and the advent of Mikhail Gorbachev, which may have been fortunate for, and congruent with, the purposes of these studies. The true test would be further, randomly assigned replications against the local, national, and international grains of a downwardly spiraling decade.

Parsimony, then, directs us back toward a largely uninvestigated but naturalistic Durkheimian social field. The potential discovery involved here could be almost as revolutionary as the opposite, more doubtful conclusion that what has been hitherto lacking in parapsychology research are large-enough numbers of simultaneous senders. In most of the above studies, the various socioeconomic indices were not correlated with each other, but only with the attendance and timing of the communal meditations. This makes it even more plausible that if the Maharishi Effect is artifactual, the only other explanation would be the common sharing of all these measures in a deeper optimism/pessimism wave to which these meditators may have been far more sensitive than the average person, who is lower in imaginative absorption. Perhaps we are not nearly as separate from each other as most of us have thought, but fail rather in the recognition of this fact. If so, then to go inward in meditation is, among other things, to resonate more fully to a collectivity of shared felt meanings.

Laboratory Parapsychology as Communal Fluctuations in Imagery

If Durkheim's collective consciousness provides the most parsimonious explanation for the Maharishi Effect, we might expect a similar interpretation to be possible for much of the laboratory-based research in parapsychology. Again, although it was not the intention of these researchers, they will have demonstrated the existence of a shared social field most readily tapped within the high-imaginative-absorption subjects and imagery-cultivation conditions used in this research.

The crucial drawback of research into extrasensory perception (ESP) has been its nonreplicability (Irwin, 1989; Alcock, 1981). This widespread failure, however, has been reversed in much of the research on dream telepathy (Krippner, 1970; Ullman and Krippner, 1970; Ullman, Krippner, and Vaughan, 1973), remote viewing (Tart, Puthoff, and Targ, eds., 1979), and, especially, telepathic imagery studies with the ganzfeld (Honorton et al., 1990; Parker and Wiklund, 1987). In the dream telepathy series, completed at Maimonides Medical Center in New York, randomly selected art prints were "sent" to laboratory subjects who were in ongoing REM sleep. Their reported dreams were later matched against the prints by both the subject and external judges — generally at levels beyond chance. Remote-viewing studies involve the matching of ongoing imagery from "receivers" with actual physical locations randomly selected for "senders" from a set of possibilities. In the ganzfeld research, senders image an art print randomly selected from sets of four, while receivers report simultaneous spontaneous imagery during exposure to white noise and a diffusely lit visual field (ganzfeld), in order to encourage imagery formation. In these latter studies, replication of significant levels of match between prints and imagery has been more the rule than the exception, even after the progressive adoption of the more stringent controls for randomization and stimulus order suggested by skeptical critics (Hyman, 1985; Parker and Wiklund, 1987; Honorton et al., 1990; Bem and Honorton, 1994) and often absent in the dream and remote-viewing studies (Marks and Kammann, 1978).

The question becomes whether the shift from nonreplicable studies based on the guessing of cards and numbers, which typified "classical" ESP research (Irwin, 1989), to these "free-response" methods based on qualitative, pictorial target materials proves the reality of an extrasensory communication. Perhaps it has instead demonstrated that certain kinds of imagery, at least, fluctuate communally in terms of a more naturalistically shared social field.[3]

The most recent meta-analyses of the ganzfeld imagery research (Honorton et al., 1990; Bem and Honorton, 1994) review several studies, all conducted by Honorton and his colleagues, which included immediate judging to rule out any potential order effects and, in most cases, "prompting" for possible matches by an experimenter also blind to the actual target sent. The mean correct identifications ranged from .24 to .67, with an average across all studies of .34 — this compared to the .25 correct that would be expected on the basis of chance alone. A key control missing from these studies, and from dream telepathy and remote-viewing research as well, is the inclusion of control sessions during which no target is actually sent, with the subjects' imagery in these sessions judged against previous experimental series, and the imagery from real and control sessions compared for any qualitative differences. Parapsychologists are very reluctant to use such controls, which are the only means of determining the actual probability of matches, because, they argue, it breaks trust with the subject and, on parapsychological theory, the control trials might still be based on precognition rather than telepathy. What this may mean, sadly for all the enthusiasm lately generated, is that the experimental method is ultimately not usable in this area.

Could the ganzfeld paradigm have fallen victim to a more sociologically sophisticated form of the confound first identified by Louis Goodfellow (1938, 1940)? Goodfellow showed that the ostensible ESP demonstrated when the Zenith Radio Show asked listeners to guess telepathically sent sequences of numbers, letters, and designs could be explained by the fact that the sequences of listener guesses were not random and showed a strong tendency to avoid symmetry and repetition, reflecting their assumptions about the nature of "chance" and allowing a significant attunement with the sequences actually sent. All significance in these results disappeared when controlled for nonrandom patterns of guessing and related communal associations unwittingly primed by the instructions. Goodfellow and Spencer-

Brown (1956, 1957) both concluded that probability estimates in ESP research should be based not on statistical probabilities per se but on the empirical (or psychological) probability of a given response or response series from experimental subjects — and, we can add, especially from those highest on imaginative absorption in image generation studies.

The empirical probabilities of a "hit" in the more recent free-response studies would then be based on the probability that certain kinds of imagery will appear in successful subjects, combined with the probability that similar forms of imagery would appear within the sets of art prints usually used in these studies. There is, in fact, considerable indication that certain subjects (high in imaginative absorption, high in dream recall) and certain forms of imagery prominent in such subjects (archetypal, psychedelic) are indeed characteristic of the successful trials in these studies (Ullman, Krippner, and Vaughan, 1973).

Susan Blackmore's (1986) descriptions of her own participation in a ganzfeld study mention her immediate impression of striking similarities between her imagery and most of the potential target pictures presented to her, with a difficult decision process in picking which was the closest match. This in itself suggests that spontaneous imagery in certain subjects and aesthetic material will tap a common, potentially shared level of imagistic consciousness. High imaginative absorbers would indeed be more likely to produce especially rich and complex imagery, more easily matched to highly imaginative pictures, and indeed these subjects are the most successful in such research (Stanford and Frank, 1991). Honorton et al.'s (1990) examples of actual hits tend to involve archetypically rich imagery, whose empirical probability of occurrence in the target stimuli has never been assessed but likely is high.

With respect to the more "successful" pictorial targets, Ullman, Krippner, and Vaughan (1973) describe certain art prints (vivid, archetypal, religious) as commonly eliciting hits, whereas others almost never did. Honorton emphasizes the special success of a short video of a tidal wave engulfing a city (although one must wonder whether this would follow from its visual synesthetic congruence with the background white noise). He also found that sets of videos were more successful (40 percent hits) than sets of simpler, static pictures (27 percent). In the absence of research on both spontaneous imagery and works of art like that of Hall and Van de Castle (1966) on the incidence of various elements and features in dreams, we can have no way of knowing whether the real probability of hits in Honorton's ganzfeld studies is a statistical .25 or something higher.

Although Daryl Bem and Charles Honorton (1994) found significant differences in selection rates for the most popularly chosen stimuli when they were actually targets versus when they were not, Ray Hyman's (1994) demonstration of a .83 correlation between hit rates and number of target repetitions in these same samples, many involving the experimenter promptings mentioned above, strongly suggests a form of the "Goodfellow Effect." Significant elevations in hits with videos versus static pictures, acquaintances as senders versus strangers, target repetitions versus one-time exposure, high subject creativity, and experimenter prompting all suggest that we have conditions in which longer, more complex image protocols would offer greater leeway for communally shared response biases in imagery preferences.

If one needs the "right" sort of target and the "right" subjects with the "right" imagery for successful results, a more parsimonious conclusion than the demonstration of ESP would be that these studies tap a "collective" level of spontaneous imagery generation such as is more or less common to art, dreams, and spontaneous imagery in imaginatively absorbed subjects. On this view, the free-response parapsychological studies have unintentionally discovered an empirical way of measuring Durkheim's collective consciousness on the level of shared presentational imagery. As with the Maharishi Effect, we should not let a rejection of the conclusions of this research obscure the genuine importance of what seems to have been demonstrated: the further inward one goes into a supposedly private and idiosyncratic imagery, the more the resulting states are potentially communal — the more coordinated we become with all others in related states. Our contemporary cognitive paradigm has been centered on the symbolic capacity of the individual mind, when that very capacity is first and foremost a phenomenon of culture and group. We have tended to believe that it is language that makes our consciousness and cognition social. Perhaps, on a still more fundamentally shared level, it is imagery and metaphor.

Spencer-Brown (1956) makes the observation that the history of psychical research has been curiously "suicidal." As soon as various of its phenomena have been sufficiently studied to be understood in terms of patterned processes, rather than remaining purely inexplicable, they are removed from the psychical to become part of a more general psychology. This was certainly true for hypnosis, and more recently for out-of-body experiences, lucid dreaming, and near-death experience. If the present view is correct, the free-response research on dream telepathy, remote viewing, and imagery in the ganzfeld, to the extent that it has actually been replicated, would become a way of operationalizing Durkheim's notion of consciousness as collective — most especially in states of high imaginative absorption. The result would be, yet again, to remove what can be "understood" and leave parapsychology with its familiar core of spontaneous experiences that by their very description are acausal and inexplicable, and so engender an intrinsic fascination in those who are directly exposed to them.

Anecdotal, utterly puzzling experiences of the paranormal are clearly experienced by people and do have a characteristic impact, which in itself can be empirically studied along with the phenomenology of these states (Green and McCreery, 1975). By virtue of their very phenomenology, however, these states lie outside of any conceivable basis in cause and effect. It is the impossibility of so understanding them that is a defining feature of their phenomenology. Jung (1955) made a considerable contribution here in coining the purely descriptive term "synchronicity" for spontaneous instances of ostensible telepathy, clairvoyance, and precognition. Synchronicity or "meaningful coincidence" covers events that are inexplicable in terms of ordinary physical and social causality and so logically must be regarded as chance, yet are so powerful in their immediate impact and sense of connection that we are subjectively compelled to attribute meaning to them. The attempt to bring these spontaneous phenomena into the laboratory introduces a strangely quixotic quality to such research, since it is attempting to produce the inexplicable through an experimental paradigm whose essence must be predictability and regularity. Jung may have been correct in his suggestion that the core of parapsychology must remain these spontaneous anecdotal occurrences, since anything we can study in the laboratory is no longer synchronicity in the acausal sense of this term. If their nature is to confound, then whatever emerges out of their study as regular and replicable has fallen out again into a naturalistic cognitive and social psychology of imagistic states.

Some Sociocultural Implications

In 1927 Heidegger suggested that we had lost our sense of "isness" — our ability to experience ourselves and our surroundings as "real" and "there" — a phenomenon both deeply personal and widely shared. It does not seem like this was a "speculation" on Heidegger's part, or the expression of a "metaphysical" belief. It was an observation. Something very similar has been enunciated by most of the foundational figures of twentieth-century social science — James, Jung, Weber, Durkheim, and, of course, Nietzsche and Kierkegaard, who saw it coming. Winnicott and Kohut saw disturbances in the sense of self at the core of contemporary psychotherapy, an inability to feel "real" and vitally "present" in the here and now, which is — as presence-openness — all that sentient beings ultimately have.

Heidegger locates the beginnings of this loss in the essentialism of later Greek thought — truth is single, and we can know it. But if it is the case that "isness," in its twin aspects of soul and community, comes to us primarily through the more powerful presentational states of waking transpersonal experience and archetypal/lucid dreams, we can find still earlier signs of such a loss within our own tradition. Heraclitus, whom Heidegger understood as still attuned to presence-openness, wrote that "the waking have one world in common, whereas each sleeper turns away to a private world of his own," and he complained that ordinary people "are as neglectful of what they do when awake as they are when asleep" (Wheelwright, trans., 1966, p. 69, 70). That would make no sense at all to a native shaman. The shaman enters into a shared, mythological "dream time" precisely in "big dreams" and vision trance — a realm communally defined and open to continual reinterpretation and redefinition with each generation (Hunt, 1989a; Tedlock, 1987). Shared dreamscapes and visions were major sources of the immediate sense of community in native peoples — a point that Heraclitus may have been the first in recorded history not to understand. Henceforth the experiential complex of shamanism was to be preserved within the western tradition only in mystery cults and periodic efflorescences of mysticism.

The predominance of prophetical religion, as reflected in the Judeo-Christian tradition, is associated with social conduct and vocation as the marks of salvation and so as the source of felt meaning and "isness." Its subsequent slow secularization over the past two hundred years has left us with the curious civic cult of the autonomous individual and his or her "success," which is about equally distant now from sense of community and vitally embodied presence. This heritage of individualism means that any subsequent turn toward the "mystical," as the available direction for renewal and opening, will be understood instead as something within, private, and closed off from others — and this not only by observers but potentially by participants as well. In such a context any move toward subjectivity must seem empty, nihilistic, or an invitation to narcissism and grandiosity. Yet presence-openness is a shared existential fact, not a process or a theory.

The difficulties in the way of this understanding of the presentational realization of presence-openness are twofold. Obviously, these "states" — all that we have left to term them — will remain narcissistic in a culture that does not offer the sort of early education in dreaming and imaginative absorption that we see in hunter-gatherer, dream-centered societies. The solution here has been apparent since the writings of William James. If presentational states help us feel real and present in the world, and if they are the most direct answer to the sensed loss of reality that brings so many into modern psychotherapy, then we, too, could help young children with their recognition, communal shaping, and sanctioning. I have commented elsewhere (Hunt, 1989a) on the readiness with which groups of grade-school children describe and share their "special" dreams and early transpersonal experiences. Written stories, poems, and drawings based on such experiences probably could approximate a grade-school version of core instruction in the humanities to match our present, more exclusive emphasis on the training of representational thought.

More serious, however, are the deficits in sense of self and self-esteem that seem to so many psychologists to follow from our ways of dealing with infants and very young children — ways that have often struck nonwestern peoples as peculiarly barbaric and unfeeling. The separation of newborn infants into an early enforced "privacy," and the failure to mirror a sense of secure presence back to the infant and very young child by adults who may lack this very quality, become the continuing source of a weakness in sense of self and being that will later require children to suppress their spontaneous imaginative states as too "out of control" and terrifying. Proclivity toward presentational states in the absence of a sufficiently strong sense of self will entail experiences that are nightmarish or may transform these "inner" states into an avenue for escape and withdrawal (Hunt, Gervais, Shearing-Johns, and Travis, 1992). Where basic self-esteem is deficient, we will be denied what are, at the very least, the pragmatic "good works" of spontaneous presentational states as direct realizations of presence-openness.

Conclusions

What have we learned, then, about consciousness — that most misleading of all fundamental concepts? Fully realized for its own sake, consciousness is very much in-the-world. It is a realization of presence into openness that on the deepest level must be sensed as compassionate, protecting, and nurturant. The basic dimensions of awareness are common to all sentient, motile creatures — so it is a "conscious-ness-with" in a way denied to us by traditional western thought. Developed in the form of presentational states in self-referential symbolic beings, consciousness *is* collective. There is no human condition more open to being shared communally than "religious experience." Traditional societies show us that. Shared presenta-tional states may indeed be the most fundamental source of a sense of community. Fully articulated in a supportive and guiding social environment, presentational states convey the sense — possibly quite accurate — that we cannot be anything other than at home in this universe and that we cannot be — as social symbolic beings — truly alone.

In an era where openness has seemed a mere "nothing" and presence a post-modern "deletion of the subject," it is perhaps worth noting that, as symbolizing beings turned around on the basic organization of ambient perception, we do have a definite structure, after all. That structure, however, rests on a perceptual dimension of presence-openness which must open us out and up in a way that cannot be finally "closed" within any conceptual system or order. Depending on whether our context becomes one of fear or hope, our horizonal openness becomes either cruel illusion and the source of our invisibility, nothingness, and driven pointlessness, or the basis of our sense of freedom and of Being as ultimately compassionate. As self-referen-tial beings, we are turned around on a fixed structure whose full realization becomes an open window into whatever we choose to *be* and to *let* encompass us.

Notes

Chapter 1: What Is Consciousness?

1. By way of synopsis we could say that the necessary asymmetry between consciousness$_1$ (interpersonal) and consciousness$_2$ (personal), described by Mead's model of symbolic cognition as a "taking the role of the other," produces something like Freud's unconscious, elicits consciousness$_4$ (reflexive) as an emergent possibility that makes consciousness$_3$ (primary awareness) partially visible, and entails a constant flux between consciousness$_7$ (integrative) and consciousness$_5$ (divided). Consciousness$_6$, as the behavioral side of an intentionally embedded and ordinarily backwardly masked consciousness$_3$, constitutes the necessary background state of arousal for all these transformations to unfold.

2. Although unintelligible without each other, the grammatical differences between first- and third-person access to experience are also open to various forms of use and exploitation in particular cultures: "How is it with feelings being private or hidden? A society in which the ruling class speaks a language which the serving class cannot learn. The upper class places great importance on the lower one never guessing what they feel. In this way they become unfathomable, mysterious" (Wittgenstein, 1992, p. 37).

Chapter 2: Cognition and Consciousness

1. Although it might be logically possible to construct a neo-Wittgensteinean model of altered states of consciousness as the epiphenomena of language and grammar, I have as yet been unable to see how such an account would actually work. That model would also have to explain, on the basis of their supposedly linguistic genesis, why subjects so uniformly insist on the difficulty of describing these states verbally *and* the experimental correlations between the propensity for such states and

measures of nonverbal spatial skills. Parsimony would seem to dictate a theory based on a nonverbal imagistic intelligence.

While Harré (1983) offers the beginnings of a "grammatical" model of states of consciousness, I do not see how this approach begins to account for the detailed phenomenologies to be covered in chapters 7, 8, and 10. He seems forced to regard such states as an attenuation of self-reference rather than its heightening.

2. Baars, along with most writers on consciousness in cognitive science and neurophysiology, tends to speak of consciousness as an "internal scanning" of *neural* areas, rather than as the perceptual awareness of an environment that Heidegger argues we lose when we substitute "consciousness" for "world." If consciousness is primarily qualitative and perceptual, it is hard to see what it could be "of" other than the world around us. We will find Gibson's approach to the ecological array to be the antidote for such implicit neurocognitive solipsism.

3. A similar account can be given of Libet's earlier (1978) demonstration of an apparent backward referral in time of conscious sensation. Subjects were able to signal with their right hand their registration of direct electrical stimulation to the cortex (in the tradition of Penfield, 1975). It required a 500 millisecond stimulation for any conscious registration of these cortically elicited sensations. With their left hand these subjects were asked to signal their immediate awareness of a perceived tactile stimulus (requiring between 100 and 200 milliseconds for most subjects). By comparing the temporal separation of the two perceptions, Libet was able to conclude that subjects "backwardly referred" the tactile stimulus to 20 milliseconds after it had actually been administered. This was well within the nonconscious first 100 milliseconds of the cortical evoked response, but not prior to the more diffuse autonomic responsiveness located in subliminal studies (Dixon, 1981). Accordingly, it seems most plausible to suggest that subjects were not "backwardly referring" at all, but locating their first conscious awareness at the point of their diffuse sense of something emerging, which will shortly be finished as a more recognizable focal awareness. After all, the awarenesses of the Würzburg introspectors may have been impalpable and vague, but they were definitely sensed enough to be timed with stopwatches. Libet may have been studying that microgenesis of perception out of which full recognition emerges but which can be diffusely sensed as such prior to that completion.

4. One of the best, if somewhat "in-house," demonstrations that the cognitive awareness system and the cognitive unconscious are coordinated as two sides of the same dimension comes from reviews of research on consciousness by Holender (1986) and Velmans (1991). Using the same widely cited studies on subliminal perception, implicit awareness, tachistoscopic masking, parafoveal vision, and dichotic listening, Holender concludes that the cognitive unconscious actually consists in micromoments of awareness that are ordinarily backwardly masked by more finished forms of consciousness. Velmans, on the other hand, refutes the view of consciousness as any sort of causal capacity in its own right by attempting to separate subjective awareness from functional attention, which he suggests can operate nonconsciously to perform all the functions attributed to a conscious awareness system. Essentially, cognitive research that one group of researchers explains in terms of "consciousness" are explained as "unconscious" by another group.

5. One of the more interesting ways of seeing Freud's "system unconscious" as not intrinsically outside awareness is to consider Matte-Blanco's (1988) attempt to formalize the features that Freud ascribed to his unconscious in terms of a more general logic of symmetry and identity. Freud's characterization of the unconscious in terms of absence of contradiction (simultaneous coexistence of contrary meanings), timelessness, and the lack of any negation is for Matte-Blanco based on a logic of "infinite sets," in which all possible sets are equivalent to each other and included within a sensed totality — the principle of identity here completely triumphant over any

analytical differentiation. Indeed, some principle of symmetricization of meaning does seem to be entailed by psychoanalytic descriptions of condensation, displacement, projection, and symbiotic identification, since they all involve the triumph of perceived identity over perceived difference. Yet it seems clear that the identity of everything with everything else is exactly the description, here fully conscious, of experiences in spontaneous mystical states. The philosopher J. N. Findlay (1970) has posited a specific logic of mysticism based on just such a principle of an enhanced identity that totally supersedes difference and diversity. If experience organized in the terms that Matte-Blanco attributes to the system unconscious can and does occur as the full expression of a conscious awareness system in its presentational aspect, then such experience is not intrinsically unconscious but more typically subordinated to the pragmatic representational symbolism of everyday life.

Chapter 3: Consciousness as Emergent

1. There is some irony in Sperry's insistence on a principle of holistic emergence in the relation of consciousness and brain, on the one hand, and his historical review of the concept of emergence itself (1987), which he painstakingly traces to his own presentation of the concept of downward control in 1964. Apparently, the sort of emergent properties often referred to as *Zeitgeist* in the history of ideas did not obtain in this particular instance. Field theoretical concepts and holism were important notions within gestalt psychology (Köhler, 1947) and systems theory (Von Bertalanffy, 1952), and while their extension to the neurophysiology of consciousness is certainly laudable, its causal status for the contemporary spread of doctrines of emergent holism is not so clear.

   To follow Italo Calvino's strategy in *Cosmi-Comics* (1968) and anthropomorphize Sperry's individual water molecules riding on the surface of a wave, certainly they will all know something big is happening, and when they see the crest forming just ahead of them, they have every right to be proud of their precursor status. But when the single molecule at the very tip of the fully poised crest — with a uniquely good view that is surely worthy of study in its own right — concludes that it caused the wave to break, well, that's too much.

2. An example of a simple nonlinear, iterative equation that can produce chaotic patterns uniquely dependent on initial values is $y \rightarrow ay^2 + c$. This signifies that the next value of y is a product of the value of y just computed (van Eerwyk, 1991). An equation of oscillating or mutual inhibition whose values bifurcate in opposite ways at a fixed point, depicting, say, predator-prey population ratios, is $x_j + 1 = rx(1 - x)$. Here values of x are substituted on the basis of previous values of x in the equation, but when the rate of change (r) reaches a value between 3 and 4, subsequent values of x will bifurcate in unpredictable and emergent ways.

3. Wittgenstein's best demonstration of the continual openness of the context of our propositional knowledge comes from *On Certainty* (1969), where he shows that there are no "atomic," incontrovertible, or fundamental propositions, as G. E. Moore had thought, of "this is my hand" and other expressions of common sense as a potentially fixed system. Wittgenstein recontextualized "this is my hand" as follows: an attacking tribe has herded all surviving males together and has ruthlessly chopped off all their right hands, which now lie in a pile in the center of the village. After the conquerors leave, the men gather around the pile. One exclaims, "This is my hand!" Another answers, "No, it's not."

4. Whereas Gordon Globus (1988) has called attention to parallels between Gibson's ambient array and Heidegger's being-in-the-world, my own approach is based on the integration of the two gradually developed by Terry Swanlund (personal communication).

5. Natsoulas (1983, 1989, 1991), whose definition of primary awareness specifically includes the "is-like" aspect of immediate sentience, nonetheless has attempted to insert a dimension of "presentational content" or "internal perceptual content" into Gibson's account of direct perception. Natsoulas is surely correct that Gibson's streaming perspective and propriolocation entail primary awareness, and Gibson himself added the introspective or self-referential attitude to perception that Natsoulas (1992) terms "reflexive seeing" and which is basic to the pictorial attitude in aesthetics. However, the explicit insertion of "internal" phenomenal content into direct perception would commit us to just the splitting of subject and object that Gibson, Heidegger, and Natsoulas himself on primary awareness would have us avoid. Only confusion can result from inserting into Gibson's account what is already there twice over.

   That said, Natsoulas's more general cognitive reading and Globus's existential-phenomenological view of Gibson fit well with Reed's (1988) exhaustive survey of direct perception and its basically phenomenological implications — especially important in the face of various attempts to turn direct perception into a physics of light refraction.

6. Richard Rorty, in his influential *Philosophy and the Mirror of Nature* (1979), cites the ancient notion of perception and thought as "mirrors" of their referents, with the attendant implications, he claims, of truth conceived as accuracy and correspondence. This, he holds, became a pernicious and misleading metaphor blocking the full development of the post-Kantian constructivism and relativism that he espouses. However, mirrors were not silvered until the 1600s. Thus the mirror metaphor that runs through ancient and medieval thought described the *transformations* of appearances in metal and liquid mirrors, rather than anything to do with accuracy or perfect correspondence (Miller, 1986). "Reflection" and "mirroring" just do not have the connotations in classical thought that Rorty finds so pernicious as metaphors of knowledge. They are actually closest to Heidegger's being-in-the-world, as an inseparable coalition of subject and object, each nested into the other and only definable in terms of that reciprocal mirroring.

7. There is considerable ambiguity in Leibnitz's characterization of "bare monads" as the lower material correspondence to sentient perception. In some accounts (*The Monadology*) bare monads are the "dazed" and "unconscious" perceptions of plants. In other places (also in *The Monadology*) he seems to imply, by utilizing his logic of an infinitesimal calculus of minute differences to annihilate all absolute categorical distinctions, that small moments of consciousness — the *petit perceptions* so anticipatory of microgenesis — somehow merge into physical reality, thus earning him the epithet "animist." Most interesting for our purposes, however, are his statements (*New System on the Nature of Substances* and *Of Communication*) that bare monads are based on *analogues* to perception and drive in the dynamic forces that organize the physical universe — as exemplified by the fluid properties of wind and fire. In this context, he even suggests that within purely physical systems the "less distinct" patterns will be analogous to the acts of perception, while the "more distinct" patterns will be analogous to the objects perceived. This is astonishingly like discussions of reciprocal "resonance zones" in nonlinear excitable systems (Othmer, 1991), in which one system of interacting waves or flow dynamics entrains the other.

Chapter 4: Consciousness as Localized

1. Only in the final editing did I discover Sass's (1992) linkage of the hyperreflexivity of schizophrenic "first rank" symptoms (see my "involuntary introspection" analysis of these in chapter 6) and overactivation in the *left* hemisphere in this condition — possible compensating for a hypoactivation of the "context" conferring presentational consciousness of the right hemisphere. My approach here was to contrast the heightened self-awareness of schizophrenia with that of medita-

tion in terms of a context of anxiety and withdrawal versus one of organismic relaxation and equilibrium. It could well be that the former reflects a heightened self-awareness of the left hemisphere, with its bizarre "spatializations" of what would otherwise be more spontaneously felt. That would then contrast with the more fluid syntheses of a right-hemisphere predominant self-awareness. Or it could also be that the impaired felt meanings of the right hemisphere in schizophrenics must still process the defensive representations of the left.

2. Jerison (1973) has developed a model of the evolution of perception which would help create the basis for later direct cross-modal translations on the higher-primate and human levels. He suggests that the evolution of early, nocturnal, forest-dwelling mammals necessitated the gradual remodeling of audition so that it could give in sequential form the sort of information provided by visual perception in diurnal reptiles. The later diurnal shift in mammalian evolution would have led to the recasting of vision in terms of the more differentiated auditory sequences previously developed, thence to inform the complex tactile-kinesthetic sensitivities needed for prehensile, treetop living. Thus each sensory modality was differentiated on the template of another. The hierarchic integration of such mutually differentiated modalities thereby becomes more plausible and likely.

  Marshall McLuhan's (1964) account of the development of symbolic media similarly pictures radio as creating an imaginary space based on sound, setting the stage for television as a passive witnessing of those sound spaces. As with Jerison, each predominating medium informs the subsequent development of the next. At roughly the same time as Geschwind, McLuhan was putting forward his own "synesthetic" model of mind and media.

3. Although the preservation of verbal mediation cannot be ruled out as a potential factor in the study by Lee et al. (1988), neither can the possibility that language itself rests on these preserved neocortical cross-modal capacities. Subsequent studies are broadly consistent with this latter view. For instance, Shaw, Kentridge, and Aggleton (1990) compared a group of Korsakoff's patients, presumed to have diffuse cortical damage, with a postencephalitic group, hypothesized to have predominantly subcortical limbic deficits. While the postencephalitic groups had a deficit in cross-modal matching, but not the Korsakoff's patients, both groups showed equally severe decrement in a naming task based on the tactile identification of unusual objects. The authors suggest that this latter task would be based on a more complex cross-modal ability to visualize tactile patterns in order to name them. Oscar-Berman, Pulaski, Hutner, Weber, and Freedman (1990), on the other hand, found cross-modal matching deficits in another Korsakoff group, and report that cross-modal deficits in patients with Alzheimer's disease and Parkinson's disease were correlated with difficulties in naming ordinary objects. On balance, we could speculate that the encephalization in human beings of a lower limbically based cross-modal *association* ability would allow the more complex cross-modal *translations* that underlie more metaphoric and linguistic capacities.

4. I have concentrated primarily on cross-modal fusions among vision, touch-movement, and vocalization as the constituents of symbolic cognition. However, Levi-Strauss's (1969) analysis of mythologies as elaborate multiple-realm classification grids also highlights the importance and human uniqueness of gustatory and olfactory qualities and their complex associations and physiognomies. Levi-Strauss's analysis of the semantic significances of the foods, smells, and tastes of cooking within traditional mythological systems could itself be used to reach conclusions about the cross-modal transformational basis of the human mind. Levi-Strauss (1974), in fact, called attention to the existence of a syntax and logic within cross-modal correspondences and to their fundamental importance in symbolism.

5. Copious cross-modal translations in dolphins, also capable of manifesting the beginnings of self-

reference, recombinatory problem solving, and symbolic communication (Herman et al., 1984), and similar arguments for the abilities of parrots (Barber, 1993), along with striking anecdotal observations on elephants (Griffin, 1984), support the idea that our evolutionary line is one version of a structural possibility open to vertebrates with highly differentiated perceptual capabilities. Something like this structural inevitability for hierarchic integration seems assumed in the television series *Star Trek: The Next Generation,* where intelligent life throughout the galaxy develops along roughly similar lines. Maybe it's true.

Chapter 5: Animal Consciousness

1. Applewhite's (1979) final summation on associational learning in protozoa is perhaps uniquely admirable within contemporary science and is worth quoting in full: "Learning (beyond habituation) has not been adequately demonstrated in protozoa. Claims of learning have either not been confirmed in replications, or controls are lacking to rule out alternative explanations to learning. In spite of this, I find no a priori reason why protozoa cannot learn. Most of the protozoan experiments reported on here are relatively simple to perform and I would encourage their replication by others. As for me, I give up" (Applewhite, 1979, p. 352).

2. Although neurotransmitters and neuromodulators have not yet been implicated in the motility and sensitivity of protozoa, their well-established presence in plants as chemical messengers may suggest a mechanism available for reuse in the development of neural networks. Jaffe (1970) found acetylcholine in the growing tips and roots of bean seedlings, which he posits would help to regulate the more gradual shifts in ion flux across cell membranes that are found in all living cells and need to be distinguished from the more sudden action potentials of neurons and protozoa. There is some evidence of a reactive sensitivity in some protozoa to neurochemicals introduced into the environment. Van Houton (1981) reviewed studies showing a specific reactivity to acetylcholine, epinephrine, and norepinephrine. This does not mean that such neuro-chemicals are a natural part of the responsivities of protozoa. They may instead interact experimentally with adenosine triphosphate (ATP) as part of the central energy metabolism of living cells.

3. Moving plants, like *Mimosa* and *Drosera,* which Darwin (1881) likened to motile animals, along with certain algae, show action potentials based also on calcium influx and potassium efflux (Applewhite, 1975; Williams and Pickard, 1972ab; Toriyama and Jaffe, 1972; Higinbotham, 1973). These action potentials show habituation with repeated stimulation and disappear altogether under ether. They are graded depolarizations rather than all-or-none discharges, and they tend to last for hundreds of milliseconds, but they do show that there is a remarkable ubiquity in the principles underlying motility in all organisms.

   Still more remarkable is the demonstration by Pickard (1972) of spontaneous depolarizing spikes in the nonmotile *Ipomea pisum* and *Xanthiam.* Unlike the action potentials in motile insectivorous plants, these do not propagate across the stalk but appear to originate in one or a very few cells. Although generally not occurring at all, when they do appear they last between 100 and 400 milliseconds and can run in trains lasting from one second up to about two hours.

   If we provisionally follow the principle that it is motility that requires sentience for its guidance, as indexed by sudden depolarizations and hyperpolarizations of cell membranes, then we are left with the possibility of a sort of diffuse sentience in moving plants — which would not have seemed strange to Darwin and his postulation of evolutionary continuity in all functions. Going further, Pickard's (1972) research could be taken as implying that this sort of diffuse periodic sentience is actually vestigial in nonmoving plants as well (in contrast to Fechner's assumption of a continuously present sentience). This leaves us on ground remarkably like that covered by Bergson (1907), who suggested that the vegetative evolutionary line sacrificed consciousness along with the free motility from which it is inseparable in return for a continuous access to nutrients. Bergson pictured plants as in a comparative "torpor," within which sentience was nonetheless latent.

4. Since there seems to be a direct current polarized from negative to positive and going from head to tail in many creatures, and from dendrites to axons (Becker and Selden, 1985), and since anesthesia and coma reverse this charge, we could speculate that this polarity betokens a felt or vital sense of being as a basic readiness for movement within all sentient organisms, with depolarizing and hyperpolarizing fluctuations in membrane current as the resonance of that "charged presence" to an ambient flowing surround. To go much further along such lines, at present, however, may risk more of a Frankensteinian model of consciousness than either author or reader might wish.

5. Although we would expect function to precede structural instantiation for recombinatory cognition, at least in principle, it is not clear that certain partial anticipations of this ability necessarily entail the same cross-modal translations that seem to be involved in higher-primate, parrot, and dolphin intelligence. For instance, consider the waggle dance of bees: a forager indicates the direction of possible new food or nest locations to those who have remained behind in the hive by means of linear movements inside the hive in relation to the position of the sun. This is often taken as an emergent recombinatory intelligence (Griffin, 1976, 1984; Gould, 1990). It is not clear, however, whether this ostensible pointing or referring behavior is truly recombinatory. It seems more like transferring one form of kinesthetic mapping (outside the hive) into another socially shared one (inside the hive) rather than something in the manner of Köhler's or Goodall's chimpanzees. Similarly, Maier and Schneirla's (1964) demonstrations of "reasoning" as opposed to association learning in rats, where rats taught one part of a problem maze on one day and another the next day managed to combine this learning to reach a blocked food source, seem to involve more the combination of two spatial maps from the same general area into a unitary map (certainly remarkable in itself), rather than the reorganizations of perception demonstrated in higher primates.

6. It may be more than ironic that Searle's complaint that computers have syntax but no semantics — that is, no "understanding" of their own programs — is echoed by Terrace (1985), who observes that signing chimpanzees have incipient semantics but no syntax. It would seem that if we had to choose the loss of one or the other capacity, most of us would have little doubt as to which would be needed in order to preserve our most essential hominid status. Current artificial-intelligence programs, while on the verge of beating grand masters at chess, have contributed nothing to our comprehension of the multiple forms of life embedded in that hallowed game.

7. This is not to deny, however, the appearance of defensive, catatonic-like stupors *and* sexual perversions in highly stressed *captive* chimpanzees, but only positive absorptive trance and affiliative sexual foreplay in the wild. Logically, then, we could contrast the present cross-modal theory with a competing "zoo" model of the human mind — from which I will forbear.

Chapter 6: William James and the Stream of Consciousness

1. In a factor analytic study, Martindale and Martindale (1988) verified Bachelard (1942) and Jung (1944) on the utility of the classical humors, temperaments based on the varying preponderance of earth, air, fire, and water, as the underlying or most inclusive typology for contemporary terms describing interpersonal relations and aesthetic experience.

2. As D'Arcy Thompson (1961) states, it is a major error to regard the golden section simply as the "curve of life," in contrast to supposedly inorganic symmetries. Rather, symmetries are charac-

teristic of structures whose parts are produced relatively simultaneously, whether organic or inorganic. This would include the margins of leaves in Thompson's account, as well as the looming "explosions" of visual surfaces in Gibson's array, not to mention the more obviously symmetrical aspects of body shapes in living organisms. Golden-section ratios and spirals, considered most generally, appear wherever change is more gradual and preceding phases exert a continued influence on succeeding ones. It would not only include plant growth and, as Thompson puts it, the "frozen" or "dead" residues of growth in animal horns and seashell spirals, but any asymmetrical dynamic process slow enough to be influenced by its initial organization. This would seem to include many spiral galaxies. Lefebvre (1990) argues that cognitive "reflection" is not just a metaphor but follows from processes that physically turn around on their point of origin. It may be that the golden section will be produced by any asymmetrical stochastic series that sustains a middle course between outward dissipation and inward collapse.

Chapter 7: Synesthesia

1. Aristotle (*On the Soul*) would presumably have been well pleased with Boernstein. We will see (chapter 9) that although Aristotle would have agreed with Boernstein that the unity of the senses was conveyed in blood, his own account of the actual capacities of the *sensus communis* includes functions that later thinkers have regarded as emergent on the human level and so would entail a hierarchic integration of already differentiated modalities.
2. Something very like this "arbitrary yet functionally instilled" basis of physiognomy in semantic meaning can be seen in the way we can imbue the pictures and names of our favorite writers with much of the significance that we attach to their theories. We do this with theorists and friends, even though we know "rationally" that a person's character is not truly expressed in their face and that we see their face "as" their life only because we already know the latter so well. Such facial physiognomizing is part of the sensed meaning others have for us, while also showing that metaphor is always polysemic and open to alternative reorganizations.
3. For Wittgenstein, too, the "seeing as" or physiognomic aspect of language, without which our thought would be "mechanical," always entails the awareness of a relative novelty and appears where the overall organization of meaning undergoes a change: "*Astonishment* is essential to a change of aspect. And astonishment is thinking. . . . Being struck is related to thinking" (Wittgenstein, 1982, pp. 73, 91). We could say that the full empirical development of Wittgenstein's later philosophy of thinking only appears with Werner and Kaplan (1963), Arnheim (1969), Lakoff (1987), Johnson (1987), and McNeill (1992). Wittgenstein, for all his functionalism and pragmatism, looked very hard at the *experience* of thinking and spent a great deal of time in describing its "is like" in a way that directly anticipates these heterodox cognitive psychologies.
4. Where my own usage tends to treat physiognomies and synesthesias as two aspects of the same cross-modal processes, involving a common kinesthetic or "vital" embodiment, Lindauer (1991) demonstrates a decided priority for the use of strictly physiognomic words ("resistant," "peaceful") over more strictly synesthetic words ("hard," "quiet") in the forced-choice descriptions of both pictures and words. He suggests a two-step developmental process by which physiognomic perception precedes strictly intersensory semantic usage. Asch and Nerlove (1960) had similarly suggested that the understanding of the interpersonal side of double-function terms like "hard" or "bitter" develops slowly in childhood, as part of overall metaphoric capacity. Lindauer's ongoing research on this issue should prove to be of great importance in locating the developmental stages in what I am treating as a common synesthetic process underlying all symbolic cognition. However, the original facial mirroring of infancy, out of which more specific cross-modal matching

abilities would seem to develop, is impossible to conceptualize at all without reference to a dynamic cross-modal translation capacity. The general use of the term "synesthesia" has the advantage of indicating such a general cross-modal process, and it is used here to imply a broad family of closely related states.

5. The sensed glow, opening out and emanating calm, that can come with meditative absorption is well depicted by the qualities of luminosity in the clear night sky about an hour before dawn. As you look toward the area in which the sun will emerge, there is at some point, along with the sense that it must have been there before this first noticing, a faint glow in the sky. The stars are still visible through the glow, and it is, as you stare now directly at "it," suddenly impossible to localize. It is not exactly in the same depth orientation as the blue sky of daylight, but it is certainly beneath and within the clear night darkness. As you continue to look, you can think that really there is no difference after all from the rest of the sky, or that it is now so subtle, what you took as so definite just before, that it may have been created simply by staring. So you look away, directly up into the starry darkness. But, no, when you look back a few moments later there it is again — an utterly subtle glow, almost with something like a definite fluffy texture, but not quite. And now it is clearly brighter than the first time you noticed it. Yet as you make your gaze more directly investigatory again, the same sequence is repeated. It must have been an illusion, after all. It didn't really exist. So you look back to the now seemingly less bright and shining stars, and out of the corner of your eye there it is again, spreading and welling forth in and as the sky, a texture without a surface, a depth without dimension, but somehow very fine to watch — gentle, allowing and giving forth the day to be. This remarkable phenomenon is mirrored in both meditative accounts of eyes-closed luminosities and experimental introspectionist accounts of luster and glow. The predawn sky has always been our best symbol of all that is promising and open and beneficent in human life.

Chapter 8: The Multiplicity of Image

1. Pylyshyn's (1984) intense skepticism about all things imaginal extends to his treatment of Mozart's assertion of his ability to "see the whole" of a work in composition "at a glance" and "hear it all at once." Since there is no specific medium in which the sequential complexity of music could be presented simultaneously, Pylyshyn takes Mozart's assertions as by definition pertaining to a logical-propositional understanding and not to direct experience. From the present point of view, it is indeed possible to experience as immediately given a simultaneous geometric-dynamic translation of the complex, sequential structure of music. Such a structure would be neither visual nor auditory but an immediately felt fusion of both, exactly as Mozart describes. Such quasi-imagistic emergents would be definitely sensed and understood but also nonlocalizable and impossible to describe in any precise terminology — again exactly what Mozart seems to be saying.

2. Rock, Wheeler, and Tudor (1989) showed the difficulty that subjects have in imaginally rotating randomly shaped bits of wire, indicating that what cannot be easily recognized in ongoing perception will not make for good imagery either. An earlier study by Rock (1983) found that subjects had some difficulty, to begin with, in recognizing such physical shapes when rotated into different orientations. Certainly for Rock, imagery is a kind of description, but this is his characterization of recognitive perception as well. Shape recognition for Rock is highly dependent on position and orientation in the vertical, in contrast to the spatial transformations so basic to Gibson's direct perception.

3. Various arguments have been made as to why such claims by scientists and inventors should not

be credited, and their imagery seen instead as the by-product of previously realized propositional knowledge (Blagrove, 1993). There has been some skepticism, for instance, about Kekule's claim that his benzene insights actually originated from his spiraling serpent imagery, because he did not report this fact at the conference where he first presented his conclusions but only many years later, when such a claim might justify his ignoring the contributions to this discovery made by others (Rudofsky and Wotiz, 1988). But Kekule is not alone, as Shepard shows, in making such claims, and despite its unorthodoxy the young Kekule apparently did report his imagery at the time (Ramsay and Rocke, 1984). The alternative for such critics would be a more gradualist model of scientific insight, with the "ah-ha" states of sudden novel meaning relegated to background importance — despite their prominence in anectodal accounts. If synesthetic imagery is simply the secondary expression of knowledge already consolidated, it is difficult to see why its implications are often so difficult to put into words and take so long to dawn.

Chapter 9: *Sensus Communis*

1. When Plotinus says that consciousness, meaning immediate self-knowledge, is a "conpercep-tion" (literally, *synaisthesis,* p. 380), this might seem identical to the present thesis of human consciousness as a synesthesia. But Plotinus means here fusion or synthesis of multiple percep-tions, with no implication that it be cross-modal. He would know of Aristotle's *coeno-aisthesis* and see it as lower, hardly the principle of the soul. Aristotle and Plotinus thus fall on either side of the thesis of this book.

2. Chidester (1992) has documented the way in which the Christian mystics Origen and Augustine understood the classical "inner sense" as the basis of a unified experience of the divine in which the light of god is able to speak. The mergence of the senses was paradoxical and so allowed for the potentiality of transcendent experience. Such experience constituted a higher "intellectual vision" superior to ordinary reason. The language of the great Christian mystics is, of course, full of the richest synesthetic references (Underhill, 1955).

3. This is perhaps the best place to distance the present approach from Julian Jaynes's elaborate reconstruction of a "bicameral mind" as evinced in Homer and Hesiod. Jaynes's approach to human consciousness differs fundamentally from the present one, yet shares a similar emphasis on metaphor and the dialogic structure of mind.

   In *The Origin of Consciousness in the Breakdown of the Bicameral Mind* (1976) Jaynes advances some novel reasons for a very traditional idea — that the fully self-referential conceptual mind is a rather recent historical creation. His account separates us from the "primitivity" charac-teristic of most traditional peoples, which for Jaynes includes Greece before 1200 B.C. Before then, he argues, no concept of mind existed, and thought actually consisted in verbal hallucina-tions in which "the gods" — later to become the self-referential linguistic capacity of the left hemisphere — told people what to do and why.

   Jaynes can only make his elaborate historical model work by ignoring the fieldwork of cultural anthropologists, since it is their almost uniform conclusion that native peoples are rather like ourselves in the most fundamental modes of consciousness. Jaynes's concept of the bicameral mind can only be made consistent with the data of cultural anthropology if first contacts with westerners almost instantaneously resulted in a switch from the previous hallucinatory mode to our form of language-based, volitional self-reference. In addition, Jaynes must ignore evidence that the form of numinous experience in hunter-gatherer shamanism is predominantly visual-spatial, not auditory. Bourguignon (1973) distinguishes the "vision trance" and emphasis on archetypal dreaming in hunter-gatherer peoples from the auditory "possession trance" that emerges in more settled peoples.

It may well be that what Jaynes is really tracing in the *Iliad* is not an original consciousness, as he seems to believe, but the language-centered developments that occur under the pressures of increasingly complex socioeconomic organization — pressures that many thinkers believe lead toward restrictions in the fullest potentialities of consciousness. Certainly hunter-gatherer peoples are dream and trance centered in a way that has often struck anthropologists. The reappearance and further development of vision trance in the various meditative traditions certainly attest to a self-referential symbolic consciousness not primarily based on the linguistic system and capable of undergoing its own specialized development in a suitable social context.

In addition to his insistence that self-consciousness is a secondary by-product of language, Jaynes (1986) is reluctant to posit any more immediate form of navigational sentience that would characterize the life-worlds of less complex, nonsymbolic organisms. I have already stressed the trade-off involved in such restrictions of consciousness and its varieties. I would prefer not to have to theorize about why protozoa look and act *as though* they are sentient, but somehow really are not. Jaynes, at this very point, clings to a methodological behaviorism that only lets us off the hook if we already accept its reductionist, eliminativist assumptions. We may do so at our peril. I would prefer that as a discipline we worry less about how far "down" to extend our empathy, with the admitted risk that we might fall into anthropomorphizing white blood cells, than that we continue a program of restricting whatever may be left of our empathic capacities to the point where various philosophical and psychological positivist writers have actually come to doubt consciousness in ourselves. The risk will be, as Heidegger saw, that we finally dismiss our own experience as unimportant.

4. Margaret Janzen, a registered nurse and massage therapist in St. Catharines, Ontario, has pointed out to me in regard to this "vertical" axis of consciousness in the Greek tradition that there is a separate "pulse" or oscillating rhythm of the cerebrospinal system, difficult to detect but distinct from the pulse rate of the cardiovascular system. Given the Greek fascination with the body, closely observed in athletics and war as well as in the slaughtering and sacrificing of animals, it seems likely that they would have noticed this different, more subtle "craniosacral rhythm" and, indeed, that it might have been part of the basis for their positing separate "horizontal" and "vertical" axes of consciousness.

Chapter 10: A Cognitive Psychology of Transpersonal States

1. There are some interesting differences among the Hindu version of the chakras in Kundalini practice, the chakras and Dumo heat activation as developed by Tibetan Buddhism, the Taoist "circulation of the light," and the Sufi lataif system — the latter being more subtle centers than the classical chakras (Almaas, 1986a). The seven chakras of classical yoga are generally energized in an ascending, transcendental sequence of activation only. The system of chakras described in Tibetan Buddhism varies between the classical seven of Indian tradition, a simplified five-chakra version, and the still more basic four-chakra account of the fourteenth-century sage Longchenpa (1976). Here, in addition, there are two sequences of activation, a descending process of the melting and gathering of energies, associated more with experiences of vital presence, and a second ascending sequence approaching the white light of the void.

The channels of the subtle body in Taoistic yoga are very differently organized. In the Taoistic circulation of the light (Luk, 1958), which at certain points does lead to out-of-body and white-light states very similar to the above accounts, the "inner" or meditative breath is visualized as drawn in down the front of the body, held, and then sent back up the spine to the head and back down again to the diaphragm — as the place for the storage of the sublimated sexual energies of vital embodiment. The centers of bodily energy are also more explicitly identified with internal bodily organs (kidney, liver, etc.) in both Taoistic and Sufi mysticism than is the case with the chakras of the central channel in Indian yogic tradition. See Mann and Short (1990) and Almaas (1986a) for a more detailed discussion of these differences.

2. A similar process seems to be involved, albeit involuntary and less benign, in conversion and confessional states associated with torture and brainwashing (Fischer, 1975). The fasting, lack of sleep, and pain from motionless sitting associated with long-term meditative retreats and combined with the cultivation of appropriate imagery can lead to especially intense moments of felt meaning which can similarly solidify one's understanding of such teachings. The key difference from brainwashing is the volitional nature of meditative practice and some understanding of the purposes of these physical hardships.

3. It might seem that Reichian bioenergetics differs from the meditative chakra traditions in outlining only the descending sequence leading to bodily vitalization and sense of felt presence. While this is literally true in terms of Reich's own writings on therapeutic practice and those of his successors (Sharaf, 1983), Reich's largely dismissed later work, in which he thought he had discovered "orgone" as the physical basis of a life energy coordinated with "cosmic" processes (Reich, 1951), does reflect, albeit metaphorically, the more impersonal and transcendent ascending sequence. The problem was that without a cultural tradition to support his later, more overtly transpersonal phase, and buffeted by disastrous political intrusions, as well as being victimized by just the narcissistic personal pathology that will also be stirred up by higher states of consciousness, he was doomed to a progressive idiosyncracy and isolation.

Chapter 11: Heidegger, Mahayana Buddhism, and Gibson's Ambient Array

1. There are, of course, some other ways of approaching a convergence of Heidegger (or existential phenomenology in general) and eastern thought. By the mid-1930s Heidegger had become aware of parallels between his attempt to revive a sense of Being within the western tradition and both Zen Buddhism and Taoism. This resulted in some collaborative studies and contacts with representatives of these traditions (Caputo, 1986; Parkes, 1987). Such parallels are important, and in some respects may have actually influenced his later, more mystical thought, but Guenther's translation of Tibetan Buddhist sources into Heideggerian phraseology, based on the identical metaphors in each, seems to me the potentially deeper resonance — and is the one pursued herein. Along a somewhat different line, Varela, Thompson, and Rosch (1991) have labored to tie together Mahayana Buddhism with cognitive psychology by way of Merleau-Ponty's (1964) approach to knowledge as vitally "embodied" and Maturana and Varela's (1987) work on the spontaneous autopoiesis or self-organization of all living systems.

2. The "mystical element" in Heidegger's later thought was hardly an addition to his earlier work but rather a making more explicit of his fundamental intentions. Caputo (1986) has demonstrated how closely Heidegger's account of the *Dasein-Sein* relationship is a naturalistic and phenomenological restatement of the mysticism of Meister Eckhart on the relation of soul and godhead. Similarly, Kisiel (1992), in analyzing the young Heidegger's essays and correspondence, has shown how his later analytic of *Dasein* was intended as an attempt to describe the structure of experience in everyday life in such a way as to show how the "transcendence" of medieval Catholicism would be its inevitable consequence.

3. The extent of this more experiential opening out of the analysis of *Dasein* from 1927 is seen in Heidegger's statement in 1964 that if *Sein und Zeit (Being and Time)* were to be published for the first time, then it would have the title *Lichtung und Anwesenheit (Opening and Presence)* (Caputo, 1986). Being is now understood as the opening or shining forth that "gives" our presence.

4. We cannot leave this discussion of Heidegger's mystical element without some mention of the recent, controversial, and often strident debate over the importance of his Nazi involvements as rector of the University of Freiburg and of his pro-Nazi speeches in 1933 and 1934. Opinions on this issue range from the view that such involvements are irrelevant to the evaluation of his philosophy, or at worst reflect a temporary aberration in his midlife development, to the stronger assertions that all his work is thereby exposed as implicitly authoritarian and fascist.

Certainly my view here, that the import of Heidegger's later thought lies in his phenomeno-logical and ultimately naturalistic restatement of the experiential core of human spirituality, means that we cannot simply ignore Heidegger's pre-war Nazism. If, at the extreme, Heidegger is to be regarded as one of the great spiritual thinkers of this century, then some accounting of such a colossal failing is surely required.

While I hope to present a psychological treatment of this matter separately, two points might be worth mentioning here. First, Heidegger's own version of Nazism shunned the crude racism and biological doctrines of Aryan supremacy that defined Nazi orthodoxy. Consistent with his romanticizing of the "authenticity" of the soldier at the front in his early writings (Kisiel, 1992), Heidegger was drawn to the Röhm faction of the S.A. — with its militaristic ideology based on the *Freikorp* veterans and its emphasis on the Black Forest youth camps that Heidegger enthusi-astically sponsored and participated in while rector (Farias, 1989). The assassination of Röhm in 1934 followed shortly on Heidegger's resignation of the rectorship and marked the end of his active involvement with the Nazis. By his own account, his later reaction to this early enthusiasm was one of "shame" (Ott, 1993).

Second, and consistent with our discussion of the close relationship between transpersonal experience and characterological "metapathologies" related to narcissistic grandiosity and emo-tional withdrawal, it should be noted that Heidegger, after his astonishing early success with *Being and Time*, by 1933 hoped to become the "spiritual Führer" of Germany — the equivalent of Hitler in the cultural sphere (Farias, 1989). Whatever the personal opportunism that was at times involved, this surely suggests the sort of metapathological complication of genuine spiritual development described by Maslow, Almaas, and Engler. Rather than invalidate the claim that the direction of Heidegger's thought follows a genuinely spiritual path, his absurd grandiosity and complete failure to understand his social-historical surroundings, with so many close Jewish students and colleagues now in danger, may rather attest to the sort of struggle with "inflation" that Jung, among others, saw as a by-product of numinous awareness.

It was Heidegger's misfortune to go through this period of grandiosity and worship of the will — so absent in his later more contemplative thought — not only during the precise years that Levinson (1978) documents as ripe for mid-life crisis, but coincident with the incipient collective insanity of Nazism — by which so many other neo-romantics, including Jung (Maidenbaum and Martin, eds., 1991), were briefly attracted. Heidegger thought that the Nazis represented a rejec-tion of technology and technological control over society (Zimmerman, 1990), which surely confirms the dangers of genuinely unpolitical people getting caught up in the enthusiasm of mass movements.

All the collective movements of the 1930s, on whatever side of whatever ideological line, seem to have elicited an essentially religious sense of inspiration that many of their adherents came to regret. Heidegger's own version of this latter was his supposedly infamous "silence" and his "shame" — not, after all, one of the more "noisy" emotions. Heidegger's continued conserva-tism and wish that National Socialism had not gone "wrong" are not "evidence" of much of anything other than that he was typical of postwar Germans of his age and social class.

5. Heidegger is phenomenologically "correct" in saying that clearings in the woods are indeed

revealed by and hidden behind the shining light they permit and "gather." This is especially striking on clear moonlit nights. Walking a familiar trail through thick woods under a full moon (any other circumstances being nearly suicidal), one will be periodically struck by strange volumic patterns of glow here and there in the distance as one inspects the woods around. The contrast with the surrounding darkness is so striking that these wellings forth can appear almost like weirdly shaped dwellings and fantastic objects. On investigation, they are the result of the gathering of moonlight within physical clearings in the woods, often too small to be easily noted as such during the daylight hours. The glow of moonlight lets these clearings become apparent as what they are — an apt metaphor for the way that the welling forth of specific events lets "isness" appear as such and at the same time obscures our awareness of this "allowing" or "gift" through our very attention to what has been given.

6. I am especially indebted to Terry Swanlund (personal communications) throughout this discussion on the location of Gibson's ambient array in relation to Heidegger's being-in-the-world. I completely agree with him that what is missing in Heidegger's analysis of presence-openness is precisely Gibson's ambient array, and that its inclusion as the common ground of humans and animals would have made Heidegger a still more revolutionary and foundational thinker.

7. Aside from the recently translated Parmenides lectures (1942), the major source for Heidegger's views on the "world-poor" nature of animals has been the untranslated 1929–30 lectures titled *The Fundamental Concepts of Metaphysics: World — Finitude — Solitude*. Extensive discussions and partial translations of this invaluable material, very much based on Heidegger's reading of Von Uexküll on the "bubble" of perception in animals, can be found in Olafson (1987), Zimmerman (1990), and Krell (1992). The latter argues, similarly to the view herein, that what Heidegger rejected, unfortunately, was the obvious link between his approach to human existence and the "life philosophies" of Bergson and Whitehead.

Chapter 12: Consciousness as Time

1. The specific envelope of flow welling forth out of horizonal openness constitutes an ever-renewed increase in pattern and energy. In that formal sense, all sentient creatures are looking "back up" the dissipative line of increasing entropy toward the principles of spontaneous self-organization that characterize both its early post-big-bang stages and the nonlinear fluid systems that are the immediate physical surround of living systems. In this formal sense, then, sentient creatures, in their charged presence before horizonal openness, are, with the alchemists, "present at creation." Again and again, intricate patterns of flow keep emerging out of a "nothing." Certainly, this is a key aspect of the dimension of time in sentient beings.

2. The very notion of a basic psychological moment has also come in for criticism. On some accounts, there is just too much variability caused by the nature of the experimental stimuli, their intensity, and sensory modality to admit of a moment of set duration that would be truly common to all research studies. If we consider such moments in terms of the more simple, peripherally based ability to detect successive versus simultaneous presentations of simple stimuli such as lights, clicks, or taps, such intervals do vary by modality, and all fall considerably short of the 100 milliseconds that seems to be the constant for central processing (Pöppel, 1988).

3. It is interesting to note a striking difference in the emotional impact of these image-driven felt meanings common to LSD-induced and meditative accounts, depending on whether the observer of these "mind moments" becomes absorbed primarily in the successive decline of each burst or in its emerging edge, perpetually welling forth out of light. The "down side," usually noticed first, comes to be felt as an elongated, "cosmic" dying. The emerging side, requiring deeper introspective sensitization, is correspondingly often sensed as "creation" itself. Thus, in Buddhist medita-

tion accounts (Goleman, 1972; Wilber, 1990) the preliminary realization of emptiness can be a horrifying sense of a ceaseless flux leading into decay and cessation, while the more fully realized experience becomes an emergent opening out or welling forth as the "gift" of luminosity. Something of this same shift is found in the change from the early Heidegger's approach to Being through "death" to his later evocative sense of "isness" as a shining or welling forth.

4. Fechner (1901), experimental psychology's perplexing "father," also put forward a psychological version of the afterlife — in third-person perspective. The dead live on in a psychic gestalt made by the sum and synthesis of all their effects on others. Thus Hitler and Jesus have very long afterlives, while most people fade out completely over a few generations even within their own families. Our first-person version is of course quite differently constituted — and lasts considerably "longer."

Chapter 13: Consciousness as Space

1. This situation is complicated by the tendency of some physicists to incorporate consciousness into quantum theory as a causal phenomenon (as reviewed by Goertzel, 1992; Goswami, 1990). They speculate that it would be consciousness itself that collapses the probabilistic wave packets of light into single particle trajectories. In effect, it is measurement that creates the reality. With Penrose (1989), I would suggest that the very closeness of the principles of subatomic fields to the organizing principles of consciousness, and the fact that our observations do *de facto* determine one outcome out of the many possible in probabilistic realms, has been confused with causation — a sophisticated version of animism.

2. This appeal to the common rooting of consciousness and physics in the hidden structures of perception should not be confused with any of the stronger versions of the anthropic principle, which would have it that we are somehow "intended" within the physical universe (see Hawking, 1990). Rather, I am saying that our nature cannot be totally inconsistent with the levels of physical reality, or else we would not exist. The question then becomes the degree — quite possibly variable — to which various levels of this reality are reflected within the perceptual capacities of creatures that must be sensitive to the organization of at least part of that universe. Our perception should be congruent with the universe within which we find ourselves and out of which we have developed, without that entailing any intention in our emergence. This leaves sufficient room, I suspect, for the idea that the function of a self-referential creature once so emerged is the witnessing of Being as such. We would be, with Jung and Heidegger, Being seeing itself. That is, after all, something we can do that cyclones and quantum fields cannot.

3. Mann (1992) makes a related point about his nonlinear dynamic models of cognitive reflexivity and the self.

Chapter 14: Consciousness as Society

1. These historical and cross-cultural precedents for the periodic resurgence of mysticism make suitable nonsense of various "new-age" speculations that the human brain is somehow evolving toward a condition of increasing openness to contemplative states. The conditions for what is happening to us seem more plausibly social-historical.

2. Of course, this is not to deny the more socially negative effects of these movements. Prophetical fundamentalisms, with their ethical absolutism, easily end up killing those who refuse to be included, while mysticism in a complex society risks a politically meaningless withdrawal from all in the world that it fails to influence.

3. The idea of a common or shared mentality in subjects as the source of significant laboratory ESP

effects also gains strength from the very implausibility of the various "physical" theories suggested to account for parapsychological phenomena. Quantum fields organized in terms of psychological processes (LeShan, 1969; Wallace, 1986; Irwin, 1989) have the difficulty of explaining why such fields would not be swamped by the noise of other high-energy particles. How *would* they preserve their integrity long enough to "communicate" through it? The only other remotely plausible physical theory posits waves based on geomagnetic and electromagnetic activity (Irwin, 1989). It is difficult to see, however, how these effects could be sustained over long-enough distances to match the more "distant" successes of many parapsychological findings. The replicated demonstrations of Persinger (Persinger and Krippner, 1989; Berger and Persinger, 1991), showing the association of significant laboratory ESP studies with low levels of background geomagnetic activity, only establish that different levels of geomagnetic activity make certain kinds of imagery experience more likely — along with numerous other, more psychological variables, like imaginative absorption.

References

Aaronson, B. 1971. Time, time stance, and existence. *Studium Generale* 24:369–87.

——. 1968. Hypnosis, time rate perception, and personality. *Journal of Schizophrenia* 2:11–41.

——. 1966. Behavior and the place names of time. *American Journal of Hypnosis* 9:1–17.

Abraham, R., and C. Shaw. 1988. *Dynamics: The geometry of behavior.* Part 4: *Bifuration behavior.* Santa Cruz: Aerial Press.

——. 1985. *Dynamics: The geometry of behavior.* Part 3: *Global behavior.* Santa Cruz: Aerial Press.

——. 1984. *Dynamics: The geometry of behavior.* Part 2: *Chaotic behavior.* Santa Cruz: Aerial Press.

——. 1983. *Dynamics: The geometry of behavior.* Part 1: *Periodic behavior.* Santa Cruz: Aerial Press.

Ach, N. 1905. Determining tendencies: Awareness. In D. Rapaport, ed., *Organization and pathology of thought.* New York: Columbia University Press, 1951, pp. 15–38.

Adams-Webber, J. 1990. A model of reflexion from the perspective of personal construct theory. In H. Wheeler, ed., *The structure of human reflexion: The reflexional psychology of Vladimir Lefebvre.* New York: Peter Lang, pp. 93–112.

——. 1979. *Personal construct theory: Concepts and applications.* New York: John Wiley.

Aihara, K., and G. Matsumoto. 1986. Chaotic oscillations and bifurcations in squid giant axons. In A. V. Holden, ed., *Chaos.* Manchester: Manchester University Press, pp. 257–69.

Alcock, J. 1981. *Parapsychology: Science or magic?* Oxford: Pergamon.

Alexander, C. N., R. W. Cranson, R. W. Boyer, and D. W. Orme-Johnson. 1987. Transcendental consciousness: A fourth state beyond sleep, dreaming, and waking. In J. Gackenbach, ed., *Sleep and dreams: A sourcebook.* New York: Garland. pp. 282–315.

Alexander, C. N., J. L. Davies, C. N. Dixon, M. C. Dillbeck, K. M. Oetzel, J. K. Muehlman, and D. W. Orme-Johnson. 1990. Higher stages of consciousness beyond formal operations: The Vedic psychology of human development. In C. N. Alexander and E. J. Langer, eds., *Higher stages of human development: Adult growth beyond formal operations.* New York: Oxford, pp. 286–341.

Allport, D. 1968. Phenomenal simultaneity and the perceptual moment hypothesis. *British Journal of Psychology* 59:395–406.

Allport, F. 1955. Theories of perception and the concept of structure. New York: John Wiley.

Almaas, A. H. 1988. *The pearl beyond price — integration of personality into being: An object relations approach.* Berkeley: Diamond Books.

———. 1986a. *Essence — the diamond approach to inner realization.* York Beach, Me.: Samuel Weiser.

———. 1986b. *The void: A psychodynamic investigation of the relationship between mind and space.* Berkeley: Diamond Books.

Anderson, J. 1978. Arguments concerning representations for mental imagery. *Psychological Review* 85:249–77.

Anderson, O. R. 1988. *Comparative protozoology: Ecology, physiology, life history.* Berlin: Springer-Verlag.

Angyal, A. 1965. *Neurosis and treatment: A holistic theory.* New York: John Wiley.

———. 1937. Disturbances of activity in a case of schizophrenia. *Archives of Neurology and Psychiatry* 38:1047–54.

———. 1936a. The experience of the body-self in schizophrenia. *Archives of Neurology and Psychiatry* 35:1029–53.

———. 1936b. Phenomena resembling lilliputian hallucinations in schizophrenia. *Archives of Neurology and Psychiatry* 36:34–41.

———. 1935. The perceptual basis of somatic delusions in a case of schizophrenia. *Archives of Neurology and Psychiatry* 34:270–79.

Angyal, A., and N. Blackman. 1940. Vestibular reactivity in schizophrenia. *Archives of Neurology and Psychiatry* 44:611–20.

Antrobus, J. 1991. Dreaming: Cognitive processes during cortical activation and high afferent thresholds. *Psychological Review* 98:96–121.

Applewhite, P. B. 1979. Learning in protozoa. In M. Levandowsky and S. Hunter, eds., *Biochemistry and physiology of protozoa*, vol. 1. New York: Academic Press, pp. 341–55.

———. 1975. Plant and animal behavior: An introductory comparison. In E. Eisenstein, ed., *Aneural organisms in Neurobiology.* New York: Plenum, pp. 131–39.

Aquinas, T. 1272. *Summa theologica.* In A. Pegis, ed., *Introduction to Saint Thomas Aquinas.* New York: Modern Library, 1948.

Arendt, H. 1978. *Thinking: The life of the mind*. Vol. 1. New York: Harcourt Brace Jovanovich.

Aristotle. 1936. *On the soul, parva naturalia, on breath*. Trans. W. S. Hett. Cambridge: Harvard University Press.

Armitage, R., R. Hoffmann, and A. Moffitt. 1992. Interhemispheric EEG activity in sleep and wakefulness: Individual differences in basic rest-activity cycle. In J. Antrobus ed., *The mind in sleep*, vol. 2. Hillsdale, N.J.: Erlbaum.

Arnheim, R. 1974. *Art and visual perception*. Berkeley and Los Angeles: University of California Press.

——. 1969. *Visual thinking*. Berkeley and Los Angeles: University of California Press.

Aron, E., and A. Aron. 1986. *The Maharishi effect*. Walpole, N.H.: Stillpoint.

Asch, S. 1961. The metaphor: A psychological inquiry. In M. Henle, ed., *Documents of gestalt psychology*. Berkeley and Los Angeles: University of California Press, pp. 324–33.

Asch, S., and H. Nerlove. 1960. The development of double-function terms in children: An exploratory investigation. In B. Kaplan and S. Wapner, eds., *Perspectives in psychological theory: Essays in honor of Heinz Werner*. New York: International Universities Press, pp. 47–60.

Aserinsky, E. 1986. Proportional jerk: A new measure of motion as applied to eye movements in sleep and waking. *Psychophysiology* 23:340–47.

Baars, B. 1988. *A cognitive theory of consciousness*. Cambridge: Cambridge University Press.

Bachelard, G. 1942. *Water and dreams: An essay on the imagination of matter*. Dallas: Pegasus Foundation, 1983.

Back, K. W. 1992. This business of topology. *Journal of Social Issues* 48:51–66.

Balint, M. 1968. *The Basic Fault*. New York: Brunner/Mazel.

Bang, M. 1991. *Picture this: Perception and composition*. Boston: Little, Brown.

Barber, T. X. 1993. *The human nature of birds*. New York: St. Martin's Press.

Baringa, M. 1990. The mind revealed? *Science* 249:856–58.

Barr, H., R. Langs, R. Holt, L. Goldberger, and G. Klein. 1972. *LSD: Personality and experience*. New York: Wiley.

Barron, F. 1969. *Creative person and creative process*. New York: Holt, Rinehart, and Winston.

Bartlett, F. 1932. *Remembering*. Cambridge: Cambridge University Press.

Becker, R., and R. Selden. 1985. *The body electric: Electromagnetism and the foundation of life*. New York: William Morrow.

Bellah, R., R. Madsen, W. Sullivan, A. Swidler, and S. Tipton. 1985. *Habits of the heart: Individualism and commitment in American life*. New York: Harper and Row.

Bem, D. J., and C. Honorton. 1994. Does psi exist? Replicable evidence for an anomalous process of information transfer. *Psychological Bulletin* 115:4–18.

Benjafield, J., and J. Adams-Webber. 1976. The Golden Section hypothesis. *British Journal of Psychology* 67:11–15.

Berger, R., and M. Persinger. 1991. Geophysical variables and behavior: Quieter annual geomagnetic activity and larger effect size for experimental PSI (ESP) studies over six decades. *Perceptual and Motor Skills* 73:1219–23.

Bergson, H. 1907. *Creative evolution*. New York: Modern Library, 1944.

———. 1889. *Time and free will*. New York: Harper and Row, 1960.

Bernard, T. 1950. *Hatha Yoga*. London: Rider.

Bertini, M., and C. Violani. 1984. Cerebral hemispheres, REM sleep, and dreaming. In M. Bosinelli and P. Cicogna, eds., *Psychology of dreaming*. Bologna: CLUEB, pp. 131–35.

Bichowski, F. R. 1925. The mechanism of consciousness: The presensation. *American Journal of Psychology* 36:588–96.

Bickerton, D. 1984. The language bioprogram hypothesis. *Behavioral and Brain Sciences* 7:173–221.

Binet, A. 1888. *The psychic life of micro-organisms: A study in experimental psychology*. Philadelphia: Albert Saifer, 1970.

Bion, W. R. 1975. *Brazilian Lectures*. Vol. 2. Rio de Janeiro: Imago Editora LTDA.

———. 1965. *Transformations*. New York: Basic Books.

———. 1963. *Elements of psychoanalysis*. New York: Basic Books.

———. 1962. *Learning from experience*. London: Heineman.

Bixby, F. 1928. A phenomenological study of lustre. *Journal of General Psychology* 1:136–74.

Blackmore, S. 1986. *The adventures of a parapsychologist*. Buffalo: Prometheus.

Blagrove, M. 1992. Dreams as the reflection of our waking concerns and abilities: A critique of the problem-solving paradigm of dream research. *Dreaming* 2:205–20.

Block, R. A. 1990. Models of psychological time. In R. A. Block, ed., *Cognitive models of psychological time*. Hillsdale, N.J.: Erlbaum, pp. 1–35.

———. 1979. Time and consciousness. In G. Underwood and R. Stevens, eds., *Aspects of consciousness,* vol. 1. London: Academic, pp. 179–217.

Blofeld, J. 1973. *The secret and sublime: Taoist mysteries and magic*. London: George Allen and Unwin.

Blumenthal, A. L. 1977. *The process of cognition*. Englewood Cliffs, N.J.: Prentice-Hall.

Boernstein, W. S. 1970. Perceiving and thinking: Their inter-relationship and organismic organization. *Annals of the New York Academy of Science* 169:673–82.

———. 1967. Optic perception and optic imageries on man. *International Journal of Neurology* 6:147–81.

———. 1936. On the functional relations of the sense organs to one another and to the organism as a whole. *Journal of General Psychology*. 15:117–31.

Bohm, D. 1980. *Wholeness and the implicate order*. London: Routledge and Kegan Paul.

Boisen, A. 1936. *The exploration of the inner world*. Harper, 1962.

Bolinger, D. 1989. *Intonation and its uses: Melody in grammar and discourse*. Stanford: Stanford University Press.

Bonke, B. 1990. Psychological consequences of so-called unconscious perception and awareness in anaesthesia. In B. Bonke, W. Fitch, and K. Millar, eds., *Memory and awareness in anaesthesia*. Amsterdam: Swets and Zeitlinger, pp. 197–218.

Boring, E. G. 1950. *A history of experimental psychology*. New York: Appleton-Century-Crofts.

———. 1942. *Sensation and perception in the history of psychology*. New York: Appleton-Century-Crofts.

Bourguignon, E. 1972. Dreams and altered states of consciousness in anthropological research. In F. L. Hsu, ed., *Psychological Anthropology*. Cambridge, Mass.: Schenkman, pp. 403–34.

———. 1973. Introduction: A framework for the comparative study of altered states of consciousness. In E. Bourguignon. ed., *Religion, altered states of consciousness and social change*. Columbus: Ohio State University Press, pp. 3–35.

Bowers, K. 1987. Revisioning the unconscious. *Canadian Psychology* 28:93–132.

———. 1976. *Hypnosis for the seriously curious*. New York: Norton.

Bowers, M. 1974. *Retreat from sanity*. New York: Human Sciences Press.

Brentano, F. 1874. The distinction between mental and physical phenomena. In R. M. Chisholm, ed., *Realism and the background of phenomenology*. Glencoe, Ill.: Free Press, 1960, pp. 39–61.

Bronowski, J. 1971. *The identity of man*. Garden City, N.J.: Natural History Press.

Brown, D., M. Forte, and M. Dysart. 1984. Visual sensitivity and mindfulness meditation. *Perceptual and Motor Skills* 58:775–84.

Brown, J. W. 1991. *Self and process: Brain states and the conscious present*. New York: Springer-Verlag.

———. 1988. *The life of the mind*. Hillsdale, N.J.: Erlbaum.

Bryant, P., P. Jones, V. Claxton, and G. Perkins. 1972. Recognition of shapes across modalities by infants. *Nature* 240:303–4.

Bugter, S. 1987. Sensus communis in the works of M. Tullius Cicero. In F. van Holthoon and D. Olson, eds., *Common sense: The foundations for social science*. Lanham, Md.: University Press of America, pp. 83–98.

Bühler, K. 1908. On thought connections. In D. Rapaport, ed., *Organization and pathology of thought*. New York: Columbia University Press, 1951, pp. 39–57.

Burnett, N., and K. Dallenbach. 1927. The experience of heat. *American Journal of Psychology* 38:418–31.

Calvino, I. 1968. *Cosmi-comics*. New York: Harcourt Brace Jovanovich.

Campbell, C. 1978. The secret religion of the educated classes. *Sociological Analysis* 39:146–156.

Capra, F. 1975. *The tao of physics*. Fontana/Collins.

Caputo, J. 1986. *The mystical element in Heidegger's thought*. New York: Fordham University Press.

Casey, E. S. 1976. *Imagining: A phenomenological study*. Bloomington: Indiana University Press.

Cattell, R. B. 1930. The subjective character of cognition and the presensational development of perception. *British Journal of Psychology,* monograph no. 14.

Céline, L. F. 1968. *Castle to castle.* Trans. R. Mannheim. New York: Delacorte.

Chambers, D., and D. Reisberg. 1992. What an image depicts depends on what an image
means. *Cognitive Psychology* 24:145–174.

———. 1985. Can mental images be ambiguous? *Journal of Experimental Psychology:
Human Perception and Performance* 11:317–28.

Chang, G. C. 1963. *Teachings of Tibetan yoga.* New York: University Books.

Chapman, J. 1966. The early symptoms of schizophrenia. *British Journal of Psychology*
112:225–51.

Chapman, L., and J. Chapman. 1980. Scales for rating psychotic and psychotic-like
experiences as continua. *Schizophrenia Bulletin* 6:476–80.

Charlot, V., N. Tzourio, M. Zilbovicius, B. Mazoyer, and M. Denis. 1992. Different
mental imagery abilities result in different regional cerebral blood flow activation
patterns during cognitive tasks. *Neuropsychologia* 30:565–80.

Chen, V. 1975. Membrane potential and behavior: Proposal of a model system. In E.
Eisenstein, ed., *Aneural organisms in neurobiology.* New York: Plenum, pp. 77–90.

Chidester, D. 1992. *Word and light.* Chicago: University of Illinois Press.

Child, I. 1985. Psychology and anomalous observations: The question of ESP in dreams.
American Psychologist 40:1219–30.

Churchland, P. S. 1988. Reduction and the neurobiological basis of consciousness. In A. J.
Marcel and E. Bisiach, eds., *Consciousness in contemporary science.* Oxford: Clarendon Press, pp. 273–304.

Claridge, G. 1972. The schizophrenias as nervous types. *British Journal of Psychiatry*
121:1–17.

Clarke, H. M. 1911. Conscious attitudes. *American Journal of Psychology* 22:214–49.

Cleary, T., ed. 1980. *Timeless spring: A Soto Zen anthology.* San Francisco: Wheelwright
Press.

Cogliolo, P., V. Romano, R. Villani, M. Duval, E. Santangelo, and R. Cuocolo. 1990.
Factors influencing the occurrence of awareness. In B. Bonke, W. Fitch, and K. Millar,
eds., *Memory and Awareness in anaesthesia.* Amsterdam: Swets and Zeitlinger, pp.
110–14.

Cook, T. 1914. *The curves of life.* New York: Dover, 1979.

Costall, A. 1993. How Lloyd Morgan's canon backfired. *Journal of the History of the
Behavioral Sciences* 29:113–22.

Coveney, P., and R. Highfield. 1990. *The arrow of time.* New York: Fawcett Columbine.

Covey, A., and L. Weiskrantz. 1975. Demonstration of cross-modal matching in rhesus
monkeys. *Neuropsychologia* 13:117–20.

Critchley, M. 1977. Ecstatic and synaesthetic experiences during musical perception. In
M. Critchley and R. Henson, eds., *Music and the brain: Studies in the neurology of
music.* Springfield, Ill.: Charles C. Thomas, pp. 217–32.

———. 1953. *The parietal lobes.* London: Arnold.

Csikszentmihalyli, M. 1990. *Flow: The psychology of optimal experience*. New York: Harper and Row.

Cutsforth, T. D. 1925. The role of emotion in a synaesthetic subject. *American Journal of Psychology* 36:527–43.

———. 1924. Synaesthesia in the process of learning. *American Journal of Psychology* 35:88–97.

Cytowic, R. 1989. *Synesthesia: A union of the senses*. New York: Springer-Verlag.

Damasio, A. R. 1989. The brain binds entities and events by multiregional activation from convergence zones. *Neural Computation* 1:123–32.

Darwin, C. 1881. *The power of movement in plants*. New York: DaCapo, 1966.

———. 1872. *The expression of the emotions in man and animals*. New York: Philosophical Library, 1955.

Davenport, R. 1976. Cross-modal perception in apes. *New York Academy of Sciences* 280:143–49.

Davenport, R., and C. Rogers. 1970. Intermodal equivalence of stimuli in apes. *Science* 168:279–80.

David-Neel, A. 1932. *Magic and mystery in Tibet*. New York: Dover, 1971.

Deikman, A. 1982. *The observing self*. Boston: Beacon Press.

———. 1971. Bimodal consciousness. *Archives of General Psychiatry* 25:481–89.

———. 1966. Implications of experimentally induced contemplative meditation. *Journal of Nervous and Mental Disease* 142:101–16.

DeJong, H. 1945. *Experimental catatonia*. Baltimore: Williams and Wilkins.

Dennett, D. 1991. *Conscousness explained*. Boston: Little, Brown.

Dennett, D., and M. Kinsbourne. 1992. Time and the observer: The where and when of consciousness in the brain. *Behavioral and Brain Sciences* 15:183–247.

Dickinson, C. 1926. The course of experience. *American Journal of Psychology* 37:330–44.

Dillbeck, M., K. Cavanaugh, T. Glenn, D. Orme-Johnson, and V. Mittlefehldt. 1987. Consciousness as a field: The transcendental meditation and TM-sidhi program and changes in social indicators. *Journal of Mind and Behavior* 8:67–104.

Dilthey, W. 1914. The understanding of other persons and their life-expressions. In P. Gardiner, ed., *Theories of history*. Glencoe, Ill.: Free Press, 1959, pp. 213–25.

Dimond, S. 1976. Brain circuits for consciousness. *Brain and Behavioral Evolution* 13:376–95.

Dixon, N. F. 1991. Hydrocephalus and "misapplied competence": Awkward evidence for and against. *Behavioral and Brain Sciences* 14:675–76.

———. 1981. *Preconscious processing*. New York: John Wiley.

Doczi, G. 1981. *The power of limits*. Boulder, Co.: Shambala.

Doricchi, F., C. Guariglia, S. Paolucci, and L. Pizzamiglia. 1993. Disturbances of the rapid eye movements of REM sleep in patients with unilateral attentional neglect: Clue for the understanding of the functional meaning of REMs. *Electroencephalography and Clinical Neurophysiology* 87:105–16.

Dowling, J. 1992. *Neurons and networks: An introduction to neuroscience*. Cambridge: Harvard University Press, Belknap Press.

Dreyfus, H. 1991. Being-in-the-world: A commentary on Heidegger's *Being and Time*. Cambridge: MIT Press.

——, ed. 1982. *Husserl, intentionality, and cognitive science*. Cambridge: MIT Press.

Dufrenne, M. 1973. *The phenomenology of aesthetic experience*. Evanston, Ill.: Northwestern University Press.

Durkheim, E. 1912. *The elementary forms of the religious life*. New York: Collier Books, 1961.

Dykes, M., and A. McGhie. 1976. A comparative study of attentional strategies of schizophrenic and highly creative normal subjects. *British Journal of Psychiatry* 128:50–56.

Eccles, J. 1990. A unitary hypothesis of mind-brain interaction in the cerebral cortex. *Proceedings of the Royal Society of London* B240:433–51.

——. 1986. Do mental events cause neural events analogously to the probability fields of quantum mechanics? *Proceedings of the Royal Society of London* B227:411–28.

Eckert, R., D. Randall, and G. Augustine. 1988. *Animal physiology: Mechanisms and adaptions*. New York: Freeman.

Edelman, G. 1992. *Bright air, brilliant fire: On the matter of the mind*. New York: Basic Books.

——. 1989. *The remembered present: A biological theory of consciousness*. New York: Basic Books.

Edelson, M. 1975. *Language and interpretation in psychoanalysis*. New Haven: Yale University Press.

Efron, R. 1990. *The decline and fall of hemispheric specialization*. Hillsdale, N.J.: Erlbaum.

Eibl-Eibesfeldt, I. 1971. *Love and hate*. New York: Holt, Rinehart, and Winston.

Eliade, M. 1964. *Shamanism*. New York: Pantheon.

Elliott, R. 1977. Cross-modal recognition in three primates. *Neuropsychologia* 15:183–186.

Engell, J. 1981. *The creative imagination: Enlightenment to romanticism*. Cambridge: Harvard University Press.

Engler, J. 1984. Therapeutic aims in psychotherapy and meditation: Developmental stages in the representation of self. *Journal of Transpersonal Psychology* 16:25–61.

Epstein, A. W., and N. N. Simmons. 1983. Aphasia with reported loss of dreaming. *American Journal of Psychiatry* 140:108–9.

Erdelyi, H. 1985. *Psychoanalysis: Freud's cognitive psychology*. New York: Freeman.

Erickson, M., and E. Rossi. 1981. *Experiencing hypnosis*. New York: Irvington.

Erikson, E. 1963. *Childhood and society*. New York: Norton.

——. 1962. *Young man Luther*. New York: Norton.

Ettlinger, G., and W. Wilson. 1990. Cross-modal performance: Behavioural processes, phylogenetic considerations, and neural mechanisms. *Behavioural and Brain Research* 40:169–92.

Evens-Wentz, W. Y., ed. 1954. *Tibetan book of the great liberation*. London: Oxford University Press.

Fairbairn, W. R. D. 1954. *An object-relations theory of the personality*. New York: Basic Books.

Farah, M. 1989. Mechanisms of imagery-perception interaction. *Journal of Experimental Psychology: Human Perception and Performance* 15:203–11.

———. 1988. Is visual imagery really visual? Overlooked evidence from neuropsychology. *Psychological Review* 95:307–17.

———. 1986. The laterality of mental image generation. *Neuropsychologia* 24:541–51.

———. 1985. Psychophysical evidence for a shared representational medium for mental images and percepts. *Journal of Experimental Psychology: General* 114:91–103.

———. 1984. The neurological basis of mental imagery: A computational analysis. *Cognition* 18:245–72.

Farah, M., K. Hammond, D. Levine, and R. Calvanto. 1988. Visual and spatial mental imagery: Dissociable systems of representation. *Cognitive Psychology* 20:439–62.

Farah, M., F. Peronnet, M. Gonon, and M. Giard. 1988. Electrophysiological evidence for a shared representational medium for visual images and visual percepts. *Journal of Experimental Psychology* 117:248–57.

Farias, V. 1989. *Heidegger and Nazism*. Philadelphia: Temple University Press.

Farthing, G. M. 1992. *The psychology of consciousness*. Englewood Cliffs, N.J.: Prentice-Hall.

Faulkner, W. 1946. The Bear. In M. Cowley, ed., *The portable Faulkner*. New York: Viking, pp. 227–363.

Febvre-Chevalier, C., A. Bilbaut, Q. Bone, and J. Febvre. 1986. Sodium-calcium action potential associated with contraction in the Heliozoan *Actinocoryne Contractilis*. *Journal of Experimental Biology* 122:177–92.

Fechner, G. T. 1901. *On life after death*. Chicago: Open Court, 1945.

Findlay, J. N. 1970. *Ascent to the absolute*. London: George Allen and Unwin.

Finke, R. 1980. Levels of equivalence in imagery and perception. *Psychological Review* 87:113–32.

Finke, R., S. Pinker, and M. Farah. 1989. Reinterpreting visual patterns in mental imagery. *Cognitive Science* 3:51–78.

Fischer, R. 1975. Cartography of inner space. In R. Siegel and L. West, eds., *Hallucinations: Behavior, experience, and theory*. New York: Wiley, pp. 197–239.

Fodor, J., and Z. Pylyshyn. 1988. Connectionism and cognitive architecture: A critical analysis. *Cognition* 28:3–71.

Ford, G. O. 1991. *Insights*. Lapis Press.

Forte, M., D. Brown, and M. Dysart. 1987. Differences in experience among mindfulness meditators. *Imagination, Cognition, and Personality* 7:47–60.

———. 1985. Through the looking glass: Phenomonological reports of advanced meditators at visual threshold. *Imagination, Cognition, and Personality* 4:323–38.

Foster, M. L. 1980. The growth of symbolism in culture. In M. L. Foster and S. H.

Brandes, eds., *Symbol as sense: New approaches to the analysis of meaning.* New York: Academic Press, pp. 371–97.

Foucault, M. 1978. *The history of sexuality.* Vol. 1. New York: Pantheon.

———. 1970. *The order of things: An archaeology of the human sciences.* New York: Pantheon.

Foulkes, D. 1985. *Dreaming: A cognitive-psychological analysis.* Hillsdale, N.J.: Erlbaum.

Foulkes, D., and S. Fleischer. 1975. Mental activity in relaxed wakefulness. *Journal of Abnormal Psychology* 84:66–75.

Foulkes, D., and M. Schmidt. 1983. Temporal sequence and unit composition in dream reports from different stages of sleep. *Sleep* 6:265–80.

Fox, O. 1975. *Astral projection: A record of out of the body experiences.* Secaucus, N.J.: Citadel.

Frazier, J. G. 1922. *The golden bough: A study in magic and religion.* London: Macmillan.

Freeman, W. 1991. The physiology of perception. *Scientific American* 264:78–85.

Freud, S. 1933. *New introductory lectures on psycho-analysis.* Trans. W. J. Sprott. New York: Norton.

———. 1930. *Civilization and its discontents.* New York: Norton, 1961.

———. 1924. The economic problem in masochism. In *Collected papers,* vol. 2, trans. J. Riviere. New York: Basic Books, 1959, pp. 255–68.

———. 1923. *The ego and the id.* London: Hogarth.

———. 1919a. *Beyond the pleasure principle.* London: Hogarth, 1950.

———. 1919b. The "uncanny". In *Collected papers,* vol. 4, trans. J. Riviere. New York: Basic Books, 1959, pp. 368–407.

———. 1915a. The unconscious. In *Collected papers,* vol. 4, trans. J. Riviere. New York: Basic Books, 1959, pp. 98–136.

———. 1915b. Repression. In *Collected papers,* vol. 4, trans. J. Riviere. New York: Basic Books, 1959, pp. 84–97.

———. 1914. On narcissism. In *Collected papers,* vol. 4, trans. J. Riviere. New York: Basic Books, 1959, pp. 30–59.

———. 1900. *The interpretation of dreams.* New York: Avon, 1965.

Friedrich, R., A. Fuchs, and H. Haken. 1991. Synergetic analysis of spatial-temporal EEG patterns. In A. V. Holden, M. Markus, and H. Othmer, eds., *Nonlinear wave processes in excitable media.* New York: Plenum, pp. 23–37.

Froehlich, W., G. Smith, J. Draguns, and U. Hentschel., eds. 1984. *Psychological processes in cognition and personality.* Washington, D.C.: Hemisphere.

Gackenbach, J., and J. Bosveld. 1989. *Control your dreams.* Harper and Row.

Gackenbach, J., W. Moorecraft, C. Alexander, and S. LaBerge. 1987. Physiological correlates of "consciousness" during sleep in a single TM practitioner. *Sleep Research* 16:230.

Gadamer, H. 1975. *Truth and method.* New York: Seaburg Press.

Gaffron, M. 1956. Some new dimensions in the phenomenal analysis of visual experience. *Journal of Personality* 24:285–307.

Galin, D. 1974. Applications for psychiatry of left and right cerebral specialization. *Archives of General Psychiatry* 31:572–83.

Galka, M. 1986. The feasibility of Guenther's Heideggerian interpretation of the Tibetan Nyingma Buddhist tradition in the *Kindly Bent to Ease Us* trilogy. St. Catharines, Ont.: Department of Philosophy, Brock University, 1986.

Gallup, G. 1977. Self recognition in primates. *American Psychologist* 32:329–38.

———. 1974. Animal hypnosis: Factual status of a fictional concept. *Psychological Bulletin* 81:836–53.

Gardner, H. 1985. *The mind's new science: A history of the cognitive revolution.* New York: Basic Books.

———. 1983. *Frames of mind.* New York: Basic Books.

———. 1975. *The shattered mind.* New York: Basic Books.

Gazzaniga, M. 1988. Brain modularity: Towards a philosophy of conscious experience. In A. J. Marcel and E. Bisiach, eds., *Consciousness in contemporary science.* Oxford: Clarendon Press, pp. 218–38.

———. 1983. Right hemisphere language following brain bisection: A 20-year perspective. *American Psychologist* 38:525–37.

Gendlin, E. 1978. *Focusing.* New York: Bantam.

———. 1962. *Experiencing and the creation of meaning.* New York: Free Press.

Geschwind, N. 1982. Disorders of attention: A frontier in neuropsychology. *Philosophical Transactions of the Royal Society of London,* B298:173–85.

———. 1981. Anatomical and functional asymmetry of the brain. Annual meeting of the Association for the Psychophysiological Study of Sleep, Hyannis, Mass., May.

———. 1965. Disconnection syndromes in animals and man. *Brain* 88:237–94:585–644.

Ghyka, M. 1946. *The geometry of art and life.* New York: Dover, 1977.

Gibson, J. J. 1979. *The ecological approach to visual perception.* Boston: Houghton Mifflin.

———. 1975. Events are perceivable but time is not. In J. T. Fraser and N. Lawrence, eds., *The Study of Time II.* New York: Springer-Verlag, pp. 295–301.

———. 1966. *The senses considered as perceptual systems.* Boston: Houghton Mifflin.

———. 1950. *The perception of the visual world.* Boston: Houghton Mifflin.

Gillespie, G. 1989. Lights and lattices and where they are seen. *Perceptual and Motor Skills* 68:487–504.

Gleik, J. 1987. *Chaos: Making a new science.* New York: Penguin Books.

Glicksohn, J. 1986. Photic driving and altered states of consciousness: An exploratory study. *Imagination, Cognition, and Personality* 6:167–82.

Globus, G. 1992a. Perceptual meaning and the holoworld. In M. Stamenov, ed., *Current advances in semantic theory.* Amsterdam: John Benjamins, pp. 75–85.

———. 1992b. Toward a noncomputational cognitive neuroscience. *Journal of Cognitive Neuroscience* 4:319–330.

———. 1990. The lucid brain. Paper presented at the Lucidity Association Conference, Chicago, July.

———. 1989. Connectionism and the dreaming mind. *Journal of Mind and Behavior* 10:179–95.

———. 1988. Existence and brain. *Journal of Mind and Behavior* 9:447–56.

———. 1973. Consciousness and brain: II. Introspection, the qualia of experience, and the unconscious. *Archives of General Psychiatry* 29:167–76.

Goertzel, B. 1992. Quantum theory and consciousness. *Journal of Mind and Behavior* 13:29–36.

Goldman-Rakic, P. 1988. Topography of cognition: Parallel distributed networks in the primate association cortex. *Annual Review of Neuroscience* 11:137–56.

Goleman, D. 1972. The Buddha on meditation and states of consciousness. *Journal of Transpersonal Psychology* 4:1–44.

Goodall, J. 1986. *The chimpanzees of Gombe: Patterns of behavior.* Cambridge: Harvard University Press.

———. 1971. *In the shadow of man.* Boston: Houghton Mifflin.

Goodfellow, L. 1940. The human element in probability. *Journal of General Psychology* 23:201–5.

———. 1938. A psychological interpretation of the results of the Zenith radio experiments in telepathy. *Journal of Experimental Psychology* 23:601–32.

Goswami, A. 1990. Consciousness in quantum physics and the mind-body problem. *Journal of Mind and Behavior* 11:75–96.

Gould, J. L. 1990. Honey bee cognition. *Cognition* 37:83–103.

Gould, S. J. 1977. *Ontogeny and phylogeny.* Cambridge: Harvard University Press, Belknap Press.

Govinda, A. 1960. *Foundations of Tibetan mysticism.* New York: Dutton.

Gray, C., P. Konig, A. Engel, and W. Singer. 1989. Oscillatory responses in the cat visual cortex exhibit inter-columnar synchronization which reflects global stimulus properties. *Nature* 338:334.

Green, C. 1968a. *Lucid dreams.* London: Hamish Hamilton.

———. 1968b. *Out-of-body experiences.* New York: Ballantine.

Green, C., and C. McCreery. 1975. *Apparitions.* London: Hamish Hamilton.

Greenwood, P., D. H. Wilson, and M. S. Gazzaniga. 1977. Dream report following commissurotomy. *Cortex* 13:311–16.

Gregerson, H., and L. Sailer. 1993. Chaos theory and its implications for social science research. *Human Relations* 46:777–802.

Greyson, B., and C. Flynn, eds. 1984. *The near-death experience: Problems, prospects, perspectives.* Springfield, Ill.: Charles C. Thomas.

Griffin, D. 1984. *Animal thinking.* Cambridge: Harvard University Press.

———. 1978. Prospects for a cognitive ethology. *Behavioral and Brain Sciences* 4:527–629.

———. 1976. *The question of animal awareness.* New York: Rockefeller University Press.

Grof, S. 1980. *LSD psychotherapy.* Pomona, Calif.: Hunter House.

Guenther, H. 1989. *From reductionism to creativity: rDzogs-chen and the new sciences of mind.* Boston: Shambhala.

——. 1984. *Matrix of mystery: Scientific and humanistic aspects of rDzogs-chen thought*. Boulder: Shambhala.

——, trans. 1976. *Longchenpa's "Kindly bent to ease us."* Vol. 1–3. Emeryville, Calif.: Dharma.

——, trans. 1971. *Gampopa's "Jewel ornament of liberation."* Berkeley: Shambhala.

——. 1963. *Life and teaching of Naropa*. London: Oxford University Press.

Guenther, H., and C. Trungpa. 1975. *The dawn of tantra*. Berkeley: Shambhala.

Gurdjieff, G. 1975. *Life is real only then, when "I am."* New York: Dutton.

Gyatso, G. K. 1982. *Clear light of bliss: Mahamudra in Vajrayana Buddhism*. London: Wisdom Publications.

Haber, R. N. 1979. Twenty years of haunting eidetic imagery: Where's the ghost? *Behavioral and Brain Sciences* 3:583–629.

Haber, R. N., and M. Hershenson. 1965. The effects of repeated brief exposures on the growth of a percept. *Journal of Experimental Psychology* 69:40–46.

Hall, C., and G. Lindzey. 1970. *Theories of personality*. New York: John Wiley.

Hall, C., and R. Van De Castle. *The content analysis of dreams*. New York: Appleton-Century-Crofts, 1966.

Hamilton, T. 1975. Behavioral plasticity in protozoans. In E. Eisenstein, ed., *Aneural organisms in neurobiology*. New York: Plenum, pp. 111–30.

Hanlon, R., ed. 1991. *Cognitive microgenesis: A neuropsychological perspective*. New York: Springer-Verlag.

Hara, R., and H. Asai. 1980. Electrophysiological responses of *Didinium Nasutum* to *Paramecium* capture and mechanical stimulation. *Nature* 283:869–70.

Harré, R. 1983. *Personal Being*. Oxford: Basil Blackwell.

Hartshorne, C. 1934. *The philosophy and psychology of sensation*. Chicago: University of Chicago Press.

Haskell, R. 1984. Empirical structures of mind: Cognition, linguistics, and transformation. *Journal of Mind and Behavior* 5:29–48.

Hawking, S. 1988. *A brief history of time*. Toronto: Bantum Books.

Hayek, F. A. 1952. *The sensory order*. London: Routledge and Kegan Paul.

Hebb, D. O. 1949. *Organization of behavior*. New York: John Wiley.

Hegel, G. W. F. 1807. *The phenomenology of mind*. Trans. J. B. Baillie. London: George Allen and Unwin, 1931.

Heidegger, M. 1982/1927. *The basic problems of phenomenology*. Bloomington: Indiana University Press.

——. 1977. *The question concerning technology and other essays*. New York: Harper.

——. 1971. *Poetry, language, thought*. New York: Harper and Row.

——. 1962. *On time and being*. New York: Harper and Row, 1972.

——. 1959a. *On the way to language*. New York: Harper and Row, 1971.

——. 1959b. *Discouse on thinking*. Hew York: Harper and Row, 1966.

——. 1956a. *The question of being*. New York: Twayne, 1958.

——. 1956b. *The principle of reason*. Bloomington: Indiana University Press, 1991.

——. 1954. *What is called thinking?* New York: Harper and Row, 1968.

———. 1942. *Parmenides*. Bloomington: Indiana University Press, 1992.

———. 1936. *Schelling's treatise on the essence of human freedom*. Athens: Ohio University Press, 1985.

———. 1928. *The metaphysical foundations of logic*. Bloomington: Indiana University Press, 1984.

———. 1927. *Being and time*. New York: Harper and Row, 1962.

Heidegger, M., and E. Fink. 1979. *Heraclitus Seminar, 1966/67*. University of Alabama Press.

Heiman, M. 1989. Neonatal imitation, gaze aversion, and mother-infant interaction. *Infant Behavior and Development* 12:495–505.

Hentschel, U., G. Smith, and J. Draguns, eds. 1986a. *The roots of perception: Individual differences in information processing within and beyond awareness*. Amsterdam: North-Holland.

———. 1986b. Subliminal perception, microgenesis, and personality. In U. Hentschel, G. Smith, and J. Draguns, eds., *The roots of perception*. Amsterdam: North-Holland, pp. 3–36.

Herman, J. H., D. Barker, P. Rampy, and H. Roffwarg. 1987. Further evidence confirming the similarity of eye movements in REM sleep and the awake state. *Sleep Research* 16:38.

Herman, L. M., D. Richards, and J. Wolz. 1984. Comprehension of sentences by bottlenosed dolphins. *Cognition* 16:129–219.

Higinbotham, N. 1973. Electropotentials of plant cells. In W. Briggs, P. Green, and R. Jones, eds., *Annual Review of Plant Physiology,* vol. 24. Palo Alto, Calif.: Annual Reviews, pp. 25–46.

Hilgard, E. 1968. *The experience of hypnosis*. New York: Harcourt, Brace and World.

Hilgard, J. 1974. *Personality and hypnosis: A study of imaginative involvement*. Chicago: University of Chicago Press.

Hillman, J. 1981. *The thought of the heart*. Dallas: Spring Publications.

———. 1978. The therapeutic value of alchemical language. *Dragonflies,* 33–42.

———. 1977. An inquiry into image. *Spring,* 62–88.

———. 1975. *Revisioning psychology*. New York: Harper and Row.

———. 1972. *The myth of analysis*. Evanston, Ill.: Northwestern University Press.

Hillman, J., and M. Ventura. 1992. *We've had a hundred years of psychotherapy — and the world's getting worse*. San Francisco: Harper.

Hoffman, R. 1986. Verbal hallucinations and language production processes in schizophrenia. *Behavioral and Brain Sciences* 9:503–48.

Hofstadter, D. 1981. Metamagical themas: Strange attractors: Mathematical patterns delicately poised between order and chaos. *Scientific American* 245:22–43.

———. 1979. *Gödel, Escher, Bach: An eternal golden braid*. New York: Basic Books.

Holender, D. 1986. Semantic activation without conscious identification in dichotic listening, parafoveal vision, and visual masking. *Behavioral and Brain Sciences* 9:1–66.

Holt, R. 1964. Imagery: The return of the ostracized. *American Psychologist* 19:254–64.

Holton, G. 1968. The roots of complementarity. *Eranos Jahnbuch* 38:45–90.

Holtzinger, B. 1990. Psychophysiological correlates of lucid dreaming. Association for the Study of Dreams, Chicago, June.

Honorton, C. 1985. Meta Analysis of PSI ganzfeld research: Response to Hyman. *Journal of Parapsychology* 49:51–91.

Honorton, C., R. Berger, M. Varvoglis, M. Quant, P. Derr, E. Schecter, and D. Ferrari. 1990. PSI communication in the ganzfeld: Experiments with an automated testing system and a comparison with a meta-analysis of earlier studies. *Journal of Parapsychology* 54:99–139.

Hood, R. W. 1975. The construction and preliminary validation of a measure of reported mystical experience. *Journal for the Scientific Study of Religion* 14:29–41.

Hoppe, K. 1977. Split brain and psychoanalysis. *Psychoanalytic Quarterly* 46:220–24.

Horowitz, M. 1970. *Image formation and cognition.* New York: Appleton-Century-Crofts.

Hughlings-Jackson, J. 1958. Evolution and dissolution of the nervous system. In J. Taylor, ed., *Selected writings of John Hughlings-Jackson,* vol. 2. London: Staples Press, pp. 45–75.

Humphrey, G. 1951. *Thinking.* New York: Methuen.

Humphrey, N. 1983. *Consciousness regained.* Oxford: Oxford University Press.

Hunt, H. T. 1989a. *The multiplicity of dreams: Memory, imagination, and consciousness.* New Haven: Yale University Press.

———. 1989b. The relevance of ordinary and non-ordinary states of consciousness for the cognitive psychology of meaning. *Journal of Mind and Behavior* 10:347–60.

———. 1989c. A cognitive-psychological perspective on Gillespie's "lights and lattices": Some relations among perception, imagery, and thought. *Perceptual and Motor Skills* 68:631–41.

———. 1986. A cognitive reinterpretation of classical introspectionism: The relation between introspection and altered states of consciousness and their mutual relevance for a cognitive psychology of metaphor and felt meaning, with commentaries by D. Bakan, R. Evans, and P. Swartz, and response. *Annals of Theoretical Psychology* 4:245–313.

———. 1985a. Relations between the phenomena of religious mysticism and the psychology of thought: A cognitive psychology of states of consciousness and the necessity of subjective states for cognitive theory. *Perceptual and Motor Skills,* monograph no. 61:911–61.

———. 1985b. Cognition and states of consciousness: The necessity of the empirical study of ordinary and non-ordinary consciousness for contemporary cognitive psychology. *Perceptual and Motor Skills,* monograph no. 60:239–82.

———. 1984. A cognitive psychology of mystical and altered state experience. *Perceptual and Motor Skills,* monograph no. 58:467–513.

Hunt, H. T., and C. Cherfurka. 1976. A test of the psychedelic model of consciousness. *Archives of General Psychiatry.* 33:867–96.

Hunt, H. T., A. Gervais, S. Shearing-Johns, and F. Travis. 1992. Transpersonal experiences in childhood: An exploratory empirical study of selected adult groups. *Perceptual and Motor Skills* 75:1135–53.

Hunt, H. T., R. Ogilvie, K. Belicki, D. Belicki, and E. Atalick. 1982. Forms of dreaming. *Perceptual and Motor Skills* 54:559–633.

Hunt, H. T., and C. Popham. 1987. Metaphor and states of consciousness: A preliminary correlational study of presentational thinking. *Journal of Mind and Behaviour* 11:83–100.

Huntley, H. 1970. *The divine proportion: A study in mathematical beauty.* New York: Dover.

Husserl, E. 1907. *The idea of phenomenology.* The Hague: Martinus Nijhoff, 1964.

———. 1905. *The phenomenology of internal time-consciousness.* Bloomington: Indiana University Press, 1964.

Hyman, R. 1994. Anomaly or artifact? Comments on Bem and Honorton. *Psychological Bulletin* 115:19–24.

———. 1985. The ganzfeld PSI experiment: A critical appraisal. *Journal of Parapsychology* 49:3–49.

Irwin, H. 1989. *An introduction to parapsychology.* Jefferson, N.C.: McFarland.

———. 1985. *Flight of mind: A psychological study of the out-of-body experience.* Metuchen, N.J.: Scarecrow Press.

Itil, T. 1970. Digital computer analysis of the electroencephalogram during rapid eye movement sleep state in man. *Journal of Nervous and Mental Disease* 150:201–8.

Jackendoff, R. 1987. *Consciousness and the computational mind.* Cambridge: MIT Press.

Jacobson, E. 1911a. Consciousness under anesthetics. *American Journal of Psychology.* 22:333–45.

———. 1911b. On meaning and understanding. *American Journal of Psychology.* 22:553–77.

Jaffe, M. J. 1970. Evidence for the regulation of phytochrome-mediated processes in bean roots by the neurohumor, acetylcholine. *Plant Physiology* 46:768–77.

Jakobson, R., and L. Waugh. 1987. *The sound shape of language.* Berlin: Mouton de Gruyter.

James, W. 1912. *Essays in radical empiricism and a pluralistic universe.* New York: E. P. Dutton, 1971.

———. 1902. *The varieties of religious experience.* Garden City, N.J.: Dolphin Books.

———. 1890. *The principles of psychology.* 2 vols. New York: Dover.

Jarvis, M., and G. Ettlinger. 1977. Cross-modal recognition in chimpanzees and monkeys. *Neuropsychologia* 15:499–506.

Jaynes, J. 1986. Consciousness and the voices of the mind. *Canadian Psychology* 27:128–48.

———. 1976. *The origin of consciousness in the breakdown of the bicameral mind.* Toronto: University of Toronto Press.

Jennings, H. S. 1906. *Behaviour of lower organisms.* New York: Columbia University Press.

Jerison, H. C. 1973. *Evolution of the brain and intelligence.* New York: Academic Press.

Johnson, M. 1987. *The body in the mind: The bodily bases of meaning, imagination, and reason.* Chicago: University of Chicago Press.

Johnson, M. K., and W. Hirst. 1992. MEM: Memory subsystems as processes. In A. Collins, S. Conway, S. Gathercole, and P. Morris, eds., *Theories of memory*. East Sussex: Erlbaum, pp. 221–48.

Johnson-Laird, P. N. 1988. A computational analysis of consciousness. In A. J. Marcel and E. Bisiach, eds., *Consciousness in contemporary science*. Oxford: Clarendon Press, pp. 357–68.

———. 1983. *Mental models*. Cambridge: Cambridge University Press.

Joyce, J. 1934. *Ulysses*. New York: Modern Library.

Jung, C. G. 1963. *Mysterium coniunctionis*. In *Collected works,* vol. 14, trans. R. F. C. Hull. Princeton: Bollingen.

———. 1959a. Archetypes of the collective unconscious. In *Collected works,* vol. 9 (1), trans. R. F. C. Hull. Princeton: Bollingen, 1960, pp. 3–41.

———. 1955. Synchronicity: An acausal connecting principle. In *Collected works,* vol. 8, trans. R. F. C. Hull. Princeton: Bollingen, 1960, pp. 418–519.

———. 1954. Psychological commentary. In W. Y. Evens-Wentz, ed., *The Tibetan book of the great liberation*. London: Oxford University Press, pp. xxix–lxiv.

———. 1953. *Two essays on analytical psychology*. In *Collected works,* vol. 7, trans. R. F. C. Hull. Princeton: Bollingen, 1960.

———. 1951. *Aion: Researches into the phenomenology of the self*. In *Collected works,* vol 9 (2), trans. R. F. C. Hull. Princeton: Bollingen.

———. 1950. A study in the process of individuation. In *Collected works,* vol. 9 (1), trans. R. F. C. Hull. Princeton, Bollingen, 1960, pp. 290–354.

———. 1946. The psychology of the transference. In *Collected works,* vol. 16, trans. R. F. C. Hull. Princeton: Bollingen, 1954, pp. 163–340.

———. 1944. *Psychology and alchemy*. In *Collected works,* vol. 12, trans. R. F. C. Hull. Princeton: Bollingen, 1953.

———. 1921. *Psychological types*. In *Collected works,* vol. 6, trans. R. F. C. Hull. Princeton: Bollingen, 1971.

Juscyk, P., and B. Earhard. 1980. The lingua mentis and its role in thought. In P. Juscyk and R. Klein, eds., *The nature of thought: Essays in honor of D. O. Hebb*. Hillsdale, N.J.: Erlbaum, pp. 155–86.

Kakise, H. 1911. A preliminary experimental study of the conscious concomitants of understanding. *American Journal of Psychology* 22:14–64.

Kandel, E. R., and J. Schwartz. 1982. Molecular biology of learning: Modulation of transmitter release. *Science* 218:433–42.

Kapleau, P., ed. 1967. *The three pillars of zen: Teaching, practice, and enlightenment*. Boston: Beacon Press.

Katz, S., ed. 1978. *Mysticism and philosophical analysis*. New York: Oxford University Press.

Kaufmann, G. 1980. *Imagery, language and cognition*. Bergen, Norway: Universitets-forlaget.

Kaye, K., and T. G. R. Bower. 1994. Learning and intermodal transfer of information in newborns. *Psychological Science* 5: 241–52.

Kerr, B., S. M. Condon, and L. A. McDonald. 1985. Cognitive spatial processing and the regulation of posture. *Journal of Experimental Psychology: Human Perception and Performance* 11:617–22.

Kerr, N., D. Foulkes, and M. Schmidt. 1982. The structure of laboratory dream reports in blinded and sighted subjects. *Journal of Nervous and Mental Disease* 170:286–94.

Khan, M. R. 1974. The use and abuse of dream in psychic experience. In *The privacy of the self*. New York: International Universities Press, pp. 306–15.

Kihlstrom, J. F. 1987. The cognitive unconscious. *Science* 237:1445–52.

Kihlstrom, J. F., and D. L. Schacter. 1990. Anaesthesia, amnesia, and the cognitive unconscious. In B. Bonke, W. Fitch, and K. Millar, eds., *Memory and awareness in anaesthesia*. Amsterdam: Swets and Zeitlinger, pp. 21–44.

Kihlstrom, J. F., D. L. Schacter, R. Cork, C. Hurt, and S. Behr. 1990. Implicit and explicit memory following surgical anesthesia. *Psychological Science* 1:303–6.

Kihlstrom, J. F., and B. Tobias. 1990. Anosognosia, consciousness, and the self. In G. Prigalano and D. Schacter, eds., *Awareness of deficit after brain injury: Clinical and theoretical issues*. Oxford: Oxford University Press, pp. 198–222.

Kinsbourne, M. 1988. Integrated field theory of consciousness. In A. J. Marcel and E. Bisiach, eds., *Consciousness in contemporary science*. Oxford: Clarendon Press, pp. 239–56.

Kisiel, T. 1992. Heidegger's apology: Biography as philosophy and ideology. In T. Rockmore and J. Margolis, eds., *The Heidegger case: On philosophy and politics*. Philadelphia: Temple University Press, pp. 1–51.

Klein, E. 1971. *A comprehensive etymological dictionary of the English language*. Amsterdam: Elsevier.

Klinger, E. 1978. Modes of normal conscious flow. In K. S. Pope and J. L. Singer, eds., *The stream of consciousness*. New York: Plenum, pp. 226–54.

Klüver, H. 1966. *Mescal and mechanisms of hallucination*. Chicago: University of Chicago Press.

Köhler, W. 1947. *Gestalt psychology*. New York: Liveright.

———. 1926. Intelligence in apes. In C. Murchison, ed., *Psychologies of 1925*. Worcester, Mass.: Clark University Press, pp. 145–61.

Kohut, H. 1984. *How does analysis cure?* Chicago: University of Chicago Press.

———. 1977. *The restoration of the self*. New York: International Universities Press.

Kolb, B., and I. Whishaw. 1990. *Fundamentals of human neuropsychology*. New York: Freeman.

Kornfield, J. 1979. Intensive insight meditation. *Journal of Transpersonal Psychology* 11:41–58.

Kosslyn, S. 1988. Aspects of a cognitive neuroscience of mental imagery. *Science* 240: 1621–26.

———. 1987. Seeing and imagining in the cerebral hemispheres: A computational approach. *Psychological Review* 94:148–75.

———. 1983. *Ghosts in the mind's machine: Creating and using images in the brain*. New York: Norton.

——. 1981. The medium and the message in mental imagery: A theory. *Psychological Review* 88:46–66.

Kragh, U. 1955. *The actual-genetic model of perception-personality*. Lund, Sweden: Gleerups.

Kragh, U., and G. Smith, eds. 1970. *Percept-genetic analysis*. Lund, Sweden: Gleerups.

Krauss, R., P. Morrel-Samuels, and C. Colasante. 1991. Do conversational hand gestures communicate? *Journal of Personality and Social Psychology* 61:743–54.

Kreezer, G. 1930. Luminous appearances. *Journal of General Psychology* 4:247–80.

Krell, D. 1992. *Daimon life: Heidegger and life-philosophy*. Bloomington: Indiana University Press.

Krippner, S., and M. Ullman. 1970. Telepathy and dreams: A controlled experiment with electroencephalogram-electro-oculogram monitoring. *Journal of Nervous and Mental Disease* 151:394–403.

Krishna, G. 1967. *Kundalini*. New Delhi: Ramadhar and Hopman.

Krueger, F. 1928. The essence of feeling: Outline of a systematic theory. In M. Reymert, eds., *Feelings and emotions*. Worcester, Mass.: Clark University Press, pp. 58–85.

Kugler, Paul. 1982. *The alchemy of discourse*. Lewisberg, Pa.: Bucknell University Press.

Kugler, Peter. 1987. *Information, natural laws, and self-assembly of rhythmic movement*. Hillsdale, N.J.: Erlbaum.

Kuhn, T. S. 1962. *The structure of scientific revolutions*. Chicago: University of Chicago Press.

Lacan, J. 1973. *The four fundamental concepts of psycho-analysis*. New York: Norton.

Laing, R. D. 1976. *The facts of life: An essay in feelings, facts, and fantasy*. New York: Pantheon.

——. 1970. *Knots*. New York: Pantheon.

Lakoff, G. 1988. Smolensky, semantics, and the sensorimotor system. *Behavioral and Brain Sciences* 11:39–40.

——. 1987. *Women, fine and dangerous things: What categories reveal about the mind*. Chicago: University of Chicago Press.

Langer, S. 1972. *Mind: An essay on human feeling*. Vol. 2. Baltimore: Johns Hopkins University Press.

——. 1942. *Philosophy in a new key*. Cambridge: Harvard University Press.

Lasch, C. 1984. *The minimal self*. New York: Norton.

——. 1978. *The culture of narcissism*. New York: Norton.

Lashley, K. S. 1960. Cerebral organization and behavior. In F. Beach et al., eds., *The neuropsychology of Lashley: Selected papers of K. S. Lashley*. New York: McGraw-Hill, pp. 529–43.

Laski, M. 1961. *Ecstasy*. Bloomington: Indiana University Press.

Lavie, P., and O. Tzischinsky. 1985. Cognitive asymmetry and dreaming: Lack of relationship. *American Journal of Psychology* 98:353–61.

Leary, T., R. Metzner, and R. Alpert. 1964. *Psychedelic experience*. New York: Academy.

Lee, G., R. Meador, J. Smith, D. Loring, and H. Flanigin. 1988. Preserved crossmodal association following bilateral amygdalotomy in man. *International Journal of Neuroscience* 40:47–55.

Lefebvre, V. 1990. The fundamental structures of human reflexion. In H. Wheeler, ed., *The structure of human reflection: The reflexional psychology of Vladimir Lefebvre.* New York: Peter Lang, pp. 5–70.

Lefebvre, V., V. Lefebvre, and J. Adams-Webber. 1986. Modeling an experiment on construing self and others. *Journal of Mathematical Psychology* 30:317–30.

Legerstee, M. 1990. Infants use multimodal information to imitate speech sounds. *Infant Behavior and Development* 13:343–54.

Lehrman, D. S. 1964. The reproductive behavior of ring doves. *Scientific American* 211:48–54.

Leibnitz, G. 1951. *Selections.* New York: Scribner.

———. 1898. *The monadology and other philosophical writings.* Oxford: Oxford University Press.

Leibowitz, H., and R. Post. 1982. The two modes of processing concept and some implications. In J. Beck, ed., *Organization and representation in perception.* Hillsdale, N.J.: Erlbaum, pp. 343–64.

Lesh, P. 1987. Interview. *Berkeley Monthly.* July.

LeShan, L. 1969. *Toward a general theory of the paranormal.* New York: Parapsychology Foundation.

Levinson, B. 1990. The states of awareness in anesthesia. In B. Bonke, W. Fitch, and K. Millar, eds., *Memory and awareness in anaesthesia.* Amsterdam: Swets and Zeitlinger, pp. 11–18.

Levinson, D. 1978. *The seasons of a man's life.* New York: Ballantine.

Levi-Strauss, C. 1974. *Tristes tropiques.* New York: Atheneum.

———. 1969. *The raw and the cooked.* Trans. J. Weightman and D. Weightman. New York: Harper and Row.

Lewin, K. 1936. *Principles of topological psychology.* New York: McGraw-Hill.

Leyton, M. 1992. *Symmetry, causality, mind.* Cambridge: MIT Press.

Libet, B. 1985. Unconscious cerebral initiative and the role of conscious will in voluntary action. *Behavioral and Brain Sciences* 8:529–66.

———. 1978. Subjective referral of the timing for a conscious sensory experience. *Brain* 102:193–224.

Lindauer, M. 1991. Physiognomy and verbal synesthesia compared: Affective and intersensory descriptors of nouns with drawings and art. *Metaphor and Symbolic Activity* 6:183–202.

Lipowski, Z. 1990. *Delirium: Acute confusional states.* Oxford: Oxford University Press.

———. 1967. Delirium, clouding of consciousness and confusion. *Journal of Nervous and Mental Disease* 145:227–55.

Lowrie, W., ed. and trans. 1946. *Religion of a scientist: Works of G. Fechner.* New York: Pantheon.

Lucas, J. R. 1961. Minds, machines, and Gödel. *Philosophy* 36:112.

Luk, C. 1988. *Taoist Yoga.* New York: Samuel Weiser.

Lukoff, D. 1985. *The diagnosis of mystical experiences with psychotic features. Journal of Transpersonal Psychology* 17:155–81.

Luria, A. 1973. *The working brain.* Harmondworth, Eng.: Penguin Books.

———. 1972. *The man with the shattered world,* trans. L. Solotaroff. New York: Basic Books.

Lynn, S. J., and R. W. Rhue. 1988. Fantasy proneness. *American Psychologist* 43: 35–44.

McCrae, R., and P. Costa. 1983. Joint factors in self-reports and ratings: Neuroticism, extraversion, and openness to experience. *Personality and Individual Differences* 4:245–55.

McGuinn, C. 1991. *The problem of consciousness.* Oxford: Basil Blackwell.

McKellar, P. 1957. *Imagination and thinking.* London: Cohen and West.

MacLean, P. D. 1973. *A triune concept of the brain and behavior.* Toronto: University of Toronto Press.

McLuhan, M. 1964. *Understanding media.* Toronto: Signet.

McNeill, D. 1992. *Hand and mind: What gestures reveal about thought.* Chicago: University of Chicago Press.

———. 1985. So you think gestures are nonverbal? *Psychological Review* 92:350- 371.

McNulty, J. 1976. Dolphin behavior and perception. Colloquium, Department of Psychology, Brock University, St. Catharines, Ont., March.

Mahler, M. 1968. *On human symbiosis and the vicissitudes of individuation.* New York: International Universities Press.

Maidenbaum, A., and S. Martin, eds. 1991. *Lingering shadows: Jungians, Freudians, and anti-semitism.* Boston: Shambhala.

Maier, N. R. F. 1931. Reasoning in humans, pt. 2: The solution of a problem and its appearance in consciousness. *Journal of Comparative Psychology* 12:181–94.

Maier, N. R. F., and T. C. Schneirla. 1964. *Principles of animal psychology.* New York: Dover.

Malraux, A. 1960. *The metamorphosis of the gods.* Garden City, N.Y.: Doubleday.

Mandelbrot, B. 1982. *The fractal geometry of nature.* San Francisco: Freeman.

Mandler, G. 1975. *Mind and emotion.* New York: Wiley.

Mann, D. 1992. A mathematical model of the self. *Psychiatry* 55:403–12.

Mann, J., and L. Short. 1990. *The body of light.* New York: Globe Press Books.

Marcel, A. 1988. Phenomenal experience and functionalism. In A. Marcel and E. Bisiach, eds., *Consciousness in contemporary society.* Oxford: Clarendon Press, pp. 121–58.

———. 1983a. Conscious and unconscious perception: Experiments on visual masking and word recognition. *Cognitive Psychology* 15:197–237.

———. 1983b. Conscious and unconscious perception: An approach to the relations between phenomenal experience and perceptual processes. *Cognitive Psychology* 15: 238–300.

Marks, D., and R. Kammann. 1978. Information transmission in remote viewing experiments. *Nature* 274:680–81.

Marks, L. 1989. On cross-modal similarity: The perceptual structure of pitch, loudness, and brightness. *Journal of Experimental Psychology: Human Perception and Performance* 15:586–602.

——. 1987. On cross-modal similarity: Auditory-visual interactions in speeded discrimination. *Journal of Experimental Psychology: Human Perception and Performance* 13:384–94.

——. 1978. *The unity of the senses.* New York: Academic Press.

——. 1975. On colored-hearing synesthesia: Cross-modal translations of sensory dimensions. *Psychological Bulletin* 82:303–31.

Marr, D. 1982. *Vision: A computational investigation in the human representation of visual information.* San Francisco: Freeman.

Martindale, A., and C. Martindale. 1988. Metaphysical equivalence of elements and temperaments: Empirical studies of Bachelard's theory of imagination. *Journal of Personality and Social Psychology* 55:836–48.

Martinez, J. 1974. Galileo on primary and secondary qualities. *Journal of the History of the Behavioral Sciences* 10:160–69.

Masling, A., R. Bernstein, F. Poynton, S. Reed, and E. Katkin. 1991. Perception without awareness and electrodermal responding: A strong test of subliminal psychodynamic activation effects. *Journal of Mind and Behavior* 12:33–47.

Maslow, A. 1971. *The farther reaches of human nature.* New York: Viking.

——. 1962. *Towards a psychology of being.* Princeton: Van Nostrand.

Matte-Blanco, I. 1988. *Thinking, feeling, and being.* London: Routledge.

Maturana, H., and F. Varela. 1987. *The tree of knowledge: The biological roots of human understanding.* Boston: Shambhala.

Mead, G. H. 1934. *Mind, self, and society.* Chicago, Ill.: University of Chicago Press.

Melara, R. 1989a. Dimensional interaction between color and pitch. *Journal of Experimental Psychology: Human Perception and Performance* 15:69–79.

——. 1989b. Similarity relations among synesthetic stimuli and their attributes. *Journal of Experimental Psychology: Human Perception and Performance* 15:212–31.

Melara, R., and L. Marks. 1990a. Dimensional interactions in language processing: Investigating directions and levels of crosstalk. *Journal of Experimental Psychology: Learning, Memory, and Cognition* 16:539–54.

——. 1990b. Processes underlying correspondences between linguistic and nonlinguistic dimensions. *Memory and Cognition* 18:477–95.

Melara, R., and T. O'Brien. 1990. Effects of cuing on cross-modal congruity. *Journal of Memory and Language* 29:655–86.

——. 1987. Interaction between synesthetically corresponding dimensions. *Journal of Experimental Psychology: General* 116:323–36.

Mellor, C. 1970. First rank symptoms of schizophrenia. *British Journal of Psychiatry* 117:15–23.

Meltzoff, A., and M. Moore. 1992. Early imitation within a functional framework. The importance of person identity, movement, and development. *Infant Behavior and Development* 15:479–505.

———. 1989. Imitation in newborn infants: Exploring the range of gestures imitated and the underlying mechanisms. *Developmental Psychology* 25:954–62.

———. 1977. Imitation of facial and manual gestures by human neonates. *Science* 198: 75–78.

Merleau-Ponty, M. 1964. *The primacy of perception and other essays*. Evanston, Ill: Northwestern University Press.

Mesulam, M. 1985. Attentional confusion and neglect. In M. Mesulam, ed., *Principles of Behavioral Neurology*. Philadelphia: F. A. Davis, pp. 125–68.

Mesulam, M., and N. Geschwind. 1978. On the possible role of neocortex and its limbic connections in the process of attention and schizophrenia. *Journal of Psychiatric Research* 14:249–59.

Miller, A. I. 1984. *Imagery in scientific thought: Creating 20th-century physics*. Boston: Birkhauser.

Miller, D. 1986. Through a looking glass: The world as enigma. *Eranos* 55. Frankfort: Insel-Verlag, 1988, pp. 349–402.

Miller, G. 1981. Trends and debates in cognitive psychology. *Cognition* 10:215–25.

Miller, I. 1984. *Husserl, perception, and temporal awareness*. Cambridge: MIT Press.

Minkowski, E. 1970. *Lived time*. Evanston, Ill.: Northwestern University Press.

Mishkin, M., L. Ungerleider, and K. Macko. 1983. Object vision and spatial vision: Two cortical pathways. *Trends in Neuroscience* 6:414–17.

Mogami, Y., and H. Machemer. 1991. A novel type of ciliary activity in *Stylonychia Mytilus*. *Journal of Experimental Biology* 161:239–55.

Montagu, A. 1962. Time, morphology, and neotony in the evolution of man. In A. Montagu, ed., *Culture and the evolution of man*. New York: Oxford University Press, pp. 324–42.

Moody, R. 1975. *Life after life*. Atlanta: Mockingbird Books.

Moreton, R. B., and W. B. Amos. 1979. Electrical recording from the contractile ciliate *Zoothamnium Geniculatum Ayrton*. *Journal of Experimental Biology* 83: 159–67.

Morgan, C. L. 1994. *An introduction to comparative psychology*. London: Walter Scott.

Moruzzi, G., and H. Magoun. 1949. Brainstem reticular formation and activation of the EEG. *Electroencephalography and Clinical Neurophysiology* 1:455–73.

Murray, E. A., and M. Mishkin. 1985. Amygdalectomy impairs crossmodal association in monkeys. *Science* 228:604–6.

Nafe, J. P. 1924. An experimental study of the affective qualities. *American Journal of Psychology* 35:507–44.

Nagel, T. 1986. *The view from nowhere*. Oxford: Oxford University Press.

———. 1974. What is it like to be a bat? *Philosophical Review* 83:435–50.

Nahm, F., D. Tranel, H. Damasio, and A. Damasio. 1993. Cross-modal associations and the human amygdala. *Neuropsychologia* 31:727–44.

Naitoh, Y., and R. Eckert. 1973. Sensory mechanisms in basis of the hyperpolarizing mechanoreceptor potential. *Journal of Experimental Biology* 59:53–65.

————. 1969a. Ionic mechanisms controlling behavioral responses of Paramecium to mechanical stimulation. *Science* 169:963–65.

————. 1969b. Ciliary orientation: Controlled by cell membrane or by intracellular fibrils? *Science* 166:1633–35.

Natsoulas, T. 1992. The ecological approach to perception: The place of perceptual content. *American Journal of Psychology* 102:443–76.

————. 1991–92. "I am not the subject of this thought." *Imagination, Cognition, and Personality* 11:279–302.

————. 1991. Consciousness and commissurotomy, III: Toward the improvement of alternative conceptions. *Journal of Mind and Behavior* 12:1–32.

————. 1989. Is consciousness what psychologists actually examine? *American Journal of Psychology* 105:363–84.

————. 1984. Towards the improvement of Gibsonian perception theory. *Journal for the Theory of Social Behavior* 14:231–58.

————. 1983. Concepts of consciousness. *Journal of Mind and Behavior* 4:13–59.

————. 1982. Conscious perception and the paradox of "blind-sight." In G. Underwood, ed., *Aspects of Consciousness,* vol. 3. London: Academic Press, pp. 79–109.

————. 1981. Basic problems of consciousness. *Journal of Personality and Social Psychology* 41:132–78.

Neisser, U. 1991. Without perception there is no intelligence. In R. G. Burton, ed., *Minds: Natural and Artificial.* Albany: State University of New York Press.

————. 1989. Direct perception and recognition as distinct perceptual systems. Paper presented to the Cognitive Science Society, Ann Arbor, Mich.

————. 1976. *Cognition and reality.* San Francisco: Freeman.

————. 1972. Changing conceptions of imagery. In P. Sheehan, ed., *The function and nature of imagery.* New York: Academic Press, pp. 233–51.

Neisser, U., and N. Kerr. 1973. Spatial and mnemonic properties of visual images. *Cognitive Psychology* 5:138–50.

Nielsen, T. 1993. Changes in the kinesthetic content of dreams following somatosensory stimulation of leg muscles during REM sleep. *Dreaming* 3:99–113.

Nietzsche, F. 1888. *The will to power.* New York: Random House, 1967.

Nigro, G., and U. Neisser. 1983. Point of view in personal memories. *Cognitive Psychology* 15:467–82.

Nisbett, R., and T. Wilson. 1977. Telling more than we can know: Verbal reports on mental processes. *Psychological Review* 5 (1):147–60.

Norris, E., and G. Ettlinger. 1978. Cross-modal performance in the monkey: non-matching to sample with edible shapes. *Neuropsychologia* 16:99–102.

Noyes, R., and R. Kletti. 1976. Depersonalization in the face of life-threatening danger: A description. *Psychiatry* 39:19–27.

O'Keefe, D. L. 1982. *Stolen lightning: The social theory of magic.* New York: Vintage Books.

Olafson, F. A. 1987. *Heidegger and the philosophy of mind.* New Haven: Yale University Press.

Olton, D. S. 1984. Comparative analysis of episodic memory. *Behavioral and Brain Sciences* 7:250–51.

Olton, D. S., J. Becker, and G. Handelmann. 1979. Hippocampus, space, and memory. *Behavioral and Brain Sciences* 2:313–65.

Onians, R. B. 1951. *The origins of European thought about the body, the mind, the soul, the world, time, and fate*. Cambridge: Cambridge University Press.

Ordal, G. 1977. Calcium ion regulates chemotactic behaviour in bacteria. *Nature* 270:66–67.

Orme-Johnson, D., C. Alexander, and J. Davies. 1990. The effects of the Maharishi technology of the unified field: Reply to a methodological critique. *Journal of Conflict Resolution* 34:756–68.

Orme-Johnson, D., C. Alexander, J. Davies, H. Chandler, and W. Larimore. 1988. International peace project in the middle east: The effects of the Maharishi technology of the unified field. *Journal of Conflict Resolution* 32:776–812.

Orme-Johnson, D., and M. Dillbeck. In press. Higher states of consciousness: The Maharishi effect. In J. Gackenbach, ed., *Higher states of consciousness*. New York: Plenum.

Orme-Johnson, D., M. Dillbeck, J. Bousquet, and C. Alexander. 1985. An experimental analysis of the application of the Maharishi technology of the unified field in major world trouble-spots. *Scientific Research on Maharishi's Transcendental Meditation and TM-sidhi programme* 4:322:2532–48.

Ornitz, E. M., and E. R. Ritvo. 1968. Perceptual inconstancy in early autism. *Archives of General Psychiatry* 18:78–98.

Ornstein, R. 1969. *On the experience of time*. Baltimore: Penguin.

Oscar-Berman, M., J. Pulaski, N. Hutner, D. Weber, and M. Freedman. 1990. Cross-modal functions in alcoholism and aging. *Neuropsychologia* 28:851–69.

Osgood, C. 1964. Semantic differential techniques in the comparative study of cultures. *American Anthropologist* 66:171–200.

Osgood, C., G. Suci, and P. Tannenbaum. 1957. *The measurement of meaning*. Urbana: University of Illinois Press.

Oswald, I. 1962. *Sleeping and waking*. New York: Elsevier.

Othmer, H. 1991. The dynamics of forced excitable systems. In A. V. Holden, M. Markus, and H. Othmer, eds., *Nonlinear wave processes in excitable media*. New York: Plenum, pp. 213–31.

Ott, H. 1993. *Martin Heidegger: A political life*. New York: Basic Books.

Otto, R. 1923. *The idea of the holy*. New York: Galaxy Books, 1958.

Ouspensky, P. D. 1949. *In search of the miraculous: Fragments of an unknown teaching*. New York: Harcourt, Brace.

Oxford English Dictionary. 1989. Oxford: Clarendon Press.

Paivio, A. 1971. *Imagery and verbal processes*. New York: Holt, Rinehart, and Winston.

Parker, A., and N. Wiklund. 1987. The ganzfeld experiments: Towards an assessment. *Journal of the Society for Psychical Research* 54:261–65.

Parkes, G., ed. 1987. *Heidegger and Asian thought*. Honolulu: University of Hawaii Press.

Patterson, R. 1990. Perceptual moment models revisited. In R. A. Block, ed., *Cognitive models of psychological time.* Hillsdale, N.J.: Erlbaum, pp. 85–100.

Pauling, L. 1989. Interpretation of so-called icosahedral and decagonal quasicrystals of alloys showing apparent icosahedral symmetry elements as twins of an 820-atom cubic crystal. *Computers and Mathematics with Applications* 17:337–39.

Peirce, C. S. 1905. Critical common-sensism. In J. Buchler, ed., *Philosophical writings of Peirce.* New York: Dover, pp. 290–301.

Pekala, R. J. 1991. *Quantifying consciousness: An empirical approach.* New York: Plenum.

Penfield, W. 1975. *The mystery of the mind.* Princeton: Princeton University Press.

Penfield, W., and P. Perot. 1963. The brain's record of auditory and visual experience. *Brain* 86:595–696.

Penrose, R. 1994. *Shadows of the mind: A search for the missing science of consciousness.* Oxford: Oxford University Press.

———. 1989. *The emperor's new mind: Concerning computers, minds, and the laws of physics.* New York: Oxford University Press.

Persinger, M., and S. Krippner. 1989. Dream ESP experiments and geomagnetic activity. *Journal of the American Society for Psychical Research* 83:101–16.

Peterson, M., J. Kihlstrom, P. Rose, and M. Glisky. 1992. Mental images can be ambiguous: Reconstruals and reference-frame reversals. *Memory and Cognition* 20:107–23.

Piaget, J. 1952. *The origins of intelligence in children.* New York: International Universities Press.

Pickard, B. 1972. Spontaneous electrical activity in shoots of *Ipomoea, Pisum,* and *Xanthium. Planta* 102:91–114.

Plato. *Theaetetus.* In *The collected dialogues of Plato,* trans. F. M. Cornford. Princeton: Princeton University Press, Bollingen Press, pp. 845–919:1961.

Plotinus. *The Enneads.* Trans. S. MacKenna. Penguin Books, 1991.

Plotkin, W. 1979. The alpha experience revisited: Biofeedback in the transformation of psychological states. *Psychological Bulletin* 86:1132–48.

Poirier, M., and H. Hunt. 1991. The microgenesis of perception and personality. Unpublished paper. Department of Psychology, Brock University, St. Catharines, Ont.

Pöppel, E. 1988. *Mindworks: Time and conscious experience.* Boston: Harcourt Brace Jovanovich.

Premack, D. 1983. The codes of man and beasts. *Behavioral and Brain Sciences* 6:125–67.

Premack, D., and G. Woodruff. 1978. Does the chimpanzee have a theory of mind? *Behavioral and Brain Sciences* 4:515–26.

Preston, B. 1993. Heidegger and artificial intelligence. *Philosophy and Phenomenological Research* 53:43–69.

Pribram, K. 1991. *Brain and perception: Holonomy and structure in figural processing.* Hillsdale, N.J.: Erlbaum.

———. 1985. Mind and brain, psychology and neuroscience, the eternal verities. In S. Koch and D. Leary, eds., *A century of psychology as a science.* New York: McGraw-Hill, pp. 700–720.

Prigogine, I. 1984. *Order out of chaos.* New York: Bantam Books.

Pylyshyn, Z. 1984. *Computation and cognition: Toward a foundation for cognitive science.* Cambridge: MIT Press.

———. 1981. The imagery debate: Analogue media versus tacit knowledge. *Psychological Review* 88:16–45.

———. 1973. What the mind's eye tells the mind's brain: A critique of mental imagery. *Psychological Bulletin* 80:1–24.

Rader, C., and A. Tellegen. 1981. A comparison of synesthetes and nonsynesthetes. In E. Klinger, ed., *Imagery,* vol. 2, *Concepts, results, and applications.* New York: Plenum, pp. 153–63.

Radner, D., and M. Radner. 1989. *Animal consciousness.* Buffalo: Prometheus Books.

Ramsay, O., and A. Rocke. 1984. Kekule's dreams: Separating the fiction from the fact. *Chemistry in Britain* 20:1093–94.

Ramsey, J., and H. Hunt. 1993. Cognitive and social determinants of metaphor. American Psychological Association, Toronto, August.

Rapp, P. E. 1986. Oscillations and chaos in cellular metabolism and physiological systems. In A. V. Holden, ed., *Chaos.* Manchester: Manchester University Press, pp. 179–208.

Reed, E. 1988. *James J. Gibson and the psychology of perception.* New Haven: Yale University Press.

Reich, W. 1951. *Cosmic superimposition.* New York: Farrar, Straus, and Giroux.

———. 1949. *Character analysis.* New York: Noonday Press.

———. 1942. *The discovery of the orgone: The function of the orgasm.* New York: Farrar, Straus, and Cudahy.

Reichel-Dolmatoff, G. 1975. *The shaman and the jaguar: A study of narcotic drugs among the Indians of Colombia.* Philadelphia: Temple University Press.

Reisberg, D., and D. Chambers. 1991. Neither pictures nor propositions: What can we learn from a mental image? *Canadian Journal of Psychology* 45:336–52.

Reissland, N. 1988. Neonatal imitation in the first hour of life: Observations in rural Nepal. *Developmental Psychology* 24:464–69.

Ricoeur, P. 1988. *Time and narrative.* Vol. 3. Chicago: University of Chicago Press.

Ring, K. 1980. *Life at death: A scientific investigation of near-death experiences.* New York: Coward, McCann, and Geoghegan.

Roche, S., and K. McConkey. 1990. Absorption: Nature, assessment, and correlates. *Journal of Personality and Social Psychology* 59:91–101.

Rock, I. 1983. *The logic of perception.* Cambridge: MIT Press.

Rock, I., D. Wheeler, and L. Tudor. 1989. Can we imagine how objects look from other viewpoints? *Cognitive Psychology* 21:185–210.

Roffwarg, H., J. Herman, C. Bowe-Anders, and G. Tauber. 1978. The effects of sustained alterations of waking visual input on dream content. In A. M. Arkin, J. S. Antrobus, and S. J. Ellman, eds., *The mind in sleep: Psychology and psychophysiology.* Hillsdale, N.J.: Erlbaum, pp. 295–349.

Romanes, G. 1883. *Animal intelligence.* Washington, D.C.: University Publications of America, 1977.

Rorty, R. 1979. *Philosophy and the mirror of nature.* Princeton: Princeton University Press.

Ross, W. D. 1959. *Aristotle: A complete exposition of his works and thought.* Cleveland: Meridian Books.

Rudofsky, S., and J. Wotiz. 1988. Psychologists and the dream accounts of August Kekule. *Journal of Human Behavior and Learning* 5:1–11.

Rumelhart, D., P. Smolensky, J. McClelland, and G. Hinton. 1986. Schemata and sequential thought processes in parallel distributed processing models. In J. McClelland and D. Rumelhart, eds., *Parallel distributed processing: Explorations in the microstructure of cognition,* vol. 2. Cambridge: MIT Press.

Ryle, G. 1949. *The concept of mind.* New York: Barnes and Noble.

Sabom, M. 1982. *Recollections of death: A medical investigation.* New York: Harper and Row.

Sacks, O. 1989. *Seeing voices: A journey into the world of the deaf.* Berkeley and Los Angeles: University of California Press.

——. 1987. *The man who mistook his wife for a hat.* New York: Harper and Row.

Sander, F. 1930. Structures, totality of experience, and gestalt. In C. Murchison, ed., *Psychologies of 1930.* Worcester, Mass.: Clark University Press, pp. 188–204.

Sartre, J. P. 1940. *Psychology of imagination.* New York: Washington Square Press, 1966.

——. 1939. A fundamental idea of the phenomenology of Husserl: Intentionality. Unpublished translation by J. Mayer of "Une ideé fondamental de la phenomenologie de Husserl," in *Situations I.* Paris: Gallimard, 1947.

Sass, L. A. 1992. *Madness and modernism: Insanity in the light of modern art, literature, and thought.* New York: Basic Books.

Savage-Rumbaugh, S., K. McDonald, R. Sevcik, W. Hopkins, and E. Rubert. 1986. Spontaneous symbol acquisition and communicative use by pygmy chimpanzees. *Journal of Experimental Psychology: General* 115:211–35.

Savage-Rumbaugh, S., J. Pate, J. Lawson, S. Smith, and S. Rosenbaum. 1983. Can a chimpanzee make a statement? *Journal of Experimental Psychology: General* 112: 457–92.

Savage-Rumbaugh, S., R. Sevcik, and W. Hopkins. 1988. Symbolic cross-modal transfer in two species of chimpanzees. *Child Development* 59:617–25.

Schacter, D. 1989. On the relation between memory and consciousness: Dissociable interactions and conscious experience. In H. Roediger and F. Craik, eds., *Varieties of memory and consciousness: Essays in honour of Endel Tulving.* Hillsdale, N.J.: Erlbaum, pp. 355–89.

Schacter, D., M. McAndrews, M. Moszcovitch. 1988. Access to consciousness: Dissociations between implicit and explicit knowledge in neuropsychological syndromes. In L. Weiskrantz, ed., *Thought without language.* Oxford: Clarendon Press, pp. 242–78.

Schanfald, D., C. Pearlman, and R. Greenberg. 1987. The capacity of stroke victims to report dreams. *Cortex* 21:1–15.

Schilder, P. 1942. *Mind: Perception and thought in their constructive aspects.* New York: Columbia University Press.

———. 1933. Experiments on imagination, after-images, and hallucinations. *American Journal of Psychiatry* 13:597–611.

———. 1924. *Medical Psychology.* New York: International Universities Press, 1953.

Schreber, D. P. 1901. *Memoirs of my nervous illness.* London: Dawson, 1955.

Schrodt, P. 1990. A methodological critique of a test of the effects of the Maharishi technology of the unified field. *Journal of Conflict Resolution* 34:745–55.

Schutz, A. 1962. On multiple realities. In *The problem of social reality,* vol. 1 of *Collected papers of Alfred Schutz.* The Hague: Martinus Nijhott, pp. 207–59.

Schwenk, T. 1965. *Sensitive chaos: The creation of flowing forms in water and air.* Bristol England: Rudolf Steiner Press.

Searle, J. 1992. *The rediscovery of the mind.* Cambridge: MIT Press.

———. 1990. Consciousness, explanatory inversion, and cognitive science. *Behavioral and Brain Sciences* 13:585–642.

———. 1980. Minds, brains, programs. *Behavioral and Brain Sciences* 3:417–57.

Segal, S. 1971. Processing of the stimulus in imagery and perception. In S. Segal, ed., *Imagery: Current cognitive approaches.* New York: Academic Press, pp. 69–100.

Seidenberg, M., and L. Petitto. 1979. Signing behavior in apes: A critical review. *Cognition* 7:177–215.

Seligman, P. The numinous in religion, art, and analytical psychology. Department of Philosophy, Brock University, St. Catharines, Ont., 1976.

Sergent, J. 1989. Image generation and processing of generated images in the cerebral hemispheres. *Journal of Experimental Psychology: Human Perception and Performance* 15:170–78.

Shafton, A. 1976. *Conditions of awareness.* Portland, Ore.: Riverstone Press.

Shapiro, D. 1983. Meditation as an altered state of consciousness: Contributions of western behavioral science. *Journal of Transpersonal Psychology* 15:61–81.

Sharaf, M. 1983. *Fury on earth: A biography of Wilhelm Reich.* New York: St. Martin's.

Shaw, C., R. Kentridge, and J. Aggleton. 1990. Cross-modal matching by amnesiac subjects. *Neuropsychologia* 28:665–71.

Shaw, R., and M. McIntyre. 1974. Algoristic foundations to cognitive psychology. In W. B. Weimer and D. Palermo, eds., *Cognition and symbolic processes.* Hillsdale, N.J.: Erlbaum, pp. 305–62.

Shaw, R., and M. T. Turvey. 1981. Coalitions as models for ecosystems: A realist perspective on perceptual organization. In M. Kubovy and J. Pomerantz, eds., *Perceptual organization.* Hillsdale, N.J.: Erlbaum, pp. 343–415.

Shaw, R., M. T. Turvey, and W. Mace. 1982. Ecological psychology: The consequence of a commitment to realism. In W. B. Weimer and D. Palermo, eds., *Cognition and the symbolic process.* Hillsdale, N.J.: Erlbaum, pp. 159–226.

Shepard, R. N. 1978. Externalization of mental images and the act of creation. In B. Randhawa and W. Coffman, eds., *Visual learning, thinking, and communication.* New York: Academic Press, pp. 133–89.

Shepard, R. N., and J. Metzler. 1971. Mental rotation of three-dimensional objects. *Science* 171:701–3.

Shukla, G. D., S. C. Sahu, R. P. Tripathi, and D. K. Gupta. 1982. Phantom limb: A phenomenological study. *British Journal of Psychiatry* 141:54–58.

Siegel, R., and M. Jarvick. 1975. Drug-induced hallucinations in animals and man. In R. Siegel and L. West, eds., *Hallucinations: Behavior, experience, theory*. New York: Wiley, pp. 81–161.

Silberer, H. 1918. The dream: Introduction to the psychology of dreams. *Psychoanalytic Review* 42 (1955):361–87.

———. 1917. *Hidden symbolism of alchemy and the occult arts*. Trans. S. E. Jelliffe. New York: Dover, 1971.

———. 1912. On symbol formation. In D. Rapaport, ed. and trans., *Organization and pathology of thought*. New York: Columbia University Press, 1951, pp. 208–33.

———. 1909. Report on a method of eliciting and observing certain symbolic hallucination-phenomena. In D. Rapaport, ed. and trans., *Organization and pathology of thought*. New York: Columbia University Press, 1951, pp. 195–207.

Singer, J. 1978. Experimental studies of daydreaming and the stream of thought. In K. S. Pope and J. L. Singer, eds., *The stream of consciousness*. New York: Plenum, pp. 187–223.

———. 1977. Ongoing thought: The normative baseline for alternate states of consciousness. In N. Zinberg, ed., *Alternate states of consciousness*. New York: Free Press, pp. 89–120.

Skarda, C., and W. Freeman. 1987. How brains make chaos in order to make sense of the world. *Behavioral and Brain Sciences* 10:161–95.

Smith, G. 1991. Percept-genesis: A frame of reference for neuropsychological research. In R. Hanlon, ed., *Cognitive microgenesis: A neuropsychological perspective*. New York: Springer-Verlag, pp. 199–211.

Smith, G., and I. Carlsson. 1990. *The creative process*. Madison, Conn.: International Universities Press.

Smolensky, P. 1988. On the proper treatment of connectionism. *Behavioral and Brain Sciences* 11:1–74.

Smythies, J. 1959. The stroboscopic patterns: II. The phenomenology of the bright phase and after images. *British Journal of Psychology* 50:305–25.

Spadafora, A., and H. Hunt. 1990. The multiplicity of dreams: Cognitive-affective correlates of lucid, archetypal, and nightmare dreams. *Perceptual and Motor Skills* 71:627–44.

Spanos, N. P., and P. Moretti. 1988. Correlates of mystical and diabolical experiences in a sample of female university students. *Journal for the Scientific Study of Religion* 27:105–16.

Spearman, C. 1923. *The nature of intelligence and the principles of cognition*. London: Macmillan.

Spencer-Brown, G. 1969. *Laws of form*. New York: Dutton.

———. 1957. *Probability and scientific inference*. London: Longmans, Green.

———. 1956. The data of psychical research: A study of three hypotheses. In G. Wolstenholme and E. Millar, eds., *CIBA foundation symposium on extrasensory perception.* Boston: Little, Brown, pp. 73–79.

Sperry, R. W. 1991. In defense of mentalism and emergent interaction. *Journal of Mind and Behavior* 12:221–46.

——. 1987. Structure and significance of the consciousness revolution. *Journal of Mind and Behavior* 8:37–66.

——. 1984. Consciousness, personal identity and the divided brain. *Neuropsychologia* 22:661–73.

——. 1979. Self recognition and social awareness in the deconnected minor hemisphere. *Neuropsychologia* 17:153–66.

Sprung, M. 1994. *After truth: Explorations in life sense.* Albany: State University of New York Press.

Stanford, R., and S. Frank. 1991. Prediction of ganzfeld ESP-task performance from session-based verbal indicators of psychology function: A second study. *Journal of Parapsychology* 55:349–76.

Starker, S. 1978. Dreams and waking fantasy. In K. S. Pope and J. L. Singer, eds., *The stream of consciousness.* New York: Plenum, pp. 301–19.

Stein, B., and M. Meredith. 1993. *The merging of the senses.* Cambridge: MIT Press.

Stein, G. 1951. *Gertrude Stein and her brother, and other early portraits.* New Haven: Yale University Press.

Stevens, P. 1974. *Patterns in nature.* Boston: Little, Brown.

Stitch, S. 1983. *From folk psychology to cognitive science: The case against belief.* Cambridge: MIT Press.

Straus, E. 1963. *The primary world of the senses.* New York: Free Press.

Stroud, J. M. 1955. The fine structure of psychological time. In H. Quastler, ed., *Information theory in psychology: Problems and methods.* Glencoe, Ill.: Free Press, pp. 174–205.

Sullivan, H. S. 1953. *The interpersonal theory of psychiatry.* New York: Norton.

Swartz, P., and L. Seginer. 1981. Response to body rotation and tendency to mystical experience. *Perceptual and Motor Skills* 53:683–88.

Tart, C. 1969. *Altered states of consciousness: A book of readings.* New York: Wiley.

Tart, C., H. Puthoff, and R. Targ, eds. 1979. *Mind at large: Institute of electrical and electronic engineers — symposia on the nature of extrasensory perception.* New York: Praeger.

Tarthang Tulku 1973. *Calm and clear.* Berkeley: Dharma.

——. 1977. *Time, space, and knowledge.* Emeryville, Calif.: Dharma.

Tedlock, B., ed. 1987. *Dreaming: Anthropological and psychological interpretations.* Cambridge: Cambridge University Press.

Tellegen, A., and G. Atkinson. 1974. Openness to absorbing and self altering experiences ("absorption"), a trait related to hypnotic susceptibility. *Journal of Abnormal Psychology* 83:268–77.

Terrace, H. S. 1985. In the beginning was the "name." *American Psychologist* 40:1011–28.

Thom, R. 1975. *Structural stability and morphogenesis*. Reading, Mass.: Benjamin.

Thompson, D'Arcy. 1961. *On growth and form*. Cambridge: Cambridge University Press.

Tiryakian, E. 1962. *Sociologism and existentialism: Two perspectives on the individual and society*. Englewood Cliffs, N.J.: Prentice-Hall.

Titchener, E. B. 1929. *Systematic psychology: Prolegomena*. New York: Macmillan.

———. 1912. Description vs. statement of meaning. *American Journal of Psychology* 23:165–82.

Toriyama, H., and M. J. Jaffe. 1972. Migration of calcium and its role in the regulation of seismonasty in the motor cell of *Mimosa Pudica L. Plant Physiology* 49:72–81.

Travis, F. 1994. The junction point model: A field model of waking, sleeping and dreaming, relating dream witnessing, the waking/sleeping transition, and transcendental meditation in terms of a common psychophysiologic state. *Dreaming* 4:91–104.

Troeltsch, E. 1931. *The social teachings of the Christian churches*. 2 vols. New York: Harper Torchbooks, 1960.

Trungpa, C. 1973. *Cutting through spiritual materialism*. Berkeley: Shambhala.

Tulving, E. 1985. Memory and consciousness. *Canadian Psychology* 26:1–12.

———. 1984. Relations among components and processes of memory. *Behavioral and Brain Sciences* 7:257–68.

———. 1983. *Elements of episodic memory*. Oxford: Oxford University Press.

Turing, A. 1950. Computing machinery and intelligence. *Mind* 59:433–60.

Tylor, E. 1871. *Primitive culture*. Vol. 1. New York: Gordon Press.

Ullman, M., and S. Krippner. 1970. *Dream studies and telepathy: An experimental approach*. New York: Parapsychology Foundation.

Ullman, M., S. Krippner, and A. Vaughn. 1973. *Dream telepathy: Experiments in nocturnal ESP*. Baltimore: Penguin.

Ullman, S. 1980. Against direct perception. *Behavioral and Brain Sciences* 3:373–415.

Underhill, E. 1955. *Mysticism*. New York: Meridian.

Utting, J. 1990. Clinical aspects of awareness during anaesthesia. In B. Bonke, W. Fitch, K. Millar, eds., *Memory and awareness in anaesthesia*. Amsterdam: Swets and Zeitlinger, pp. 259–71.

Van de Castle, R. 1986. ESP in dreams: Comments on a replication "failure" by the "failing" subject. Annual meeting of the Association for the Study of Dreams, University of Virginia, Charlottesville, June.

Van der Maas, H., and P. Molenaar. 1992. Stagewise cognitive development: An application of catastrophe theory. *Psychological Review* 99:395–417.

Vanderwolf, C. H., and T. E. Robinson. 1981. Reticulo-cortical activity and behavior: A critique of the arousal theory and a new synthesis. *Behavioral and Brain Sciences* 4:459–514.

Van Dusen, W. 1972. *The natural depth in man*. New York: Harper and Row.

Van Eenwyk, J. R. 1991. Archetypes: The strange attractors of the psyche. *Journal of Analytical Psychology* 36:1–25.

Van Holtoon, F. 1987. Common sense and natural law: From Thomas Aquinas to Thomas

Reid. In F. Van Holthoon and D. Olson, eds., *Common sense: The foundations for social science*. Lanham, Md.: University Press of America, pp. 99–114.

Van Houton, J. 1979. Membrane potential changes during chemokinesis in *Paramecium*. *Science* 204:1100–1103.

Van Houton, J., D. Hauser, and M. Levandowsky. 1981. Chemosensory behavior in protozoa. In M. Levandowsky and S. Hunter, eds., *Biochemistry and physiology of behavior*, vol. 4. New York: Academic Press, pp. 67–124.

Varela, F., E. Thompson, E. Rosch. 1991. *The embodied mind: Cognitive science and human experience*. Cambridge: MIT Press.

Varela, F., A. Toro, E. John, and E. Schwartz. 1981. Perceptual framing and cortical alpha rhythm. *Neuropsychologia* 19:675–86.

Velmans, M. 1991. Is human information processing conscious? *Behavioral and Brain Sciences* 14:651–726.

Vico, G. 1744. *The new science*. Trans. T. Bergin and M. Fisch. Ithaca, N.Y.: Cornell University Press, 1970.

Von Bertalanffy, L. 1952. *Problems of life*. New York: Wiley.

Von Hornbostel, E. 1927. The unity of senses. In W. Ellis, ed., *A sourcebook of Gestalt psychology*. New York: Humanities Press, 1967, pp. 210–16.

Von Uexküll, J. 1934. A stroll through the world of animals and man. In C. Schiller, ed., *Instinctive behavior*. New York: International Universities Press, 1957, pp. 5–80.

Vowles, D. 1970. Neuroethology, evolution, and grammar. In R. Aronson, E. Tobach, D. Lehrman, and J. Rosenblatt, eds., *Development and evolution of behavior: Essays in memory of T. C. Schneirla*. San Francisco: Freeman, pp. 194–215.

Vygotsky, L. 1962. *Thought and language*. Cambridge: MIT Press.

Wagner, S., E. Winner, D. Cicchetti, and H. Gardner. 1981. "Metaphorical" mapping in human infants. *Child Development* 52:728–31.

Walker, P., and S. Smith. 1984. Stroop interference based on the synesthetic qualities of auditory pitch. *Perception* 13:75–81.

Wallace, K. 1986. *The neurophysiology of enlightenment*. Fairfield, Iowa: Maharishi International University Press.

Walsh, R. 1992. The search for synthesis: Transpersonal psychology and the meeting of East and West, psychology and religion, personal and transpersonal. *Journal of Humanistic Psychology* 32:19–45.

———. 1977. Initial meditative experiences. *Journal of Transpersonal Psychology* 9:151–92.

Washburn, M. 1917. *The animal mind: A text-book of comparative psychology*. New York: Macmillan.

Weber, M. 1922. *The sociology of religion*. Boston: Beacon, 1963.

———. 1915. The social psychology of the world religions. In H. Gerth and C. W. Mills, eds., *From Max Weber: Essays in sociology*. New York: Oxford University Press, 1946, pp. 267–301.

Weimer, W. B. 1982. Ambiguity and the future of psychology: Meditations Leibniziennes.

In W. B. Weimer and D. Palermo, eds., *Cognition and the symbolic process*. Hillsdale, N.J.: Erlbaum, pp. 331–60.

Weiskrantz, L. 1988. Some contributions of neuropsychology of vision and memory to the problem of consciousness. In A. J. Marcel and E. Bisiach, eds., *Consciousness in contemporary science*. Oxford: Clarendon Press, pp. 183–99.

Weiskrantz, L., E. Warrington, M. Sanders, and J. Marshall. 1974. Visual capacity in the hemianopic field following a restricted occipital ablation. *Brain* 97:709–28.

Werner, H. 1961. *Comparative psychology of mental development*. New York: Science Editions.

———. 1956. Microgenesis and aphasia. *Journal of Abnormal and Social Psychology* 52:347–53.

Werner, H., and B. Kaplan. 1963. *Symbol formation*. New York: Wiley.

Westley, F. 1978. "The cult of man": Durkheim's predictions and new religious movements. *Sociological Analysis* 39:135–45.

Wheeler, R. H., and T. D. Cutsforth. 1922b. Synaesthesia and meaning. *American Journal of Psychology* 33:361–84.

———. 1922a. Synaesthesias: A form of perception. *Psychological Review* 29:212–20.

———. 1921. The role of synaesthesia in learning. *Journal of Experiential Psychology* 4:448–68.

Wheelwright, P., ed. 1966. *The presocratics*. New York: Odyssey.

Whitton, J., H. Moldofsky, and F. Lue. 1978. EEG frequency patterns associated with hallucinations in schizophrenia and "creativity" in normals. *Biological Psychiatry* 13:123–33.

Wicker, F., and C. Holahan. 1978. Analogy training and synesthetic phenomena. *Journal of General Psychology* 98:113–22.

Wilber, K. 1990. Two patterns of transcendence: A reply to Washburn. *Journal of Humanistic Psychology* 30:113–36.

———. 1984. The developmental spectrum and psychopathology: Part I. Stages and types of pathology. *Journal of Transpersonal Psychology* 16:75–118.

———. 1980. *The Atman project*. Wheaton, Ill.: Theosophical Publishing House.

Williams, S., and B. Pickard. 1972a. Receptor potentials and action potentials in *Drosera* tentacles. *Planta* 103:193–221.

———. 1972b. Properties of action potentials in *Drosera* tentacles. *Planta* 103:222–40.

Wilson, S., and T. Barber. 1981. Vivid fantasy and hallucinatory abilities in the life histories of excellent hypnotic subjects: preliminary report with female subjects. In E. Klinger, ed., *Imagery*, vol. 2, *Concepts, results, and applications*. New York: Plenum, pp. 133–49.

Winnicott, D. W. 1971. *Playing and reality*. New York: Basic Books.

Wittgenstein, L. 1992. *Last writings on the philosophy of psychology*. Vol. 2. Oxford: Basil Blackwell.

———. 1982. *Last writings on the philosophy of psychology*. Vol. 1. Chicago: University of Chicago Press.

———. 1980. *Remarks on the philosophy of psychology*. 2 vols. Oxford: Basil Blackwell.

———. 1969. *On certainty.* New York: Harper.

———. 1953. *Philosophical investigations.* New York: Macmillan.

Wolf, F. 1990. *Parallel universe: The search for other worlds.* New York: Touchstone.

Wood, D. C. 1975. Protozoa as models of stimulus transduction. In E. Eisenstein, ed., *Aneural organisms in neurobiology.* New York: Plenum, pp. 5–23.

———. 1972. Generalization of habituation between different surfaces of *Stentor. Physiology and Behavior* 9:161–65.

Woodworth, R. S. 1906. Imageless thought. *Journal of Philosophy, Psychology, and Scientific Method* 3:701–8.

Woodworth, R. S., and H. Schlosberg. 1954. *Experimental psychology.* New York: Holt, Rinehart, and Winston.

Yates, J. 1985. The content of awareness is a model of the world. *Psychological Review* 92:249–84.

Zaleski, C. 1987. *Otherworld journeys: Accounts of near-death experience in medieval and modern times.* New York: Oxford University Press.

Zaparoli, G., and L. Reatto. 1969. The apparent movement between visual and acoustic stimulus and the problems of intermodal relations. *Acta Psychologica* 29:256–67.

Zeeman, E. C. 1977. *Catastrophe theory: Selected papers 1972–1977.* Reading, Mass.: Addison-Wesley.

———. 1976. Catastrophe theory. *Scientific American* 234 (4):65–83.

Zimmerman, M. 1990. *Heidegger's confrontation with modernity: Technology, politics, art.* Bloomington: Indiana University Press.

Zubek, J. 1969. *Sensory deprivation: Fifteen years of research.* New York: Appleton-Century-Crofts.

Index

Aaronson, B., 249

Abraham, R. H., 55, 57, 270, 273

Action potential of neuron, 101–6

Adams-Webber, J., 132

Addison, J., 185

Agnosia, 4

Alchemy, 121, 124–27, 136, 187, 192, 262, 310n1

Alexander, C. N., 77, 150, 286

Almaas, A. H., xiii, 194, 201, 204, 209–11, 213, 218, 227, 307n1, 308n1

Altered states of consciousness. *See* Transpersonal states

Ambient optic array. *See* Ecological array

Amnesia, 32, 37, 79, 83

Anderson, J., 162

Anesthesia, 37, 76, 123, 250, 303n4

Angyal, A., 45, 200–202, 205, 209

Animal consciousness: bees, 303n5; and blindsight, 17, 32; compared with plants, 5, 302–3nn2–3; and cross-modal transformations, 84–87, 107, 303n5; debate over, 93–96; dolphins, 107, 109, 301–2n5, 303n5; Heidegger versus Buddhists on, 231–34, 310n7; memory, 80; mirror behaviors, 106,

107; parrots and songbirds, 107, 302n5, 303n5; protozoa, 5, 96–106, 302–3nn1–3; rats, 303n5; self-awareness in higher apes, 84, 106–12; signing by higher apes, 86, 107–108, 303nn5–6

Animism, 124, 234–35, 262

Antrobus, J., 56

Aphasia, 4, 32–33, 156

Applewhite, P., 99, 302n1, 302n3

Aquinas, T., 182–83, 196, 234

Archetypes, 135–36

Arendt, H., 182, 183, 186, 196, 231

Aristotle, 81, 179, 180–85, 188–91, 195, 196, 304n1, 306n1

Armitage, R., 170

Arnheim, R., xii, 9, 23, 125, 144, 151, 171–76, 196, 209, 251, 267, 304n3

Artificial intelligence, 4, 16, 26, 35, 51, 55, 59–63, 244, 303n6

Asch, S., 11, 124, 174, 209, 211, 304n4

Augustine, 3, 195, 306n2

Baars, B., 4, 8, 26, 31–32, 33, 36, 55, 63, 74, 75, 298n2

Balint, M., 216